Double Jeopardy

Double Jeopardy

The History, the Law

George C. Thomas III

NEW YORK UNIVERSITY PRESS

New York and London

NEW YORK UNIVERSITY PRESS
New York and London

Library of Congress Cataloging-in-Publication Data
Thomas, George C. (George Conner), 1947–
Double jeopardy : the history, the law / George C. Thomas, III.
p.   cm.
Includes bibliographical references and index.
ISBN 0-8147-8233-7 (cloth : acid-free paper)
1. Double jeopardy—United States—History. I. Title.
KF9245 .T48 1998
345.73'04—ddc21   98-25367
                              CIP

New York University Press books are printed on acid-free paper,
and their binding materials are chosen for strength and durability.

Manufactured in the United States of America

10 9 8 7 6 5 4 3 2 1

To Frank W. Miller
Mentor, Scholar, Teacher
Who showed me the way to double jeopardy

Contents

Acknowledgments

When I wrote my LL.M. thesis at Washington University in St. Louis in 1983, I began to think about writing a book on double jeopardy. In the intervening fifteen years, more people helped me than I can possibly thank. But I would be remiss if I did not name a few.

My LL.M. and J.S.D. thesis committee (Professors Kathleen Brickey, Ed Imwinkelried, and Frank Miller) gave me the right amount of guidance mixed with grief.

I had the benefit of excellent research assistants; Howard Baum, Nick Costantino, David Griffin, Lynn Miller, and Rebekah Wanger provided particular support to the double jeopardy project. A brave and talented group of Rutgers students served as guinea pigs for the manuscript in the fall of 1995 by taking my seminar on double jeopardy. Their thoughts and critiques helped shape the final version.

The book was also shaped by a University of Pennsylvania criminal law workshop and a Rutgers faculty colloquium. Both groups asked provocative, probing questions, some of which I have only partly answered. Many readers offered helpful comments outside the colloquium or workshop context: Roger Abrams, Gary Francione, Doug Husak, Greg Mark, Michael Moore, and Stephen Morse. The comments of two anonymous reviewers were also extremely helpful. My colleague Ron Chen translated, with skill and patience, many Latin sources for me.

Much support (ranging from financial to friendship) came my way from Roger Abrams and Peter Simmons, my deans at Rutgers Law School, and Choong Soon Kim, my department chair at the University of Tennessee at Martin.

My first research assistant at Rutgers, Marsha Wenk, worked closely with me as an early version of the current blameworthiness theory began to take shape in 1987 and 1988. She continued to critique and help shape my thinking on double jeopardy until her untimely death in 1995.

As with all human projects, this one required not a little luck and much assistance from others, only some of whom I have named here. I thank everyone and appreciate the luck.

Introduction

The United States Supreme Court has failed to achieve a stable interpretation of the Double Jeopardy Clause. This is surprising because the American double jeopardy prohibition partakes of a Western legal concept that is both ancient and fundamental. A specific bar against double jeopardy has existed in the common law at least since the confrontation between Henry II and Saint Thomas Becket in 1164. More generally, laws against changing a final judgment can be traced to the Code of Hammurabi.

At one level, a bar against double jeopardy is a self-evident protection that is inevitable in any legal system. No legal system can survive without some bar against relitigating the same issue over and over. And if there is to be a bar against multiple determinations of the same question, why should the number of permissible determinations be anything other than one? Once a tribunal has determined the facts and law, there is no reason to think that a second tribunal would be any more likely to reach the "right" or "just" outcome (however we might define those terms). Indeed, if two tribunals returned different verdicts in the same case, there would be no a priori reason to prefer one to the other, and thus no reason to prefer a second trial's outcome to the first.

Viewed in this way, stripped to its core, there is nothing difficult or controversial about double jeopardy. If D is convicted or acquitted of murdering his ex-wife, he cannot again be tried for the murder of his ex-wife. The Double Jeopardy Clause captures this self-evident principle in an arcane formulation: "nor shall any person be subject for the same offence to be twice put in jeopardy of life or limb." The clause thus forbids a second "jeopardy of life or limb" for the "same offence."[1]

At the core, both "jeopardy" and "same offense" have a self-evident, uncontroversial meaning. The self-evident meaning of "same offense" is "identical offense." First-degree premeditated murder is the same offense as first-degree premeditated murder, of course, but not much else is obvious about the same offense question. Felony murder is a killing in the commission of a felony (for example, robbery, rape, kidnapping). Suppose *D* is acquitted of premeditated murder; can he be charged later with felony murder for the same killing? Could he be charged with kidnapping if convicted of premeditated murder? Could he be charged with kidnapping if convicted of felony murder based on kidnapping? Moreover, there is a civil/criminal distinction that is worrisome. O. J. Simpson was tried for the civil tort of killing his ex-wife and her friend Ronald Goldman after being found not guilty of the same murders in a criminal trial. Why is this not double jeopardy? The self-evident meaning of same offense is not ultimately helpful.

The self-evident meaning of "twice in jeopardy" is a second criminal trial. But if a second criminal trial is always a second jeopardy, a judge could never declare a mistrial without triggering a double jeopardy bar, regardless of how many errors had infected the trial and regardless of how much the defendant wanted a mistrial. Moreover, appellate courts could never reverse convictions and remand for a new, error-free trial. (Indeed, this complaint was lodged by the Framers against James Madison's original language forbidding more than one trial for the same offense, as I discuss in chapter 2.) Judges would be loathe to declare mistrials and reverse convictions under that regime, and defendants would be harmed. It appears again that something other than the self-evident meaning must be sought.

Even if we accept the self-evident meaning of "twice in jeopardy" as more than one trial, the Clause does not prohibit all second jeopardies, just second jeopardies of "life or limb." Literally construed, this additional parameter limits double jeopardy protection to capital offenses and offenses with the nonexistent penalty of amputation. So a strict self-evident meaning of second jeopardy would limit the Double Jeopardy Clause to capital offenses. There is no historical evidence to support that reading of the language.

Finding an understanding of same offense or second jeopardy beyond the self-evident reading is not an easy task. Some examples will introduce the difficulties. In Case One, the defendant caused two deaths in an automobile accident. He pled guilty to the traffic offense of failure to reduce speed to avoid an accident and was later prosecuted for involuntary manslaughter. There is no doubt that a guilty plea is a conviction and no doubt that an unreversed conviction is the end of one jeopardy. The issue, then, is whether failure to yield is the same offense as vehicular homicide. Holding that they were the same offense, the state court dismissed the manslaughter prosecution.[2] The United States Supreme Court reversed because the state courts had misapplied the prevailing test of same offense, but the Supreme Court suggested that the offenses would be the same if based on the same failure to yield.[3]

Should a traffic offense bar a manslaughter prosecution? One question is whether offenses are the same because based on the same criminal conduct. Another question is whether a traffic offense can be a "life or limb" offense under the Double Jeopardy Clause. If the answer is yes to both of these questions, then the state court was right to bar the manslaughter prosecution.

In Case Two, the defendant was arrested and charged with federal drug charges. The government also brought forfeiture proceedings against his house and farm, on the ground that some of the drug offenses occurred there. The forfeiture proceedings were civil in nature and thus proceeded separately from the drug prosecution. Stressing the inherently remedial nature of civil forfeiture, the Supreme Court held that forfeiture did not bar the criminal charges.[4] Though this seems to make good sense, notice the odd conjunction with Case One: forfeiture of one's house and farm does not bar a criminal charge based on the same underlying conduct, but paying a traffic ticket might be a bar. Something very odd seems to be going on here.

In Case Three, the defendant robbed a federally insured bank in Illinois. He was acquitted of federal bank robbery charges and was then prosecuted in state court for the same bank robbery. The Supreme Court held that the state and federal governments are different sovereigns with different interests to protect and that, therefore, each can prosecute separately from the other regardless of the overlap in conduct or statutory elements.[5] Even if a state and federal crime had identical elements, the Court held, they would not be the same offense. Logically, this is a difficult proposition to defend. Moreover, a question arises as to whether either government intends that result and, ultimately, whether this type of dual prosecution can be defended as the best reading of the Constitution.

In Case Four, the prosecutor announced ready, and the jury was sworn. A few minutes later, the prosecutor moved for a mistrial on the ground that one of his key witnesses had not been subpoenaed and might not appear. The trial judge granted the mistrial over defense objection. The Supreme Court held that this mistrial was the end to one jeopardy and that the government could not bring another jeopardy for the same offense.[6] But would the result be the same if the mistrial had been based on a faulty indictment? Or on defense counsel's inappropriate opening argument?[7]

Case Five brings together the jeopardy and same-offense issues in a more complex setting. A prosecution for armed robbery ended because the jury was hung—that is, could not agree on a verdict. The trial court denied a motion for acquittal in which the defendant claimed that the state's case was legally insufficient to convict. Could the state bring another trial for armed robbery without allowing the defendant to appeal the trial court's ruling on the sufficiency of the state's case? If the state could proceed with a second trial for the identical offense, it must be because the hung jury did not end the first jeopardy. No second jeopardy can exist until the first jeopardy has ended. To answer the hung jury jeopardy question, the Court relied on an 1824 case that was logically inapposite.[8] Not to worry; Justice Rehnquist brushed off the illogic of the Court's position by citing "Justice Holmes' aphorism that 'a page of history is worth a volume of logic.'"[9] The rest of the Court's hung jury analysis is similarly superficial.

If the defendant were permitted to appeal the denial of his motion for acquittal, a resolution in his favor would be a finding that the state did not produce enough evidence to submit the case to the jury. The appellate court would be holding that the trial judge should have directed a verdict of acquittal.[10] An acquittal of armed robbery, of course, would bar a new charge of armed robbery based on the same robbery. Assuming a successful appeal in Case Five, the next question is whether the state could reprosecute the same robbery under a different statute—for example, a statute forbidding robbery in a dwelling.[11]

Is armed robbery the same offense as robbery in a dwelling? The Court has failed to provide an analytic structure for the same-offense question; the commentators have failed as badly. The difficulty is finding a referent for "same offense" other than "identical offense." We have some idea what "freedom of speech" or "trial by jury" means. But what does "same offense" mean in the Double Jeopardy Clause? Well, it means same offense.

In 1990 the Court attempted to ground the same-offense inquiry by fashioning a new rule that essentially asked whether the proof of offense A would require proof of offense B in the particular case.[12] In Case Five, for example, proof of the armed robbery would also prove robbery in a dwelling. But in 1993 the Supreme Court overruled itself; offenses are the same, the Court held, only if one is *necessarily* included in the other.[13] As armed robbery *can* be proved without proving robbery in a dwelling, and vice versa, they are not the same offense under the Court's current rule.

Rarely, if ever, has the Court changed its mind so quickly about a constitutional guarantee. Cynics will likely think the quick change is more indicative of politics than lack of consensus about double jeopardy. Both cases were 5-4 decisions, and the two leading liberal members of the Court, Justices Brennan and Marshall, were replaced by more conservative Justices in the time that elapsed between the two cases. But that does not explain the badly splintered conservative wing in the 1993 case; Justice Scalia wrote for the majority in overruling the earlier case, but only Justice Kennedy joined the part of Scalia's opinion applying the same-offense test to the various charges. Three Justices argued for an even stricter application of the test and different results for some charges.[14] The outcome endorsed by the largest number of Justices, ironically, was that of the earlier case, which drew support from the four dissenters.[15]

It is to be expected, of course, that members of the Court will routinely challenge each other's constitutional interpretation. This is part of their interpretive function. But something more underlies the disputes over the Double Jeopardy Clause: the Court is without a conception of double jeopardy beyond the narrow self-evident meaning. The Court's disagreement over what the Double Jeopardy Clause means at the level of doctrinal application is thus merely symptomatic of the Court's inability to articulate double jeopardy first principles.

In 1988 I offered a first principle, arguing that the concepts of same offense and second jeopardy should be understood to prevent multiple procedural outcomes of singular substantive criminal law blameworthiness.[16] In this book, I elaborate and expand the blameworthiness concept of double jeopardy. Though I defend my account mostly at a theoretical level, it has the added virtue of being historically linked to the views of Sir William Blackstone. I find in Blackstone, albeit with some amplification, a conception of double jeopardy that is based on procedural and substantive blameworthiness.

One of the Framers argued that part of Madison's proposed double jeopardy prohibition was unnecessary because "the courts of justice would never think of trying and punishing twice for the same offence."[17] But before we can give voice to this noble principle, we must know when the trial and punishment is "twice" and when the offense is the "same." That is the goal of my book.

Blackstone provides, of course, only a starting point, albeit a more helpful one than the text of the Clause, the Court's doctrine, or the modern commentators. From this starting point, the analysis proceeds by examining substantive and procedural blameworthiness. I conclude that since the legislature creates statutory criminal blameworthiness and the procedure for determining that blameworthiness, the legislature is the ultimate source of guidance on when offenses are the same and when the first jeopardy has ended. Though no one has yet made the argument in this fashion, it is the account of double jeopardy that is truest to its long, stable history.

I began the task of developing my blameworthiness account in chapter 1 by putting the interpretational issue in its theoretical context.

1

The Road Back to Blackstone
An Overview of the Argument

Blackstone was almost certainly the source of the Double Jeopardy Clause language. The Supreme Court noted that a bar against double jeopardy "was carried into the jurisprudence of this Country through the medium of Blackstone."[1] Blackstone stated a centuries-old common law view of double jeopardy, which is (I argue) the most defensible conception today, more than two hundred years later. But the growing procedural and substantive complexity of modern law has made the application of the common law principles devilishly difficult. Blackstone did not have to deal with federal sentencing guidelines, for example, and the number of criminal offenses today is a thousand times larger than when English double jeopardy law was in its infancy. "At the end of the thirteenth century, apart from treason and three offenses which were fast falling into the category of misdemeanors, there were but six felonies."[2] The difficulties of discerning when two offenses are the "same offense" are markedly reduced when one has a universe of six or seven offenses, rather than one of 7,000.[3]

This chapter sketches the argument that the rest of the book makes in more detail. Ultimately, the argument requires understanding Blackstone's conception of double jeopardy and how that conception applies to the radically different modern criminal procedure. First, I introduce three models of double jeopardy protection as a way of organizing the argument.

Three Double Jeopardy Models

The Court has explicitly rejected the first of the three models, though commentators sometimes write wistfully as if the model were still viable. This model, attractive to those who fear legislative excess, finds in the

Double Jeopardy Clause a substantive limitation on how the legislature can define crimes and fix punishments.

Model 1: A Substantive Double Jeopardy Clause

A double jeopardy protection can be primarily about punishment, limiting the number of punishments that the substantive law can authorize for particular wrongdoing. Indeed, as we see in chapter 2, Thomas Becket's attempt to limit the king's power to punish clerics already convicted in ecclesiastical courts was early evidence of a double jeopardy principle. But, as we also see, that limitation on the lawgiver's power to define crimes and fix penalties was decisively rejected in the thirteenth century. The reasons used to reject it eight hundred years ago are still valid today.

In modern times, it is the legislature, not the monarch, that creates criminal blameworthiness. Model 1 thus views double jeopardy as a substantive limitation on the legislature. The legislature is free to create crimes and authorize punishments, under this model, as long as the result is not impermissible multiple punishment. Model 1 assumes that the Double Jeopardy Clause has a substantive component that tells us when punishments are impermissibly multiple. But what would that component be? One might argue that any time a defendant is punished "twice" for the same offense, he has suffered impermissible multiple punishment. Even that apparently obvious principle turns out to be controversial and complex. Legislatures often authorize both a fine and a jail term for a single criminal violation. If the judge imposes both penalties, has the defendant been punished in violation of the Double Jeopardy Clause?

Perhaps a Model 1 proponent would argue that a fine and jail term do violate double jeopardy. If so, what about a fine and community service? Or a fine and probation? Or probation and community service? It seems unlikely that the Double Jeopardy Clause would forbid the judge to impose probation and community service, yet there is no principled basis to distinguish those sanctions from a fine and a jail term. All four sanctions require the defendant to do something as a consequence of having been found guilty of a criminal violation.[4] Suffering a judicially imposed consequence for a criminal violation, even community service, must be a punishment. If not, why would the legislature authorize it as a sanction for a criminal violation? Thus, the Model 1 proponent is forced to argue that the imposition of probation and community service is multiple punishment.

But our intuitions resist the argument that probation and community service for the same criminal violation is impermissible multiple punishment. The reason, I believe, has to do with long-standing allocation of institutional responsibility to design and impose appropriate penalties. We expect the legislature to define crimes and fix penalties. We expect judges to impose from a range of penalties those that are most appropriate. In accomplishing the task of fashioning the proper punishment, flexibility is a virtue. In some cases, community service is sufficient punishment. In others, a prison sentence is necessary. And in cases where the public purse is also harmed, both a fine and a prison sentence are necessary to achieve a proportional punishment.

To take an example that is not strictly about judicial discretion, President Ford decided that Richard Nixon had "suffered enough" by having to resign the presidency, a "sentence" that would be unavailable for the rest of us. Whether or not one agrees with President Ford's pardon of Nixon, the point is that flexibility permits the sentencer leeway to construct a sentence that takes into account unusual or even unique characteristics of the offender. Any principle that says the legislature can authorize, and the judge can impose, only a single kind of penalty seems too arbitrary, too rigid.

Our intuitions here are manifested in sentencing theory. Different theoretical models of sentencing have been offered over the centuries, ranging from a pure retributive model to a pure rehabilitation model, including various combinations of retribution, deterrence, incapacitation, and rehabilitation. Retribution is probably the oldest sentencing theory; it can be found in the Old Testament (an eye for an eye) as well as in the Code of Hammurabi. Kant was perhaps its most passionate and best advocate. To show his dedication to retribution as the sole justification for punishment, Kant offered a hypothetical in which an island community was going to leave the island forever. The community has to decide what to do with convicted murderers in prison awaiting execution. One choice is to leave the murderers behind on the island. They can harm none other than themselves (Kant assumes they cannot escape). But he insists that justice requires that "the last murderer lying in the prison ought to be executed before the resolution was carried out. This ought to be done in order that every one may realize the desert of his deeds, and that blood guiltiness may not remain upon the people; for otherwise they might all be regarded as participators in the murder as a public violation of justice."[5]

Deterrence is probably a more modern, and certainly a more utilitarian, justification for punishment. The theory is to set punishments at a level that will deter the individual offender from repeating his offense, and the general population from committing it for the first time. These goals are called, respectively, special and general deterrence. Incapacitation is related to deterrence, except that it focuses only on the dangerousness of the individual offender. The more likely he is to recividate, the longer the sentence should be.

Rehabilitation is a theory currently out of favor, in part because it permits the most flexibility on the part of the judge, and the public has become dissatisfied with excessive judicial discretion in sentencing. Determining what sanction will have the best chance of rehabilitating an offender is a wholly individualized determination. Probation might be the best rehabilitative tonic for a first-time offender, but a repeat offender might need a fine and a prison term.

With a single possible exception, all of these theories and combinations of theories require at least some flexibility in sentencing. Retribution might seem to offer a "one size fits all" approach—for each crime there might be a Kantian punishment that is uniquely appropriate—but this would work only if the substantive criminal law were narrowly tailored to reflect Kantian harms. Modern United States criminal law has broad offense definitions and expansive notion of accomplice liability, thus requiring individualized sentences even under the retributive model. For example, a youth who drives the getaway car for what he thinks is a burglary may be guilty of murder if his partners kill a janitor in the building. But it is difficult to argue that he is as blameworthy as the killers. Indeed, the Supreme Court has focused on lesser blameworthiness to derive limitations on accomplice liability from the Eighth Amendment's ban on cruel and unusual punishment.[6]

Incapacitation, special deterrence, and rehabilitation all focus on the individual offender and thus, by definition, require flexibility in sentencing. The only theory that does not require attention to individualized sentencing is the general deterrence goal of discouraging those who have yet to commit crime. Presumably, the question of optimal general deterrence is unrelated to the characteristics of the particular offender; after all, general deterrence failed by definition in the case before the court. Thus, a single sentence for murder is presumably justified by general deterrence goals, without regard to the failure of that sentence to satisfy retributive, incapacitative, or special deterrence goals in the case of our young getaway driver. The general deterrence message is "Don't drive a getaway car for a burglary because you might wind up guilty of murder." Thus, a system based wholly on general deterrent goals would likely need only a single sentence for each crime.

But general deterrence is an unsatisfying justification if used in isolation. General deterrence requires penalties to be arranged according to the temptation to commit crimes. Because few of us are tempted to commit murder, and many of us are tempted to take recreational drugs or cheat on our income taxes, a sentencing system built solely on general deterrence would have higher penalties for drug possession and income tax evasion than for murder. We reject this system because our ideal of justice is driven in large part by retribution and, to a lesser extent, by incapacitation and special deterrence. Murder will always carry the greatest penalty, despite its relative rarity, because it is the most harmful to society—so harmful that Kant wanted to kill the convicted murderers rather than strand them on the island.

It is quite likely, therefore, that general deterrence adherents would accept at least some flexibility in sentencing to take account of individual distinctions in blameworthiness and the need for incapacitation. As long as retribution, incapacitation, and special deterrence play a role in our instincts about sentencing, legislatures should be encouraged to provide alternative forms of sentences (fines, jail, probation, community service), and judges should be encouraged (with or without formal sentencing guidelines) to concoct the appropriate sentence by using one, some, or all of the alternatives. To find a countervailing, absolute ban on this kind of sentencing flexibility is to read far too much into the Double Jeopardy Clause.

Indeed, the Supreme Court has never held that imposition of a legislatively authorized fine and prison term for the same offense violates the multiple punishment component of the Double Jeopardy Clause. But if this clear case of double punishment is not impermissible "multiple punishment," why would two consecutive prison terms be "multiple punishment" if they are clearly authorized by the legislature? The answer, the Court provided in *Missouri v. Hunter*,[7] is that no combination of clearly authorized penalties constitutes multiple punishment under the Double Jeopardy Clause. Thus, Missouri could constitutionally authorize a second conviction and consecutive sentence for using a weapon to commit robbery (one conviction and sentence for robbery; the second conviction and consecutive sentence for using a weapon to commit the robbery).

Hunter, decided over only two dissents, is a clear refutation of a Model 1 substantive limitation on the power of the legislature to decree more than one conviction for the "same offense" in a single trial. If the legislature speaks clearly enough, two convictions in one trial (or three or four, for that matter) are not "multiple punishment" for purposes of the Double Jeopardy Clause. Oddly enough, after rejecting Model 1, the Court seems poised to accept a variant of this model based on little more than a jurisprudential reflex. The Justices who support a more expansive view of double jeopardy seem willing to find a limitation on the legislature in an amalgam of loose language in earlier cases, and the conservatives are attracted by what appears to be a literal reading of the constitutional text. But, as I show later, this Model 2 is flawed for the very same reason the Court rejected Model 1.

My view is that *Hunter* is the only defensible framework for a double jeopardy/multiple punishment framework. I argue in the next two sections for an expansion of the *Hunter* analysis to include successive prosecution theory and the civil/criminal distinction.

Model 2: A Partly Substantive Double Jeopardy Clause

If the Double Jeopardy Clause does not forbid the legislature the power to decree the number of penalties, or convictions, that can attend the same offense in a single trial, the next question is whether it limits the power of the legislature in the context of successive prosecutions. At first glance (and, I argue, on deeper analysis as well), it would seem that the power to "define crimes and fix penalties" is the power to have as many substantive criminal offenses as the legislature wants for particular conduct. After all, by what standard could a court judge whether the legislature had divided conduct too finely, created too many offenses out of one "indivisible" course of conduct? What would an "indivisible" course of conduct look like? As then-Justice Rehnquist noted in rejecting this notion: "To the extent that this . . . thesis assumes that any particular criminal transaction is made up of a determinable number of constitutional atoms that the legislature cannot further subdivide into separate offenses, 'it demands more of the Double Jeopardy Clause than it is capable of supplying.'"[8]

Once we know how many substantive offenses have been committed by the defendant's conduct—and this question *Hunter* answers by deferring to legislative intent—any other limit on the prosecutor must be a limit on obtaining authorized penalties in more than one trial. One such limit is the joinder law of the jurisdiction. Joinder law, which is nonconstitutional in nature, is a procedural mechanism that sometimes requires trying in one trial offenses arising out of the same conduct. Model 2 essentially holds that the Double Jeopardy Clause overrides the legislature's ability to define different substantive offenses. Stated differently, Model 2 finds in the Double Jeopardy Clause an additional, constitutionally based form of mandatory joinder.

There are two sets of arguments against the proposition that double jeopardy sometimes bars separate trials for legislatively separate offenses. Ironically, the arguments are held by Justices on opposite ends of the judicial philosophy spectrum ("liberal" to "conservative"). On the "liberal" end of the spectrum, we hear about the policy of not harassing criminal defendants by repeated prosecutions for the same conduct. This, to be sure, is the argument underlying nonconstitutional joinder provisions that sometimes require trying together offenses that arise from the same conduct. But the double jeopardy issue is whether that sound policy is embedded in the Double Jeopardy Clause. As chapter 2 shows, this policy argument is unpersuasive if we have a good account of when the legislative has truly authorized separate penalties. The antiharassment policy is also an untenable construction of the language of the Double Jeopardy Clause, which, after all, forbids more than one jeopardy for the same "offense," not for the "same conduct" or "same transaction" or "same episode."

Ironically, the reliance on constitutional language to avoid the liberal antiharassment argument leads the conservative side of the Court also to miss the essence of double jeopardy. Focusing on the language about "twice in jeopardy," Justice Scalia argues that the Double Jeopardy Clause is wholly inapplicable in the single trial/multiple punishment context. While this is a permissible reading of the language, it is not the best reading of the history of double jeopardy, again as we see in chapter 2. More important, Scalia's focus on carving the multiple punishment doctrine out of double jeopardy has led him to accept blindly the proposition that the clause must limit the number of trials the legislature can authorize. There is no reason in logic or history or language that the latter proposition follows from Scalia's multiple punishment argument.

The Court has never held that the Double Jeopardy Clause forbids a prosecutor to seek two trials in the *Hunter* situation—when the legislature clearly meant to create different substantive offenses that would be the same offense under the Court's mechanical same-offense test. Moreover, Scalia's endorsement of that proposition is limited to a single footnote.[9] Thus, the Court still has time to realize that the reason to reject Model 1 also applies to Model 2. The Double Jeopardy Clause has no substantive component that somehow denies to the legislature its prerogative to have as many substantive offenses, and trials, out of the same conduct as it wants. Policies about harassing prosecutions, while sound enough, do not transform the Double Jeopardy Clause into a rule of mandatory joinder.

If double jeopardy is not a substantive limitation on the legislature when it defines crimes and creates penalties in the single-trial context (*Hunter*), symmetry and logic dictate that double jeopardy is never a limit on the legislature. Of course, one can reject symmetry and logic and hold that the Framers meant to fasten double jeopardy on the legislature to prevent it from acting in derogation of the double jeopardy principle when "true" double jeopardy questions arise—that is, when one jeopardy has ended and another is threatened. This is Scalia's view. Unfortunately, as the rest of this book details, there is no acceptable way to define either "offense" or "jeopardy" without ultimately relying on what the legislature intended. Our culture, legal and otherwise, gives us a rough idea of when a punishment is "cruel and unusual." Culture gives us a benchmark of "unreasonable searches and seizures." It tells us roughly when a witness has been "compelled to be a witness against himself." It tells us precisely nothing about when offenses are the same and when a jeopardy has become "twice." To arrive at a definition, we need the legislature. But if we need the legislature to flesh out our understanding of double jeopardy, we cannot avoid deferring entirely to the legislature when it speaks clearly to double jeopardy issues. That, at least, is the thesis of my book.

Model 3: A Procedural/Derivative Double Jeopardy Clause

Consistent with Blackstone's conception of double jeopardy, discussed in the next section, Model 3 limits the role of the Double Jeopardy Clause to ensuring the integrity of the legislative prerogative about "offense" and "jeopardy." In effect, this model teaches that double jeopardy is a procedural limitation on prosecutors and judges, but not a substantive limitation on the legislature. This model takes seriously what the Court said in 1977 in *Brown v. Ohio*: "The legislature remains free under the Double Jeopardy Clause to define crimes and fix punishments."[10]

Emphasizing that double jeopardy does not have a substantive component makes clear that it functions as a crude form of sentencing control (or guideline). Like modern statutory sentencing systems, double jeopardy provides legislative limits on how judges can sentence defendants. Double jeopardy provides a crude, either/or limitation—either the judge can sentence both for auto theft and joyriding, or the judge cannot. Despite its lack of fine gradations, which we expect in modern sentencing schemes, the Model 3 view of double jeopardy is remarkably similar to sentencing theory.

Like sentencing theory, double jeopardy applies uniformly whether penalties for violating different substantive offenses are sought in one trial or in two. Commentators and judges have perceived an independent concern with successive prosecutions[11] because of the obvious (and trivial) limitation on prosecutors that follows from the multiple punishment limitation. If a judge cannot impose two convictions for offense *A* and offense *B*, prosecutors cannot seek two trials for *A* and *B*. While this is true, it tells us nothing more important than that prosecutors cannot seek *any* penalty if the legislature did not intend the defendant's conduct to merit a penalty.

Consider statutory rape, defined as sexual intercourse with a person age 14–16 by someone who is at least two years older than the victim. A day before her sixteenth birthday, Allison has sex with Andy on his fourteenth birthday. Whatever our view of the morality involved, the legislature has spoken: Allison is not guilty of statutory rape, and the prosecutor may not seek her conviction. If the prosecutor does seek to convict Allison, the judge has no choice but to dismiss the indictment because Allison did not commit the substantive offense of statutory rape.

Now assume the legislature defines offense *A* so that it is an aggravated form of *B*, intending that actors who violate both *A* and *B* should be convicted of either offense but not both. If the prosecutor charges both in a single trial, and the jury convicts, the judge can impose but one conviction. This is the crucial multiple punishment limitation that derives from the Double Jeopardy Clause. It also follows that, once a conviction for either A or B exists, the prosecutor cannot prosecute the other, just as the prosecutor cannot prosecute Allison in the previous example—neither Allison nor our A-B offender has committed a crime for which the legislature intends prosecution.

This way of viewing the successive prosecution doctrine makes it derivative of the multiple punishment protection, precisely the opposite view from that of Justice Scalia. The Supreme Court seems to have recognized the derivative nature of successive prosecution theory in *Brown*, when it said:

> If two offenses are the same under this [same-offense] test for purposes of barring consecutive sentences at a single trial, they necessarily will be the same for purposes of barring successive prosecutions. Where the judge is forbidden to impose cumulative punishment for two crimes at the end of a single proceeding, the prosecutor is forbidden to strive for the same result in successive proceedings.[12]

To be sure, the Court confused matters by saying, earlier in the opinion, "Where successive prosecutions are at stake, the [double jeopardy] guarantee serves 'a constitutional policy of finality for the defendant's benefit.'"[13] I address the "constititutional policy of finality" in the next chapter. For now, suffice to say that the defendant who committed A-B has finality expectations no different from Allison. Allison can count on not being prosecuted for statutory rape because she did not commit statutory rape. Our A-B defendant can count on not being prosecuted for both A and B because he has not committed an act that makes him prosecutable for both crimes.

The task of defending Model 3 begins in the next section, where we meet the strongest contrary argument: that the Double Jeopardy Clause should be a substantive limitation on the legislature, like the Fourth Amendment, the Sixth Amendment, and the rest of the Fifth Amendment. The legislature cannot authorize unreasonable searches and seizures, or put limits on the constitutional right to counsel or confrontation, or permit defendants to be compelled to testify against themselves. Why, then, is the legislature the sole source of the substance of the Double Jeopardy Clause? Putting the question in less friendly terms, as some have done, why is the legislature free to act without the constraint of the Double Jeopardy Clause?

Why the Legislature?

I can imagine a skeptic who would say my legislative-prerogative thesis puts too much power in legislatures who pander to the crime fear in the populace.[14] Alternatively, the skeptic might deny the positivism that is at the heart of my thesis, opting instead for some natural law understanding of double jeopardy.[15] The skeptic would say that to defer completely to the legislature somehow denies the Double Jeopardy Clause the independence befitting a constitutional right. The skeptic might concede that the legislature controls what counts as a completed jeopardy. The end of jeopardy has always been understood as a verdict and, in this century, certain kinds of mistrials. Moreover, the legislature has little lattitude in defining verdicts because of the overarching right to a jury trial and the right to be found guilty beyond a reasonable doubt.

But the skeptic would draw the line at defining "offense." She would insist that the power to define double jeopardy offense belongs to judges. Judges are best situated to uncover "the consciousness and spirit of a community which, in turn, is embedded in its customs and practices."[16] These "customs and practices" give shape to the definitional inquiry. Judges are charged with defining "search," "seizure," "cruel and unusual punishment," and "coercion," to name a few difficult constitutional concepts. Why not "offense"?

The double jeopardy argument set out in this book does not deny judges their interpretative function. Indeed, the account offered here is the only one that provides judges an overarching, hard-edged principle to use in discharging that function. But it limits the range of the interpretive function to determining how the legislature meant to assign criminal blameworthiness.

The defense of this limit on judicial interpretation is partly linguistic: "offense" has no referent other than the legislative enactment. Concepts like "coercion" and "cruel" have cultural referents that exist independent of the legislature. A law seeking to define compulsion, for example, could not supplant judicial interpretations of what it means to be compelled to be a witness against oneself. "Offense" is different; there is no referent beyond what the offense-creating institution has done. We might say that it is immoral to lie or cheat. But we cannot say that it is an "offense," in the double jeopardy sense or the criminal law sense,[17] until the appropriate institution has made it an offense.

The linguistic argument intertwines with the historical and functional argument. With rare exception, the double jeopardy principle has always operated as a limitation on prosecutors and judges but not on the lawgiver; it is only the legislature (the lawgiver) that is institutionally competent to create legal blameworthiness. My argument crucially depends on the premise that the purpose of the Double Jeopardy Clause is to limit the number of blameworthiness determinations. Both Martin Friedland and Jay Sigler relegate prevention of multiple convictions to a secondary status because both believe that the principal function of double jeopardy is to prevent "the unwarranted harassment of the accused by multiple prosecutions."[18] That premise might cause one to reject the legislature as the ultimate source of double jeopardy limitations because one might naturally view the legislature as just another source of potential harassment.

Chapter 2 considers, and rejects, harassment as a double jeopardy policy that exists independent of the policy limiting the number of judgments to those authorized by the legislature. If I am right to reject harassment as an independent double jeopardy policy, no institution other than the legislature can give meaning to jeopardy and to same offense. To be sure, common-law judges were principally responsible for these tasks in the pre-1792 world. But common-law judges performed many functions that we now assign to the legislature. More significant, even in the world where judges gave meaning to jeopardy and same offense, an occasional statute usurped the judicial role by permitting second trials or punishments in particular categories of cases,[19] and none of these statutes were overruled by courts or criticized by any of the commentators, including the oft-critical Blackstone.

Using legislative intent to determine the right number of penalties is easy to defend when the issue arises in a single trial. The question of how many penalties the particular conduct deserves is otherwise beyond the capacity of judges to answer. Begin with the related question of the quantity of punishment a particular defendant or offense deserves (without regard to the appropriate number of penalties). In the Eighth Amendment cases involving a single penalty, the Court has been hard pressed to answer the desert question. This is the reason the Court has essentially limited the Eighth Amendment proportionality analysis to cases involving the death penalty.[20] It is possible, though not easy, to develop a metaphysical answer to the question of whether a particular crime deserves the death penalty.[21] It is almost impossible to defend a desert position on penalties less than death. Does possession of 650 grams of cocaine deserve forty years in prison? No, I do not believe so (even though the Court has approved life in prison without parole for this offense).[22] Can I demonstrate that forty years is cruel and unusual punishment? Probably not. Even if I could, what would the answer be to thirty-nine years? Or thirty-eight years? And so forth.

Shifting to multiple penalties, the desert question is no easier to answer. Consider entry into a federal bank with intent to rob it, and aggravated bank robbery (robbery with a dangerous weapon). The first offense is punishable by fifteen years, the second by twenty-five years. If the judge imposes consecutive sentences totaling forty years, does this defendant have a valid claim of multiple punishment? Assuming forty years for aggravated bank robbery is not an excessive *single* penalty, it would be an excessive *multiple* penalty only if Congress did not intend both penalties to apply.[23] From a functional perspective, therefore, the multiple punishment analysis begins with legislative intent.

Legislative intent is the right analytic approach to multiple punishment, both for the pragmatic reason that no other analytic structure exists and because it is the best functional structure. Though accounts of general moral or ethical blameworthiness can be developed and defended, the only blameworthiness that concerns the criminal justice system is wholly contained within the criminal prohibition. The legislature is the author of that prohibition and thus of that blameworthiness.

To see that this is so, consider what a metaphysical blameworthiness account would say about *mala prohibita* offenses—those that are thought to prohibit morally neutral but potentially harmful acts, such as driving without a license. There are dozens, if not hundreds, of criminal statutes that proscribe conduct that would be considered morally neutral on mainstream accounts of morality—engaging in homosexual conduct, sale of obscenity to adults, public drunkenness, vagrancy, gambling, and (perhaps) prostitution. If conduct is morally neutral, the statutory criminal blameworthiness in these offenses must necessarily be found in what Michael Moore calls the "bad state of affairs" that the legislature intended to prevent.[24] Thus, gambling is a crime because it may harm the family of the gambler by depriving them of necessary money. Public drunkenness is a crime because it upsets the sensibilities of upstanding citizens. But if morally neutral criminal blameworthiness is found not in the conduct itself but in a social problem the legislature seeks to address, on what theory is traditional criminal blameworthiness (e.g., murder, robbery, theft) found in the conduct rather than in the legislative description and prohibition of that conduct?

Driving without a license is a blameworthy, forbidden act because the legislature wants to promote highway safety, and prohibiting this morally neutral conduct is an overinclusive way of accomplishing that goal. Drunk driving is a blameworthy act for the same reason and irrespective of the moral status of driving drunk (which is surely different from driving without a license). The argument seems irresistible that criminal blameworthiness, as opposed to moral fault, is exclusively the function of legislative creation. Thus, the criminal blameworthiness of engaging in homosexual conduct, for example, is constructed in the same manner as the criminal blameworthiness of murder—by consulting the statutory language forbidding the conduct, and without regard to metaphysical notions of wrongful or harmful acts.

This is but another way to say that legislatures today do what judges did in Blackstone's day. In 1769 most criminal offenses were the product of judicial decision. Common-law judges created and refined the criminal "code" over the centuries, carving out subcategories of offenses as necessary—creating manslaughter as a crime distinct from murder, for example, to distinguish its lesser blameworthiness.[25] Judges eventually relinquished to the legislature the role of defining crimes. With the role of defining crimes comes the role of defining jeopardy offenses. It is that simple.

To claim that all double jeopardy theory ultimately collapses into the "black hole" of legislative intent is not to suggest that this intent is easy to uncover. Nor do I have (or need) a new method of ascertaining the relevant intent. Indeed, part of the argument here is that the legislature so rarely makes its intent known on double jeopardy issues that courts must resort to presumptions to decide these questions. Chapters 6 and 8 develop and defend a set of presumptions about when offenses are the same and when jeopardy ends. But, if the legislature makes its intent clear, this intent overcomes any presumptions offered in this book or previously created by courts. Requiring the legislature to speak clearly to rebut double jeopardy presumptions solves the problem of how to ascertain legislative intent that is ambiguous, vague, or nonexistent. The practical value of this approach has been recognized in the Australian Crimes Act, which "requires that the legislature specifically intend double punishment" for the same act before it can be imposed.[26]

The theory offered here is simply that the legislature creates substantive blameworthiness and thus inevitably controls how it is to be parceled out (same offense) and when one determination procedurally stands for that blameworthiness (the end of jeopardy). Once the confusion about double jeopardy having a substantive component is cleared up, the analysis can profitably focus on how best to determine legislative intent on "same offense" and on "twice in jeopardy."

The Court's View of Legislative Prerogative

I detail the specific doctrinal evidence in favor of the legislative-prerogative thesis in chapter 3. Here I offer more general doctrinal support, first drawing from areas outside double jeopardy. Then I use two somewhat unusual double jeopardy cases to show that my Model 3 account has more explanatory power than the Model 2 view, which limits successive prosecutions even when the legislature meant to create separately punishable offenses.

Outside the double jeopardy context, the Court has recognized that the legislature operates with only minimal limitations on its power to define crimes and fix penalties; these limitations are embedded in due process and in the Eighth Amendment prohibition of cruel and unusual punishment. For example, the issue in *Patterson v. New York*[27] was whether in a murder prosecution the state had to prove the absence of "extreme emotional disturbance," a general affirmative defense created by a different code section. Patterson argued that homicide consisted of the elements of homicide plus the proof that he had *not* acted under extreme emotional disturbance. To permit the legislature to characterize extreme emotional disturbance as a defense, rather than as a (negation of) one element of the crime itself, Patterson argued, had the effect of undermining the due process right to be proven guilty of the offense beyond a reasonable doubt. The Court responded that Patterson's "offense" was what the legislature defined in the homicide code section and did not include the negation of affirmative defenses defined elsewhere in the criminal code. The key to *Patterson* is that the legislature retains the prerogative to decide what constitutes a criminal offense and what constitutes a defense to that crime.

Even closer to the double jeopardy context, the issue in *Schad v. Arizona*[28] was whether a guilty verdict could stand if the state presented two different theories of liability, one requiring direct proof of mens rea (premeditated murder) while the other presumed mens rea once the actus reus was proven (felony murder). It was possible, Schad argued, that six jury members thought he committed the underlying felony but lacked premeditation and six others thought he premeditated but did not commit the underlying felony. In that situation, half the jury would have acquitted of felony murder and half would have acquitted of premeditated murder. How, then, Schad argued, could his verdict be constitutional?

As the Court recognized, Schad was not really arguing about jury unanimity or proof beyond a reasonable doubt. The jury unanimously found Schad guilty of first-degree murder beyond a reasonable doubt because Arizona defined first-degree murder in the alternative (premeditated or felony murder). Thus,

> petitioner's real challenge is to Arizona's characterization of first-degree murder as a single crime as to which a verdict need not be limited to any one statutory alternative, as against which petitioner argues that premeditated murder and felony murder are separate crimes as to which the jury must return separate verdicts. The issue in this case, then, is one of the permissible limits in defining criminal conduct.[29]

The limits to the legislature's prerogative to define criminal conduct is to be found in a "distillate of the concept of due process with its demands for fundamental fairness and for the rationality that is an essential component of that fairness."[30] In determining whether a particular statute satisfies this due process "distillate," the Court began "with a threshold presumption of legislative competence to determine the appropriate relationship between means and ends in defining the elements of a crime."[31]

Why this heavy dose of deference? The answer is allocation of institutional responsibilities and competence. The difficulty is in trying to determine whether there are "really" two offenses when the legislature said it was creating only one offense. As the Court put it: "Judicial restraint necessarily follows from a recognition of the impossibility of determining, as an *a priori* matter, whether a given combination of facts is consistent with there being only one offense."[32] The same difficulty infects the double jeopardy same offense analysis—how can a court know "as an *a priori* matter" whether what a defendant did is "really" only one crime even though the legislature has defined it as two? *Schad* suggests that, for due process purposes, there is a presumption that the legislature has made the right choice. My argument in this book is that, for double jeopardy purposes, the presumption is conclusive as long as the legislature expresses itself clearly.

If the legislature satisfies due process "fundamental fairness" and "rationality," *Schad* holds that it may define one crime as it pleases. The legislative deference rationale of *Schad* suggests the prerogative to define two (or more) crimes to permit successive prosecution and cumulative punishment, again as long as the legislature satisfies the Eighth Amendment and the *Schad* standard of "fundamental fairness" and "rationality." Because those standards are found outside the Double Jeopardy Clause, however, we can state the principle derived from *Schad* as follows: the Double Jeopardy Clause contains no substantive limitation on the legislative prerogative. If any given combination of statutes satisfies the Eighth Amendment and due process, Model 3 double jeopardy requires only that courts have good reason to believe that the legislature meant both statutes to apply to the defendant's conduct. In that event, both penalties can be applied consistent with the Constitution.

Two examples from the Court's double jeopardy jurisprudence show the explanatory power of Model 3. Oddball cases often make good tests of the concepts behind doctrine, and *Ohio v. Johnson*[33] is an oddball case. The state charged two pairs of greater- and lesser-included offenses, murder/manslaughter and robbery/theft. At arraignment, the defendant offered to plead guilty to the lesser charges in each pair. Though the prosecutor objected, the judge accepted the guilty pleas to the lesser charges and dismissed the greater charges as violative of double jeopardy.

The Court held, 7-2, that double jeopardy did not forbid the state from proceeding on the greater charges. But finding a rationale in traditional doctrine, which tracks Models 1 and 2, was not easy. The Court had to distinguish *Brown v. Ohio*,[34] its seminal same-offense case that held that a lesser-included offense is always the same as the greater offense. It distinguished *Brown* by limply arguing that Johnson had "only offered to resolve part of the charges brought against him, while the State objected to disposing of any of the counts against respondent without a trial."[35] This is true enough, but the Court did not explain why the *defendant*'s actions should change the meaning of "same offense." If a greater- and a lesser-included offense are *always* the same offense, as *Brown* certainly suggests, Johnson should have won (this was the argument of Justices Stevens and Marshall in dissent).

And if greater- and lesser-included offenses are not always the same offense, which is implicit in *Johnson*, we need an account of when to ignore the included-offense test. The Court's weak account in *Johnson* echoes dicta from a Justice Black opinion (inapposite on the merits) about preventing the harassment of defendants. Presumably, Johnson had not been harassed, because it was his idea to plead guilty to the lesser charges and the prosecutor objected on the spot. While this works to explain *Johnson* as a gloss on Model 2's view that "same offense" has a content independent of legislative intent, harassment is what I call a "soft-edged" principle—one that does not provide much guidance to courts. I also argue that harassment is a due process concept, based on what the *Schad* Court termed a "distillate" of "fundamental fairness" and "rationality." Doctrines that are indistinguishable from due process should be removed from double jeopardy and relocated to the Due Process Clause.

Model 3 operates much more cleanly here. We ask whether the legislature authorized judges to accept plea bargains over the prosecutor's objection, thereby preventing the state from proceeding with trial. In this country, the decision of whether to proceed with trial belongs to the prosecutor, not the judge. Suppose the judge had told the prosecutor, "I don't think you should bring these greater charges, though I have not heard the evidence and cannot enter a judgment of acquittal. So I will dismiss with prejudice the greater charges." It seems clear to me that the legislature did not authorize this kind of judicial oversight, which is the effect of what the judge did in *Johnson*.

If a review of the state rules of procedure bears out this assessment, then the judge has acted in derogation of the legislative prerogative that prosecutors decide which charges to bring to trial. Since double jeopardy, under Model 3, operates only to enforce legislative judgments (actual or presumed) about "offense" and "jeopardy," it cannot be deployed in derogation of the legislative scheme. Johnson loses under Model 3, just as he does under Model 2, but he loses because double jeopardy is simply inapplicable to oppose legislative judgments, rather than because of some vague notion that he was not harassed.

The difference between this model and the first two is fundamental: under Model 3 defendants receive, as double jeopardy protection, no more convictions than the legislature has authorized, either by virtue of the way the legislature has defined "offense" or by virtue of how the legislature meant for one exposure to jeopardy to end. But there is no substantive component of double jeopardy that limits the legislature. If the legislature created an offense that *always* required reprosecution of conduct underlying another offense, and made it clear that reprosecution is what it intended, Model 3 says that the double jeopardy inquiry is at an end. We do not have to agonize over whether the legislature is permitted to create two cumulatively punishable substantive criminal law offenses.

The Supreme Court considered a statute very close to the one just hypothesized in *Garrett v. United States*.[36] The unusual federal offense of "continuing criminal enterprise" (CCE) requires proof of predicate felonies (along with other elements). While these felonies do not *have* to be manifested in prior convictions, they usually are (because that makes the prosecutor's job easier and because it is usually the prior charges and convictions that tip off the authorities to the existence of the criminal enterprise). Garrett was convicted in federal court in the state of Washington for importing marijuana. He was later prosecuted in Florida for CCE. The Government offered the Washington felony conviction as part of its CCE proof. These are the same offense under the included-offense test because CCE always requires proof of other felonies, here the Washington felony.[37]

In analyzing the double jeopardy same-offense question, the majority began by asking whether Congress intended to create "separate" offenses, with neither being a "substitute" for the other.[38] This is the right way to phrase the legislative-intent question. The question, as the Court realized, is *not* whether Congress meant to create an offense in addition to the predicate felony offenses; of course Congress meant to do that. The key question is whether Congress meant for the CCE offense to operate *separate* from the predicate felonies, rather than as a substitute for them. One way Congress could have envisioned the problem is as follows: if someone commits a sufficient number of predicate felonies, then we want that person convicted of CCE in lieu of the other, presumably lesser, predicate felonies. If Congress meant that, of course, it did not mean to create separate offenses.

The answer to the separate-offense question is the answer to my Model 3 question about legislative intent to create different double jeopardy offenses. Having gotten off to a good Model 3 start, the Court in *Garrett* quickly complicated matters, rephrasing the inquiry as three separate questions: (1) whether Congress intended to create offenses that could be prosecuted separately; (2) whether the Double Jeopardy Clause bars separate prosecution of these offenses; and (3) whether the Double Jeopardy Clause bars cumulative punishment of these offenses. On a Model 3 view, this is the same question asked three different ways. Once a court determines that Congress did (or did not) create separate criminal law offenses, we also know how many prosecutions and punishments are permissible under the Double Jeopardy Clause. The Court's opinion in *Garrett* is, by comparison, a Gordian knot of different strands of analysis.

Read one way, *Garrett* suggests that legislative intent is the only relevant criterion.[39] But after holding that Congress intended to create offenses that could be prosecuted separately, the Court then went on to discuss at length whether the Double Jeopardy Clause would permit the authorized separate prosecutions and cumulative punishments. The opinion is puzzling even on its own terms. After concluding that the Double Jeopardy Clause permitted separate prosecutions, because CCE is an exception to the normal *Brown v. Ohio* application of the lesser-included-offense test, the Court treated as undecided the issue whether cumulative punishments were permitted. But on any coherent view of double jeopardy, deciding that two offenses may be prosecuted separately necessarily answers the question of whether the Double Jeopardy Clause permits cumulative punishments. What kind of constitutional scheme would permit separate prosecutions and then forbid the penalty sought in the second trial?

The Court's failure to apply a Model 3 analysis to the successive-prosecution question led it to a convoluted, unsatisfying analysis. The Court distinguished "typical" applications of the included-offense test because *Garrett's* criminal conduct continued after the first conviction. Though the majority is right, the point is both obvious and trivial. If a defendant is convicted of conspiracy, and the conspiracy continues after the conviction, the defendant can be tried again for the subsequent conspiratorial conduct. This distinction is less apt in *Garrett*, as the dissent pointed out, because *all the conduct for which Garrett was prosecuted* was over by the time of the first trial.[40]

Rather than respond to the dissent's point on conduct, Justice Rehnquist wrote for the Court, "One who insists that the music stop and the piper be paid at a particular point must at least have stopped dancing himself before he may seek such an accounting."[41] This analogy hardly qualifies as an answer to the dissent and only demonstrates the emptiness of the conceptual Model 2 double jeopardy universe. The Court seemed to mean its "paying the piper" metaphor to answer some kind of generalized fairness question—whether it was fair for the government to charge these offenses in separate indictments. Six members of the Supreme Court found no unfairness, citing the relatively small part the Washington felony played in the five-and-one-half-year continuing criminal enterprise.[42] Three members of the Court found unfairness, at least in part because the CCE case could have been proven using other offenses alleged in the CCE indictment.[43] This kind of analysis is precisely why double jeopardy is in such a mess today. On what basis could anyone judge which position best manifests a vague double jeopardy policy against unfairness?

It is better to start over. Starting over, in my view, means returning to the history and policies underlying double jeopardy. Though Blackstone was far from the beginning of double jeopardy history, his 1764 summary is the most complete, satisfying statement of the doctrine and policy yet written.

Blackstone's Double Jeopardy

Blackstone wrote at length about double jeopardy in his *Commentaries.* Though some of the meaning will be unclear at present, in part because of the differences between the eighteenth-century legal system and procedure and those in use today, we can begin by quoting Blackstone on double jeopardy. A particularly jarring anachronism must be noted: the use of "appeal" in Blackstone's day meant a prosecution by a private citizen, to be distinguished from the king's indictment. It is difficult to keep out of one's mind the modern usage of appealing to a higher court, and I thus occasionally use brackets to remind the reader of Blackstone's meaning. To make Blackstone's contribution more apparent, I break it into parts and pause to show how it fits with a modern conception of double jeopardy. All of this, however, is by way of summary. The rest of the book explains and defends a blameworthiness conception of double jeopardy more fully. Blackstone begins:

> Special pleas in bar . . . are of four kinds: a former acquittal, a former conviction, a former attainder, or a pardon. There are many other pleas which may be pleaded in bar of an appeal [a private prosecution]; but these are applicable to both appeals and indictments.
>
> I. First, the plea of *autrefoits acquit,* or a former acquittal, is grounded on this universal maxim of the common law of England, that no man is to be brought into jeopardy of his life or limb more than once for the same offence. And hence it is allowed as a consequence, that when a man is once fairly found not guilty upon any indictment or other prosecution, before

any court having competent jurisdiction of the offence, he may plead such acquittal in bar of any subsequent accusation for the same crime. Therefore an acquittal on an appeal [private suit] is a good bar to an indictment on the same offence. And so also was an acquittal on an indictment a good bar to an appeal, by the common law; and therefore, in favor of appeals, a general practice was introduced not to try any person on an indictment of homicide till after the year and day, within which appeals may be brought, were past; by which time it often happened that the witnesses died, or the whole was forgotten. To remedy which inconvenience, the statute 3 Hen. VII. c.1 enacts, that indictments shall be proceeded on immediately at the king's suit, for the death of a man, without waiting for bringing an appeal; and that the plea of *autrefoits acquit* on an indictment shall be no bar to the prosecuting of any appeal.[44]

In Blackstone's day, the private prosecution (the appeal) was a criminal trial, simply brought by a different prosecutor. Indeed, at common law it was the preferred method of prosecuting crime, as it had been for a thousand years or more. This can be seen in the common-law rule that the king had to wait a year and a day before bringing an indictment in order to let the private prosecutor have the first opportunity. At least one thirteenth-century commentator (Britton) treated the private appeal and the king's indictment as separate realms, permitting both to go forward.[45] But by the time of Coke (mid-1600s), the law was clear that a verdict in either type of prosecution was a bar to the other, as the year-and-a-day rule makes plain. Blackstone notes the single exception—the Henry VII statute permitting the king to proceed on a homicide indictment immediately without an acquittal barring the private appeal. This suggests that by the time of Henry VII, the monarch was sufficiently interested in controlling prosecutions that the private appeal was beginning to lose its prominence.

Over time, the private appeal withered—today it seems odd even to think of a private citizen prosecuting crime.[46] Its place was taken by a more prominent role for the king's indictments and the civil tort action. Today, as suggested earlier and detailed in chapter 4, there is no overlap between civil tort and crime, just as there was no overlap in Blackstone's day when a homicide indictment produced an acquittal. Today, as long as an action is civil—making this distinction is the subject of chapter 4—there is no bar to a criminal prosecution based on the same conduct.

Returning now to Blackstone:

2. Secondly, the plea of *autrefoits convict*, or a former conviction for the same identical crime, though no judgment was ever given, or perhaps will be, (being suspended by the benefit of clergy or other causes) is a good plea in bar to an indictment. And this depends upon the same principle as the former, that no man ought to be twice brought in danger of his life for one and the same crime. Hereupon it has been held that a conviction of manslaughter, on an appeal or an indictment, is a bar even in another appeal, and much more in an indictment for murder; for the fact prosecuted is the same in both, though the offences differ in coloring and in degree. It is to be observed that the pleas of *autrefoits acquit* and *autrefoits convict*, or a former acquittal and former conviction, must be upon a prosecution for the same identical act and crime.[47]

Blackstone's view of greater- and lesser-included offenses is manifested today in the Court's same-offense test, most clearly articulated in *Brown v. Ohio*. The idea that conviction of a lesser offense bars prosecution of the greater has been accepted in a line of cases extending back in time between *Brown* and Blackstone.[48] Notice that the plea of *autrefois convict* is actually broader in one way than that of *autrefois acquit*: the Henry VII exception to the year-and-a-day rule did not apply to *autrefois convict*. The common-law view of double jeopardy was roughly as follows: if a defendant was convicted of the same act and crime by either a private citizen or the king, it was an end to the matter (more on this in relation to *autrefois attaint*). If, on the other hand, a defendant was acquitted, there was the chance of an erroneous acquittal (because "witnesses died, or the whole was forgotten"). This risk of error justified an exception when the king proceeded first in a homicide case and an acquittal resulted.

With that single difference to one side, Blackstone noted the similarity between the two pleas: "It is to be observed that the pleas of *autrefoits acquit* and *autrefoits convict*, or a former acquittal and former conviction, must be upon a prosecution for the same identical act and crime." Of course, he is using "identical act and crime" in a loose way because he gave as an example the offenses of murder and manslaughter. They are identical only in that manslaughter is necessarily included in murder. Again, this suggests the Court's greater- and lesser-included offense test from *Brown*. Though I will suggest modifications to the greater- and lesser-included offense test, it is far better than any other test, certainly far better than the "identical-offense" test recently offered by Akhil Amar and

Jonathan Marcus.[49] Once again, Blackstone had the right idea about double jeopardy.

In the next section, Blackstone contrasts *autrefois acquit* and *autrefois convict* with a much broader plea. Recall that he ended the prior discussion by noting that the pleas of former acquittal and former conviction "must be upon a prosecution for the same identical act and crime." Now he continues:

> But the case is otherwise, in
>
> Thirdly, the plea of *autrefoits attaint,* or a former attainder, which is a good plea in bar, whether it be for the same or any other felony. For wherever a man is attainted of felony by a judgment of death, either upon a verdict or confession, by outlawry, or heretofore by abjuration, and whether upon an appeal or an indictment, he may plead such attainder in bar to any subsequent indictment or appeal for the same or for any other felony. And this because, generally, such proceeding on a second prosecution cannot be to any purpose; for the prisoner is dead in law by the first attainder, his blood is already corrupted, and he hath forfeited all that he had; so that it is absurd and superfluous to endeavor to attaint him a second time. But to this general rule, however, as to all others, there are some exceptions; wherein *cessante ratione, cessat et ipsa lex* [the reason ceasing, the law ceases]. As, 1. Where the former attainder is reversed for error, for then it is the same as if it had never been. And the same reason holds where the attainder is reversed by parliament, or the judgment vacated by the king's pardon, with regard to felonies committed afterwards. 2. Where the attainder was upon indictment, such attainder is no bar to an appeal [private prosecution], for the prior sentence is pardonable by the king; and if that might be pleaded in bar of the appeal, the king might in the end defeat the suit of the subject by suffering the prior sentence to stop the prosecution of the second, and then, when the time of appealing is elapsed, granting the delinquent a pardon. 3. An attainder in felony is no bar to an indictment of treason; because not only the judgment and manner of death are different, but the forfeiture is more extensive and the land goes to different persons. 4. [omitted].[50] And from these instances we may collect that a plea of *autrefoits attaint* is never good but when a second trial would be quite superfluous.[51]

Much of this discussion is anachronistic. There is no modern analog to the plea of *autrefois attaint* because its very premise is no longer viable—that a felony judgment corrupts the blood and causes forfeiture of all property and rights (becoming "dead in law," to use Blackstone's arresting metaphor). With that kind of draconian, permanent change in status, little wonder that a single attaint could be pled in bar of an indictment for any other felony, not just the same offense. As Blackstone explained, "it is absurd and superfluous to endeavor to attaint him a second time" if the attaint is still in effect.

The reader might wonder why the common law developed a plea of *autrefois convict* if it had the generally broader plea of *autrefois attaint.* The reason was procedural; several mechanisms permitted a convicted felon to avoid having judgment imposed. In these cases, the proper plea was *autrefois convict,* former conviction (without judgment). When *autrefois attaint* faded from use, *autrefois convict* became the proper plea for all cases that sought to use a former conviction to bar a second trial. Like the plea of former acquittal, former conviction was a good plea only if the offenses were the same.

Two wrinkles in the law of attaint still have relevance, however. First, an attaint upon an indictment barred another indictment but not a private appeal; again, this demonstrates the separate nature of the private suit, which still exists today, albeit in modified form, in the distinctiveness of the tort and the criminal systems. Blackstone's rationale for this exception also explains the distinct tort/criminal systems: if the king pardons the conviction after the time for appeal has passed, the private citizen is left without a remedy. This explains why, for example, the families of Nicole Simpson and Ronald Goldman could obtain a multimillion-dollar civil judgment against O. J. Simpson despite his acquittal in the criminal case.

Second, notice the effect of the attaint being reversed—the same effect today of almost all appellate reversals: the defendant may be tried again "[w]here the former attainder is reversed for error, for then it is the same as if it had never been." The difficulty of getting a former attainder reversed explains Blackstone's preference for when pardons should be pleaded in bar:

> 4. Lastly, a *pardon* may be pleaded in bar; as at once destroying the end and purpose of the indictment by remitting that punishment which the prosecution is calculated to inflict. There is one advantage that attends pleading a pardon in bar, or in arrest of judgment, *before* sentence is passed, which gives it by much preference to pleading it *after* sentence or attainder. That is, that by stopping the judgment it stops the attainder and prevents the corruption of the blood, which when once corrupted by at-

tainder cannot afterwards be restored otherwise than by act of parliament.[52]

The influence of Blackstone can be seen in Supreme Court opinions and early American law review commentary. In 1883 the law review commentary summarized the same offense universe in a way that both Blackstone and the current Supreme Court would understand and endorse. Charles Batchelder recapitulated the rules of former jeopardy as follows:

> 1. That a conviction or acquittal of the whole crime bars further prosecution for the whole or any part of the crime.
>
> 2. That a conviction of an included offence on an indictment for the greater crime bars further prosecution for the whole or any part of the crime.
>
> 3. That a conviction or acquittal of an included offence on an indictment for the included offence only is a bar to the further prosecution of the whole or any part of the crime.[53]

Batchelder's summary is manifested in the holding and mode of analysis in *Brown v. Ohio*, almost one hundred years after Batchelder wrote his summary and more than two hundred years after Blackstone published his *Commentaries*. The consistency of double jeopardy law from Blackstone to the present suggests that "same offense" is captured in some kind of greater-lesser-offense relationship. To explain the precise nature of that relationship requires the first seven chapters of this book. The next section shows the explanatory power of Model 3, informed as it is by Blackstone's double jeopardy principles.

Applying Blackstone and the Three Models

The question of when offenses are the same can usefully be viewed as a substantive criminal law problem—a threshold double jeopardy issue. There is no reason to be concerned about the twice-in-jeopardy question if the offenses are not the same.

Criminal Law Offense Definitions

Jay Sigler asserts that the "same offense" question is the "greatest puzzle in state double jeopardy law," one that also "seems to bedevil the federal courts."[54] One law student comment perhaps said it best in its title:

Two Centuries of Judicial Failure in Search of a Standard.[55] Though Sir Matthew Hale presented dozens of examples of when offenses were or were not the same offense,[56] Blackstone spent little time on this point. Indeed, he seemed to view the question as almost self-evident when he noted that murder and manslaughter were "the same identical crime" because "the fact prosecuted is the same in both, though the offenses differ in coloring and in degree." The "same offense" part of Blackstone's conception seems to turn on whether the crimes involved the same "fact." Nineteenth-century courts were attracted to this idea. Many sought to determine "same offense" by trying to decide whether "the same act" was prosecuted more than once.[57]

To the extent this inquiry demanded an account of "same act" existing in the universe, it was doomed to failure. In a highly influential student note about double jeopardy, Larry Simon drew on J. L. Austin to state, "Whether any span of conduct is an act depends entirely upon the verb in the question we ask. A man is shaving. How many acts is he doing? Is shaving an act? Yes. Is changing the blade in one's razor an act? Yes. Is applying lather to one's face an act? . . . Yes, yes, yes."[58]

This critique is effective only against a metaphysical account of "act."[59] But there is no reason to use a metaphysical account in double jeopardy analysis. A more defensible account is to locate "act" in the legislative description of the prohibited conduct. Indeed, it is possible that Blackstone saw "fact prosecuted" as "fact prohibited by the criminal law." This account makes it possible to defend a "same act" definition of same offense.

When deciding how to understand "acts" prohibited by the criminal law, the most obvious source would be the statutory language. If a statute were to make "shaving" a crime, for example, courts would have to determine what the legislature meant by "shaving." The legislative history might be helpful, or the context in which the word appears in the statute. Presumptions (for example, the so-called "rule of lenity")[60] may have to be pressed into service. Whatever the outcome, whatever difficulties it entails, it is a very different inquiry from the one Simon had in mind, and it is not subject to Austin's metaphysical critique.

The Supreme Court has adopted at least two presumptions about "same offense," as we see in chapter 2. The Court has also held that these presumptions are rebuttable by clear evidence of contrary legislative intent, at least when the issue is whether offenses tried together in a single trial are the same. While the Court's conception is a reasonable starting point, it is radically incomplete and sometimes produces answers that cannot be justified. The Court held in 1958 that selling the same quantity of narcotics can be three double jeopardy offenses: selling not from the original package, selling not pursuant to a written order, and selling with knowledge of unlawful importation.[61] This is a rather puny conception of legislatively decreed "same act." The Court held in 1980 that rape and murder are the same offense.[62] This seems too robust.

The task in chapter 5 is to offer a better justification for the Court's fuzzy same-offense picture by showing that legislative intent, and presumptions about legislative intent, are the ultimate source of guidance on the same offense question. Chapter 5 also refocuses the same-offense picture by including some additional offense pairs and excluding others that the Court has included. Finally, it improves the clarity of the picture by unifying the successive prosecution problem with that of multiple punishments in a single trial.

The same offense problem is, of course, not the only double jeopardy problem. Many other problems can be lumped together as twice-in-jeopardy double jeopardy issues, discussed in the next section.

Twice in Jeopardy

In Blackstone's day, questions about second jeopardies had to do with the kind of trial outcome—a conviction with judgment, conviction without judgment, or acquittal. To shift Blackstone into modern times, we have but to rephrase the outcome question. Did the defendant receive an outcome (verdict, sentence, guilty plea) that the legislature intended to count as a final determination of blameworthiness? If so, that defendant has completed a procedural jeopardy, and a new jeopardy for the same offense cannot be instituted.

The focus on the legislative definition of what constitutes a final outcome parallels the view offered so far that privileges the legislative definition of offenses in terms of proscribed acts. There is much work yet to be done to defend this view of double jeopardy as premised on legislative prerogative. In sum, the argument is that double jeopardy protects procedurally what the legislature creates in the substance of its criminal law and its criminal procedure.

Here again, the Supreme Court has made a good start in understanding double jeopardy based on presumed legislative intent, holding that a dismissal bars a new trial for the same offense only if the dismissal is equivalent to an acquittal.[63] This makes sense because the legislature would not have intended a defendant to face a second trial after the first trial has ended in what amounts to an acquittal. Keeping the focus on what the legislature would have intended permits easy resolution of cases in which the defendant procures an acquittal by fraud. Finding virtually no case law, David Rudstein turned to the treatises, which suggest that double jeopardy does not protect when the acquittal is obtained by fraud.[64] Bishop, for example, was clear that "[t]here is direct English authority, and there are numerous judicial *dicta*, English and American" supporting that proposition.[65] Though the Supreme Court has not intimated an answer to the fraud question, a legislative intent theory suggests that the treatises are correct.

In the absence of fraud, acquittals always bar a second trial, and the Court has been sensitive to the reality that "acquittals" can occur in contexts other than a not-guilty verdict at trial. For example, consider an appeal that produces a finding in the defendant's favor on guilt—a reversal on the ground of insufficient evidence.[66] In this context, the Court has held that an outcome that is equivalent to an acquittal (a finding that the state produced insufficient evidence to convict) should be treated as an acquittal. The Court has also held that an acquittal of criminal offense #1 can create a collateral estoppel bar against criminal offense #2 even though the two offenses are not the same offense.[67] (A moment's reflection discloses that of course the two offenses are not the same offense; if they were, there would be no need for a separate doctrine of collateral estoppel.) Collateral estoppel is nothing more than an application of the rule that a substantive determination as to criminal blameworthiness always bars a new proceeding. One way to think of outcomes that are not strictly verdicts but nonetheless resolve the criminal blameworthiness question in the defendant's favor is that they are "acquittal-equivalents." If the jury acquits S of robbing victim #1 when S claims that the victim was mistaken about the robber's identity, that jury has implicitly acquitted S of robbing victim #2 at the same time and place.

On Blackstone's account (and Justice Story's as well), double jeopardy protects only against new trials following verdicts, which the Court has extended to include any determination that the defendant was not guilty. The implication of this principle is that outcomes that are neither verdicts nor acquittal-equivalents should not be treated as jeopardy bars. Thus, the typical mistrial—an order terminating a trial because of prejudicial errors in the proceeding—could never be a jeopardy bar because it does not resolve the issue of defendant's guilt. But the Court so far has refused to follow this logic or to follow Blackstone and Story. In an effort to prevent procedural unfairness to defendants where mistrials were granted too hastily, the Supreme Court has attempted to identify a standard by which a mistrial can be judged a jeopardy bar even when it does not resolve the defendant's guilt. This attempt has not gone well. The test currently in use is whether the first trial ended because of a "manifest necessity," a standard that Stephen Schulhofer describes as a "thoroughly deceptive misnomer, perhaps not rivaled even by the Holy Roman Empire."[68]

Moreover, to define the end of jeopardy without drawing on an understanding of "verdict" forces one to draw an arbitrary line about when jeopardy begins. If we are going to investigate the fairness of the prosecutor's mistrial motion, we have to know when the trial has proceeded far enough that the unfairness becomes a double jeopardy problem. That arbitrary line is when the jury is sworn (or, in a trial to the judge, when the first witness is sworn).[69] If, on the other hand, we understood verdicts as the only way jeopardy ends (Blackstone's and Story's understanding), there would be no need to worry about when jeopardy begins. If the criminal process produces a finding in the defendant's favor on the facts of the criminal offense, it is a verdict and an end to jeopardy without regard to when in the process the finding occurred.

Keeping the focus on the actual nature of the outcome (without regard to its label) helps provide coherence to a confused mistrial case law. Oddly enough, the Court permitted a defendant to bar a second trial because the prosecutor failed to subpoena an important witness[70] but did not permit defendants to show that a hung jury (one that cannot agree on a verdict) was based on insufficient evidence.[71] Why should a defendant be in a better position vis-à-vis the Double Jeopardy Clause if the prosecutor failed to subpoena a witness than if the state presented its entire case and failed to introduce sufficient evidence even to submit the case to a jury? It makes no sense. Indeed, the Court seemed to acknowledge the lack of logic in the hung jury case. The mistrial rule, the Court intoned, "has its own sources and logic."[72] Moreover, "Justice Holmes' aphorism that 'a page of history is worth a volume of logic' sensibly applies here."[73]

If, rather than follow the Court's unique logic, we stay with Blackstone and Story, the Court has been both too generous and too strict in its mistrial cases. The Court has been too generous in creating a mistrial doctrine separate from acquittal equivalence, causing great doctrinal incoherence in the bargain as courts struggle to put a meaning on "manifest necessity." The Court has been too strict in refusing to permit a defendant to show that a hung jury is based on legally insufficient evidence, while permitting convicted defendants to gain double jeopardy protection if they show insufficient evidence underlying the conviction. Why should a hung-jury defendant be in an inferior double jeopardy position when compared to a convicted defendant?

With procedural jeopardy understood as turning on an accurate characterization of the initial outcome, many of the complexities of modern criminal procedure become irrelevant, and what appear to be difficult cases are quite simple. For example, the Model 3 view of double jeopardy functions as a crude limitation on sentencing, by limiting the number of convictions. But Model 3 double jeopardy has no other implications for sentencing, despite sentencing procedures that might raise jeopardy issues under the fairness approach that animates the other two models. The federal sentencing guidelines permit a defendant's sentence to be enhanced on the basis of uncharged conduct. A double jeopardy question is whether this uncharged conduct can later be prosecuted as a criminal offense. It is easy to see why this raises double jeopardy concerns: the government is using the same conduct twice, once to enhance the defendant's sentence and once to obtain an additional conviction. Is this fair? Is it a form of prosecutorial harassment?

Model 3 operates more cleanly here. If a court's lodestar were fairness (preventing harassment), who knows whether double jeopardy permits the uncharged conduct to be prosecuted later? But Model 3 clearly permits a later prosecution for uncharged conduct because Model 3 requires a verdict (or acquittal-equivalent) to trigger double jeopardy protection. Nothing about increased sentencing is a verdict that is separate from the verdict which serves as the basis for the sentence. The Court agreed,[74] though it used a slightly different rationale because it has yet to accept explicitly Model 3.[75]

Now consider a variation. Suppose the defendant is tried for two offenses, acquitted of one, convicted of the other, and the federal prosecutor seeks to prove the "acquitted" conduct to enhance the sentence on the conviction. That this would pass the fairness test seems unlikely. After all, the defendant could legitimately claim that she is being made to prove her innocence a second time.[76] What is fair about that? But Model 3 permits the government to prove this conduct. Sentencing is not a verdict—cannot lead to a verdict—and thus it is not a jeopardy that is forbidden by the acquittal. The defendant has been found guilty of only one offense;

nothing about being found guilty of one offense, and sentenced for that offense, can ever be double jeopardy under Model 3. Of course, this is just another way to say that the legislature can have whatever sentence and however many convictions that it wants (consistent with due process and the Eighth Amendment). The Court agreed, again using a somewhat different analysis.[77]

Model 3 also explains why there is no jeopardy bar to a new trial following a typical appellate reversal (on grounds other than sufficiency of evidence)[78] and why double jeopardy does not prohibit resentencing to a higher sentence following a retrial and new conviction.[79] Assume a defendant received a ten-year sentence, appealed the conviction, and secured a reversal on grounds that have nothing to do with the sufficiency of the evidence. As the Court has recognized, this defendant has no double jeopardy claim against a new trial. There is no extant verdict that would give rise to a jeopardy claim. Moreover, if this defendant is reconvicted, double jeopardy does not prohibit a longer sentence. The Court's metaphor in justifying this result is instructive: the "slate has been wiped clean."[80] Precisely. There is no verdict manifesting blameworthiness for the conduct in question. The state may, therefore, retry the defendant and sentence her to any sentence permitted by law—at least as far as double jeopardy is concerned.[81]

Guilty pleas should be treated no differently from any other kind of verdict. A guilty plea is a conviction that is an end to further jeopardy for that offense (assuming it is not overturned on appeal). If, however, a defendant wishes to make his guilty plea conviction conditional on providing testimony against another defendant, there is nothing in the Double Jeopardy Clause that prevents the state from enforcing the contract.[82] By vacating the first conviction, the state puts the defendant where he would have been if there had been no guilty plea in the first place; there is no verdict to manifest his blameworthiness and thus no bar to the state proceeding with a trial.

So far, then, the Model 3 argument is quite straightforward, at least in its outlines. If a criminal prosecution ends in a verdict, or an acquittal-equivalent, the defendant may not be charged again for the same offense as long as the first outcome remains undisturbed by the defendant. Though much work remains to be done to fill in the details of the "same-offense" picture, it is roughly whether the legislature meant the two statutes to proscribe the same criminal act. As the legislature almost never discloses its intent on these matters, we have to develop a series of presumptions about likely legislative intent. These presumptions draw heavily on the philosophy of action.

One more category of questions awaits us, chameleon issues that could be described as same offense or as twice-in-jeopardy issues. Rather than try to force these issues into one or the other category, let us think of them as separate from the issues of same offense and jeopardy.

Other Double Jeopardy Issues

One perplexing issue in criminal law generally is finding the dividing line between civil sanctions and criminal penalties. An example that is close to the line is an action denominated as civil in which the government seeks treble damages for an intentional tort.[83] Outside double jeopardy, the issue has purely procedural implications. If a proceeding is civil, the defendant is not entitled to a jury or to the standard of proof beyond a reasonable doubt. Moreover, an indigent defendant is not entitled to counsel at government expense.

But as double jeopardy cannot arise until the first jeopardy is ended, the civil/criminal double jeopardy issue has deeper implications. If the first proceeding—the intentional tort action, for example—is determined to be criminal, the defendant cannot be tried for the parallel criminal offense (assuming the tort and criminal offense meet the relevant test for same offense). In this way, the civil/criminal issue has substantive implications, as it controls the total sanctions that can be imposed for the conduct that gives rise to potential civil and criminal liability.

This problem has proved particularly nettlesome for the Court in the last two decades. The Court made a brave start on the problem in 1989,[84] but the dicta from that decision have caused a flood of new cases seeking to use civil sanctions to forestall criminal trials or punishments. In 1994 the Court withdrew some of the robust dicta from the earlier case, insisting that it is only the truly rare civil sanction that constitutes double jeopardy punishment.[85] And in 1997 the Court essentially reversed the troublesome 1989 precedent.[86]

A Model 3 account of double jeopardy solves this problem easily and along the lines the Court finally adopted in 1997. As the legislature determines both what counts as a verdict and when offenses are the same, a civil and criminal offense can never be double jeopardy for the same offense, no matter how much overlap in the offense definitions. The legislature, in enacting both a civil and a criminal sanction, must have wanted both to apply.

An issue that is controversial, but hardly perplexing, is the Court's "dual sovereignty" doctrine. Under this formalistic view of the relationship between the states and the federal government (as well as the relationships between the states and between Indian tribes and the federal government), each sovereign retained the power to punish criminal acts without regard to whether the other sovereigns have tried or punished the same crimes.[87] This, then, is a truly easy double jeopardy issue for the Court: each sovereign may proceed, and no issues even arise about same offense or whether the first trial ended in a criminal verdict.

A Model 3 account, premised as it is on legislative prerogative, agrees that each sovereign has this power, but the relevant question is whether each sovereign intended to use the power to punish in addition to the other sovereign(s). If the sovereign stated its intent to proceed (or not), that would be the end of the matter. Since an expression of this intent is almost always missing, the task for Model 3 is to formulate presumptions about that intent. A useful way to begin is to examine the early opinions of the Supreme Court. The most persuasive argument in those early opinions presumes that neither the federal government nor the states would want to proceed in addition to the other.[88] Moreover, the best evidence on the original intent of the Framers, as Paul Cassell has shown, is that they would have understood the Double Jeopardy Clause to forbid overlapping state and federal prosecutions.[89]

The argument presented in this book is that double jeopardy is a procedural overlay on the substantive criminal law that defines blameworthiness and on the law of procedure that defines criminal verdicts and dictates when those verdicts can be sought by prosecutors. The legislature has the power to define crimes, set punishments, and create a procedural system in which some outcomes (but not others) are final. This legislative prerogative requires that judges and prosecutors respect the substantive law of crimes and the rules of criminal procedure but nothing more.

"Legislative prerogative" is not a new double jeopardy idea. In *Brown v. Ohio*, the Court held that joyriding and auto theft defined the same Ohio offense.[90] The Court defended its holding by noting that it resulted from the way the state courts construed the crimes defined by the legislature. The Court hastened to add: "The legislature remains free under the Double Jeopardy Clause to define crimes and fix punishments; but once the legislature has acted courts may not impose more than one punishment for the same offense and prosecutors ordinarily may not attempt to secure that punishment in more than one trial."[91] Unfortunately, this language is ambiguous. The Court might have meant a robust legislative prerogative that gives the legislative carte blanche simply to state that offense *A* is different from offense *B*. Or the Court could have meant a more restrained kind of prerogative, one that merely states a truism: legislatures draft statutes, containing elements that, when construed by courts, lead to a result that may or may not be what the legislature wanted.

Even if *Brown* meant legislative prerogative in the robust sense, the theory sketched here, and defended throughout the book, is the first attempt to use legislative prerogative as a unifying conception for all of double jeopardy. I hasten to stress what I have said already in this chapter: legislative prerogative is the theoretical construct within which I create a series of presumptions about likely legislative intent. Because the legislature almost never makes its intent known, these presumptions are the principal focus of the book, and decide almost all the cases. Thus, the role of courts is no less central in a double jeopardy world built on legislative prerogative than a world in which courts create the concepts of "same offense" and "jeopardy" out of thin air. The difference is that a double jeopardy conception built on legislative prerogative has a sturdy foundation that can repel attacks easily directed at other double jeopardy theories.

The balance of the book is a defense of a view of double jeopardy based on legislative prerogative, as well as the set of presumptions necessary to make it work. The defense necessarily involves comparisons with other conceptions of double jeopardy. Because comparisons require value judgments, it is useful to briefly sketch the jurisprudence that underlies these value judgments. That is the subject of the next section.

The "Edges" of Law

Legal doctrine requires locating what can be called the "edges" of law— the beginning and the ending of the law's reach. Some rules have harder "edges" than others; hard-edged rules have relatively few close cases at the margin of the law's reach. The law against driving more than fifty-five miles per hour has completely hard edges. Problems of proof and potential defenses aside, a driver is either going more than fifty-five mph, or she is not. There are zero cases at the margin. A law against traveling at an excessive speed, or against reckless driving, has softer edges because a larger universe of contested cases can be imagined. The Fourth Amendment requirement that a search or seizure be "reasonable" has very soft edges indeed, leading to a jurisprudence that can fairly be characterized as baroque.[92]

Some have argued that soft-edged laws present judges the opportunity to create individual outcomes responsive to the underlying policy or goals manifested in a particular law. The "legal realists" from the 1920s and 1930s made policy analysis the centerpiece of their judicial approach. The legal realist method, which is still taught in law schools and heavily influences judges, is to identify explicitly the policies and values manifested in the law and then seek to decide the case in a way most consistent with these policies and values. Indeed, some legal realists argued that judges can get along better with policy analysis than by following a set of hard-edged rules. Felix Cohen said in 1935: "The age of the classical jurists is over. . . . The 'Restatement of the Law' by the American Law Institute is the last long-drawn-out gasp of a dying tradition."[93]

But Cohen's view has not prevailed. It seems unlikely that even the most exacting analysis of policies and values can replace rules. If a statement of policy could replace rules, then all criminal procedure rules could be replaced by Kafka's policy command inscribed by the needles of the Harrow as a means of executing its last victim. The command was "Be Just."[94] If one rejects "Be Just" as a replacement for the Bill of Rights and the rules of criminal procedure, it must be because there is value in having hard-edged rules that both guide and limit judges in dispensing justice.

The critical legal studies scholars from the 1970s and 1980s undermined the part of the legal realist enterprise that manifested faith in judges. Critical theory partisans agreed with the realists that law has surprisingly soft edges—is largely "indeterminate," in their terminology—permitting judges often to decide cases for reasons other than the law's rule. Some of these writers seemed to suggest that law is wholly indeterminate, that it never compels a particular outcome. For example, Gary Peller and others argued that the constitutional provision requiring that the President be at least thirty-five years of age is indeterminate.[95]

Critical theory parted company with most legal realists in arguing that this indeterminacy is (or can be) pernicious because it permits judges to impose their own personal biases or vision of justice.[96] "All law is masked power" is Owen Fiss's summary.[97] On this account, to make judges the ultimate arbiter of justice is to invite injustice.

Critical theory suggests a value in making law as determinate as possible. Law can be made more determinate—more predictable in application—by making its edges harder. Because predictability is a virtue in law, if all other factors are roughly equal, constitutional interpretations should favor hard-edged doctrine. All other factors equal, therefore, courts should eschew balancing tests that leave the outcome of cases in doubt until a judge weighs various policies or values to arrive at the right result for each unique case.

To be sure, many Supreme Court opinions make explicit use of balancing tests; Justice O'Connor seems particularly enamored of them.[98] This is, in part, because few laws can have edges as sharp as the fifty-five-mph law. To fill in the gaps, to answer the questions left in doubt in what Richard Posner calls the "open" areas of law,[99] courts must identify and apply the underlying policy goals of the law they are interpreting. Fourth Amendment doctrine currently permits police to search a residence without a warrant if they have sufficient reason to believe that a life is in jeopardy.[100] This kind of doctrine has very soft edges, and we would not want it any other way. We want police to err on the side of searching if they believe they can save a life, and we are perfectly content to let courts review these decisions with a very soft standard.

Most judges and scholars would agree, however, that if everything else is roughly equal, hard-edged rules or doctrines are preferable. In the Fourth Amendment area we might, for example, prefer a harder-edged rule to govern when police can conduct body cavity searches of school children for drugs. In controlling the risks created by reckless driving, a speed limit may be a more appropriate tool than an offense of reckless driving. The issue is always whether the soft edges are necessary to accomplish what the legislature intends.

One critique easily made of double jeopardy doctrine is that some of it has unnecessarily soft edges—for example, much of the "manifest necessity" doctrine that determines when the first jeopardy has ended. As the Court implicitly observed in *Arizona v. Washington*,[101] "manifest necessity" either means what it literally says (that there was no choice but to terminate the trial) or has no real content beyond what the Court has tried to supply in a series of cases. *Washington* rejected the literal meaning, and courts continue to struggle to decide how to apply "manifest necessity" cut off from its literal meaning. What does "necessity" mean if not "necessary"?

But the preference for hard-edged rules is not limitless. The Supreme Court has, since 1824, held that a hung jury always permits a second trial. This is a very hard-edged rule; it has no exceptions. Rules, however, can be both hard-edged and wrong. This is the limitation in my stated preference for hard-edged rules: "everything else" must be "roughly equal."

What is not "equal" in the Court's hung-jury rule is that the universe of outcomes does not correspond with the best statement of double jeopardy policy. This reliance on policy is not the rejection of rules espoused by the legal realists but is, rather, the use of policy to choose among various hard-edged rules. A second kind of critique, therefore, depends on comparing the outcomes of the Court's doctrine with double jeopardy policy. Later chapters make this kind of critique not only of the Court's hung jury rule but also of the Court's mechanical, hard-edged test for same offense, as well as some scholarly conceptions of double jeopardy.

Choosing one rule over another thus requires a judge to consider the interplay between the value of hard edges—predictability—and the degree to which the outcomes under each rule seem to be consistent with the rule's underlying policy and goals. The interplay is complex and itself subject to a claim of indeterminacy. A judge might, for example, prefer a rule with slightly softer edges if it avoids a subset of outcomes that are contrary to the policy that supports the rule. This is my argument against both the Court's hung-jury rule and its same-offense test. But is there a principle to justify any particular trade-off of predictability for a slightly more satisfying set of outcomes?

I believe that such a principle or set of principles can be developed. Indeed, the jurisprudence sketched here is similar to that of Ronald Dworkin and can probably be defended as Dworkin defended his.[102] But my book is about the history, policy, and doctrine of double jeopardy, not about jurisprudence. I am content to rest the remainder of my argument on the following general principles. First, all things being roughly equal, hard-edged rules are to be preferred over rules with softer edges. Second, in deciding whether all things are roughly equal, judges must understand as completely as possible the policy and values manifested in the rule. Using policy to evaluate a rule is a tricky business, of course, because statements of policy themselves must be reasonably hard-edged to be helpful. The call to "Be Just" does not permit a judge to evaluate very many rules. We must therefore seek a relatively hard-edged policy statement to guide our double jeopardy inquiry.

"Legislative prerogative" as tentatively described in this chapter is a policy statement that is relatively hard-edged, but is it the best policy statement that can be articulated? That is the subject of the balance of the book.

2

Double Jeopardy Policy and History

Part of the argument in the preceding chapter was that rules cannot be evaluated without a relatively hard-edged statement of the overarching policy and goals. This chapter seeks to identify the plausible statements of double jeopardy policy and then to choose the one that most closely fits the parameters developed in chapter 1. After a single "best" policy is tentatively identified, I turn to double jeopardy history to justify and illuminate that policy statement.

Double Jeopardy Paradigm and Policies

A paradigm case can often tell us a fair amount about the policies that are served by the rule manifested in the paradigm. For example, English cases in which the king sent his officials to break into and search the shops of printers help us understand the constitutional guarantees of free press and freedom from unreasonable searches and seizures. Unfortunately, the double jeopardy paradigm is not as helpful.

A Double Jeopardy Paradigm

The paradigm double jeopardy case has very hard edges. If state X prosecutes D for the premeditated murder of V and the jury reaches a verdict of guilty or not guilty, double jeopardy forbids state X to conduct a second trial of D for the premeditated murder of V. This outcome would be double jeopardy under any of the models identified in chapter 1. Model 1 presupposes a substantive double jeopardy role that limits the legislature regardless of how it seeks multiple penalties; Model 2 assumes that the legislature can impose any number of penalties in a single proceeding if it clearly states its intent but not in successive prosecutions. Model 3 concludes that the definition of "same offense" and "twice in jeopardy" is wholly up to the legislature but requires clarity of expression when multiple penalties attend the same conduct.

There is no reason in the paradigm case to assume that the legislature meant to create more than one offense or to authorize more than one jeopardy for the premeditated killing of V. In this simple case (and, it turns out, in many others), the three models produce the same result. Because the rule prohibiting what the state attempted to do in the paradigm case has such hard edges, no cases manifesting the rule exist in recent times, though we can find some in the thirteenth century.[1]

Double jeopardy in this paradigm application produces a result that is not only satisfying but also inevitable in any system of justice that values repose and finality. One could say that no prosecutor would be so stupid as to bring a second charge for the very same statutory offense after a jury verdict. But double jeopardy does the work here; the reason no prosecutor would bring a second trial on these facts is that the legal rule is clear and its enforcement not in doubt. Indeed, as late as 1970, the Court reversed a conviction because the prosecutor twice prosecuted almost identical robberies, frankly admitting that he used the first trial as a "dry run" for the second.[2]

Once we depart the double jeopardy paradigm, however, we are without adequate guidance. In large part, the lack of guidance results from the narrow and unilluminating nature of the core paradigm. Other constitutional rights have either cores that encompass most of the outcomes suggested by their underlying policies or core paradigms that provide a mode of inquiry applicable to cases outside the core. Examples of the first category, those with expansive cores, are the right to counsel, the right to a jury trial, the right (in federal court) to a grand jury indictment, the right to be free from unreasonable searches, and the various First Amendment rights (free speech, freedom of religion, freedom from an established religion, freedom of association). We can find a few difficult cases at the margin of free speech or the right to a jury trial, but the basic paradigm case includes almost all of the cases the right seems likely to have been intended to cover.

Examples of the second category, those with narrow paradigms that nonetheless suggest an approach to other cases, include the right against compelled self-incrimination, the right to confront the state's witnesses, and the right against cruel and unusual punishment. Though few confessions are literally compelled—one almost always has a choice to answer or not to answer police questions—the paradigm suggests the wrongfulness of using or threatening force against someone to produce an answer. This logical entailment suggests the answer to self-incrimination cases that do not involve classic compulsion—for example, deprivation of food or sleep, the use of threats, or relentless questioning for thirty-six straight hours.[3] Similarly, the right to confront witnesses has a paradigm (the defendant being present when the state's witnesses testify) that is rarely an issue itself but helps shape the inquiry when the state seeks to rely on testimony in another forum or on hearsay testimony from an unavailable witness. "Cruel" and "unusual" are about as difficult to define as "compel," but we possess a cultural image of "cruel and unusual" punishments (torture, public humiliation) that helps answer cases outside the core paradigm—for example, conditions of prison confinement.

The core double jeopardy paradigm, on the other hand, is both narrow and so far has failed to provide the Court with adequate logical implication. Part of the inquiry is whether a mistrial or dismissal is the end of jeopardy, thus making another trial a second jeopardy. The end of jeopardy in the paradigm case is a verdict. We would need to decide whether dismissals and mistrials are roughly like a verdict. Unfortunately, the Court has largely ignored this analogy, in one case so confusing the issue as to hold that jeopardy ended with any dismissal based on facts outside the indictment.[4] Until the Court recognizes the logical entailment of verdict-like endings, we should expect continuing confusion in the jeopardy cases.

The paradigm meaning of same offense is the literal same statutory offense. What is roughly like "same statutory offense"? Again, it is difficult to know. A criminal offense comes into existence only when the legislature enacts a statute. If the legislature creates two statutes and they are not identical, it is plausible to argue that they are not the same offense. Why would the legislature waste its time creating two offenses that are the same offense?

Two commentators have recently embraced the "plain meaning" concept that "same" means "identical,"[5] but the Supreme Court has never considered this narrow reading (nor did Blackstone). Instead, the Court has opted for a more expansive view that an offense is the same as its necessarily included offenses. The mechanical test manifesting this view requires courts to compare statutory offense elements. Thus, offense (1,2,3) is the same as (1,2), (2,3), and (1,2,3,4) but not the same as (1,4). The theory here is that if proving one offense always proves another, the legislature meant the two as alternative bases of criminal liability, rather than as distinct criminal liabilities.

While the included-offense rule is not a bad start toward a defensible, hard-edged same-offense rule, it suffers from three major problems. First, some results are very unsatisfying. Two examples come from felony murder. The Court's test pronounces felony murder a different offense from premeditated murder, meaning that a defendant can be twice prosecuted and convicted for a single killing. On the other hand, felony murder is, on the Court's test, the same offense as the underlying felony, which means that an actor can rape and kill, or rob and kill, and be guilty of only one offense. Both of these results seem wrong, but so far we lack a policy reason to explain this intuition.

The second problem with the included-offense test is that the Court has applied it in different ways, depending on whether the defendant faces one trial or two. This, of course, is the doctrinal origin of Model 2, which assumes that the Double Jeopardy Clause limits the legislature when successive prosecutions are involved but not when multiple outcomes attend a single trial. The Court has failed to articulate a persuasive justification for this difference in application. The third flaw is related to the second: the included-offense test is an incomplete account of same offense. For example, it tells us nothing about offense overlaps between state and federal law, and between quasi-criminal "civil" offenses and the criminal code. But the most vexing lack of guidance attends the problem of dividing conduct into discrete offenses. Is it one assault or two if X slaps Y twice? If X steals five items from the top of a dresser, does the number of theft offenses depend on whether X took all the items at once, or one at a time; does it matter if X left the room each time and then returned? The included-offense test has no relevance for this conduct dimension of the same offense problem, and Court's cases offer little guidance.

The lack of a set of hard-edged double jeopardy policies has left the Court with a largely ad hoc double jeopardy doctrine. Why does a hung jury mistrial always permit a second trial? Because the Court has done it that way since 1824. Why does the Court cling to the included-offense test as the only means of defining same offense? Because the Court used the test to solve one piece of the same-offense puzzle in 1932 and has never faced the reality that the test was not intended to be a global solution to defining same offense.

In chapter 1 I suggested that we can benefit from taking the road back to Blackstone—but not because Blackstone's understanding informed the thinking of the Framers. Nor do I believe that Blackstone necessarily understood double jeopardy policy better than anyone today. Rather, my claim is that when we carefully examine the underlying policy issues, Blackstone's double jeopardy rules are a better match than the Court's doctrine or anything the commentators have proposed.

Traditional Understanding of Double Jeopardy Policy

As noted briefly in chapter 1, the Court sometimes resorts to a fairness test in evaluating double jeopardy claims. The Court tries to provide meaning to this vague notion by focusing on the idea of prosecutorial harassment. This idea comes from the widely quoted and eloquent language of Justice Black in *Green v. United States*: "the State with all its resources and power should not be allowed to make repeated attempts to convict an individual for an alleged offense, thereby subjecting him to embarrassment, expense and ordeal and compelling him to live in a continuing state of anxiety and insecurity, as well as enhancing the possibility that even though innocent he may be found guilty."[6]

That this rationale is quoted so often suggests that it expresses some underlying truth about double jeopardy. Yet upon close examination, the florid language is not very illuminating. How are we to understand Black's statement? The standard interpretation focuses on the harm of forcing a defendant to endure a second trial, a harm the Court refers to as "harassment." Superficially, this interpretation is appealing, as well as consistent with Black's concern about "embarrassment, expense and ordeal" and the "continuing state of anxiety and insecurity."

But concern with harassment can be understood in two ways, which turn out to be either hopelessly flawed as a policy matter or hopelessly soft-edged. Concern with harassment could be understood in terms of Madison's original double jeopardy language, which prohibited "more than one trial or punishment for the same offence."[7] So understood, this is a hard-edged rule with a serious policy flaw: no excuse for ending a trial could ever permit a second trial for the same offense, and judges would be loathe to grant a mistrial. This would force defendants to proceed to verdict even when trials are infected with obvious, reversible error. Moreover, as "no second trial" means "no second trial following an appellate reversal," appellate courts would also be loathe to reverse convictions, no matter how badly flawed they were. In this scheme, defendants would have almost no protection against trial errors that lead to flawed convictions because courts would be unlikely to permit defendants to avoid or reverse a conviction.

As I explain later in this chapter, the Framers identified this very problem with Madison's hard-edged rule prohibiting more than one trial or punishment for the same offense. To avoid this problem, one might understand "harassment" to be a general policy that requires judges to decide whether a defendant has been unduly harassed by the second prosecution. This is the way the Court has understood Black's rationale, at least in the context of determining when a mistrial ends one jeopardy.

As the Court has allowed the mistrial doctrine to develop, preventing harassment is not hard-edged enough to withstand my critique of soft-edged rules. The Court refers to a defendant's interest in mistrial cases as the "valued right to have his trial completed by a particular tribunal."[8] Stephen Schulhofer has developed an elaborate mistrial construct that seeks to give doctrinal voice to this "valued right."[9] After reviewing nearly two hundred appellate mistrial cases,[10] Schulhofer concluded that mistrials trigger either a deferential or a strict level of scrutiny, depending primarily on how late in the trial the mistrial occurs.[11] The later the mistrial occurs and the greater the defendant's interest in completing the trial, the greater the potential harm that will come to a defendant in a new trial, and the less significant is the prosecutor's claim of disadvantage in being forced to complete the flawed trial. This rule, while attractive in a way, obviously has very soft edges.

Another flaw in the standard interpretation of Black's double jeopardy rationale is its unitary focus on harassment. This focus leaves unaddressed the single most complex problem in double jeopardy: deciding when two offenses are the same offense. It also leaves unaddressed the problem of how to decide when the state can impose more than one verdict in a single trial. For a brief three-year period, the Court attempted to use the policy of preventing harassment by successive prosecutions as a partial way of understanding same offense.[12] On this account, which the Model Penal Code has explicitly adopted, the harm of repeated prosecutions should cause the definition of same offense to be more expansive than when the state seeks more than one verdict in a single trial. In the Model Penal Code, for example, the state is forbidden generally to reprosecute the same conduct but may impose more than one conviction for the same conduct in a single trial.[13]

Following the Model Penal Code, commentators began to argue that the problem of successive prosecutions is different from, and more serious than, that of multiple punishments. Jay Sigler's comments are typical. He refers to the "failure to distinguish between the question of multiplicity of trials and multiplicity of punishments" as manifesting a "confusion" which "runs counter to the root meaning of double jeopardy, either as a historical matter or as a problem of setting public policy."[14]

There are two insurmountable problems to using harassment policy to inform our understanding of same offense. First, it provides only a partial answer; it has nothing to say about the definition of same offense in a single trial. Thus, we are forced to identify another policy for single-trial, multiple-punishment issues. The Model Penal Code rejects a conduct test in this context, focusing instead on the elements of the offenses and the harm sought to be avoided.[15]

The second problem is more fundamental. Michael Moore has argued that it is meaningless to talk about the harassment of a second trial.[16] A second criminal trial, like a first trial, is always unwanted and burdensome. But that tells us nothing about whether it is permitted by the Double Jeopardy Clause. There is no necessary connection between harassment and the number of verdicts the Clause permits. If the Double Jeopardy Clause permits two verdicts for the same conduct, as the Court now concedes the legislature can authorize regardless of how similar the offenses may appear, why should it matter if those verdicts are obtained in one trial or two? What double jeopardy harm occurs if the prosecutor decides to obtain the authorized number of verdicts in two trials? The next subsection develops this argument in the context of a misstep that the Court took in 1990 on its same-offense journey.

The Brief, Unhappy Life of *Grady v. Corbin*

In 1932 the Court explicitly fashioned a test for determining when Congress had intended to create cumulatively punishable offenses. *Blockburger v. United States* held that offenses should not be *punished* separately when one is necessarily included in the other—for example, offense (1,2) is the same as (1,2,3) but not the same as (2,3). *Blockburger* implicitly left open whether any limit exists on how many trials the prosecutor can institute to seek authorized penalties. In 1889 the Court had held in *In re Nielsen*[17] that a conviction of cohabitation barred a new trial for adultery. Notice that *Nielsen* is not consistent with *Blockburger*—at least not on the traditional understanding of the offenses of adultery and cohabitation. Each of these offenses required proof of an element the other did not—adultery required proof of marriage and cohabitation required proof of living together. Despite this distinctiveness in the statutory elements, *Nielsen* applied a double jeopardy bar.

Because *Nielsen* involved successive prosecutions and *Blockburger* did not, it was possible to argue that the Court intended different tests of same offense for the different procedural contexts.[18] In 1977 the Court put these two cases together in a way that suggested different analytical approaches for multiple punishment and successive prosecutions. In *Brown v. Ohio*[19] the Court held that joyriding and auto theft were the same offense because, as construed by the Ohio courts, joyriding was a necessarily included offense of auto theft. After reaching this uncontroversial conclusion, the Court seemed to go out of its way to note that *Blockburger* was "not the only standard for determining whether successive prosecutions impermissibly involve the same offense."[20]

The Court quoted language from *Nielsen* to the effect that the Double Jeopardy Clause forbids a second prosecution for one of the "incidents" of a crime already prosecuted.[21] It stated the idea more clearly in a footnote: "Even if two offenses are sufficiently different to permit the imposition of consecutive sentences, successive prosecutions will be barred in some circumstances where the second prosecution requires the relitigation of factual issues already resolved by the first."[22]

The two-tier test of same offense was born. In 1980 the Court began to flesh out its suggestion of a two-tier test. The Court in *Illinois v. Vitale* stated in dicta that a "substantial claim" of double jeopardy would arise if a traffic conviction was used as a necessary part of a later manslaughter prosecution.[23] In 1990, in *Grady v. Corbin*,[24] the Court squarely held that double jeopardy analysis must be accomplished by a two-tier inquiry when successive prosecutions are involved.[25] The first tier is *Blockburger*'s included-offense test. If offenses are the same under that test, the matter is at an end. But if *Blockburger* finds the offenses to be different, a more fine-grained inquiry must be conducted into the relationship between the offenses charged. In *Grady*, the Court held that a conviction for drunk driving barred a later prosecution for reckless manslaughter that would require proof of the same drunk driving.[26]

The difference between *Grady* and *Blockburger* is subtle but significant. *Grady* asks whether any offense that is part of an earlier criminal judgment must be proved in the second trial. *Blockburger*, on the other hand, asks whether one of the statutory offenses always requires proof of the other offense. Thus, on the facts of *Grady*, reckless manslaughter would not always require proof of drunk driving, and the two were not the same offense under *Blockburger*, but this particular reckless manslaughter would require proof of the offense of drunk driving for which the defendant had already been prosecuted, making the offenses the same under *Grady*. It is in this sense that *Grady* is a more fine-grained inquiry than *Blockburger*.

The exclusive reliance on *Blockburger* in single trials created a same-offense asymmetry between single trials and successive prosecutions. But it was unclear what theory of same offense was at work in *Grady*. On *Grady*'s two-tier approach, the Double Jeopardy Clause permitted a defendant to be twice convicted and punished in one trial for what would have been the same offense if the state had tried the charges separately. The defendant in *Grady*, for example, could have been convicted of both drunk driving and reckless manslaughter if the state had tried the charges together. What was the same would not be the same if tried in a single trial. But how does the Double Jeopardy Clause accomplish that result? How is it that "same offense" is a chameleon that changes meaning in different procedural contexts?

The most sophisticated defense of *Grady* is that of Anne Bowen Poulin, who argues that *Grady* extended the mistrial rationale from the jeopardy context to supplement the *Blockburger* "same offense" protection.[27] She concludes that the Court saw fragmented prosecutions based on the same conduct as another category of potential harassment even when the offenses were not the same *Blockburger* offense. Professor Poulin argues that mistrial cases trigger an interest in "closure," which she correctly distinguishes from the interest in finality that arises in verdicts.[28] According to Poulin, *Grady* limits the state's "ability to fragment prosecution" and thus advances the defendant's interest in closure. Poulin admits that "*Grady* pushes the interest in closure to its limits."[29] Nonetheless, she endorses *Grady* because of her view that closure is a separate double jeopardy interest from verdict finality.

My double jeopardy account holds that double jeopardy protects verdict finality and nothing else. Thus, I reject closure as a separate double jeopardy interest and, necessarily, reject Poulin's defense of *Grady*.[30] In contrast to Poulin's careful analysis, most commentators support a two-tier approach by a reflexive quote of Justice Black's concern about the vexatious harms that arise uniquely in successive prosecutions—anxiety, expense, embarrassment, and greater risk of an erroneous conviction. While these concerns are valid, they have nothing to say about the right definition of same offense. One way to talk about Black's concerns is in the context of mandatory joinder of offenses that arise from the same conduct or transaction. Writing about the English approach, Friedland notes that the rule against unreasonably splitting a case "is sometimes discussed in terms of a trial judge's discretion to prevent an abuse of the process of the Court, rather than as a positive rule of law."[31] At least four advisory groups in this country recommend mandatory joinder as a legislative solution to vexatious prosecutions.[32] Either approach is better than trying to locate a rule of constitutional joinder in the Double Jeopardy Clause.

The Supreme Court has consistently rejected a reading of the Double Jeopardy Clause that creates constitutional mandatory joinder, despite Justice Brennan's tireless support of a "same transaction" test, which at one time or another also attracted the votes of Chief Justice Warren and Justices Douglas and Marshall. While an obvious problem exists in defining "transaction," which Justice Brennan acknowledged, the general shape of the idea is clear enough. It requires the state to join, in one trial, all charges arising from the same transaction. In effect, the criminal transaction is functioning as a single "offense," making any factually included offense the same offense.

Despite the merits of compulsory joinder, which are many, the same-transaction test is a flawed definition of same offense. Nothing in the text, history, or rationale of the Double Jeopardy Clause remotely suggests that all offenses committed in a single "transaction" must be tried together or not at all.[33] The constitutional question is whether offenses are the same, not whether the transaction is the same.

The Court has long understood these questions to be different. In 1887, in *Ex parte Henry*,[34] for example, the statute permitted the government to charge up to three mail fraud offenses if committed within a six-month period; the judge could, however, enter but one sentence if the government joined charges. Henry argued that by virtue of the permissive joinder provision, Congress intended only one punishment for all acts of mail fraud committed in any six-month period. But the Court drew a distinction between the number of offenses committed and how they may be prosecuted: "there is nothing whatever in [the joinder provision] to indicate an intention to make a single continuous offence . . . out of what, without it, would have been several distinct offences, each complete in itself."[35]

The two questions are not interchangeable unless the argument is that "offense" means "criminal transaction," an argument that has obvious linguistic and historical difficulties. There is also a policy issue: the equivalence of "offense" and "transaction" would forbid more than one conviction from the same transaction even if sought in one trial. What this means, borrowing the words of Chief Justice Burger, is that "that the second and third and fourth criminal acts are 'free'" if part of the same transaction, which "does not make good sense and . . . cannot make good law."[36]

Implicit in Burger's concern is that the same-transaction test diminishes the legislative power to create offenses. In the same-transaction test, the criminal actor and the prosecutor define double jeopardy offense by the manner in which the crimes are committed and charged. To state that proposition is to reject it. If one abandons the argument that double jeopardy "offense" equals "transaction," to avoid Burger's powerful critique, one is forced to defend the position that the Double Jeopardy Clause contains two protections, one against two convictions or trials for the *same offense* and one against two trials for the same *criminal transaction*. Finding the latter protection in the language of the Clause is a problem of the first magnitude.

The argument is untenable. The Double Jeopardy Clause does not, as some have read Justice Black to say, protect against harassing prosecutions. It protects against multiple consequences for the same offense. As Eli Richardson puts it, the Clause prohibits more than one jeopardy *for* the same offense, rather than more than one jeopardy *involving* the surrounding facts of the case against the defendant.[37] Prohibiting more than one jeopardy for the same offense, of course, sometimes results in a bar against harassing prosecutions, but that is an effect of the double jeopardy prohibition and not a basis for interpreting the Double Jeopardy Clause. The Clause is satisfied if the second trial or conviction is for a different offense, regardless of the prosecutor's motives or the effects on the accused.

Grady was a middle ground between the same transaction test and *Blockburger*.[38] It looked to the statutory offense as prosecuted, rather than to the elements as written, and was thus more expansive than *Block-burger*. But *Grady* insisted that offense inclusion could exist only within a greater statutory offense, rather than within a judicial construct called a "transaction."

To see the difference, assume that a trial for manslaughter follows a traffic fine for speeding. These offenses are the same under the same-transaction test if the driving and accident are viewed as the same transaction. They would never be the same under *Blockburger* because manslaughter does not always prove speeding. They might or might not be the same under *Grady*. They would be the same if the state must rely on speeding to prove the manslaughter mens rea; they would not be the same if the state relied on some other evidence of reckless behavior—for example, drunk driving.

Though *Grady* is a better approach than the same transaction test, its underlying premise is flawed in the same way. Any two-tier definition of "same offense" in the Double Jeopardy Clause leaves the Court open to Justice Scalia's sarcasm: how can a single prohibition of "same offense" mean two different things? Indeed, only three years after *Grady* was decided, the Court put it out of its misery. In *United States v. Dixon*,[39] the Court retreated all the way to *Blockburger*, holding that its included-offense test supplies the definition of "same offense" whether the question arises in one trial or two.[40]

Problems remain in the wake of *Dixon*; one problem is figuring out its holding.[41] Four Justices argued that *Grady* should not be overruled.[42] Of the remaining five, only Justice Kennedy agreed with all of Justice Scalia's applications of *Blockburger*. Chief Justice Rehnquist, joined by Justices O'Connor and Thomas, found Scalia's interpretation of *Blockburger* too generous.[43] Akhil Amar and Jonathan Marcus suggest that Scalia, "upon reflection," should change his mind about the "preposterous" outcome in *Dixon*.[44] I return to the *Dixon* doctrinal point in chapter 6.[45] The more fundamental problem with *Dixon*, as I hope to demonstrate, is that *Block-burger* simply provides too many intuitively wrong outcomes to be used as the basic double jeopardy test.

But the Court was right in *Dixon* to reject the two-tier test of same offense. The real problem with *Grady* is not its failure to rely on *Block-burger* but, instead, its underlying premise that the prosecution of substantively different offenses is somehow restrained by the Double Jeopardy Clause.

Double Jeopardy Unity: Rejecting Greater Protection against
Successive Prosecutions

All two-tier tests of same offense are incoherent, not just the same-transaction test or the *Grady* test. It is a little strange that the Court has rejected both of these tests and still seems to adhere to the *Brown* view that there exists a greater protection against successive prosecutions. Michael Moore has argued that the problem is not with the particular test used to provide greater protection against successive prosecutions; the problem is with the underlying concept.[46]

As Moore recognized, if offenses are truly different, successive prosecutions cannot be vexatious. It would not, for example, be thought vexatious to try R separately for robbing V on Wednesday and Z on Friday because no one doubts that these offenses are different. Indeed, R might very well move for separate trials if the state sought to try both robberies in a single trial. Thus, if the Court had a good account of when offenses are truly different, rather than superficially different, it would be odd to say that different offenses could be punished cumulatively but not prosecuted separately. Offenses would either be the same or not, and, if not, they could be treated as different offenses in every sense.

In Moore's words:

> The time, expense, and embarrassment of a criminal trial are harms to every criminal defendant, but they are harms we obviously are and should be willing to inflict on a defendant sometimes, else we'd never prosecute anyone. Similarly, the knowing infliction of these harms on a defendant by a prosecutor cannot always amount to harassment; it is only where these harms are inflicted on a defendant for no good reason that a prosecutor is harassing a defendant. When offenses are not truly the same, there is a good reason for a defendant to have to suffer the harms of criminal trials more than once, and there is a good reason for a prosecutor to knowingly inflict them more than once. That reason is "insuring that the guilty are punished." If a defendant has truly done more than one wrong, he deserves more than one punishment. Hence, conviction for an earlier wrong should not bar a second prosecution for the second wrong. The embarrassment, time, and expense of a second trial are no reason to bar the second prosecution, nor can such a prosecution be called harassment.[47]

The contrary argument assumes a substantive role for "harassment" in double jeopardy analysis. It assumes that judges are capable of determining when someone has been unduly harassed even though the legislature authorized multiple penalties for the particular conduct. The difficulty with this argument is that it simply assumes that multiple trials are harassment and, beyond quoting Justice Black's famous *Green* language, does nothing to establish why defendants are harassed by legislatively authorized penalties.[48]

One approach that avoids the difficulty of measuring "harassment" is to argue that the Clause forbids disproportionate punishments. On this view, the Clause forbids a second penalty that produces disproportionate punishment because we want to prevent disproportionate punishment (whether imposed in one trial or in more than one trial).[49] There is nothing wrong with the notion that the Constitution should protect against disproportionate punishments. Doctrinally, this protection should logically reside in the Eighth Amendment, which forbids both "cruel and unusual punishments" and "excessive fines." Conceptually, as argued in chapter 1, there is no defensible basis to determine which legislatively authorized penalties are excessive. When Professor Amy Ronner argues that "even legislatively authorized punishments" can be "excessive and disproportionate,"[50] she owes the reader an account of how judges would make that determination.

Nancy King agrees with Michael Moore, and with me, arguing in favor of a legislative deference approach which is

> premised on the belief that by referring to "offence," the Framers intended that prosecutors and judges adhere to legislative choices regarding the appropriate classification of conduct into culpable units. . . . Legislatures could be trusted to divide wrongdoing into appropriate units for punishment and prosecution, but prosecutors and judges could not necessarily be trusted to respect those choices. Under this view, if Congress intends to create two separate offenses by enacting two separate provisions, then the Fifth Amendment does not prevent prosecutors from seeking successive penalties under both, regardless of how similar or even identical the two provisions appear.[51]

In short, eliminating "unfairness" or "harassment" is a separate concern from preventing more than one trial for the same offense. Eli Richardson puts it this way, referring to the crimes in *Dixon*: "After all, successive prosecutions for criminal contempt and the underlying crime could be considered unfair and unduly burdensome even if *not* for the same offense."[52] I agree with Moore, King, and Richardson. Commentators, and courts, make a category mistake when they assume that same offense should have two different meanings, depending on the potential for harassment inherent in the context of successive prosecutions.

Moore locates his attack on two-tier tests in an account that argues for the primacy of action theory to unravel same offense problems. Though action theory plays a role in structuring the presumptions I use in the absence of clear legislative authorization (see chapter 5), the present account recognizes the primacy of legislative intent, thus agreeing with King that the Framers intended this model and that it is implicit in the Clause itself. On a legislative-prerogative view of double jeopardy, the procedural context in which offenses are prosecuted (one trial or two trials) is irrelevant for institutional reasons. If same offense can be located by discerning legislative intent, and if the legislature is sufficiently clear that two offenses define distinct criminal blameworthiness, prosecutors are entrusted with the decision of whether or how they obtain two convictions, and judges are institutionally beside the point. No one argues, for example, that carjacking cannot be prosecuted separately from the offense of embezzling money that was used to buy the gun used to commit the carjacking. No one makes that argument because there is no doubt that embezzling and carjacking define different criminal law offenses, albeit joined temporally on the facts of this hypothetical.

What we are missing, what this book hopes to provide, is an account of same offense that provides intuitively satisfying answers to the same-offense question. If the answers to the same-offense inquiry can be sufficiently satisfying, courts will be more likely to abolish all vestiges of a two-tier test of same offense. Courts will be free to recognize that offenses that are different substantively are always different for double jeopardy purposes as well. An example that caused English courts confusion is burglary and larceny. These offenses are substantively different because the burglar need not proceed inside and commit the larceny. Because these are substantively different offenses, the prosecutor should be permitted to try them together or separately, limited only by the jurisdiction's procedural rules on joinder of offenses.

On the other hand, the offenses of felony murder and premeditated murder are not substantively different, despite that result under the *Blockburger* test. Similarly, it seems unlikely that robbery in the nighttime and robbery from a dwelling are substantively different. Chapters 3 through 6 will develop analytical tools to answer the question of substantive difference. For the present, the point is simply that substantively different offenses should be capable of being prosecuted and punished in any way permitted by the jurisdiction's rules about joinder and consecutive sentences. Double jeopardy has no role to play.

We are left, then, to conclude that the standard interpretation of Black's rationale as preventing harassment may tell us something, but not very much, about the jeopardy dimension of the problem and tells us nothing useful about the same offense problem. We do not, however, have to reject Black's vision of why we prohibit double jeopardy. Rather, an alternative interpretation is possible, one that focuses on the functional instead of the rhetorical.

An Alternative Double Jeopardy Policy

Recall Black's formulation in *Green*: "the State with all its resources and power should not be allowed to make repeated attempts to convict an individual for an alleged offense, thereby subjecting him to embarrassment, expense and ordeal and compelling him to live in a continuing state of anxiety and insecurity, as well as enhancing the possibility that even though innocent he may be found guilty." There are two harms identified here. One harm is the general harassment noted earlier; the other harm is the specific risk that an innocent defendant will be convicted.

Black offered no principle to decide when the general harm triggers a jeopardy bar. He may have seen the general harm as simply a description of why double jeopardy prohibits the specific harm. That is, perhaps the "embarrassment, expense and ordeal" of a second trial that compels a defendant "to live in a continuing state of anxiety" is wrong only when the first trial has ended in a way that makes further proceedings a threat to an innocent defendant.

Defendants can be "innocent" in two very different ways, as the facts of *Green* suggest. A defendant can be innocent in the commonsense understanding borne of too many bad television shows: the police arrested and the state prosecuted the wrong person. This can be termed "factual innocence." It is more likely, however, that a defendant will be innocent of the particular degree of the offense that the state has charged—a form of legal innocence. On the facts of *Green*, the jury found the defendant guilty of second-degree murder when the charge was first-degree murder. The Court held that Green was therefore innocent of first-degree murder, and no new indictment charging that crime could proceed.[53]

There is another, more subtle way in which a defendant can be legally "innocent" of the degree of offense. Criminal offenses are simply mechanical ways to categorize and organize judgments about criminal blameworthiness. Once the legislature identifies particular conduct that creates criminal blameworthiness, one question is whether that conduct can give rise to any other statutory criminal blameworthiness. If it can, the legislature either meant the two determinations of blameworthiness to be distinct or for one to merge into the other. If the legislature intended a merged or singular blameworthiness for the conduct, only a single conviction can be imposed, regardless of how many overlapping statutes might proscribe that conduct.

Assume, for example, the legislature enacts two statutes, one that proscribes selling heroin without a written order and one that proscribes selling heroin not in the original stamped package. Assume, further, that the legislature means the conduct of selling heroin in violation of both statutes to result in a conviction of either (1) or (2), but not both. On this reading of legislative intent, a defendant convicted of (1) is "innocent" of (2) and vice versa.[54] While this is not an obvious usage of "innocent," it is a consequence of substantive criminal law.

Indeed, as the Court has acknowledged, judges cannot impose more convictions than the legislature intended, whether or not one considers double jeopardy.[55] The Due Process Clause would not permit unauthorized convictions. In this context, the Double Jeopardy Clause functions merely as an outgrowth of substantive criminal law and the procedural allocation of responsibility between legislatures and judges. The point to this book is to expand that point to all of double jeopardy and to claim that the Double Jeopardy Clause in all contexts is nothing more (or less) than the equipose that exists between substantive criminal law and the procedure that the legislature creates for imposing judgments about criminal blameworthiness. On this view, the only function of any double jeopardy doctrine is to identify the best methodologies for "reading" relevant legislative intent.

One hard-edged double jeopardy policy consistent with Black's quote would thus be to prevent convictions of innocent defendants, on either usage of "innocence"—factual or legal innocence. Though it is coherent to talk about defendants being legally "innocent" of a degree of offense or a type of blameworthiness, it is more natural to speak of unauthorized judgments. Assume, for instance, that the legislature meant larceny blameworthiness to merge into robbery blameworthiness. We can then say that a defendant who is convicted of both robbery and larceny has suffered an unauthorized conviction, which the judge must not enter or the appellate court must vacate.

Acquittals pose a special case when viewing double jeopardy as a prohibition of unauthorized judgments. Legislative intent about how many convictions are authorized is not directly relevant to whether the state can follow a finding of no blameworthiness with a second trial seeking to prove the same alleged blameworthiness. One could reasonably assert, however, that the legislature does not intend the state to relitigate the factual basis of acquittals.[56] A more difficult question would be the Double Jeopardy Clause response if a legislature passed a statute authorizing proceedings that follow an acquittal, a question that concerns us in chapter 9. Accepting for the moment that no legislature wishes to authorize a second factual determination following an acquittal, we can call these proceedings unauthorized.

In addition, some trial outcomes short of a formal verdict might imply that further proceedings are unauthorized. An example is a dismissal with prejudice on the ground that the state's evidence was insufficient to permit any rational trier of fact to convict. This outcome, of course, lacks only the formal status of a verdict. But there may be other, less obvious ways in which a dismissal or mistrial can be viewed as equivalent to a finding of factual or legal innocence. Consider, for example, a case in which the prosecution discovers after trial has begun that its physical evidence has been lost and its only eyewitness has left the jurisdiction. A mistrial here seems calculated to avoid an inevitable acquittal and thus can be viewed as equivalent to acquittal. So viewed, of course, further proceedings would be unauthorized on the assumption that the legislature does not intend acquittals to be relitigated.

Thus, a working statement of double jeopardy policy is that double jeopardy protects against unauthorized judgments of criminal blameworthiness. A policy of preventing unauthorized judgments about blameworthiness seems compelling from a systemic perspective and is consistent with our notions of due process as well as double jeopardy. In chapter 1 I stated a preference for hard-edged statements of policy as a way to evaluate the outcomes produced by a hard-edged rule. The policy of preventing unauthorized judgments about blameworthiness is a much more hard-edged policy than that of preventing the generalized harm of harassing prosecutions. We can imagine an inquiry that would provide a fairly accurate division between defendants based on the likelihood of acquittal. We can also develop tools to tell us how many convictions the legislature authorized for particular conduct. But harassment, like beauty, is pretty much in the eye of the beholder.

Two examples will clarify the working policy statement. Jenkins filed a motion for an acquittal because the law changed after he had engaged in the conduct in question.[57] The trial judge, sitting as fact finder, heard the case and then dismissed the indictment on the ground that it would be unfair to apply the change in the law to Jenkins. The Government sought to appeal the district court's holding on retroactivity. Would the defendant be harassed, within the double jeopardy policy against harassment, if the appeal were permitted?

The Court held yes. Seven members relied on the ground that a successful appeal would require new fact-finding by the district court upon remand, and this additional fact-finding would violate the double jeopardy policy as articulated by Justice Black: "the State with all its resources and power should not be allowed to make repeated attempts to convict an individual for an alleged offense."[58] This reading of "harassment" is close to Madison's hard-edged rule that the state can have only one trial or punishment per offense. But it did not last long; three years later, the Court overruled *Jenkins* and held that a second fact-finding does not always constitute harassment.[59] The Court is on the right track here. A second fact-finding should be a second jeopardy only if the first trial ended in a way analogous to a verdict. The Court has applied this principle inconsistently in its second jeopardy case law.

For a same-offense example of my proposed double jeopardy policy, consider *Brown v. Ohio*.[60] Nathaniel Brown took a car that did not belong to him, kept it for nine days, and was arrested in a different county. He pled guilty to the misdemeanor of joyriding and served a thirty-day jail sentence. He was later indicted for auto theft and joyriding. Prior to trial, the prosecutor dropped the joyriding charge, apparently conceding that the second joyriding charge was the same offense as the joyriding for which Brown had already been punished. At least as a matter of offense definitions, this is an obvious and hard-edged part of same-offense doctrine. Joyriding must be definitionally the same offense as joyriding. Brown objected to the auto theft prosecution as well but lost in the state courts.

In deciding the definitional issue, the Supreme Court applied its *Blockburger* test: if either statutory proscription necessarily includes all the elements of the other, they are the same offense. This rule has relatively hard edges because offense 1 will either include all the elements of offense 2 or it will not.[61] The Court does not ask whether elements are functionally the same, only whether they are literally the same. Applying *Blockburger* to the crimes as construed by the state courts, auto theft included all the elements of joyriding, and they were definitionally the same offense.

But *Brown* is more challenging that this description indicates. The same offense issue has two dimensions: definition and conduct. Offenses must be the same both in definition and conduct before they are the same double jeopardy offense. In *Brown*, even though joyriding is definitionally the same offense as joyriding, it is not the same offense if based on sufficiently different conduct. Joyriding *X*'s car on Monday is a different offense from joyriding *Z*'s car on Tuesday. Joyriding *X*'s car on Monday is different from stealing *W*'s car on Wednesday. As we see in more detail in chapter 5,[62] the conduct dimension was the state's strongest argument that the *Brown* offenses were different.

The Court has stated that the conduct issue—which it sometimes refers to as determining the proper "unit of prosecution"—turns exclusively on what the legislature meant to constitute one offense. While this is the right way to view the same offense problem, it is not very helpful. Is driving two women across the state line for immoral purposes one violation of the Mann Act or two? Is wounding two federal officers with a single shotgun blast two assaults or one? These questions concern us in chapter 5. Here, the point is simply that the questions are difficult, and the Court's same conduct "rule" has very soft edges.

Lacking a clear rule about when offenses are the same in terms of conduct, should a judge allow a felony trial for auto theft on the facts of *Brown*? The Supreme Court held, over three dissenting votes, that the conduct was the same "unit" and thus the auto theft conviction violated double jeopardy. Policy analysis is not helpful in hardening the edges of the conduct rule. Two competing policies exist. Defendants should face judgment on their full criminal blameworthiness; if Brown cannot be tried for auto theft, then he has escaped judgment on the extra blameworthiness entailed by the felony of auto theft (the intent to steal the car rather than merely to joyride in it). Another policy is to prefer a single determination of blameworthiness rather than piecemeal determinations—what I have called the policy against harassment. A judge's task in a case like *Brown* could be to balance the policy in favor of full judgments against the policy not to harass. But which policy should prevail?

The elasticity of current double jeopardy policy can be seen in the criticisms directed at the Court's analysis in *Brown*. On the facts of *Brown*, the policy in favor of judgment on all blameworthiness argues for a result (permitting the second trial) different from the policy against harassment, but the Court's opinion has nevertheless been criticized on both policy grounds. Peter Westen and Richard Drubel criticize the Court for not considering the full-judgment question of whether Brown had faced conviction for the more culpable element of auto theft.[63] Akhil Amar and Jonathan Marcus criticize the Court's analysis as insufficiently sensitive to whether the prosecutor was at fault for the second trial.[64] Putting these criticisms together, double jeopardy policy looks something like this: defendants can be retried for a greater offense as long as the fragmented prosecutions were not the prosecutor's fault.[65]

The troubling aspect of using harassment policy to inform same-offense analysis, at least for someone who values hard-edged rules, is that the outcome depends on the prosecutor's motives in bringing two trials. It may be old-fashioned, but it seems to me that auto theft and joyriding are either the same offense on a set of facts or they are not. If they are the same offense, they are the same offense, even if the prosecutor has the most benevolent motives in bringing two trials—indeed, regardless of whether the charges are brought in one trial or two. If two offenses are the same and the prosecutor chooses to bring the lesser one first, the legislative scheme for punishment may have been thwarted, but prosecutors routinely exercise discretion to seek lesser punishment than the legislature authorized. The same offense remains the same offense.

In sum, I believe courts should reject a global double jeopardy policy of preventing harassment of defendants and adopt, in its place, the relatively hard-edged double jeopardy policy of preventing unauthorized judgments about blameworthiness. Necessarily, courts would also reject mandatory joinder as a policy that exists independent of the equivalence between singular blameworthiness and a single judgment. While mandatory joinder is a good idea, it is different from the idea manifested in my reading of double jeopardy policy.[66]

A policy that makes blameworthiness central to double jeopardy analysis must rely on legislative intent. This focus sets my account apart from all others; while the Court and a few commentators realize the role legislative intent necessarily plays in the single-trial same-offense issue, no one has yet identified the central role legislative intent plays in all of double jeopardy analysis. On my account, legislative intent is crucial in determining whether offenses are the "same" in successive prosecutions as well as single trials and whether a defendant is placed "twice in jeopardy" by a particular proceeding.

Bishop argued that firing a single shotgun blast that struck fifty persons would be a single battery.[67] His argument was not based on legislative intent. He believed that courts defined "offense" by drawing on natural law concepts like "same act."[68] My argument in this book is to the contrary. It is the legislature, and only the legislature, that determines what counts as double jeopardy for the same offense.

I thus adopt, as a working hypothesis, that double jeopardy forbids more than the legislatively authorized number of convictions for given conduct and also forbids redetermination of an outcome that is final under the legislative procedural system.[69] The next section elaborates on this hypothesis by stating it as a principle and developing two presumptions to serve the principle.

A Double Jeopardy Principle and Two Presumptions

The principle that underlies this book is a restatement of the hypothesis developed in the preceding section. Double jeopardy is a procedural and not a substantive protection. There are no independent double jeopardy norms to tell us when offenses are the same (or different) or when a jeopardy is ended and a new one begun. The legislature determines all of these substantive issues, and courts have but to divine legislative intent. Though the legislature rarely makes its intent known, there are two examples of the legislature speaking clearly on double jeopardy issues. In the early part of the twentieth century, the Connecticut legislature authorized appeals from acquittals if the appeal was based on errors of law, rather than on the jury's fact-finding.[70] In effect, the state legislature created a system in which jeopardy did not end with an acquittal that was infected with certain legal errors. In the 1980s the Missouri legislature spoke to the same-offense aspect of double jeopardy, authorizing a second conviction and sentence based on what would otherwise be the same offense under the traditional included-offense test.[71]

In both cases, the United States Supreme Court deferred to the clear statement of legislative intent. My account in this book is based on the principle that courts should always so defer. This legislative-prerogative principle is at first glance disconcerting because few other potential limits exist on the legislative power to define crimes and authorize penalties. The Eighth Amendment forbids "excessive fines" and "cruel and unusual punishments," but the latter limitation is almost never applied to any penalty other than death. Some conduct—such as free speech and the freedom of religion—is protected by other amendments and thus cannot be criminalized. But, in the vast majority of cases, the legislature is free to define crimes and authorize penalties as it sees fit under other constitutional doctrines, and my principle removes any doubt about whether the Double Jeopardy Clause is a limit on legislative power. This makes the legislative-prerogative principle controversial, at least in the "same-offense" context.

Legislative prerogative is of less consequence to the issue of when one jeopardy ends and another one begins. Unlike questions about same offense, where little in the Bill of Rights limits legislative power, substantial limits exist on the legislature's ability to define a criminal verdict. It could not, for example, require a trial to a judge or permit a jury verdict by majority vote; both of these changes would violate the right to trial by jury. Nor could the legislature change the burden or quantum of proof without violating due process. Moreover, courts and scholars are more accustomed to looking to the legislature for the definition of "verdict."

Because divining relevant legislative intent is usually very difficult, presumptions are necessary to allow courts to infer legislative intent on jeopardy and same offense. The shape and content of the presumptions occupy much of this book. The overarching principle that the legislature is the sole source of substantive double jeopardy protection is of fundamental importance—it has never been offered as an organizing double jeopardy principle—but the scarcity of evidence of legislative intent means that almost all cases will be resolved by the presumptions, and getting the presumptions right is thus pragmatically more important than the principle of legislative prerogative.

A Presumption about the End of Jeopardy

On the jeopardy issue, an authorized-judgment account presumes that jeopardy ends only with a verdict or with a trial outcome that suggests an acquittal would have resulted. Historically, as I show in the next section, double jeopardy pleas have traditionally required a verdict. The first Supreme Court case finding a jeopardy bar in a verdictless outcome did not occur until 1963. It was *Downum v. United States.*[72]

Downum is best understood as manifesting the second part of the authorized judgment presumption: some trial outcomes suggest that an acquittal would have resulted had the case continued. The prosecutor moved for a mistrial in *Downum* because his key witness on two of the counts was not available. The prosecutor's characterization of the witness as "key" and the very act of moving for a mistrial on the ground of a missing "key" witness suggest that the government's case was likely to give rise to a reasonable doubt. Chapter 8 has more to say about outcomes that suggest acquittal avoidance. For the present, it serves to note that in the limited context of acquittal avoidance, prosecutorial harassment of a defendant sounds in double jeopardy. An authorized judgment presumption must incorporate a protection against that narrow subset of prosecutorial harassment because otherwise the protection against reprosecuting acquittals would be undermined.

As I develop in detail in chapter 8, there are other situations in which a verdictless outcome must be characterized as an acquittal. The Court has explicitly recognized three of these categories. We saw earlier the *Green* principle that a conviction of second-degree murder impliedly acquits of the first-degree murder that was charged.[73] Similarly, an appellate reversal for insufficient evidence leaves no formal verdict in place, but the Court has unanimously held it to constitute an acquittal bar to another trial.[74] Finally, a dismissal that resolves the factual elements of the offense in the defendant's favor functions as an acquittal despite the lack of a formal verdict.[75] For example, dismissal on the ground of entrapment or insanity is a fact-based favorable resolution of the charge that bars a second trial.

The jeopardy presumption thus tracks closely the Court's outcomes, albeit with a different analytical structure. It also has a simple, straightforward structure: jeopardy ends only with a formal verdict or an outcome that can fairly be characterized as an acquittal.

A Presumption about "Same Offense"

On the same-offense issue, we begin by recognizing that the legislature creates criminal blameworthiness by proscribing conduct. An authorized-judgment principle presumes equivalence between one legislatively proscribed blameworthy act and singular blameworthiness. Stated differently, each legislatively proscribed blameworthy act is one, and only one, double jeopardy offense. This presumption is subject to an exception for some cases involving multiple harms from a single act, a point that is developed in chapter 5. But, in all other cases, the number of legislatively proscribed blameworthy acts always equals the number of double jeopardy offenses the legislature meant to create. This presumption is developed and defended in more detail in chapter 5, which includes an account of the relationship between blameworthy acts and harm.

The "same-offense" presumption uses *legislatively proscribed* acts to make clear that the number of *metaphysical* acts has nothing to do with how many judgments are authorized. Justice Blackmun confused metaphysical and proscribed acts in his *Brown* dissent, arguing that Brown must have committed more than one driving episode during the nine days he possessed the car that he stole.[76] This is undoubtedly true but irrelevant. The double jeopardy question is not the metaphysical-act question. The number of times Brown got into and out of his car has nothing to do with the number of "takings" of a car that occurred. Unless one of the statutes used an unusual definition, taking a car and keeping it for nine days is a single taking.[77] If "taking" is the relevant proscribed act, Brown should have been convicted only once, as the Court held.

The same-offense presumption uses the number of *blameworthy* acts because the proscription of acts unconnected to blameworthiness is unlikely to signal legislative intent to create cumulatively punishable offenses (distinct blameworthiness). Chapter 5 explores this idea in depth. For now, the following example suffices: the offense of "committing robbery while waving a flag" should be the same offense as "committing robbery while singing 'The Star-Spangled Banner.'" Waving a flag and singing are distinct acts, but the blameworthiness in both offenses is captured by the act of robbing, and there is thus only one blameworthy act. For convenience, I sometimes refer to the same-offense presumption as "act equals offense." When I do this, I speak elliptically. I mean, in every case, that "one legislatively proscribed blameworthy act equals one offense." The full formulation is awkward to work into a sentence.

The act-equals-offense presumption thus does double duty in double jeopardy analysis. It helps sort through the definitional issue to produce consistent results. For example, the act presumption concludes that one killing is only one murder, even though the included-offense test can (oddly enough) reach a different result.[78] Similarly, the act presumption concludes that rape and felony murder based on rape are two offenses, even though the Court has reached a different result.[79]

The act-equals-offense presumption also solves the conduct dimension of the same-offense problem. The key is to realize that there is no metaphysical connection between act and offense. What counts for the double jeopardy theory offered in this book is the legislatively proscribed blameworthy act. Once we determine, by reference to actual intent or a presumption, the number of blameworthy acts the legislature meant to create from the defendant's conduct, we have the answer both to the offense definition and the "unit of prosecution" issue. We know, in short, whether Nathaniel Brown taking a car is definitionally one offense— whether the blameworthy act in the statutory offense of auto theft is the same as in the statutory offense of joyriding—and we also know whether by keeping the car for nine days, Brown committed more than one offense of either joyriding or auto theft.

The value of a double jeopardy account that can solve both dimensions of the same-offense problem with a single inquiry is alone reason to give it serious consideration.[80] In addition, overwhelming historical evidence supports my account and my statement of double jeopardy policy. What follows is the evidence that the lawgiver has traditionally determined when outcomes are completed jeopardies for a singular offense— that is, when a determination binds judges and prosecutors. Historical evidence also supports my two double jeopardy presumptions: (1) jeopardy ends only when there is a verdict or an outcome suggesting an acquittal; (2) "offense" is equivalent to "proscribed act."

Double Jeopardy Evolution to 1792

Much evidence exists of a double jeopardy bar on prosecutors and judges, but there is almost no evidence that the bar extended to the lawgiver. Double jeopardy binds prosecutors by forbidding them from relitigating acquittals or seeking more convictions than the legislature has authorized. It binds judges by forbidding them from imposing an unauthorized additional penalty or changing a verdict once it is final. But it would bind the lawgiver only if it limited his or its ability to define crimes or determine what counts as a verdict.

Legislative prerogative regarding offense and jeopardy is so pervasive that direct evidence of it is hard to uncover. But much indirect evidence exists. With a single exception, dating from 1170, there is no evidence of *any* authority denying legislative power to define offense and verdict. The one authority who, for a brief time, was successful in denying the law-giver's power in this context was the Pope. No English court ever attempted to curtail the legislative prerogative, and no English treatise writer ever suggested that the legislative prerogative should be curtailed.

Double Jeopardy Law before Henry II

In the earliest legal systems, law came from the monarch or, what may be the same, from the deity. The notion of error or lack of power would have been difficult to imagine. No one likely questioned the blameworthiness created in Hammurabi's laws or the Ten Commandments. Indeed, the Bible goes to considerable length to make clear that the Ten Commandments came from God.[81] The role of human judges was to "declare the statutes and laws of God."[82]

Some writers have found a (surely self-imposed) biblical limitation on God's power to define blameworthiness, but the interpretation is not without difficulty. In Nahum, an Old Testament book, one passage states that "affliction shall not rise up the second time."[83] This is the passage that Saint Jerome interpreted in A.D. 391 to mean that God does not twice punish the same act,[84] and this interpretation became a canon-law maxim that manifests the act-equals-offense presumption: "Not even God judges twice for the same act."[85]

While supporting the one-act-equals-one-offense presumption, this maxim contradicts the overarching principle of legislative prerogative if it is read to imply a limitation on the lawgiver's power. But Saint Jerome's interpretation is dubious. The entire verse in the King James version reads, "What do ye imagine against the Lord? he will make an utter end: affliction shall not rise up the second time." In context, the phrase seems to mean that God does not punish twice for the same act because the first punishment will make "an utter end" of God's enemies and thus be superfluous.[86] The New English interpretation is ever clearer: "No adversaries dare oppose him twice; all are burnt up like tangled briars."[87]

The better interpretation of this passage, then, is that God does not judge twice because it is unnecessary. The principle of superfluity also underlies *autrefois attaint*, a common-law plea in bar that held that a conviction of felony and a judgment on that conviction barred a new trial for any other felony, whether committed before or after the attainder. The basis for this principle was the idea that the new proceeding, in Blackstone's words, "cannot be to any purpose; for the prisoner is dead in law by the first attainder, his blood is already corrupted, and he hath forfeited all that he had; so that it is absurd and superfluous to endeavor to attaint him a second time."[88]

The creation of blameworthiness—whether by a deity, a king, or judges defining a common law felony—seems to have been unquestioned in this early period. But humans could err in prosecuting and rendering judgment. Thus, limits were needed on prosecutors and judges. A gruesome but effective way of preventing a second trial by the same prosecutor after an acquittal can be found in the first law of the Code of Hammurabi: "If a man has accused a man and has charged him with manslaughter and then has not proved [it against] him, his accuser shall be put to death."[89] A less draconian arrangement binds judges to a single verdict in the fifth law of the Code of Hammurabi:

> If a judge has tried a suit, given a decision, caused a sealed tablet to be executed, [and] thereafter varies his judgement, they shall convict that judge of varying [his] judgement and he shall pay twelve-fold the claim in that suit; then they shall remove him from his place on the bench of judges in the assembly and he shall not [again] sit in judgement with the judges.[90]

Though this mechanism is less effective than denying judges power to change a verdict—the modern res judicata rule[91]—it seeks the same goal.

Greek law bound both the prosecutor and the judge to the original verdict, as can be seen in the oft-quoted remark of Demosthenes in 355 B.C. that the "laws forbid the same man to be tried twice on the same issue."[92] If "same issue" meant "same act," as seems likely, the act-equals-offense presumption was established in early Greek law well before Saint Jerome found it in Nahum.

In the Roman Republic, a magistrate's acquittal barred further proceedings of any kind,[93] but a magistrate's conviction could be appealed to an assembly of the Roman people.[94] The rationale was given by Polybius: "The people alone judges in cases of life and death."[95] The implication is that the people are sovereign and never err when attributing blameworthiness in individual cases. The prosecutor and judge make mistakes in individual cases, and the sovereign (the people) is responsible for correcting those errors. If the sovereign cannot err in individual attribution of blameworthiness, it is difficult to imagine how it can err in creating blameworthiness in the first place.

The demise of the Roman Republic and the ascendancy of the emperors impaired the sovereignty of the people, as would be expected. One manifestation of that impairment was that an acquittal was no longer binding on the prosecutor.[96] While clearly an "infringement" on the principle "that the verdict of a competent court of justice is unalterable,"[97] it did not last. By the time of the Digest of Justinian, the law prohibited a second charge following acquittal, while still allowing appeal from a conviction.[98]

Becket and Henry II

Two different and somewhat parallel court systems existed in twelfth-century England: ecclesiastical and royal. In addition to spiritual matters (such as the ordination of clerics), the ecclesiastical courts claimed jurisdiction over "all personal causes, criminal or civil, in which a clerk was the accused or the defendant."[99] The only penalty that could be imposed on clerics, regardless of the crime they committed, was degradation in ecclesiastical courts. No forfeiture of the offender's goods to the king was permissible.

Henry II asserted in the Constitutions of Clarendon (1164) that clergy were also subject to the king's punishment.[100] Saint Thomas Becket opposed Henry, relying on Saint Jerome's interpretation of Nahum.[101] Because Becket was willing to add imprisonment as an additional penalty in the ecclesiastical courts, his notion of double punishment stated a "principle condemning not two punishments but two judgments."[102] Pollock and Maitland viewed this principle as "highly technical,"[103] but it raises the double jeopardy question in its pure form. The pure question is not whether punishments are multiple in a literal sense—as we saw in chapter 1, modern statutes often authorize a fine and imprisonment—but whether more than one judgment of criminal blameworthiness can be based on one criminal act. This is still the right question to ask, on the account offered in this book.

Henry II prevailed on the issue, although he got off to a bad start. Four of Henry's knights murdered Becket in 1170, but the king's problems with the Church did not end. The Pope condemned the punishment provision of the Constitutions of Clarendon. Unwilling to disobey the Pope (this was, after all, roughly four centuries before Henry VIII would break with the Pope), Henry was "compelled to renounce, although in carefully guarded terms," his argument that a degraded cleric could be sentenced in the royal court.[104]

But Becket's successor agreed with Henry that lay offenders who murdered clerics should be subject to hanging by the state as well as excommunication from the church.[105] From this concession that some dual judgments were permissible, Henry extracted a compromise from a papal legate in 1176 that permitted state punishment of clerics who violated certain statutory laws.[106] A subsequent decree of Innocent III "ordained that the forgers of papal letters should be handed over" to the lay power for its criminal judgment.[107]

Innocent III thus effectively abandoned Becket's hard-won principle against dual secular and sectarian judgments for the same criminal act. As Pollock and Maitland conclude, "If once it be allowed that there is here no breach of the fundamental maxim which requires that a man be not punished twice for one offense, then there remains no more than a question about the relative gravity of offences:—is, for example, the forgery of a decretal a worse crime than a murder?"[108]

It was not just dual punishments that were occurring but dual judgments as well. The state could not know whether its own laws were violated without some sort of procedural hearing. Thus, by 1250, despite the objection of the Church, the king's courts routinely conducted a trial to determine whether the goods of the cleric should be forfeited to the Crown before transferring the accused to the spiritual courts.[109]

Pollock and Maitland conclude that Becket's interpretation of canon law to prohibit multiple judgments was palpably erroneous.[110] A legislative-prerogative principle agrees. Henry II was right in 1164 when he first asserted the right to punish clerics who violated the king's law. The lawgiver cannot violate any principle forbidding multiple punishment or multiple judgments. Fully authorized punishments and judgments cannot be multiple.

One could argue that it is multiple punishment when each of two coordinate sovereigns imposes a penalty. But that assumes one of the sovereigns is not really sovereign with respect to the relevant group of wrongdoers—the assumption that Becket and the Pope probably made in 1164 (that the church was the true sovereign with respect to clerics). As long as both sovereigns are truly sovereign in respective spheres, each can impose the penalties it wishes.[111] The only question is whether the sovereign whose penalty is last imposed has clearly authorized it in addition to the penalty of the other sovereign. Chapter 6 considers this argument in greater detail with respect to the federal-state issue in the United States.

Though Becket lost in his attempt to create a universal rule that one act can be punished but once, a remnant of his argument—the plea of "benefit of clergy"—continued to play a role in the development of double jeopardy doctrine for centuries. The rationale of "benefit of clergy" was a hybrid. The remnants of Becket's argument against dual judgments appear as a limit on the power of the state to punish someone who was "allowed his clergy" for that crime. The secular conviction was valid (which permitted forfeiture of the offender's goods[112] and thus presumably satisfied the king), but without the criminal punishment otherwise imposed (usually capital punishment).[113] As long as the conviction stood, benefit of clergy was a bar against further secular proceedings for the same offense. Ironically, Becket's position against dual judgments in the secular and ecclesiastical courts became part of the common law of double jeopardy in the secular courts.

Key to benefit of clergy was the existence of a criminal judgment. This evidence supports the jeopardy presumption that the first jeopardy ends with judgment. An offender who claimed benefit of clergy could bar a second secular judgment even though he had never been criminally punished, by relying on the first judgment. The lawgiver defined verdict in terms of judgment, and a conviction with clergy (but without punishment) was therefore sufficient to be a plea in bar to a second jeopardy. Benefit of clergy manifested both of my double jeopardy presumptions— that a single judgment prohibits a second trial for the same proscribed act[114] without regard to the nature and number of punishments imposed.

One Act, One Offense

Elaborate double jeopardy pleas were recognized shortly after Becket argued that only one judgment could attend one act.[115] At least four kinds of double jeopardy claims can be found in cases from the king's courts in the first four years of the thirteenth century. These cases routinely applied the bar of former acquittal (adjudged quit)[116] and former conviction[117] to forbid prosecutions. Moreover, a case from 1202 seemed to draw a parallel between acquittal and the plea of former dismissal (withdrawal) of a murder prosecution, holding that the latter would bar a second prosecution.[118] One case articulated an early version of issue preclusion (collateral estoppel), finding a prosecution null, in part, because the victim had previously declared before the "serjeant of the hundred" that he had not been injured.[119]

The remedy in all these thirteenth-century cases was that the appeal (the prosecution) was "null" or that the defendant was "quit" of the appeal. Because a discharge or finding of "quit" would preclude a second appeal, English law by 1300 permitted four pleas that resemble modern double jeopardy (former acquittal, former conviction, dismissal, and issue preclusion). The next evolution in double jeopardy pleas further compromised the one judgment/one act rule. Just as the existence of parallel church and state court systems undermined the one-judgment principle in the twelfth century, two overlapping systems of criminal prosecution led to further erosion of the principle. From the thirteenth to the eighteenth centuries, a criminal act could be prosecuted either by the king's indictment or by private prosecution by the victim. Return of stolen goods was one of the sanctions the appeal made available, but death was also an available sanction. Beginning as a supplement to the private appeal, undoubtedly designed as a way to raise revenue, the king's indictment gradually displaced the appeal as the most common form of prosecution. But for centuries the two forms were roughly of equal stature, thus creating much opportunity for dual criminal judgments.

The reason parallel prosecution systems eroded the act-equals-offense presumption is not hard to fathom. The very existence of different systems indicates different interests to protect. The individual victim of theft or robbery wanted his property returned; the king wanted the offender's lands and also wanted to rid the kingdom of the wrongdoer.

The evidence suggests that during the thirteenth century, when the king instituted few prosecutions, there was double jeopardy unity between the appeal and the indictment: a conviction or acquittal of either kind of suit barred the other suit. This can be seen most clearly in Bracton's treatise, completed by the end of 1256.[120] In the context of trial by battle, Bracton wrote:

> If he has been appealed by several of one deed and one wound [*de uno facto et una plaga*], and successfully makes his defence against one, he will depart quit against all the other appellors, also as regards the king's suit, because he thereby proves his innocence against all, as though he had put himself on the country and it had exonerated him completely.[121]

Bracton phrased double jeopardy protection as against more than one appeal or indictment for the same "deed" (the Latin *facto*) in several places.[122] Other thirteenth-century commentators reflect similar usage. Fleta also used same "deed" (*facto*).[123] The *Mirror of Justices* noted that only one punishment can be based on one "trespass" (the French *trespas*).[124] Britton's usage was more modern—same "felony" (the French *la felonie*),[125] but there is no indication he used "felony" to mean anything other than "act" or "trespass." Thus, the early common law seemed to view the double jeopardy protection as against more than one judgment for the same act.

As early as the sixteenth century, there was judicial recognition that the number of criminal acts was more important than the number of offenses with different names. In 1591 the King's Bench noted, as an unremarkable proposition, that "if a man commits murder, and is indicted and convicted or acquitted of manslaughter, he shall never answer to any indictment of the same death, for all is one and the same felony for one and the same death, although murder is in respect of the circumstance of the forethought malice more odious."[126]

It is the same death that brings unity to the same offense question, not the murder/manslaughter distinction. This led Blackstone to make a similar observation about murder and manslaughter—"for the fact prosecuted is the same in both, though the offenses differ in coloring and in degree."[127] The early evidence supports a presumption that one act equals one offense.

Bracton's rationale for stating that neither the king nor a private party could proceed after an acquittal was that the defendant "thereby proves his innocence against all, as though he had put himself on the country and it had exonerated him completely."[128] Bracton saw the "country" as the relevant victim, explicitly including the private prosecutor and the king. This is similar to Becket's view that clerics owed allegiance to only one sovereign. Just as Becket's unity was doomed when secular justice became more important than sectarian justice, Bracton's unity was doomed as the king's prosecutors began to assume a role different from that of wronged individuals. Thus, the king's right to prosecute criminally for wrongs done society, and the victim's right to restitution, would fragment the unitary view that one act can lead to only one secular judgment.

By Sir Edmund Coke's day, Bracton's unity was fraying, and the divergence between criminal punishment and restitution was under way. Private plaintiffs could bring an appeal for robbery despite a former attainder (a felony judgment with punishment), and this principle eventually broadened into a complete separation between civil and criminal spheres for purposes of double jeopardy. No one claims that the result of a criminal trial should bar a tort suit or vice versa, even if both are based on the very same act.

Henry II and Fraudulent Acquittals

Henry II sought not only to decree a secular punishment for clerics, a matter of defining crimes and fixing penalties, but also to assert authority over the procedural mechanism by which outcomes are judged as the end of jeopardy. Though he would be temporarily stymied in his effort to authorize punishment for clerics, Henry successfully pursued another group who was escaping justice: defendants acquitted by the ordeal. The ordeal, which dates at least as far back as Ur-Nammu, c. 2050 B.C.,[129] consisted of various mechanisms that invited God to pass judgment. In Blackstone's words, the idea was "that God would always interpose miraculously to vindicate the guiltless."[130] The accused might, for example, be forced to carry hot iron or be cast into water. If his hand showed evidence of burning or he floated, he was adjudged guilty.[131]

Maitland's evidence suggests that acquittals by the ordeal were often part of a settlement between the private prosecutor and the accused, permitting the accused to avoid forfeiture of his lands to the king.[132] This type of informal accommodation is certainly consistent with human nature. Henry II would not, of course, be happy at this turn of events, which, like the situation with the clerics, was costing the Crown money.

Henry first acted in the Assize of Clarendon (1166), only two years after the controversial Constitutions of Clarendon. One decree was that those who were "absolved by the law" must nonetheless depart the realm and "abjure the king's lands" if "they have been of ill repute and openly and disgracefully spoken of by the testimony of many and that of lawful men." If they returned "except by the mercy of the lord king," they would "be seized as outlaws."[133]

This law seems directed at fraudulent acquittals. It applies only on the testimony of "many . . . lawful men" that the defendant was of "ill repute." Henry deprived this category of acquittals of their essential quality as an acquittal. Stated differently, Henry was redefining "acquittal" not to include this category of outcomes.

Ten years later, in the Assize of Northhampton (1176), Henry's concern about the ordeal was explicit, and he limited his repudiation of acquittals to those obtained "at the water" (by the ordeal of water) for "murder or some other base felony."[134] No evidence exists of any criticism that Henry somehow lacked the authority to put limitations on what constituted an acquittal. None of the commentators raised any concern with Henry's acquittal rule, including the enigmatic but quite critical commentator who wrote *The Mirror of Justices* in the next century. It appears that Henry's authority to define acquittal, and thus the end of jeopardy, was unquestioned.

With the exception of the idiosyncratic period when Becket was challenging Henry II, therefore, the early law recognized no double jeopardy limits on the lawgiver. The lawgiver could define blameworthiness and could decree what outcomes counted as complete.

Post–Henry II Statutory Changes

Statutes from 1487 to 1576 confirm that the lawgiver did not labor under double jeopardy limitations. A 1487 statute sought to avoid a 1482 case requiring the King's indictment to wait a year and a day after the felony in order to give the (preferred) private appeal time to proceed.[135] To make the waiting period unnecessary, the statute permitted a private appeal in murder cases without regard to the outcome of the king's suit.[136] This rule contradicts the law stated by Bracton,[137] and Friedland claims that it "totally disregarded the [double jeopardy] principle."[138] My view is that the 1487 statute is consistent with a different double jeopardy principle: that no limits exist on the sovereign's authority to define what counts as a criminal verdict. The king was merely withdrawing criminal verdict status from private appeals for murder.

Similarly, a 1534 statute of Henry VIII provided for reprosecution in English courts of Welsh defendants who were initially acquitted or fined in Welsh courts.[139] Again, the effect is to change the verdict status for this class of outcomes. Jill Hunter concludes: "Presumably the purpose of this Act was to ensure that Welsh criminals did not benefit from unjustified favourable treatment at the hands of Welsh juries and it was considered less radical to allow a second English prosecution than to dominate the Welsh courts directly."[140] The 1534 statute treated one category of outcomes more favorably; an attaint resulting from a conviction of felony was a bar to an appeal if the offender's attaint (and tax to the king) was accepted by the king's court. It is clear that the sovereign was in control of the definition of verdict in Welsh as well as English courts.

Also changing what counted as a verdict bar to another proceeding were the statutes limiting benefit of clergy. Blackstone and Coke make clear that this plea was favored by judges. The plea eventually expanded to include a large group of defendants. Initially the plea was available only to those who wore clerical garb, later to anyone who could read,[141] and, in Blackstone's day, to any first offender who was willing to substitute a lesser punishment for capital punishment[142] (and who would not be willing?).

Henry VII curtailed the plea in 1487 by limiting a second grant of benefit of clergy only to those who had proof of "his letters of his Orders."[143] No commentator suggested that the king lacked this power. Building on the success of his father, Henry VIII denied benefit of clergy to a long list of offenses, including premeditated murder, petty treason, and a wide variety of robberies.[144]

Elizabeth I later extended this list to include rape, burglary, and larceny from the person.[145] Expanding on Henry VII's limitation on second grants of clergy, a 1576 statute denied clergy for all subsequently committed felonies.[146] A related development, contained in the same statute, permitted judges to incarcerate a defendant who claimed clergy for a period of up to one year for "further Correction." This gave judges the power to require secular punishment before a judgment of clergy would constitute a bar to further proceedings, thus changing the definition of a benefit-of-clergy verdict.

By Blackstone's day, the notion of statutory limitations on benefit of clergy was so well accepted that he could remark, almost in passing, that "very many" felonies "are ousted of clergy by particular acts of parliament."[147] No commentator questioned the validity of these numerous statutory limitations on double jeopardy rights. Indeed, Lord Holt, C.J., noted in 1697 that the statute of Henry VII permitting both an appeal and indictment for murder was "severe in overthrowing a fundamental point in law, in subjecting a man that is acquitted to another tryal, which is putting his life twice in danger for the same crime."[148] Despite his obvious opposition to the idea, Holt did not question the right of the lawgiver to effect this fundamental change in the common law. Holt must have thought that the lawgiver could define procedural and substantive blameworthiness as it saw fit.

One might argue that this historical evidence is inapposite, coming as it does from a system that recognizes the primacy of Parliament and has no written Constitution. There is, of course, no direct parallel between the British experience and our Double Jeopardy Clause. But the British evidence shows that in a system where judges made most of the law, including the fundamental unwritten constitutional law, the prerogative of the sovereign to define procedural and substantive blameworthiness has been recognized for eight centuries. The indirect parallel to the American experience is that our judges, who do not make criminal law, have nothing to do with creating procedural or substantive blameworthiness in the context of the Double Jeopardy Clause.

Despite losing the initial skirmish with Becket and the Pope over the royal power to subject clerics to secular punishment, Henry II was vindicated by history. A king is no different from Moses or God. Sovereigns can define blameworthiness to be what they wish.

The Common-Law Pleas in Bar

The common-law pleas of double jeopardy evolved into quite complex legal rules. By the seventeenth century, the most important plea was *autrefois attaint* (former attainder) for the same offense. This plea comes from the notion that a criminal's blood is "attainted" by an act of treason or felony. With a single statutory exception, a judgment of "outlawry" based on the attaint, as long as it "standeth in force," barred another suit for the same offense by either the king (an indictment) or by a private person (an appeal).[149] On this point, Coke followed Bracton's expansive view that drew no distinction between claims adjudicated in an appeal and those in the king's suit.

The statutory exception was, as we have seen, Henry VII's 1487 statute permitting appeal of homicide despite prior attainder.[150] Thus, the complete rule stated by Coke was that *autrefois attaint* bars trial for the same felony by the king in all cases and by a private citizen in all except homicide cases.[151] Coke noted the two asymmetries created by the statute—if the private suit went first, former attaint barred the king's suit but not vice versa and former attaint barred an appeal or the king's suit for felonies other than homicide.[152] Support for a legislative-prerogative principle is found in Coke's placid acceptance of the statutory erosion of the act-equals-offense rule that had been in place since Bracton (1250).

The 1487 statutory abrogation demonstrates that the sovereign can define when a judgment bars further proceeding. In areas unaffected by legislation, Coke's common-law pleas support my act-equals-offense presumption if "same felony" is read to mean "same act." This reading is controversial but, I think, correct. The internal evidence is quite strong. First, in discussing the plea of *autrefois attaint* for appeals of murder, Coke repeatedly uses "same death" rather than "same felony" or "same murder" when describing a good plea. For example: "*Autrefoitz attaint de murder* is a good plea to an indictment . . . of petit treason of the same death, for in effect it hath the same judgement, and the self same forfeiture. So likewise if a man be attainted of manslaughter, it is a good bar to an indictment of murder of the same death, *et e converso.*"[153] Coke repeats this usage of "same death" in place of "same felony" when discussing a different plea, *autrefois acquit* (former acquittal).[154]

The conceptual linkage between offense and act can also be seen in Coke's discussion of the effect of pardon. If an attainted defendant was pardoned and thus not executed, his attaint barred a prosecution for any other felony, whether committed before or after the attainder.[155] The theory is sound: if the criminal's blood was attainted by conviction of felony, in the words of Coke, "by the attainder he was *mort in ley* [legally dead]; and in that case he had the judgement due for felony, viz, *sus. per col* [hanging by the neck]."[156]

The pardon avoided the judgment of death, but it did not change the legal status of the offender; he could not be appealed or indicted for any other felony, with three exceptions. First, "if the party attainted of felony had committed high treason before his attainder, he shall answer to the treason notwithstanding his attainder of felony, because the king by the treason was intitled to have the forfeiture of all his lands."[157] Second, "being attainted of felony, if he commit treason afterwards, he shall answer thereunto, because it is of higher nature then the felony."[158] Third, the private plaintiff could still appeal for robbery committed before the attaint. "But the party [victim] may have his appeal of robbery, for a robbery done before the felony, whereof he was attainted, because in the appeal he is to have restitution of his goods, besides judgment of death."[159] Though there was obviously a mix of rationales justifying these exceptions to the broad attainder rule, the triggering mechanism was always that a particular kind of blameworthy act was done before or after the attaint, rather than some abstract difference in the offense descriptions.

There was yet another overlapping plea: *autrefois convict* (former conviction).[160] This plea did not apply where judgment was imposed or where the offender was pardoned. In those cases, the offender could plead former attainder or former pardon against any other felony, with the exceptions mentioned earlier. The plea of former conviction was useful, then, only in cases in which judgment was suspended for some reason, usually because of benefit of clergy. Its protection was less expansive than that of former attainder; by Blackstone's day, former conviction was limited to barring "the same identical crime."[161]

Though Justice Scalia reads "crime" here to mean "statutory offense,"[162] Blackstone read it differently. In describing this plea, Blackstone made quite clear that the focus was on blameworthy acts and not on offense descriptions: "Hereupon it has been held that a conviction of manslaughter, on an appeal or an indictment, is a bar even in another appeal, and much more in an indictment of murder; for the fact prosecuted is the same in both, though the offenses differ in coloring and in degree."[163]

Blackstone summarized the common-law jeopardy pleas in a "universal maxim of the common law of England, that no man is to be brought into jeopardy of his life more than once for the same offence."[164] This summary uses "offense," to be sure, but that usage must be read in conjunction with his "same-act" example about murder and manslaughter. The "universal maxim" led, quite directly, to the American Double Jeopardy Clause.

The Double Jeopardy Clause

Twenty years after the publication of Book IV of Blackstone's *Commentaries*,[165] James Madison proposed a double jeopardy bar that avoided Blackstone's common-law language. Madison's clean-cut language was: "No person shall be subject, except in cases of impeachment, to more than one punishment or one trial for the same offence."[166] Madison's conception is elegant. A defendant can be forced to endure only one trial for the same offense. Regardless of how soon the trial ends, no new trial for the same offense can go forward.[167]

We do not know whether Madison saw "same offence" in terms of blameworthy acts, in part because this aspect of his formulation was not controversial. Controversy arose, however, over the "jeopardy" aspect of Madison's language. The Framers expressed concern about the implication of Madison's language on the right of a defendant to appeal.[168] If defendants could not have more than one trial, perhaps convictions obtained in an unfair manner would not be reversed on appeal because that could permit guilty defendants to escape justice.

Economical though Madison's conception was, the Framers rejected it. The clarity of Madison's formulation allowed the Framers to predict potential problems; as a solution, they turned to the vague contours of the common law. The final Double Jeopardy Clause language, "nor shall any person be subject for the same offence to be twice put in jeopardy of life or limb," is strikingly similar to Blackstone's "universal maxim of the common law of England, that no man is to be brought into jeopardy of his life more than once for the same offence."[169]

The Double Jeopardy Clause was far simpler than the common law; no attainder-like protection was available for other crimes; no benefit of clergy was available; there was no recognition of dual systems of criminal prosecution with complex exceptions depending on which system first produced a verdict. The problem with the Double Jeopardy Clause is that, without the common law superstructure to provide meaning, it was difficult to understand what was prohibited.

Had the Framers stayed with Madison's language and made clear that defendants could appeal (and, presumably be retried following successful appeals), they would have had a provision with relatively hard edges. We would still have uncertainty about when offenses are the "same," but that was far less of a problem in 1789 than today. With respect to the "jeopardy" side of the problem, a prohibition of more than one trial is much easier to interpret than a prohibition of more than one jeopardy. Jeopardy implies risk,[170] and it is thus possible that a defendant is in jeopardy from the moment the trial begins or, indeed, even earlier in the criminal process, perhaps following indictment. But if jeopardy is pushed far enough back in the temporal scheme, it becomes more difficult to justify treating an early end to jeopardy as a bar to another trial.

Indeed, if jeopardy is pushed only as far back as the beginning of trial—what Madison's formulation seems to entail—there will be pressure on trial judges not to grant mistrials and on appellate judges to permit retrials despite a mistrial. It would have been difficult for judges to justify a second trial if Madison's language had been adopted—since it specifically barred more than one trial, but "jeopardy" is sufficiently elastic that judges can invent concepts like Justice Holmes's "continuing jeopardy."[171] The current rule that jeopardy "attaches" at the beginning of trial but does not necessarily end when the trial ends is a form of "continuing jeopardy." This rule leads to great uncertainty about when a mistrial bars a second trial. Its edges are very soft. In chapter 8 I argue that a relatively hard-edged rule can be substituted for the Court's mistrial rule and that its universe of outcomes is more satisfying in policy terms.

Blackstone's "universal maxim" was a convenient alternative to determining exactly what should be the limitations on more than one trial for the same offense, but it led to two centuries of confusion. The next chapter summarizes that confusion. One principle is clear from the history of double jeopardy—the sovereign could define criminal wrongdoing however he pleased and could determine whether and how one outcome barred a further criminal judgment. While that may not sound like much of a contribution from history, neither the Supreme Court nor the commentators have recognized even this modest enhancement of clarity in double jeopardy theory. And, as the rest of the book demonstrates, the principle of legislative prerogative can go far in structuring a complete account of double jeopardy.

3

Standard Double
Jeopardy Approaches

This chapter examines the largely failed efforts of the
Supreme Court to find a coherent set of double jeopardy doctrines. The
first three sections in the chapter coincide with the legislative-prerogative
principle and supporting presumptions developed in chapter 2. Then I
briefly describe the best of the solutions offered by commentators. None
is any better than the Court's efforts, save that of Michael Moore,[1] and
Moore's theory can be usefully deferred to chapter 5 for its relevance in
developing a detailed set of presumptions about the same-offense issue.

The jeopardy aspect of the problem is a good place to start, partly because it is easier to describe than the same-offense problem. Moreover,
trying to determine when jeopardy ends is where the Court began. No
Supreme Court case reached the merits of a same-offense claim until
1887.[2] As early as 1824, however, the Court was deciding jeopardy-related
cases. That 1824 case is today universally understood to state a test for determining when a mistrial ends jeopardy. But this may be a modernist
misreading of the 1824 case; that Court, after all, relied on Blackstone's
pleas in bar, and these pleas offered no protection in the absence of a verdict.

Interpreting "Jeopardy"

As long as the courts understood double jeopardy to incorporate Blackstone's pleas in bar, they were on firm interpretational ground, whatever
one might think of the underlying policy issues. A mistrial would never
bar a second trial, irrespective of the linguistic implications of "jeopardy,"
if defendants had to show a former conviction or acquittal as a threshold
requirement of a Blackstone-like jeopardy plea. When *United States v.*

Perez[3] was decided in 1824, the Court was only thirty-three years from the Bill of Rights ratification and only fifty-five years from the publication of Book IV of Blackstone's *Commentaries.* The presence of a strong Blackstone influence is not surprising, particularly on so astute a scholar as Justice Story, the author of *Perez.*

The jury was unable to agree in Perez' capital case and was discharged by the trial court "from giving any verdict upon the indictment, without the consent of the prisoner, or of the attorney for the United States."[4] Story noted "some diversity of opinion and practice on this subject, in the American courts,"[5] but the Supreme Court seemed to find the issue quite easy. Perez could not prevail because he had "not been convicted or acquitted, and may again be put upon his defence."[6] This certainly sounds as if the Double Jeopardy Clause was limited to Blackstone's pleas of former conviction and former acquittal. So limited, of course, the mistrial doctrine would be easy to apply, just as it would have been under Madison's prohibition of more than one trial. The sets of outcomes would be different under the two approaches, because Blackstone's emphasis was on verdict rather than trial, but both rules are hard edged.

The twentieth-century reading of *Perez* is precisely the opposite from what Story seems to have intended. Rather than incorporate Blackstone's hard-edged requirement of a verdict to end jeopardy, modern courts have used *Perez* to justify a mistrial rule that has extremely soft edges—edges so soft they are almost invisible. The modern mistrial rule purports to protect the "valued right" of each defendant to each jury but, unlike Madison's proposed language, operates without any substantive principles to guide the inquiry. It seems likely that the modern mistrial rule is a product of the general movement in the twentieth century toward seeking justice in individual cases. This movement has favored soft-edged rules that give judges discretion to decide for defendants when injustice seems pronounced. The legal realist approach discussed in chapter 1 is an outgrowth of this movement.[7] The question remains, however, how courts managed to use *Perez* to achieve the rule demanded by modern legal culture.

Looking for rules that promise perfect justice in individual cases, courts read Story's dicta as if they were part of the holding. The dicta seem much more likely, however, to be Story's effort to give guidance to trial courts about how to exercise what he viewed as their unreviewable discretion. Following the remark that because *Perez* lacked a conviction or acquittal, he "may again be put upon his defence," Story wrote:

We think, that in all cases of this nature, the law has invested courts of justice with the authority to discharge a jury from giving any verdict, whenever, in their opinion, taking all the circumstances into consideration, there is a manifest necessity for the act, or the ends of public justice would otherwise be defeated. They are to exercise a sound discretion on the subject; and it is impossible to define all the circumstances, which would render it proper to interfere. To be sure, the power ought to be used with the greatest caution, under urgent circumstances, and for very plain and obvious causes; and, in capital cases especially, courts should be extremely careful how they interfere with any of the chances of life, in favor of the prisoner. But, after all, they have the right to order the discharge; and the security which the public have for the faithful, sound and conscientious exercise of this discretion, rests, in this, as in other cases, upon the responsibility of the judges, under their oaths of office.[8]

Story could hardly have been clearer that the decision to discharge a jury when it could not agree on guilt or innocence is completely discretionary with the trial judge. The manifest necessity discussion seems intended to impress upon trial judges the seriousness of the decision to discharge a jury. Or perhaps Story was suggesting how seriously judges already take this responsibility as a way of justifying the Court's refusal to impose a standard of review. But, in either event, he said clearly that discharge was the right of trial judges, the only limitation being their oaths of office.

It is really quite perverse that *Perez* is now known and cited as the case establishing the principle that trial courts can discharge a jury only upon a finding of manifest necessity, which finding can be reviewed in the appellate system. That may be a better system than the one Story envisioned, but it is decidedly not Story's system. When he used the "manifest necessity" language, he modified it with "in their [trial judges'] opinion." Moreover, no reason existed to mention that judges were limited by their oaths of office if Story intended for appellate courts to review the mistrial decisions of trial courts.

More evidence in favor of a Blackstonian interpretation of *Perez* is Justice Washington's presence on the *Perez* Court (the decision was unanimous). The year before, while sitting as a circuit judge, Washington had rejected a mistrial bar to a second trial on the ground that "the jeopardy spoken of in [the Fifth Amendment] can be interpreted to mean nothing short of the acquittal or conviction of the prisoner, and the judgment of the court thereupon."[9] Washington's statement seems clear enough, and his joining of the *Perez* opinion suggests at least how he viewed Story's language about "manifest necessity."

The most telling evidence that *Perez* manifests a Blackstonian, verdict-or-nothing proposition about the ending of jeopardy is Story's treatment of *Perez* nine years later in his *Commentaries on the Constitution*.[10] Story wrote there that the Double Jeopardy Clause "does not mean, that [a person] shall not be tried for the offense a second time, if the jury shall have been discharged without giving any verdict." In that case, Story concluded that the defendant's "life or limb cannot judicially be said to have been put in jeopardy." As authority for that proposition, Story cited Blackstone, Justice Washington's opinion quoted earlier, and *Perez*.[11] However others have understood *Perez*, Story understood it to state Blackstone's rule requiring a verdict to end jeopardy.

Many years after the Court began to use manifest necessity as a test for appellate review, it admitted doubt that Story intended to state a double jeopardy rule. In *Crist v. Bretz*,[12] the Court sought to justify "manifest necessity" as a rule necessary for the "administration of federal criminal justice."[13] While conceding that Story might not have meant to locate manifest necessity in the Double Jeopardy Clause, the Court insisted that Story meant to state a rule that, whatever its origin, could be conveniently packaged into the modern Double Jeopardy Clause.[14] But no rule is apparent in Story's *Perez* opinion, except the rule that there is no rule. Trial courts decide whether to grant mistrials; appellate courts have no role to play.

The modernist use of "manifest necessity" as a standard for reviewing mistrials granted by trial courts has not gone well. For many years, the Court ignored the indefiniteness of the standard, perhaps assuming that decades of case law would provide some meaning to the meaningless. In 1978 the Court gave up and acknowledged that "manifest necessity" does not provide sufficient guidance. In *Arizona v. Washington*,[15] the issue was whether the trial judge violated the Double Jeopardy Clause when he granted the prosecutor's motion for mistrial to cure improper remarks made in defense counsel's opening argument. In discussing the *Perez* "test," the Court wrote,

> Mr. Justice Story's classic formulation of the test has been quoted over and over again to provide guidance in the decision of a wide variety of cases. Nevertheless, those words do not describe a standard that can be applied mechanically or without attention to the particular problem confronting

the trial judge. Indeed, it is manifest that the key word "necessity" cannot be interpreted literally; instead, contrary to the teachings of Webster, we assume that there are degrees of necessity and we require a "high degree" before concluding that a mistrial is appropriate.[16]

The Court tells us that, in the manifest necessity standard, it is "manifest" that "necessity" cannot be interpreted literally. Is this a joke? And what does the Court mean by a "high degree" of "necessity"?

The Court acknowledged that, in the case before it, "some trial judges might have proceeded with the trial after giving the jury appropriate cautionary instructions."[17] Well, if it was not only possible but plausible to continue the trial, there can be no doubt that the "high degree" of "necessity" was missing in *Washington*. But that would be wrong.

The Court conceded that "[i]n a strict, literal sense, the mistrial was not 'necessary.'" But, the Court, continued, the "overriding interest in the evenhanded administration of justice requires that we accord the highest degree of respect to the trial judge's evaluation of the likelihood that the impartiality of one or more jurors may have been affected by the improper comment."[18] This time the Court articulated a standard phrased in terms of "highest degree."

In sum, a mistrial is a jeopardy bar unless justified by a "high degree" of necessity. But because the Court has no idea how to apply that standard, it developed a deferential attitude toward what judges do: appellate courts must accord the "highest degree of respect" to a trial judge's estimate of the effect of trial error on the jury. As we should expect, the "highest" degree standard trumps mere "high degree," and Washington lost his manifest necessity claim. Whenever a judge grants a mistrial to cure prejudicial error heard by the jury, the highest degree of respect for the trial judge's evaluation will always (or almost always) provide the high degree of necessity to justify a mistrial.

The *Washington* gloss on "manifest necessity" can be read as a pragmatic reinstatement of Blackstone (and my reading of Story's opinion in *Perez*) for this category of mistrials: defendants are going to lose mistrial claims in which prejudicial error is heard by the jury and the judge decides the best course of action is to grant a mistrial. But if this is the set of results we want, why not achieve it more directly (and honestly) by requiring a verdict to end jeopardy? The *Washington* gloss on *Perez* could manifest a policy that mistrials are necessary unless they interfere with a likely acquittal—which would not have been the case in *Washington*—but the Court has never put the policy in this way. Thus, courts are left on their own to puzzle out if they should ever refuse to give the "highest degree or respect" to the trial court's mistrial judgment.

Moreover, *Washington* provides no guidance for mistrials that do not involve the jury hearing prejudicial error. What kind of respect is due the trial judge in those cases? The Court has provided only the vaguest of clues, which I will seek to explicate in Chapter 8. Chapter 8 also contains an argument that the best mistrial formulation begins with the hard-edged Blackstone-Story rule and then amends the rule in a way that makes clear when double jeopardy policy requires a different outcome: when the mistrial manifests a likelihood of acquittal had the trial gone to verdict. The resulting rule is both more sensitive to double jeopardy policy and far more determinate than the present manifest necessity "rule." "Manifest necessity" should be reburied in the original grave dug by Joseph Story.

Beyond "manifest necessity," the Court has done little damage in the jeopardy area. The mechanical concept of jeopardy "attaching" is unnecessary if my jeopardy presumption is followed, but "attachment" has rarely produced an unjustified result. The Court also demonstrated confusion for a short time about when a dismissal should count as a jeopardy bar—in 1975 the Court unanimously held that any dismissal barred a second trial that would require new factfinding, but overruled that case by a 5-4 vote three years later.[19] If only verdicts or endings like verdicts are an end to jeopardy, the Court was right the second time to reject this rule, which is based on preventing generalized harassment and not on protecting the defendant's right to proceed when an acquittal is likely.

But the Court has otherwise been sensitive to the fine distinctions between an outcome that has resolved the defendant's blameworthiness and one that has not. *Burks v. United States*[20] is a good example. The defendant moved for a new trial after conviction, on the ground that the state presented insufficient evidence of his sanity and, therefore, that the trial judge should have directed an acquittal. The court of appeals agreed; it vacated the conviction and granted the motion for a new trial at which the state and defendant would have a new chance to litigate the sanity issue.

The Supreme Court considered conflicting precedents in *Burks*. The earliest Supreme Court case on criminal appeals held that a successful appeal (in that case on the ground of an insufficient indictment) removed the conviction as a bar to a second trial.[21] A second kind of precedent supporting the court of appeals was the rule that "a defendant who *requests* a new trial as one avenue of relief may be required to stand trial again, even when his conviction was reversed due to failure of proof at the first trial."[22] The theory behind this rule is simple: by reversing and remanding, an appellate court is simply giving a defendant what he requested.

On the other side was the precedent that an acquittal always bars a new trial. The reason *Burks* was not an easy case, of course, is that the trial judge did not grant the motion for a directed verdict of not guilty. The appellate court held that the judge should have granted the motion, but does that have the same double jeopardy effect as the trial judge granting the motion?

The two events might be different on the following argument. When the trial judge grants a motion for acquittal, he is acting as a surrogate for the jury; he has heard the evidence, witnessed the demeanor of the witnesses, and his ruling that no conviction could result is informed in a way that no appellate decision could be. When an appellate court rules that the judge should have granted a motion for acquittal, perhaps the case should be resubmitted for a new fact-finding.[23]

Burks easily distinguished the precedent about flawed indictments. An error in an indictment is different in kind from an error in failing to grant a directed verdict; the first error goes to the procedure for determining guilt and innocence, the second to the very question of guilt and innocence in the case presented by the state. The second precedent, giving the defendant the new trial that he requested, was more difficult to distinguish. This doctrine had direct support in Supreme Court cases and thus could have resulted in the Court denying certiorari on the grounds that the case was an easy one. The Court had to reason to a conclusion that the easy answer was the wrong one. The easy answer seems, at one level, fair. How is a defendant injured if a court gives him exactly what he requested?

But this precedent is logically defective. Writing for a unanimous Court, Chief Justice Burger noted that an appellate reversal for insufficient evidence "means that the government's case was so lacking that it should not have even been *submitted* to the jury. Since we necessarily afford absolute finality to a jury's *verdict* of acquittal—no matter how erroneous its decision—it is difficult to conceive how society has any greater interest in retrying a defendant when, on review, it is decided as a matter of law that the jury could not properly have returned a verdict of guilty."[24]

This quote discloses the premise that underlies the Court's decision. The Court assumed that an acquittal by a jury is always the end of jeopardy. As this has been the rule since A.D. 1200, it required no more than a passing mention—"[s]ince we necessarily afford absolute finality to a jury's verdict of acquittal." Once that premise is securely in place, however, everything else about *Burks* follows nicely.

Burks thus supports a presumption that jeopardy ends only upon a formal verdict or an outcome that demonstrates the defendant should have been (or would have been) acquitted. If the Court simply applied the same rule to mistrials, it would have a coherent jeopardy principle. But trapped as it is in the modernist misreading of *Perez*, the Court does not seem even to appreciate that mistrials, dismissals, and reversals on lack of evidence can be analyzed under the same substantive framework—whether the defendant was denied an acquittal to which he was entitled. This doctrinal unity manifests the same policy against erroneous convictions.

In sum, the Court's jeopardy jurisprudence suffers largely from a failure to understand mistrials as a type of dismissal that should be analyzed by looking to the substantive effect of denying the defendant a chance to proceed to verdict. A more difficult task for the Court has been finding clarity in the "same offense" part of the Double Jeopardy Clause. To find both clarity and a test sensitive to double jeopardy policy is a daunting challenge.

Interpreting "Same Offense"

Defining "jeopardy" is not easy, but linguistics and a long-accepted common law understanding are available to assist the inquiry. There are no similar aids to interpreting "same offense." Bishop agreed, noting that the "same-offense" decisions are even more "discordant" than the twice-in-jeopardy cases.[25] Jay Sigler predicts that, without recodification of the substantive criminal law, "the problem is virtually insoluble."[26] The problem is serious but not insoluble. Linguistics is not helpful, as we have seen, because the most logical referent suggested by "same offense" is "same statutory offense." Alternatively, same offense could include only greater- and necessarily-included offenses, but this, too, suffers from problems of overinclusiveness and underinclusiveness. Moreover, the *Blockburger* definitional test has absolutely nothing to say about limits on dividing the relevant conduct to prove multiple counts. Is robbing six victims a single offense? One would think not. Is stealing four items from a dresser a single larceny? One would think so. But we have no rule for this aspect of same offense.[27]

History offers some clues to the best understanding of same offense, and we can begin there.

Early Definitions of Same Offense

The thirteenth-century commentators—Bracton, Britton, Fleta, and the author of *The Mirror of Justices*—did not perceive a "same offense" problem. The self-evident nature of "same offense" in the 1200s reflected the rudimentary nature of criminal law at that time, which recognized only a few broad categories of conduct as separate crimes. This, of course, is consistent with an act-equals-offense presumption.

Hale has the most comprehensive discussion of same offense prior to 1800. He recognized that different offenses can occur close together. But he saw the distinctiveness of acts as the key.

> If A commit a burglary . . . and likewise at the same time steal goods out of the house, if he be indicted of larceny for the goods and acquitted, yet he may be indicted for the burglary notwithstanding the acquittal. And *e converso*, if indicted for the burglary and acquitted, yet he may be indicted of the larceny, for they are several offenses, tho committed at the same time.[28]

Hale offered a test of sorts for determining when offenses may be separate, though closely connected in terms of acts: "burglary may be where there is no larceny, and larceny may be where there is no burglary."[29] A version of Hale's test was eventually adopted by the Supreme Court in the 1915 case of *Morgan v. Devine*: "the test is not whether the criminal intent is one and the same and inspiring the whole transaction, but whether separate acts have been committed with the requisite criminal intent and are such as are made punishable by the act of Congress."[30]

While the distinctiveness in blameworthy acts is critical to an act-equals-offense presumption, "act" here is not the metaphysical "act" that some courts (and some commentators) assume. Indeed, even if we could avoid the skeptical critique Austin lodged against metaphysical accounts of acts (as Michael Moore tries to do in *Act and Crime*), we would still be left with odd double-jeopardy results. An example is the Court's very first same-offense case, *In re Snow*.[31] The issue was whether Snow could be prosecuted for three counts of cohabitation with the same women over an unbroken period of thirty-five months, all of which occurred before the first indictment.[32] It is, of course, true that different cohabitations are different offenses, just as different robberies are different offenses. To cohabit with person X in 1990 must be a different offense than to cohabit with person Z in 1991. Otherwise, a person who committed one particular statutory offense could commit other violations of the same statutory provision "for free," since only one double-jeopardy offense would be committed. Similarly, cohabiting with X in 1988 must be a different offense than cohabiting with X in 1990 if the actor did not cohabit with X in 1989.

Recognizing this obvious truth, the prosecutor in *Snow* sought to create different "acts" of cohabitation by dividing the thirty-five-month period of cohabitation into three distinct periods. This division makes the conduct at least technically distinct. As cohabitation required living with a woman, it includes smaller periods of time. Perhaps Snow "cohabited" each time he returned home after an absence of any period of time. Or perhaps he committed an infinite number of metaphysical cohabitations because there were an infinite number of points during the thirty-five months when he could have terminated the cohabitation.

The Court rejected at least the second of these interpretations, noting:

> The division of the two years and eleven months is wholly arbitrary. On the same principle, there might have been an indictment covering each of the thirty-five months, with imprisonment for seventeen years and a half and fines amounting to $10,500, or even an indictment covering every week, with imprisonment for 74 years and fines amounting to $44,400; and so on, *ad infinitum*, for smaller periods of time.[33]

The Court seemed to appreciate that the issue was the scope of the *proscribed* act created by the statute: "There can be but one offence between such earliest day [of cohabitation with the same women] and the end of the continuous time embraced by all of the indictments."[34] This puts a particular reading on "cohabitation," but it is a plausible reading. Implicit in the *Snow* opinion is that this is the reading that Congress meant.

Two years later, the Court turned to the same-offense definitional problem, with yet another case applying the federal antipolygamy provisions to the Utah territory. (These cases suggest that the Court was uncomfortable with the enforcement of the antipolygamy laws.) In *In re Nielsen*,[35] different statutory crimes were involved: adultery and cohabitation. The question is whether looking at the way the acts are proscribed in each statute is helpful in resolving the same-offense question.

Each offense required proof of an element the other did not—adultery required proof of marriage to a third person, and cohabitation required proof of living together as man and wife. This distinctiveness of statutory elements makes the offenses separate under the necessarily-included-offense test, but *Nielsen* held that a conviction of cohabitation barred a trial for adultery. Many explanations for *Nielsen* have been offered, but the soundest is that both statutes proscribed the same blameworthy act.

Determining which elements proscribe acts and which proscribe what the Model Penal Code calls "attendant circumstances" is no easy matter, as I show in chapter 5. For the present, it is enough to note, as the Court did, that both adultery and cohabitation have sexual intercourse as their central conduct element. Whether "living together" is an additional act and, if so, whether it is a blameworthy act are nice questions, but the Court read the statutes to be directed at sexual intercourse outside marriage: "Living together as man and wife is what we decided was meant by unlawful cohabitation under the statute. Of course, that includes sexual intercourse. And this was the integral part of the adultery charged in the second indictment, and was covered by and included in the first indictment and conviction."[36]

If both offenses proscribe sexual intercourse outside marriage, these offenses fail Hale's test, for there could not be proof of adultery (sex outside marriage) without proof of cohabitation (sex outside marriage). Stated differently, the act of sex outside marriage with particular partners is the same blameworthy act as sex outside marriage with those same partners.

If *Nielsen* is read in this fashion, it is consistent with the inclusion test of both Hale and Blackstone. By 1911 the Court still saw the key question as whether each offense proscribed the same blameworthy act. Like many state courts at the time, the Supreme Court in *Gavieres v. United States* sought to uncover the "gist of the offense" proscribed by two different municipal ordinances.[37] The Philippines ordinances prohibited (1) behaving in an indecent manner in a public place, and (2) insulting or threatening public officials. As the Court noted, the *proscribed* act of behaving in an indecent manner is not the same as the *proscribed* act of insulting or threatening public officials. It did not, therefore, matter that in the particular case one act happened to violate both ordinances. As I discuss in chapter 5, seeking the "gist" or "gravamen" of the offenses is consistent with my blameworthy-act account of same offense. Thus, *Gavieres* is at one level consistent with both *Nielsen* and my account. But in applying the act-based "gist" principle, the Court phrased the test as if *any* distinct element made the "gist" different,[38] which was inconsistent with the state court approach and with *Nielsen*.[39]

The difference between these applications of the "gist" test may appear unimportant (may have appeared so to the *Gavieres* Court), but it is crucial in many cases, particularly those that involve modern statutes with many elements.

The *Blockburger* Solution

The best example of the difference between what the *Gavieres* Court seemed to permit, on the one hand, and what Hale and Blackstone seemed to envision, on the other, is *Blockburger v. United States*.[40] The Court held that sale of narcotics *not from the original stamped package* could be punished in addition to sale of the same narcotics *not pursuant to a written order* because neither offense was included within the other. Each required a distinct element, indicated by italics. If, however, both offenses in *Blockburger* proscribe the blameworthy act of selling narcotics[41] and if "same offense" means "same blameworthy act," these offenses would be the same offense.

Not so under *Blockburger*, which treats the presence of the distinct elements of "not from the original stamped package" and "not in pursuance of a written order" as evidence that Congress intended to create cumulatively punishable crimes.[42] Justice Scalia claims that the *Blockburger* test is historically and textually indicated as a definition of same offense. As this book makes clear, Scalia is right about much in double jeopardy. But he is wrong about *Blockburger*.

Scalia asserts a textual argument on behalf of *Blockburger* that is clever but ultimately unsatisfying. He argues that "if each [offense] contains an element the other does not, *i.e.*, if it is possible to violate each one without violating the other, then they cannot constitute the '*same* offence.'"[43] To evaluate Scalia's argument, we first examine its buried premise that all offense elements are created equal when considering what constitutes a double jeopardy offense. But there is nothing in the language of the Double Jeopardy Clause that compels that conclusion, just like there is nothing in the Clause that is helpful in separating civil "offenses" from criminal offenses. To defend Scalia's account, one must accept that a single armed robbery in a dwelling is constitutionally transformed into two robberies in a state that proscribes "armed robbery" separately from "robbery in a dwelling." Or that it is two robberies when a robber wearing a white shirt robs a victim on Sunday in a state proscribing "robbery while wearing a white shirt" and "robbery on Sunday."

Not all "offenses" are double jeopardy offenses (torts are not, for example). There is, then, no reason to accept as inevitable Scalia's premise that all offense elements in a concededly criminal offense are capable of making offenses different under the Double Jeopardy Clause.

Obviously recognizing that his textual argument is not conclusive, Scalia turns to English history. The authority on which he relies for long-standing acceptance of *Blockburger* is the 1796 case of *King v. Vandercomb*.[44] But Scalia's use of *Vandercomb* does not withstand even a superficial critique. He quotes a statement from the opinion that is the "precise equivalent of our statement in *Blockburger*."[45]

What he fails to quote is the English court's formulation of the principle that it deduces from the common law, which is demonstrably not the *Blockburger* test. Near the end of its opinion, the English court wrote, "These cases establish the principle, that unless the first indictment were such as the prisoner might have been convicted upon by proof of the facts contained in the second indictment, an acquittal on the first indictment can be no bar to the second."[46]

This is not *Blockburger* for several reasons. It applies only to acquittals, and it relies on the contents of the indictment rather than the statutory (or common law) elements. *Blockburger* operates on the statutory elements and applies regardless of whether the first trial ended in a conviction or an acquittal.[47] Moreover, the *Vandercomb* formulation appears to make the order of prosecution crucial, while *Blockburger* applies regardless of the order of prosecution.

On *Vandercomb*'s literal holding, if a greater offense is prosecuted first, no bar would arise to a necessarily-included offense because the defendant could not have been convicted under the first indictment on proof of the lesser offense.[48] For example, *Vandercomb*'s holding would permit the state to prosecute murder and then manslaughter; the facts of manslaughter would not convict of murder. The state could not prosecute, however, in the order of manslaughter and murder. The facts of murder as contained in the second indictment would convict of manslaughter. So the state could prosecute murder-manslaughter but not manslaughter-murder.

This is an idiotic same-offense test; Friedland is more charitable, calling *Vandercomb* "totally unreasonable."[49] The fatal flaw is that it ignores the principle of correlative identity. When *A* is the same offense as *B*, *B* must always be the same offense as *A*. If one were going to dispense with this correlative principle, it would be in the direction opposite from the one *Vandercomb* chose: manslaughter and murder could conceivably be different offenses if prosecuted in that order, because manslaughter leaves unprosecuted an element in the greater offense of murder. Not so in the direction of murder-manslaughter. Once the greater offense is proven, all the elements of the lesser are always proven. *Vandercomb* gets it backwards, making offenses the same when at least one element has never been prosecuted and different when all elements are reprosecuted.

Yes, the *Vandercomb* court at one point phrased a test consistent with *Blockburger*. But what inference can be drawn from that when the court phrased a different test as the principle on which it based its holding? That the English courts were floundering in 1796 for a satisfactory account of same offense is further indicated by *Vandercomb*'s reinterpretation of *Turner's Case*. The court in *Turner's Case* found an acquittal of the burglary of *T*'s house and stealing the goods of *T* to be a bar to the charge of burglary of *T*'s house and stealing the goods of *H*.[50] The *Vandercomb* judges classified this statement of law as a "manifest mistake" and pronounced themselves not bound by it since it was not the holding in *Turner's Case*.[51]

To find in *Vandercomb* a basis to assert a long-standing acceptance of *Blockburger* is, therefore, to ignore the English confusion over same offense that is manifest in *Vandercomb* itself. No *Blockburger* understanding of same offense existed in Blackstone's day or at the time the Double Jeopardy Clause was written. *Blockburger* is neither logically entailed by the constitutional text nor historically indicated.

Scalia's attempt to ground *Blockburger* in the Court's early jurisprudence is only marginally more successful. To be sure, *Gavieres* applied a version of *Blockburger* when it held that disorderly conduct is not the same offense as insulting a public official.[52] But one gets the same result by comparing proscribed blameworthy acts, which were different in *Gavieres*.

To assert, as Scalia does, that the 1902 case of *Burton v. United States*[53] is support for *Blockburger* is simply a mistake. The Court merely held in *Burton* that two acts of receiving money would be two offenses under a statute that prohibited certain receipts of money. An obvious difficulty with Scalia's argument that *Burton* presaged *Blockburger* is that both charges were made under the same statutory offense, which means the only same-offense issue is how the prosecutor divided up the conduct (the *In re Snow* issue) and not whether two statutes define the same offense. To be sure, *Burton* applied *Vandercomb* to the language in the indictment, concluding that "the jeopardy is not the same when the two indictments are so diverse as to preclude the same evidence from sustaining both."[54] This analysis is gratuitous and, more important, focuses on the particular way the offenses are charged, a test that Scalia has rejected.[55] How Scalia finds support in *Burton* for his understanding of *Blockburger* is mysterious.

Blockburger has nothing to say about the *Burton* kind of case. Comparing different offense descriptions has nothing to do with the conduct dimension of same offense. For example, the issue in *Snow* was the proper number of convictions of cohabitation for a single thirty-five-month period of living with the same women. That issue cannot be decided by comparing the elements in two statutes, for there is only one statute.[56]

If *Blockburger* is used in this context, then either (1) multiple charges under a single statute are always the same offense, which is obviously wrong, because robbery of *X* cannot be the same offense as robbery of *Z*, or (2) the *Blockburger* formulation should be expanded to examine the underlying indictment. While (2) is more appealing than (1)—and usually gives the right results in cases with more than one victim—it remains seriously flawed. Looking at the contents of the indictments, Martin Friedland has noted, makes the result of a double jeopardy plea "often depend on the manner in which the indictments happen to be framed."[57] So, for example, drunk driving would be the same offense as vehicular homicide if the latter indictment alleged killing by drunk driving and not if the indictment simply alleged killing by reckless driving. But the Court has essentially abandoned that approach, insisting that *Blockburger* be applied only to the statutory formulations.[58]

If the Court is right that *Blockburger* should be applied only to the statutory formulation (and in chapter 5 I agree with the Court on this point), then *Blockburger* provides answers to only half the same-offense puzzle. Of course, whether *Blockburger* has the pedigree of precedent, logical entailment, or historical inevitablity, whether it solves all the puzzle or only part of it, the Court can read it into the Double Jeopardy Clause. *Miranda v. Arizona*[59] is a good example of a solution that does not depend on a long-accepted textual meaning. The only requirement for these Court-constructed solutions is that they work—that is, that they are relatively hard edged and offer a reasonable fit between the policies and the results produced.

Though *Blockburger* is mostly hard-edged,[60] it fails to deliver a set of results consistent with double jeopardy policies.[61] *Blockburger's* failures are documented throughout the book, but the conceptual flaw can be summarized in the following hypothetical criminal offenses: (1) selling narcotics on Sunday; (2) selling narcotics from an automobile; (3) selling narcotics that have been unlawfully imported; (4) selling narcotics within a thousand feet of a church; (5) selling narcotics that have not been inspected by the FDA; (6) selling narcotics without having a state pharmaceutical license. On the *Blockburger* analysis, all six of these offenses are different double jeopardy offenses.

The actor who sells unlawfully imported narcotics from an automobile on Sunday, within a thousand feet of a church, without FDA inspection, and without the proper license can be prosecuted and punished six separate times. And, of course, there is no reason to stop at six. We could make it a separate crime to sell narcotics on street corners, in certain areas of the city, at night, to buyers who are not already addicted, to buyers who are unemployed, to buyers who are younger than twenty-five, to more than one buyer in a single transaction, to buyers who have crossed state lines in the past twenty-four hours, to buyers who have not passed a certified drug education course at the high school level, to buyers who are not physicians—.

Stop. It cannot be that every element is a relevant part of the double jeopardy offense description. Moreover, whatever the value of *Blockburger's* definitional test as a starting point, it is unresponsive to the same-conduct question, and the Court's approach to the latter issue is both ad hoc and unsatisfying.

Two related claims underlie this chapter and the rest of the book. First, the Supreme Court has missed the point of why a mistrial should be a double jeopardy bar to a second trial, abandoning Blackstone's pleas in bar in favor of a test with edges so soft it fails to deliver answers. Second, the Court has not understood its own same-offense precedents, which carried over Blackstone's and Hale's premise that one proscribed blameworthy act could be only one offense.

Now that we have examined the Court's doctrinal approach to jeopardy and same offense, we can examine the Court's approach to the overarching principle of legislative prerogative. With a single blind spot, caused by the slavish devotion to the notion that double jeopardy prevents harassment, the Court has acknowledged the legislative-prerogative principle in its double jeopardy cases.

The Supreme Court's View of Legislative Intent

The earliest Supreme Court double jeopardy case, in 1820, involved dual sovereignty.[62] Dual sovereignty, as I discuss in more detail in chapter 6, permits a state and the federal government to prosecute and punish the same offense. In the process of analyzing this issue, Justice Washington's opinion announcing the Court's judgment seems to say that the Double Jeopardy Clause same-offense analysis is wholly dependent on legislative intent. Despite his view that penalties could not be imposed on the same offense by both the state and federal government, he noted that a *single* legislature could "impose upon the same person, for the same offense, different and cumulative punishments" because that would be "the will of the same body to do so" and there would be "no opposition of wills."[63]

The only way to make sense of Washington's theory is to understand it as imputing legislative intent. If a single legislature imposes different penalties on the same offense, Washington was willing to infer that the legislature intended all the penalties to apply. But Washington was apparently not willing to infer that different legislatures were aware of what the other was doing. Whatever the value of these presumptions, which I consider in chapter 6, the point here is that at least one member of the 1820 Court viewed the creation of distinct criminal blameworthiness to be wholly a legislative prerogative.

If the legislature can impose as many different and cumulative punishments as it wishes, it obviously can define the end of jeopardy any way it pleases.

Legislative Intent on the End of Jeopardy

A legislative-prerogative principle is relatively uncontroversial when applied to defining the end of jeopardy. This is so for two reasons. First, legislatures usually create same-offense problems inadvertently, by criminalizing the same conduct in several overlapping criminal statutes without specifying how those statutes should relate to each other. But legislatures do not go around enacting hundreds of statutes regulating verdicts.

Once a process for producing verdicts is set in place, there is little need to revisit it. Thus, we are much more likely to get a considered legislative view of what constitutes the end of jeopardy.

Legislative prerogative here is not controversial for another reason I have already noted—the legislature is hemmed in here by other Bill of Rights guarantees—right to trial by jury, to be found guilty beyond a reasonable doubt, and so forth. Moreover, the legislature has much less reason to decrease the protections attending verdicts than it does to enact harsh new penalties that can be cumulated. Though some defendants (including some highly publicized defendants) seem to escape "justice" with an acquittal against the weight of the evidence, there is little concern with the accuracy of acquittals generally. We have, in this regard, come a long way since Henry II was concerned about fraudulent acquittals by the water ordeal.[64] Thus, the legislative view about the end of jeopardy is almost certainly going to manifest the common-law view of verdict. No controversy can be found in that view.

So it is only in the peripheral areas that the issue of legislative intent presents a live end-of-jeopardy issue. An example is the unusual procedure in *Swisher v. Brady*.[65] The Maryland juvenile system required a master to enter proposed findings of fact that were reviewed by the juvenile judge, who entered judgment after either accepting or rejecting the master's findings. In *Swisher*, the master made findings of fact that were favorable to the juvenile, and the judge rejected them. The juvenile appealed the adverse judgement, claiming that the master's favorable findings of fact were equivalent to an acquittal, thus barring government conduct seeking to disturb the blameworthiness determination. The Supreme Court did not agree. At first blush, this seems wrong: favorable findings of fact seem functionally the same as an acquittal.[66]

But "functionalism" is a mostly failed legal realist approach. Trying to make different things look the same by examining the overarching policies permits good lawyers to make competing arguments that are almost equally good, and it permits courts the luxury of choosing the argument they think best in the particular case. As one commentator conceded when rejecting a double jeopardy historical analysis in favor of a functional one, "[A] functional approach may not make double jeopardy questions easier to resolve, particularly when a court must balance the defendant's interest against the state's prosecutorial interest."[67] Quite so. If hard-edged rules are set in place and followed, greater certainty can be achieved.

Except in the rare case when the prosecutor terminates a trial that likely would have resulted in an acquittal, the account of jeopardy offered in this book does not ask whether anything is functionally the same as anything else. It asks the more basic question: is this a verdict? That question has a procedural, not a functional, answer. The procedural answer is that a verdict is the outcome to which the process ascribes "verdict status." In Maryland, the process did not define the master's proposed findings of fact as a verdict, and the Double Jeopardy Clause contains no independent basis to ascribe "verdict status" to this event.[68]

Because of the procedure created by the Maryland legislature, the judge could accept the master's findings or reject them, but the case is not over, the verdict is not rendered, until the judge acts. If juveniles had the right to a jury trial,[69] the Maryland procedure would be unconstitutional under the Sixth Amendment. And the Court noted that the only issue raised in the lower courts was double jeopardy,[70] concluding that "if there are any objections to such a system, they do not arise from the Double Jeopardy Clause."[71] There can be no double jeopardy harm because there is but one verdict under the procedural law of the jurisdiction.

When the Court got a chance to examine legislative prerogative in the context of defining the end of jeopardy, it decided the issue correctly. In the same-offense area, the results are more muddled. The Court has granted the primacy of legislative intent in part of the same offense doctrine, but not all of it. But when the Court has directly faced legislative prerogative in a same-offense context, it has always held in favor of the primacy of legislative intent.

Legislative Intent on Same Offense

Following Justice Washington's 1820 opinion in the dual sovereignty case, the Court did not again address the role of legislative intent in defining same offense for more than one hundred years. When the Court addressed the issue again, Justice Brandeis spoke for a unanimous Court, in *Albrecht v. United States*.[72] In answering the question of whether possessing untaxed liquor was the same offense as selling it, Brandeis wrote: "There is nothing in the Constitution which prevents Congress from punishing separately each step leading to the consummation of a transaction which it has power to prohibit and punishing also the completed transaction."[73] Brandeis and Washington can easily be counted in the camp of those who subscribe to the primacy of legislative intent in the same-offense context.

The issue did not arise again until the 1960s, when the Court began to draw a distinction between multiple punishment (more than one conviction imposed in a single trial) and successive prosecutions. The suggestion, often drawing on Justice Black's famous dicta about the embarrassment, expense, and anxiety caused by successive prosecutions, was that a greater protection existed against successive prosecutions.

In the 1977 case of *Brown v. Ohio*, the Court went to considerable length to explain both the role of legislative intent in evaluating multiple punishments and how that relates to the successive prosecution issue. The Court began with multiple punishment: "Where consecutive sentences are imposed at a single criminal trial, the role of the [Double Jeopardy Clause] is limited to assuring that the court does not exceed its legislative authorization by imposing multiple punishments for the same offense."[74] The Court then reiterated the rationale for its legislative intent analysis, while hinting at the connection between legislative intent and successive prosecution doctrine:

> [T]he Fifth Amendment double jeopardy guarantee serves principally as a restraint on courts and prosecutors. The legislature remains free under the Double Jeopardy Clause to define crimes and fix punishments; but once the legislature has acted courts may not impose more than one punishment for the same offense and prosecutors ordinarily may not attempt to secure that punishment in more than one trial.[75]

This analysis implies the proper relationship between the multiple punishment and successive prosecution doctrines.[76] We begin with the notion of defining crimes and fixing punishments (creating criminal blameworthiness). This tells us when offenses are the same. The successive prosecution issue is simply whether reason exists to permit the prosecutor to use two trials to secure the singular blameworthiness judgment that is permitted. (What these reasons might be concerns us in chapters 8 and 9. One obvious example is a situation in which the defendant successfully resists joinder of two offenses that are the same offense.)[77]

To be sure, *Brown* did not state the implication of same-offense unity between multiple punishment and successive prosecution as I just did. Quite the contrary. *Brown* suggested that the greater harms of successive prosecution might lead to a different, and more expansive, test of same offense.[78] But *Brown* made clear that the analysis at least begins with legislative intent.

In 1980 the Court applied *Brown* to a federal multiple punishment issue. Acknowledging that the Double Jeopardy Clause protects "against multiple punishments for the same offense," the Court reiterated the *Brown* teaching: "the question whether punishments imposed by a court after a defendant's conviction upon criminal charges are unconstitutionally multiple cannot be resolved without determining what punishments the Legislative Branch has authorized."[79] The Court used a similar formulation the next year in *Albernaz v. United States*, adding one sentence: "Where Congress intended, as it did here, to impose multiple punishment, imposition of such sentences does not violate the Constitution."[80]

It is difficult to be much clearer than the *Albernaz* opinion, but if there is any doubt as to the Court's meaning, it is dispelled by the opinion of Justice Stewart, concurring in the judgment (joined by Justices Marshall and Stevens). These Justices read *Blockburger* to state a constitutional rule. While agreeing with the *Albernaz* outcome, because *Blockburger* pronounced the offenses to be different, Stewart criticized the majority's assertion about legislative intent: "These statements are supported by neither precedent nor reasoning and are unnecessary to reach the Court's conclusion."[81] On Stewart's view, "No matter how clearly it spoke, Congress could not constitutionally provide for cumulative punishments unless each statutory offense required proof of a fact that the other did not, under the criterion of *Blockburger v. United States*."[82]

The state courts in Missouri failed to get the *Albernaz* message, even when the United States Supreme Court vacated and remanded more than one hundred Missouri cases for noncompliance with this dicta.[83] The state court intransigence led to the ultimate test of the *Albernaz* reasoning. Stewart was right that, prior to 1983, the legislative intent analysis merely reinforced the *Blockburger* result. What was needed was a case in which legislative intent was clear and contrary to *Blockburger*.

Missouri v. Hunter,[84] involving a statute that defined a new state crime of armed criminal action, was that case. Like felony murder, armed criminal action required proof of an underlying crime. Clear legislative intent to cumulate penalties for the underlying crime and armed criminal action was set out in the latter statute: "The punishment imposed pursuant to this [statute] shall be in addition to any punishment provided by law [for any other crime committed with a firearm]."[85] On the Supreme

Court's felony murder application of *Blockburger*, however, the armed criminal action statute defined the same offense as the underlying crime that it required.[86] The issue of legislative prerogative was joined.

The Supreme Court turned its *Albernaz* reasoning into a holding with ease. Only Justices Marshall and Stevens dissented.[87] The Court noted the state court's emotional formulation of the issue:

> Until such time as the Supreme Court of the United States declares clearly and unequivocally that the Double Jeopardy Clause . . . does not apply to the legislative branch of government, we cannot do other than what we preceive to be our duty to refuse to enforce multiple punishments for the same offense arising out of a single transaction.[88]

The Court responded: "This view manifests a misreading of our cases. . . . [W]e need hardly go so far as suggested to decide that a legislature constitutionally can prescribe cumulative punishment for violation of its first degree robbery statute and its armed criminal action statute."[89]

Whether *Hunter* is right turns out to be a question about limiting the form of punishment. If the rule were that the legislature cannot turn a single robbery into more than one offense, regardless of how clearly it spoke, that would not stop the legislature from achieving the same result through its punishing power. In *Gore v. United States*,[90] for example, the Court upheld consecutive sentences based on a single sale of narcotics that violated three statutes that proscribed different ways of selling narcotics. The Court noted that Congress could have created a three-tier sentencing scheme that authorized a sentence of fifteen years in prison for selling drugs (1) not in the original package, (2) not pursuant to a written order, and (3) with knowledge of its unlawful importation. The authorized punishment could then be reduced by five years for each aggravating circumstance not present, creating a sentencing scheme indistinguishable from the consecutive sentences in *Gore*.

Should the Double Jeopardy Clause forbid in one form what Congress can clearly accomplish in another? If the legislative intent to cumulate penalties on the same act is "crystal clear,"[91] the difference between doing it in one statute or in multiple statutes is the existence of more than one conviction. Obviously, the legislature can authorize the same penalty either way. Though multiple convictions create more onerous collateral consequences (e.g., parole eligibility, habitual offender status), the clarity of the legislative intent makes this difference constitutionally irrelevant. If the legislature wants two convictions, then it wants whatever collateral consequences attend two convictions, and it can have those consequences as long as the total punishment is not cruel and unusual under the Eighth Amendment.[92]

So the question comes down to the following: is there anything in the Double Jeopardy Clause definition of "offense" that precludes the legislature from authorizing two convictions for a *Blockburger* greater and lesser offense? The answer is negative on the Court's *Hunter* analysis and on the argument presented in this book. Though *Hunter* implies that successive prosecutions for these offenses would be forbidden by *Blockburger*, that remains an open question.

A robust legislative-prerogative principle implies that legislative intent solves the same-offense problem in both contexts. The Court's earliest and seminal multiple-punishment case, *Ex parte Lange*,[93] is consistent with this view. The statute in *Lange* prescribed a fine of not more than two hundred dollars or imprisonment for not more than one year. Notwithstanding the disjunctive phrasing of the statute, the judge sentenced Lange to the maximum fine and the maximum imprisonment. After Lange paid the fine and served five days of the jail term, the judge vacated the original sentence and resentenced Lange to a single sanction of a year's imprisonment.

The Court read the disjunctive phrasing of the statute literally and held that Lange's payment of the fine was a fully executed alternative penalty that deprived the judge of the power to later sentence Lange to a jail term.[94] Justice Scalia is right to observe that the *Lange* Court mixed due process and double jeopardy notions.[95] Given the Court's construction of the statute, the Court could simply have held (and in places did seem to hold) that due process prohibited the imposition of both penalties. About a hundred years later, the Court noted the obvious: "The Due Process Clause of the Fourteenth Amendment . . . would presumably prohibit state courts from depriving persons of liberty or property as punishment for criminal conduct except to the extent authorized by state law."[96]

But the *Lange* Court drew an explicit (and I think correct) parallel between a judge imposing two punishments based on one conviction and a judge imposing two convictions for the same offense. If the latter is barred by double jeopardy, the Court reasoned, so is the former. The Court observed that it was not the threat of a second trial but, instead, "the punishment that would legally follow the second conviction which is the real danger guarded against by the Constitution."[97]

This reading of *Lange* suggests that the protection against more than one trial for the same offense is derived from the protection against more than one judgment for the same offense. In the past thirty years or so, the opposite relationship has been asserted by many commentators (myself included), as well as by the Court.[98] Indeed, as we saw in chapter 2, the Court patched together dicta from various cases and held in *Grady v. Corbin* that a greater protection exists against successive prosecutions than against multiple punishment. The nature of this greater protection was, as *Brown* intimated, a more expansive definition of same offense that essentially prohibited reprosecuting the same conduct.

In chapter 2 I endorsed Michael Moore's view that double jeopardy protection does not vary by single trial/successive prosecution context.[99] As we do not think it vexatious to prosecute successively for embezzlement and assault, for example, we should not think it vexatious to prosecute for two offenses arising out of the same transaction as long as we have a good account of when offenses are truly different. Justice Scalia dissented in *Grady* and wrote the opinion in *Dixon*, overruling *Grady*. Nonetheless, Scalia seems to believe that a greater double jeopardy protection exists in successive prosecutions.

But what would greater protection look like? Scalia suggests that it would be an inflexible *Blockburger* test that could not be rebutted by legislative intent.[100] There are two arguments that can be made here. First, on Moore's view, it makes no sense to treat successive prosecutions of truly different offenses differently from how we treat multiple punishments for those offenses. Second, the Court has for the past twenty-five years characterized *Blockburger* as a way of discerning legislative intent.[101] How is it that a tool for discerning legislative intent somehow becomes a *limit* on the legislature?

If Scalia denies that *Blockburger* is a tool of statutory construction, then he is left without a principle to use in the single trial/multiple punishment analysis. If he admits that *Blockburger* is a tool to infer legislative intent, he must argue that it also functions as an inflexible rule in the context of successive prosecutions. But this is a truly odd position: a tool to infer legislative intent sometimes (somehow) becomes a rule of constitutional law that can deny actual legislative intent. As Eli Richardson puts it, viewing *Blockburger* as having a dual nature is a "strange characterization."[102]

Moreover, there is no historical reason to create greater protection against successive prosecutions. The common law sought to prohibit multiple punishment, not successive prosecutions. The crux of the dispute between Henry II and Becket was the right of the royal courts to sentence clerics; there was no apparent concern with the harm of successive prosecutions. The common law as it developed from the twelfth century focused on the harm of the punishment. The reason former attainder was the broadest common-law plea was that the offender received the ultimate punishment and was thus *mort in ley* (dead in law). The new proceeding, in Blackstone's words, "cannot be to any purpose; for the prisoner is dead in law by the first attainder, his blood is already corrupted, and he hath forfeited all that he had; so that it is absurd and superfluous to endeavor to attaint him a second time."[103] No second trial was permissible because further punishment would be superfluous, not because there was a need for a protection against successive prosecutions.[104]

This can be seen in the existence of the plea of former conviction, a plea that was available only when no judgment (and hence no punishment) had been imposed. As noted in chapter 2, the plea of former conviction offered a much less expansive protection. But if the crux of double jeopardy protection were directed against successive trials, rather than multiple punishments, no reason existed to treat convictions differently depending on whether punishment was imposed.

Then why did Blackstone and the Framers use "twice in jeopardy"? The answer lies in the procedural law of this time. A felony could not be joined with a misdemeanor until 1915; no conviction of a misdemeanor could be entered if a felony was charged; a defendant who was charged with a misdemeanor could not be convicted if the facts showed a felony; judges typically required the prosecutor to elect one felony offense if the indictment showed more than one.[105] The combined effect of these procedural rules, all of which were in effect in Blackstone's day, was to prevent multiple convictions in a single trial and thus to restrict the pleas in jeopardy to the second trial context.

So it is not surprising that no reference to multiple convictions in a single trial can be found in Coke, Hale, Blackstone, or Hawkins. The question about applying the double jeopardy pleas in a single trial would simply never have arisen. But the underlying rationale of not trying a defendant twice for the same offense was to avoid more than one punishment for the same offense. Madison's original double jeopardy language was to that effect, forbidding "more than one punishment or trial for the same offense."[106] The Court was thus right in *Lange* to draw a parallel between multiple trials for the same offense and multiple convictions in the same proceeding:

> For of what avail is the constitutional protection against more than one trial if there can be any number of sentences pronounced on the same verdict? Why is it that, having once been tried and found guilty, he can never be tried again for that offence? Manifestly it is not the danger or jeopardy of being a second time found guilty. It is the punishment that would legally follow the second conviction which is the real danger guarded against by the Constitution.[107]

Policy strongly supports the *Lange* unity between multiple punishment and successive prosecution. If two felony judgments of guilt could not be obtained in two trials, it would make no sense to allow them in one trial. Once the *Lange* unity is accepted, it requires unity in analyzing questions of multiple punishment and successive prosecution. On a legislative-prerogative account, both issues can be solved with legislative intent. It is a fundamental conceptual error to use legislative intent in the multiple punishment doctrine and then cast the successive prosecution doctrine adrift with the inferior *Blockburger* test.

The reason the Court created the ill-fated *Grady* test in 1992 is that *Blockburger* does not provide enough protection against successive prosecutions. But that means, on a unitary view of same offense, that *Blockburger* does not provide enough protection against multiple punishments. The solution is not to give more protection against successive prosecutions, as Scalia is apparently willing to do, but to give more (and more coherent) protection than *Blockburger* provides against multiple punishment.

If all same-offense questions are answered by reference to legislative intent, the Double Jeopardy Clause still has a "plain meaning" that should please Justice Scalia. A legislative-prerogative account reads "same offense" to mean "what the legislature meant to be punished once." This is just another way of saying that the legislature creates substantive criminal offenses and thus necessarily controls by means of substance the procedural question of when offenses are the same. Offenses are the same when the legislature meant only one conviction to result; offenses are not the same when the legislature meant to authorize multiple convictions. It is just that simple.

Scalia's view that *Blockburger* is an inflexible limit on successive prosecutions causes doctrinal difficulties. Recall *Garrett v. United States*[108] from chapter 1. Decided before Scalia joined the Court, *Garrett* found that the *Blockburger* test pronounced the "compound" offense of engaging in a continuing criminal enterprise (CCE) and the "predicate" felony of a drug offense as the same double jeopardy offense.[109] The Court then held that *Blockburger* created a presumption about same offense, which was rebutted by expressions of contrary congressional intent under the facts of *Garrett*. But, on Scalia's view, Congress could not, regardless of the clarity of its intent, permit separate prosecutions of offenses that were the same *Blockburger* offense.

This outcome is particularly suspect with respect to CCE and similar offenses (such as RICO). As the Court noted in *Garrett*, it is extremely unlikely that Congress meant to create an offense that is aggravated because it includes prior crimes and then forbid prosecution of the aggravated offense if one of the prior crimes has been prosecuted.[110] Yet this odd result is precisely the one dictated by Scalia's view that *Blockburger* is an inflexible definition of same offense when separate trials are involved.

If legislative intent is an integral part of the analysis in successive prosecution cases, it must be the source of same offense. How could a court consider legislative intent and then decide the case in a contrary fashion? What would be the basis to ignore legislative intent? It cannot be *Blockburger*, which is a tool for divining legislative intent. It cannot be some metaphysical notion of harassment, for that is too indeterminate to provide concrete answers to real cases. The legislature thus determines not only what constitutes blameworthiness but also when blameworthiness is to be considered singular.

So far this chapter has identified the problems with Supreme Court doctrine on the three crucial jeopardy issues: the principle of legislative prerogative and the two presumptions that serve that principle (one proscribed blameworthy act is presumed to be only one double jeopardy offense, and jeopardy does not end without a verdict or an outcome that suggests that an acquittal would have resulted). Now we can examine briefly what other commentators have offered as solutions to the problems identified in this chapter.

Double Jeopardy Reform Proposals

Given the inconsistencies and complexities demonstrated so far, one might think that the woods would be full of proposals to bring coherence to double jeopardy. Oddly enough, that is not true. Only two books take double jeopardy doctrine as their subject. Both books accept the 1962 Model Penal Code view that the overriding double jeopardy policy is to prevent harassing prosecutions. Both books describe the then current law of double jeopardy (both were published in 1969) and offer occasional critiques and prescriptions. But neither book offers a framework for analysis that is significantly different from the 1962 Model Penal Code.

Martin Friedland's book is an excellent comparative law study on double jeopardy, but its normative thrust is to require mandatory joinder as a way of solving the harassing prosecution problem in England and Canada. Jay Sigler's book contains a wealth of material on state and federal approaches to many double jeopardy issues, along with frequent trenchant observations. Ultimately, however, Sigler views the Double Jeopardy Clause "as a series of problems in social policy."[111] He criticizes courts for not "fac[ing] the critical policy issues which lie deep beneath the surface" of double jeopardy law.[112] He criticizes reliance on "the 'same offense' dogma,"[113] by which he seems to mean the courts' failure to substitute policy statements for the language of the Clause. In place of "same offense dogma," Sigler calls for "a more complete consideration of the social policies which underlie double jeopardy."[114] While Sigler is right that the Court has not solved the same-offense problem, his reliance on underlying policies is unhelpful.

An example of what Sigler considers useful policy analysis is Justice Black's statement of double jeopardy policies. Sigler identifies it as an exception to the refusal of courts to face the deeply buried policy issues.[115] But answers to complex, specific double jeopardy questions cannot be found anywhere in Black's exhortations about "embarrassment, expense and ordeal" or living in a "continuing state of anxiety and insecurity."[116] Like Friedland, Sigler recommends a mandatory joinder solution.[117]

But my project is not about how to avoid double jeopardy problems through statutory solutions such as mandatory joinder. My project is to find the best constitutional interpretation of "jeopardy" and "same offense." Neither Friedland nor Sigler offers an account of how best to interpret these concepts.

The law review commentary is disappointing. For example, Larry Simon's student note, *Twice in Jeopardy*, is an example of the power and failure of skepticism. Prior to the publication of *Twice in Jeopardy* in 1969, decades of court decisions and academic commentary had suggested that there was (or could be) some relatively clear answer to the question of when two offenses were the same, and Simon blew apart this smug view of double jeopardy in a tour de force. He was right to conclude that double jeopardy doctrine was filled with "fictions and rationalizations" that are "the characteristic sign of doctrinal senility."[118] He was right to skewer courts for the idea that double jeopardy rules were "expressions of self-evident moral principles."[119] Concluding that the answers are not self-evident does not, of course, help in finding a useful set of principles.

It is here, at the stage of providing principles, that Simon's skeptical effort flounders. In the area of successive prosecutions, he, too, recommends mandatory joinder.[120] To solve the single-trial problem, Simon borrows the proposal of Otto Kirchheimer and argues that convictions under different statutes should be permitted only when courts believe that the statutes were designed to prevent distinct social evils.[121] Though this idea is conceptually helpful, its edges are far too soft to be useful as a doctrinal rule.

Peter Westen and Richard Drubel would avoid double jeopardy difficulties by rejecting all rules about twice in jeopardy and same offense. Courts should recognize instead that the Double Jeopardy Clause generates a set of values that can be arranged in a hierarchical manner. Paying close attention to this hierarchy of values in the context of each case will lead judges to reach the right result, whether the issue is same offense or second jeopardy.[122]

The Westen-Drubel hierarchy of double jeopardy values puts a premium on jury nullification, thus elevating an acquittal over a conviction as a bar to a second trial. The least important double jeopardy value, they assert, is finality. The middle value is a rebuttable presumption against double punishment, which they define as punishment that exceeds the total amount authorized by the legislature.

This legal realist solution thus does not protect against double jeopardy for the same offense. Rather, it protects absolutely jury nullification. In a few cases, it preserves finality, though Westen and Drubel offer no guidance beyond joining the chorus condemning generalized harassment of defendants by multiple trials. The Westen-Drubel solution protects against double punishment to the extent one can figure out what punishment was authorized by the legislature and then only as a deduction from the total authorized by the greater offense.

While Westen and Drubel offer a useful description of the Court's doctrine, it is necessarily limited by that doctrine and thus partakes of the

Court's flawed conceptual framework.[123] To the extent the Court has failed in its double jeopardy project, Westen and Drubel have failed as well.

If complexity and the lack of hard-edged rules is the problem with much of the current approach to double jeopardy, Akhil Amar and Jonathan Marcus have the antidote—a genuine identity test based on the "plain meaning" of same offense.[124] Their basic rule is so clear that no one could have serious problems applying it. The only offense that is the same as first-degree premeditated murder is first-degree premeditated murder. But this approach offers almost no protection against double jeopardy. The medicine is worse than the disease.

The Amar-Marcus approach is more protective than it first appears because it embraces the Court's implied acquittal doctrine—a prosecution for murder, for example, that results in a manslaughter conviction implicitly acquits that defendant of murder.[125] Amar and Marcus would also supplement double jeopardy protection by finding mandatory joinder (prohibition of vexatious prosecutions) in the Due Process Clause. Finally, they relocate collateral estoppel in the Due Process Clause as well.

Once all the relocating to the Due Process Clause is done, Amar and Marcus have a plain-meaning test of same offense. Inevitably, though, the same offense issues left in their conception of the Double Jeopardy Clause are trivial. First-degree premeditated murder is the same as first-degree premeditated murder; yes, of course. A conviction of manslaughter on a trial of first-degree premeditated murder acquits of murder; but otherwise no other offense is the same as first-degree premeditated murder, not felony murder or second-degree murder or aggravated murder, and certainly not manslaughter.

Blackstone was of a different mind on this issue, as we have seen, noting that a conviction under a manslaughter indictment was a jeopardy bar to a murder trial.[126] One might contend that we can improve on Blackstone's understanding and that, in any event, prosecutors are rarely going to bring manslaughter and murder trials separately. I doubt that we can improve on Blackstone's understanding of very much about double jeopardy, and the pragmatic response misses the point of finding the best conception of same offense. Moreover, anyone wishing to change the rule about lesser included offenses must contend not only with Blackstone but also, as we saw in chapter 1, with a line of cases and authorities from Blackstone to the present.[127] As Bishop said in 1923, the name of the offense "in the two indictments may differ, and within our constitutional guaranty the offences be the same."[128] To justify rejecting more than two centuries of settled law would require a showing that the replacement doctrine is much better. Amar and Marcus offer, at best, a different justification for the same doctrine and at worst a jumbled due process test that would produce even less clarity than the Court has provided.

Perversely, a plain-meaning approach to same offense requires Amar and Marcus to force much of what has been thought for centuries to be double jeopardy into a soft-edged due process analysis. This is the worst of both worlds. Amar and Marcus achieve a plain meaning of same offense that is far too narrow to replicate the common-law protection. Then they leave the rest of Blackstone's double jeopardy protection mired in due process, to be solved with a vexatious-prosecution analysis that has almost no contours or bounds.

For example, Amar and Marcus express uncertainty about whether their due process test would bar successive prosecutions for the greater-lesser offenses of auto theft and joyriding that the Court found to be the same offense in *Brown*. In their own words,

> The state's reasons for two trials did not seem particularly malicious, but sounded in local autonomy: the police in one county, where defendant was caught, apparently did not know of the plans of the prosecutor from another county, where defendant had stolen the car nine days earlier. Under an intent-based due process analysis, the state's actions might pass muster as nonvexatious; but under a stricter effects-based due process test, the fact that a highly organized state could have brought a single case might be enough for Brown to win.[129]

The state's reasons did not "seem particularly malicious" and therefore the state's actions "might pass muster," but, then again, on a different version of their test, Brown "might" have won. This due process swamp must be avoided if double jeopardy doctrine is to have coherence.[130] Moreover, unless they are willing to argue for a plain-meaning interpretation of "jeopardy of life or limb," Amar and Marcus achieve only a partial double jeopardy plain meaning.[131] This is hardly enough to justify rejecting the line of cases and authorities from Blackstone to *Brown*, as well as the certainty of a single conviction for a single homicide.

To this point, I have argued for the plausibility of a legislative-prerogative account of double jeopardy. In this account, "same offense" means "same legislatively created blameworthiness." Now a new difficulty arises. I do not believe, for example, that the legislature intends assault to be a different offense than assault with intent to murder, yet these offenses do not describe precisely the same blameworthiness. Similarly, premeditated murder describes a greater blameworthiness than manslaughter; yet there is only one killing and, Blackstone thought, only one offense.

I need an account of legislatively created criminal blameworthiness that tracks legislative intent to create distinct offenses as opposed to overlapping offenses. The difference between the two is suggested in the terminology: distinct offenses manifest blameworthiness that the legislature meant to be separately punishable; overlapping offenses are merely alternative ways of prosecuting the same blameworthiness. Murder and manslaughter are examples of alternative, overlapping offenses. Murder and rape are examples of distinct offenses.

Justice Rehnquist recognized in *Garrett* the double jeopardy difference between offenses that are distinct and those that are overlapping alternatives. He wrote, "In view of this legislative history, it is indisputable that Congress intended to create a separate CCE offense. One could still argue, however, that having created the separate offense, Congress intended it, where applicable, to be a substitute for the predicate offense."[132]

A second analytic problem has to do with what counts as double jeopardy blameworthiness. Two judgments cannot manifest the same offense unless both judgments are for an "offense" in the first place. Tort law and regulatory law create a type of blameworthiness, as does the motor vehicle code, but it is not clear that this type of fault is same-offense blameworthiness.

Because understanding what constitutes double jeopardy blameworthiness is helpful in developing my account of distinct blameworthiness, the first task is to untangle tort and crime, as well as regulatory offense and crime. I take on that task in chapter 4. Then, in chapter 5, I address the problem of separating distinct blameworthiness from merely overlapping blameworthiness.

4

"Life or Limb" Blameworthiness

The Double Jeopardy Clause does not forbid all multiple judicial outcomes. It forbids only second jeopardies "of life or limb." Even without reliance on the "life or limb" text, it is self-evident that double jeopardy protection does not apply to all forms of blameworthiness. We would be justly surprised if told our tort suit for damages could not proceed because the tortfeasor had already pleaded guilty to a crime that manifested the same blameworthiness.

We would be surprised because the divergence between crime and tort can be traced at least as far back as Britton, whose treatise was published around 1290.[1] Britton cautioned that a defendant acquitted as against private prosecutors is not necessarily "not guilty of what is laid to their charge" and thus should be prosecuted on "our" (the king's) "behalf."[2] The modern rule permits both a civil and a criminal suit to proceed, regardless of whether the first proceeding ends in favor of or against the accused and regardless of whether the civil or the criminal case goes first.[3]

Unsurprisingly, locating the line between "civil" and "criminal" offenses is far from easy. A civil fraud prosecution may threaten liquidated damages that are hugely disproportionate to the loss caused by the wrongdoing; many regulatory offenses partake of both civil and criminal rationales. Reckless driving, for example, carries a penalty, typically a fine. Risk creation in driving is without doubt blameworthy, because of the potential harm to others, but is this double jeopardy blameworthiness?

Until 1997 the Court made quite a mess of the line between "civil" and "criminal"—once admitting that the "problem has been extremely difficult and elusive of solution."[4] In 1997 *Hudson v. United States*[5] adopted a strategy that restores clarity and coherence to the civil/criminal dichotomy. *Hudson* manifests the legislative-prerogative thesis that underlies my entire double jeopardy account. But before I present the solution, I sketch the nature of the problem.

The Language of the Double Jeopardy Clause

Though the Court has never seen the civil/criminal problem in terms of the literal meaning of the Double Jeopardy Clause, its "life or limb" language is a good starting place. As I argued in 1990, it seems unlikely that a civil judgment, even one that has elements of criminal punishment, could ever be characterized as "jeopardy of life or limb."[6] Thus, close attention to constitutional language suggests that the effort to decide which civil sanctions should be treated as criminal for double jeopardy purposes was wrongheaded from the beginning.

The "beginning" of this ill-fated venture was not the unanimous decision in *United States v. Halper*[7] that the Court has now essentially repudiated.[8] A hundred years earlier, the Court contemplated a robust double jeopardy crossover between civil sanctions and criminal penalties. In *Coffey v. United States*,[9] the Court held that a criminal acquittal barred a civil suit brought on behalf of the government. The Court also discussed favorably a lower court case holding that a conviction for the criminal offense of conspiracy to defraud the United States barred the government's civil suit to recover a penalty for the lost taxes.[10]

Coffey explained the earlier case: "The two alleged transactions were but one; and it was held that the suit for the penalty was barred by the judgment in the criminal case. The decision was put on the ground that the defendant could not be twice punished for the same crime, and that the former conviction and judgment were a bar to the suit for the penalty."[11] Oddly, Bishop did not mention *Coffey* when he concluded confidently in 1923 that, while double jeopardy applies to misdemeanors, it does not apply "to actions for the recovery of penalties."[12] A "life or limb" approach to understanding the scope of the double jeopardy protection agrees with Bishop rather than *Coffey*. But how are we to understand "life or limb"?

The earliest recorded use of "life or limb" appears in the Magna Carta, where it described trial by battle,[13] a species of criminal trial in which the defendant's life and limb were literally in jeopardy.[14] Since trial by battle was, by the eighteenth century, a "long forgotten procedure of the dark ages,"[15] the Framers almost certainly did not have the Magna Carta use in mind. Other evidence suggests that the Framers did not mean "limb" to be taken literally. Death replaced amputation and mutilation as the usual punishment for felons in England as early as the thirteenth century.[16] Moreover, when debating the prohibition of cruel and unusual punishment, its opponents in the First Congress conceded that it would bar amputation. Questioning the wisdom of prohibiting cruel and unusual punishments, Samuel Livermore stated that "villains often deserve whipping, and perhaps having their ears cut off; but are we in future to be prevented from inflicting these punishments because they are cruel?"[17] If Livermore's view of the scope of the Eighth Amendment was correct, there is no reason to believe the Framers would have implicitly signaled acceptance, in the Double Jeopardy Clause, of a type of punishment that they simultaneously forbade in the Eighth Amendment. The historical argument for taking "limb" literally is thus difficult to maintain, though Sigler implicitly accepts it.[18]

Moreover, to require a literal "jeopardy of life or limb" would have been a major restriction of the protection offered by Madison's original language, which made "trial" or "punishment" the prohibited outcomes. As noted in chapter 2, the concern expressed on the House floor was not that the scope of protection was too expansive but, rather, that Madison's language might deter an appellate court from reversing a conviction obtained in an unfair manner.[19] During the debate on this point, Egbert Benson rephrased Madison's protection as "no man's life should be more than once put in jeopardy for the same offence." This is virtually identical to Blackstone's formulation of the "universal maxim of the common law of England, that no man is to be brought into jeopardy of his life more than once for the same offence."[20] Benson used "life" as the object of jeopardy, just as Blackstone did. But Benson did not intend to limit double jeopardy protection to "life" because, when seeking to describe the "humane intention of the clause," he returned to Madison's language, claiming that the intent was "to prevent more than one punishment."[21]

Indeed, Benson moved to strike "or trial" from Madison's formulation and thus to limit the prohibition to more than "one punishment." In supporting that motion, Roger Sherman of Connecticut stated that "the courts of justice would never think of trying and punishing twice for the same offence."[22] Again, the focus seemed to be on punishment in general and not any specific form or gravity of punishment.

Benson's motion to strike "or trial" from Madison's language failed, and Madison's original proposal was reported out of committee and later approved by the full House. But the Senate approved a Double Jeopardy Clause that echoed Blackstone's universal maxim, with the expansive addition of "or limb" to Blackstone's jeopardy of "life." The Senate language was: "nor shall any person be subject to be put in jeopardy of life or limb, for the same offense."[23] For reasons forever lost to us, the conference committee agreed to language close to the Senate version.[24]

The final language, then, read "nor shall any person be subject for the same offence to be twice put in jeopardy of life or limb."[25] A fairly solid inference from this drafting history is that the Framers intended to expand the protection when they added "or limb" to "life" but that they did not mean "limb" to be taken literally. No one had insisted on limiting the clause to capital offenses, and it seems likely that the Framers simply wanted to broaden the protection to noncapital offenses by adding "or limb." As Madison was a member of the conference committee that rejected his "punishment" language, there is no reason to believe he would have quietly agreed to a change that greatly reduced the protection of his original proposal.

Rejecting the literal meaning leaves "life or limb" unclear. One approach is to suppose that the Framers merely meant to reinstate Madison's concept of punishment. This has been the Court's working assumption for more than a century, but it did not prove a helpful concept until recently.

The Court's Pre-Hudson *"Criminal Punishment"* Doctrine

In 1873 the Supreme Court decided in *Ex parte Lange* that the Double Jeopardy Clause applied to all threats of criminal punishment—in effect, that a "jeopardy of life or limb" is the risk of a criminal penalty.[26] This seems the best reading of Madison's original language—"punishment," in Madison's formulation, probably meant "criminal punishment."

But we do not know what "criminal punishment" is. Perhaps it had a self-evident quality in 1873. In the meantime, however, legislatures have created much new blameworthiness. On Michael Moore's count, "a criminal code typically prohibits approximately 7,000 types of actions."[27] A substantial number of the new offenses are in the nature of regulatory or "strict liability" offenses that were unknown in 1873.

In *Halper*, the Court held that sixty-five counts of civil fraud constituted a "criminal" penalty that could not be sought following a criminal fraud conviction for the same fraud. The Court relied on the disparity between the money obtained by the fraud ($585) and the minimum liquidated damages that would attend conviction on all counts ($130,000) to conclude that the civil fraud prosecution was punitive and not remedial.

Viewed as punitive, the "civil" proceeding was substantively criminal and thus, a unanimous Court held, barred by the Double Jeopardy Clause.

Halper was an easy case; the minimum statutory damages were 220 times the amount obtained by fraud. It is difficult to view the prosecutor's use of the civil statute under these circumstances as anything other than punitive. But as Stanley Cox has noted, "*Halper*'s assumptions and implications are far-reaching."[28] Indeed, "[i]f *Halper*'s message is taken seriously, many civil and criminal prosecutions could fall, because under current statutes, both civil and criminal prosecutors often try to punish the same conduct."[29] Defense lawyers made *Halper*-based arguments that many administrative sanctions were double jeopardy punishments—for example, driver's license revocation;[30] other license suspensions,[31] including the suspension of a funeral director's license;[32] civil banking penalties;[33] and the eviction of tenants.[34] It is even possible, under a robust reading of *Halper*, for a wrongful death tort judgment to be viewed as a criminal punishment, thus undermining the parallel tort/crime systems that have been in place for centuries.[35]

Yet another example of the "far-reaching" implications of *Halper* is *Department of Revenue of Montana v. Kurth Ranch*,[36] where the Court split 5-4 over whether a tax on the possession of illegal drugs is a criminal penalty barred by criminal conviction for the same drug possession. The *Kurth Ranch* majority concluded that the tax was punitive and thus a criminal penalty. The penalty was being collected in a second proceeding that was, the Court noted in passing, "the functional equivalent of a successive criminal prosecution."[37] Thus, despite clear legislative intent to impose the tax in addition to the criminal sanction, the Double Jeopardy Clause required that the tax "be imposed during the first prosecution or not at all."[38]

Scalia used *Kurth Ranch* as an opportunity to recant his original support for the *Halper* concept, arguing in dissent that a civil proceeding could never be functionally criminal unless it was actually criminal. Scalia here recovers the historical rationale reported by Bishop: double jeopardy extended to felonies and misdemeanors, but not to actions "for the recovery of penalties because *these are not criminal proceedings*."[39] Though Bishop gave no test for "criminal proceedings," the Court developed a seven-part test in *Kennedy v. Mendoza-Martinez*.[40] The issue in *Kennedy* was whether deprivation of citizenship was a criminal punishment that required the procedural protections of the Fifth and Sixth

Amendments. The Court held that it was, relying on seven factors. One factor was the sole basis for the Court's test in *Halper*: whether the sanction "will promote the traditional aims of punishment—retribution and deterrence."[41] Others included whether "the sanction involves an affirmative disability or restraint, whether it has historically been regarded as a punishment, whether it comes into play only on a finding of scienter," whether "an alternative purpose to which it may rationally be connected is assignable for it, and whether it appears excessive in relation to the alternative purpose assigned."[42]

Most of these factors are helpful to Scalia's claim that the seven-part *Kennedy* test would not characterize a tax proceeding as criminal.[43] A tax is not a "restraint," nor is it an "affirmative disability" in a punitive sense. Taxes have not been historically regarded as punishment, and the duty to pay taxes arises without regard to criminal intent ("scienter"). There is an alternative purpose that is "rationally connected" to the tax (various governments heavily tax alcohol and cigarettes). The only *Kennedy* factors in favor of treating the tax proceeding as a criminal trial are that the tax serves traditional criminal law goals (retribution and deterrence) and is applied to conduct that is already a crime. On balance, though, the *Kennedy* factors suggest that a tax proceeding is not a criminal proceeding.

This would also be the result from applying a legislative-prerogative view of the role of legislative intent in double jeopardy analysis. Recall Justice Washington's 1820 view that the legislature can have as many penalties as it wants.[44] If my legislative-prerogative principle is right, then Stanley Cox is wrong that double jeopardy provides limits on government's ability to have two (or more) penalties for the same conduct. Because the Montana statute explicitly contemplates the tax being imposed following criminal sanctions, the tax statute is not the same legislatively authorized offense as the criminal statute. Nancy King has argued that *Kurth Ranch* strikes a discordant note when compared to *Dixon* (the case that overruled *Grady*).[45] *Dixon* used an inference from the *Blockburger* test to permit two avowedly criminal trials for the same conduct. Yet in *Kurth Ranch*, the explicit legislative intent to create separate offenses was ignored, and a tax was held an impermissible criminal penalty.

This seems truly odd. Explicit legislative intent to create cumulative sanctions cannot justify a tax, but implicit intent can justify a prison term. Indeed, to suggest that a proceeding to collect taxes places a defendant's "life or limb" in jeopardy is a linguistically startling proposition.

There is no risk of incarceration and, therefore, no sense (metaphorical or otherwise) in which the taxpayer's limbs are in jeopardy.

When law gets that far removed from common usage and common understanding, it cries out for correction.[46] David Rudstein would meet me halfway; he argues that a civil proceeding is not a jeopardy and thus the state could always bring a civil proceeding first and then a criminal one.[47] The state could not bring a punitive civil suit following a conviction, on Rudstein's view, because he accepts *Halper*'s assessment that dual punishments are barred irrespective of legislative intent.

But Peter Henning has demonstrated the incoherence of the *Halper* rationale.[48] There is so much wrong with *Halper* that Henning's critique consumes twenty-eight pages and is too detailed to summarize adequately here. Suffice to say that Henning agrees with me that a civil penalty is simply not a criminal punishment for purposes of the Double Jeopardy Clause. Moreover, Henning asks, what does proportionality have to do with double jeopardy? Double jeopardy in no other context depends on measuring the quantity of the penalty; rather, it is a "categorical prohibition" of "repeated trials and unauthorized sanctions."[49] Henning's critique is powerful, in my view leading to a legislative-prerogative thesis: if Congress wanted both a civil penalty and a criminal conviction for the same act of fraud, that is the end of the double jeopardy analysis.[50]

If my legislative-prerogative thesis is right, *Halper* must be wrong. And the Court in 1997 explicitly rejected the *Halper* analysis, using legislative prerogative as the basis for the decision.

Rethinking the Problem

The issue in *Hudson v. United States*[51] was whether the Double Jeopardy Clause barred criminal prosecution of defendants for "essentially the same conduct" that had led to "monetary penalties and occupational disbarment."[52] The government initially assessed civil money penalties against defendants for making bank loans in an improper manner. Defendants agreed to pay fines of $12,500 to $16,500 and not to "participate in any manner" in future banking affairs without written consent of the government. Defendants were later indicted for three criminal charges: conspiracy, misapplication of bank funds, and making false bank entries.

Though I find the *Hudson* analysis a vast improvement over *Halper*, *Hudson* is itself unconventional. As Justice Stevens correctly noted in his concurring opinion, the Court could have avoided the *Halper* issue by holding that the criminal offenses were not the same *Blockburger* offenses as the civil offenses—each required proof of an element that the others did not.[53] For some odd reason, the Court seems to forget or confuse the same-offense requirement when applying the Double Jeopardy Clause to civil sanctions. There was, for example, no reference to "same offense" in either *Halper* or *Kurth Ranch*.

Confusion was also manifested in *Kansas v. Hendricks* when the Court remarked obscurely: "The *Blockburger* test . . . simply does not apply outside of the successive prosecution context."[54] This statement is flatly wrong. *Blockburger* itself was a single-trial case, and the Court has cited and relied on *Blockburger* many times for its presumption about congressional intent to impose cumulative penalties in a single trial.

Perhaps the Court meant in *Hendricks* that *Blockburger* does not apply when the issue is whether a civil sanction is a double jeopardy punishment. If this is what the Court meant, it is enigmatic and puzzling. Remember that the issue is whether the double jeopardy multiple-punishment doctrine forbids a civil sanction after a defendant has already been convicted of a criminal offense. But the only way the Double Jeopardy Clause can bar the civil sanction is if the two offenses are the same offense. Otherwise, the Clause by its literal language does not apply.

That the Court seems to forget or confuse the same-offense requirement when applying double jeopardy across the civil-criminal divide probably speaks volumes about the lack of conceptual fit. Justice Stevens is right in his separate *Hudson* opinion that offenses must be tested by *Blockburger* before there is any concern about multiple punishments arising in the civil and criminal spheres. So tested, the offenses in *Hudson* would not have imposed multiple punishments for the same offense, and the convictions could have been affirmed without mentioning *Halper*.[55]

But conceding Stevens's technical point, it is clear from the other opinions, especially that of Justice Scalia, that the Court wanted to finish the job of overruling *Halper* that it had begun the year before in *United States v. Ursery*.[56] *Ursery* held that civil forfeiture is not a double jeopardy punishment (the items forfeited were a house, in one case, and the proceeds of drug transactions, in the other). The Court stressed the inherently remedial nature of forfeiture[57] and, more important, read *Halper* narrowly.[58] *Ursery* was correctly decided. As Stefan Cassella noted prior to *Ursery*, "For two hundred years, it was unquestioned that civil forfeiture did not implicate the Double Jeopardy Clause."[59] Cassella recommended returning the law to its historic understanding, as *Ursery* did.

The question remaining after *Ursery* was whether the retrenchment on *Halper* would be limited to civil forfeiture. This is where *Hudson* comes in. If one were willing (as the Court has been) to blithely ignore the same-offense requirement in these civil/criminal cases, the *Halper* mode of analysis gave the *Hudson* defendants a good chance to use the civil penalties to bar the criminal trial (indeed, the district court ruled that the monetary penalties constituted double jeopardy punishment). *Halper* defined punishment as a sanction that "cannot fairly be said solely to serve a remedial purpose, but rather can only be explained as also serving either retributive or deterrent purposes."[60] This definition does not screen out many trivial offenses. Most regulatory offenses serve deterrent purposes. The fine for double parking, for example, hardly serves a remedial function; its purpose is to deter double parking. While license revocations serve a remedial purpose, do they not also serve as a deterrent and as a punishment?[61] As Peter Henning noted, *Halper's* broad definition of punishment created "enormous uncertainty" about whether civil and criminal sanctions could ever be imposed for the same conduct.[62]

The Court in *Hudson* agreed that *Halper's* analytical structure was flawed and "ill considered" and had "proved unworkable."[63] It adopted a legislative-prerogative presumption: the legislature's preference for a civil or criminal "label" for the sanction will control unless there is the "clearest proof" that the sanction is punitive despite the legislative intent to the contrary. This legislative preference can be express or implied. *Hudson* makes clear that the legislature can have both a civil and a criminal penalty, in the absence of the "clearest proof" that the civil penalty is actually criminal.[64]

The rebuttable nature of the *Hudson* presumption is inconsistent with my robust legislative-prerogative thesis but is unlikely to have much pragmatic effect, given the requirement of "clearest proof" that a penalty civil in form is substantively criminal. By adopting the seven-part *Kennedy* test that Justice Scalia endorsed in his *Kurth Ranch* dissent, the Court has made it difficult for defendants to show the "clearest proof" that a sanction is punitive. Most of the *Kennedy* factors are not satisfied by penalties less severe than incarceration.

Risk of incarceration is also consistent with a "life or limb" understanding of when double jeopardy applies. We can begin with history.

Early English law permitted defendants to purchase emendment (atonement) for some crimes by pecuniary compensation to the injured party (the *bot*) and to the king (the *wite*).[65] But emendment was not available for serious crimes.[66] The rationale underlying this principle was that "by the gravest, the unemendable, crimes, a man 'forfeited life and member and all that he had.'"[67] Although the definition of which crimes could be emended varied over time,[68] it included only serious offenses. Thus, the "life or limb" concept in the Double Jeopardy Clause could well have referred to crimes for which a defendant forfeited "life and member," not in a literal sense but in the metaphorical sense that denied him the possibility of paying compensation in lieu of "punishment."

Halper misconceived what is unique about crimes when compared to other statutory prohibitions. The question is not whether a particular law seeks to deter conduct—indeed, contract law also seeks to deter certain kinds of conduct—but whether that conduct is deserving of condemnation. Condemnation manifests retribution (deserved punishment), rather than deterrence.

Figuring out which statutory penalties fall on the condemnation side of the line is no easy matter unless we have a mechanical test. In determining the roughly analogous question of whether Sixth Amendment cases involve a "criminal prosecution," the Court has drawn two mechanical lines. On the issue of whether a trial is a criminal prosecution for purposes of the right to a jury trial, the Court explicitly used the "gravity" of an offense as part of its analysis. The Court noted that the "penalty authorized by the law of the locality may be taken 'as a gauge of its social and ethical judgments' of the crime in question."[69] Based on this criterion, the Court drew a distinction between "serious" crimes, which required a jury trial, and "petty" offenses, which did not. The Court drew the "gravity" line for jury trials at imprisonment of six months.[70]

But six months' imprisonment is not a good "life or limb" line. In the jury trial context, the dividing line was based not on whether conduct deserved condemnation but, rather, on whether the crime was "serious." By beginning with the idea that some crimes (petty ones) did not require a jury trial, the Court was dividing the world of crime into two parts. But it seems likely that all crimes manifest condemnation. Perhaps a better marker for crime versus noncrime would be whether the conduct is punishable by a jail sentence. While the line between incarceration and other sanctions might not always prove a true measure of condemnation—some states might authorize a few days in jail for trivial offenses—there is value in having a clear, easily administered line.

This suggests that a better Sixth Amendment analogy is the right to counsel, rather than the right to a jury trial. In *Argersinger v. Hamlin*,[71] the Court held that incarceration created a right to appointed counsel. The Court later identified as the "central premise of *Argersinger* . . . that actual imprisonment is a penalty different in kind from fines or mere threat of imprisonment" and then remarked that this premise "is eminently sound and warrants adoption of actual imprisonment as the line defining the constitutional right to appointment of counsel."[72]

The *Argersinger* rule is backward-looking: judges may not incarcerate a defendant who has been denied the right to counsel. But in the double jeopardy context, the rule must be forward looking. Jeopardy implies risk, without regard to the actual outcome. The prohibition of double jeopardy is intended to prevent the second exposure to risk. For this reason, the Court has held that an interlocutory appeal must be granted a defendant who raises a double jeopardy objection to a second trial.[73] Thus, the "mere threat of imprisonment" should justify treating an offense as a "life or limb" offense.

Incarceration seems qualitatively different from penalties that do not include incarceration.[74] Moreover, incarceration captures what is unique about criminal punishment—its retributive, unemendable nature. Fines resemble civil law outcomes in tort, but incarceration is uniquely criminal and uniquely lacking in remedial or compensatory goals. In holding the Double Jeopardy Clause applicable in juvenile delinquency hearings, a unanimous Court noted that the consequences of these hearings included both the stigma associated with having committed a criminal act "and the deprivation of liberty for many years."[75] Thus, whether one seeks to define "criminal punishment," as the Court has done, or attempts to equate double jeopardy blameworthiness with condemnable conduct, as this chapter has done, the end result should be the same: the Double Jeopardy Clause protection is triggered only if both offenses authorize incarceration.

If either offense does not authorize incarceration, the second trial or punishment cannot be a second jeopardy of life or limb and is therefore permissible. If both offenses authorize incarceration, that is not, of course, the end of the inquiry; there is still the issue of whether the two offenses are the same offense. That is why *Kurth Ranch* is doubly wrong: it not only missed the nonjeopardy status of the tax proceeding but also held that the two proceedings were for the same offense, despite the legislative intent to authorize both.

Does my legislative-prerogative thesis mean that *Halper* was wrongly decided? Not necessarily. The prosecutor's use of a civil offense in *Halper* arguably manifested retribution rather than deterrence. But, if so, he was using the civil fraud statute in a way not intended by the legislature. There is no reason for a legislature to enact a civil fraud and a criminal fraud statute unless the two have different purposes. The self-evident difference is that criminal fraud serves retribution and deterrence, while civil fraud serves the goals of compensation and deterrence.

Read this way, *Halper* suggests that "life or limb" blameworthiness can occur in two ways. One is that a statute creates "life or limb" blameworthiness by proscribing conduct that deserves condemnation, signaling this purpose, I have suggested, by authorizing incarceration. But if *Halper* is right—and the result is intuitively satisfying—prosecutors can use a statute that does not proscribe "life or limb" blameworthiness in a way that condemns the conduct and seeks retribution for it. When prosecutors use civil statutes in that manner, the Double Jeopardy Clause should apply.

This second "life or limb" usage is necessarily a case-by-case determination for which no easy rule exists. The heavy presumption should be that no proceedings involve jeopardy unless brought under a statute that authorizes incarceration. Exceptions would be, in the words of *Halper*, "the rare case" where "the civil penalty sought in the subsequent proceeding bears no rational relation to the goal of compensating the Government for its loss."[76] In this very narrow category of cases, it would seem that prosecutor has abused the intent of the legislature by using a nonjeopardy statute to achieve retribution. Limited to this very narrow category of "life or limb" application of a nonjeopardy statute, *Halper* can be defended.

Moreover, *Halper* does not have to fall in order to take down *Kurth Ranch*. The difference between the two is that the prosecutor in *Halper* used a nonjeopardy statute in a way contrary to what the legislature intended. In *Kurth Ranch*, the legislature explicitly contemplated imposition of the tax following criminal sanctions. There was, then, no reason even to reach the issue of how to characterize the sanction. On Michael

Moore's insight, two offenses are the same (or different) regardless of whether prosecuted together or separately.[77] On my legislative-prerogative view, clear legislative intent to punish cumulatively always creates different offenses.[78] Combining these insights, I argue that the tax should have been upheld in *Kurth Ranch*, whether or not it was viewed as a "life or limb" penalty. As Justice Washington noted, the legislature can have as many penalties as it wants; in this book, I add only that we must have good reason to believe the legislature intended more than one penalty. The statute in *Kurth Ranch* provides this assurance, and the Court should have stopped at that stage of the analysis.

The Civil/Criminal Issue in Broader Context

The civil/criminal issue, like all others connected with my double jeopardy account, ultimately turns on legislative intent. If, for example, the legislature provides that it does not want both a "civil" and a "criminal" sanction to apply, no one would argue that both should apply. In this context, to apply both would be to punish without legislative authorization, which, as Scalia points out, is a violation of due process.[79] The harder case is that in which the legislature states that it wants both sanctions to apply—the *Kurth Ranch* situation. On a legislative-intent account of double jeopardy, however, clear legislative intent means that both sanctions can be imposed. Why would intent to punish not be given effect in the same way as intent not to punish?

If the legislature intends both sanctions, the Court has held that they cannot be for the same offense when imposed in a single trial, and the civil/criminal question is irrelevant. The only way in which my legislative-prerogative account is substantively different than the Court's double jeopardy doctrine is that the Court continues to suggest that the Double Jeopardy Clause may somehow operate independent of legislative intent in the context of successive prosecutions. Because criminal and civil sanctions are very unlikely to be imposed in a single proceeding, the civil/criminal issue takes on the character of successive prosecutions and thus raises the issue of whether successive prosecutions should be treated differently for purposes of the "same offense" analysis.

The Court's labored seven-part test that can rebut the *Hudson* presumption would be totally unnecessary if "same offense" had the same meaning in successive prosecutions that it does in single trials. If that were true, *Missouri v. Hunter* would mean that the legislature can have as many penalties for the same conduct as it wants. Thus, on my account, there would be no possibility to rebut the *Hudson* presumption that the legislature can authorize both a civil penalty and a criminal punishment.

Drawing the statutory "life or limb" blameworthiness line at authorized incarceration easily resolves the civil/criminal dichotomy. Because civil statutes do not authorize imprisonment, they can never create "life or limb" blameworthiness unless the prosecutor abuses the civil nature of an offense, as in *Halper*. This argument is fully consistent with *Ex parte Lange*'s holding that "life or limb" means "criminal penalty."

This argument is also consistent with the constitutional text. If "life or limb" is 1792 shorthand for criminal penalties that could not be avoided by paying a fine (unemendable penalties), it would include offenses that are crimes for purposes of the Sixth Amendment "criminal prosecution" requirement. Prosecutions for crimes punishable by incarceration seem likely to meet the *Kennedy* test for "criminal prosecution." Incarceration would involve an affirmative restraint and would have historically been regarded as a punishment. And, in all likelihood, any crime that authorizes incarceration would require some form of criminal intent (scienter) and would promote retribution and deterrence over remedial goals.

Limiting double jeopardy protection to offenses that proscribe "life or limb" blameworthiness has practical advantages. The more serious the offense, the more likely that the prosecutor's office is on notice of the existence of the charge and pending prosecution. If the prosecutor goes ahead with a prosecution for a less serious offense—but one that authorizes incarceration—the state can be charged with having made an election of that offense rather than a more serious one.[80] But if the first "prosecution" is for a civil offense or a regulatory offense that fails to provide for incarceration, no bar would arise to a criminal prosecution, thus avoiding the unseemly result of a traffic fine barring a trial for vehicular homicide.[81] Judges naturally recoil from applying the Double Jeopardy Clause to permit minor traffic offenses to substitute for serious felonies.[82]

Reading "life or limb" as a floor for double jeopardy blameworthiness is conceptually satisfying; "life or limb" is an explicit part of the Double Jeopardy Clause and, understood as referring to offenses that authorize incarceration, it is consistent with the line the Court has drawn in defining the right to counsel in "all criminal prosecutions." Now that we have a floor for double jeopardy blameworthiness, the next task is to understand when the legislature intended distinct double jeopardy blameworthiness and thus different offenses.

5

Singular/Distinct Blameworthiness

The argument to this point is that double jeopardy "offense" can be understood only in terms of the "life or limb" blameworthiness the legislature intends to create. We must next understand when the legislature intends to create distinct blameworthiness and thus different offenses. Ultimately, we need a test that determines whether the blameworthiness in two statutes, or two violations of a single statute, is singular or distinct. If it is distinct, no double jeopardy bar exists to imposing a punishment for each distinct blameworthiness, and no bar exists to seeking that punishment in two proceedings.

"Distinct" in this context means something other than "different." The blameworthiness of felony murder is different from that of premeditated murder, for example, because the former includes commission of the underlying felony. But that difference in blameworthiness does not necessarily suggest that the legislature meant the blameworthiness of first-degree felony murder to be distinct from that of first-degree premeditated murder. If this were the best reading of legislative intent, a killer could be tried and convicted twice for first-degree murder for a single killing, hardly a satisfying outcome.

Many nineteenth-century courts used a blameworthiness test, albeit under the guise of comparing the "gravamen" of offenses. As Susanah Mead has observed, this test "had the potential for striking a balance between the act and offense, because it focused on the conduct of the defendant as it related to the social interests sought to be protected." Examining the proscribed conduct in light of the social interests is just another way of asking what blameworthy conduct the legislature sought to proscribe.

I argue that singularity of blameworthiness is best understood as the convergence of harm singularity and act singularity. This, of course, requires an account of "act" and an account of "harm." It is my basic thesis that legislatures write statutes with some form of this act/harm singularity as a background assumption for the dividing line that separates distinct blameworthiness from singular blameworthiness.

A Basic Account of Blameworthiness

The standard account of criminal liability requires (1) an act, (2) mens rea, (3) attendant circumstances, and (4) harm.[2] Because it is the goal of the criminal law to prevent harm—consider the traditional common-law crimes of murder, robbery, and rape—we can usefully begin by equating blameworthiness with the causing of harm. But what does it mean to cause harm? Joel Feinberg devoted four excellent volumes to the problem of defining the moral limits of the criminal law,[3] and his definition of harm is useful: a wrongful setback to the interests of a person.

Harm is not a sufficient condition for blameworthiness. Feinberg explicitly states his account of harming to include the mens rea and act requirements—one must act to cause the harm and be sufficiently responsible for the act and harm.[4] Focusing on the act requirement for the moment, some misfortunes in life do not permit us to ascribe blameworthiness to a human actor because no one acted to bring them about. Random chance and Mother Nature do not give rise to wrongful setbacks.

Moreover, some acts are harmful only because of the circumstances that exist when they are committed—for example, consensual sexual intercourse with a person under a certain age or who is unconscious and thus incapable of consenting. When the presence of the circumstance is what gives rise to the harm, the two cannot be separated conceptually. The "victim" has suffered no setback to her interests if she is of age and gave her consent. Of course, some circumstance elements are not connected to harm—for example, the requirement in some federal crimes that a state line be crossed.

It seems that blameworthiness is related to act and harm (with harm understood to include the circumstances that contribute to the harm). This is hardly surprising, but still incomplete. Some acts that cause harm are not blameworthy because the actor did not have a culpable mental state. If *D* bumps *V* accidentally, *D* is not blameworthy for *V*'s fall. But if *D* intended to kill *V* while making it look like an accident, we would say that *D* had a culpable mental state that proves the felony of assault with intent to kill.

As one would expect, the standard account of criminal liability thus states the conditions of blameworthiness: act, mens rea, harm (with harm understood as including the circumstances that give rise to harm). Stating an account of criminal blameworthiness is not enough. Because any double jeopardy project is ultimately about singularity, we need an account of how these elements combine to create singular or distinct blameworthiness. One place to begin that project is to focus on the singularity of acts, in effect returning to the nineteenth-century gravamen-of-offense test. As Susanah Mead described the test: "If the gravamen, or principal act, necessary to violate each statute was the same, then the offenses were the same for double jeopardy purposes."[5] The focus was on the "principal act" and thus on whether the two offenses manifested what I call "act singularity."

Act Singularity

In considering the role that "act" plays in criminal blameworthiness, we can safely ignore the controversial possibility that criminal liability can arise in the absence of an act, with act defined as a volitional movement.[6] These questions are important in substantive criminal law but not in formulating a basic account of when legislatively proscribed criminal blameworthiness should be considered distinct.

Action Theory: Act-Types and Act-Tokens

This chapter draws heavily from action theory, a metaphysical enterprise that seeks to state the conditions under which one act is distinct from another. This is a surprisingly difficult task, one that has given rise to a skeptical view of its utility. Recall Larry Simon's critique involving the number of "acts" contained in the "act" of shaving.[7] But, as Michael Moore has recognized, we should not dismiss action theory because it fails to provide self-evident answers.

Moreover, Simon's use of action theory confuses acts that exist in the world with blameworthy acts proscribed by the legislature. A double jeopardy theory does not need an account of when acts in the universe are distinct; it merely needs an account that determines how many legislatively proscribed acts have occurred. While this is not an easy task, it is easier than the metaphysical enterprise.

The necessary relationship between "act" and "offense" has for centuries been one of the irreducible principles in substantive criminal law. The common law has long held that criminal liability requires proof of a voluntary act that is proscribed by law.[8] The last sentence states two different kinds of act requirements. Proof of a voluntary act requires that an actor have committed a particular act at a certain time and in a certain place. The requirement that the act be proscribed by law is satisfied by showing that the particular act fits the act description contained in the criminal prohibition.

Action theory draws the same distinction between descriptions of acts, called universals or act-types, and particular acts in the world, called event-particulars or act-tokens. Act-types are found in statutory proscriptions. The offense of larceny consists, in part, of the act-type of taking and the act-type of carrying away. Each particular instance of an act-type is known as an act-token. The larceny at the Watergate Hotel was an act-token.

Some form of action theory is deeply embedded in existing judicial approaches to same offense. The form it takes may constitute bad metaphysics, as Moore occasionally charges,[9] but action theory is part of our intuition about blame and responsibility. For example, no one doubts that the statutory offense of larceny from a person is the same offense as the statutory offense of larceny from a person, as long as the same larceny (the same taking) underlies both charges. Right away, we see an action theory problem. What if the actor removed the victim's wallet and returned five minutes later to take his watch? Are there two takings, two offenses, or only one? Courts have struggled with this issue, as we see later, but at least they ask the right set of questions. Did the actor remove the wallet and watch by one "act" of larceny?

Courts have failed to see that action theory can also provide the answer to the equally difficult question of whether different statutory prohibitions define the same offense. Early courts struggled with the question of whether burglary and larceny are the same offense when the larceny is used to prove the requisite intent in burglary. This issue, superficially at least, looks different from two charges of larceny. In the burglary/larceny context, two statutory formulations exist and can be laid side by side. The difficulty, however, is the lack of a way of comparing the offense descriptions for "sameness." Courts, using a variety of analyses, eventually decided that burglary and larceny were not the same offense. But the real reason these offenses are not the same is that the burglary "ends" when the threshold is crossed; the larceny is therefore a subsequent and different act.[10]

Now compare the statutory offense of larceny from the person with that of larceny at night. There are two questions. First, are the statutory act-types the same? If so, are the different charges based on different act-tokens? Obviously, committing larceny from the person on Tuesday is a different offense from committing larceny at night on Friday. The reason is that different act-tokens occurred. Thus, whatever the relationship between statutory act-types, different act-tokens always render offenses different. This must be true because two act-tokens of the very same act-type are two offenses—for example, two robberies, two larcenies, two rapes.

Similarly, if the two statutory act-types are different, they proscribe different offenses, and we need not worry about whether separate act-tokens occurred. Rape is a different act-type from murder, and it should not matter (I later argue) that the act-token of rape also caused the victim's death (arguably the same act-token).

If, however, the statutory act-types are the same and only a single act-token of that act-type occurred, there is singular criminal blameworthiness and thus only one double jeopardy offense. Let us assume, for the moment, that larceny at night is the same act-type as larceny from a person. On that assumption, if a thief takes property from the victim's pocket at night, the account developed here presumes that it is one offense even though proscribed by different statutes. *Blockburger* presumes otherwise, because the distinct element in each larceny offense makes them different whether or not those distinct elements manifest blameworthiness.

Blockburger permits judges to answer the same-offense question without thinking about substantive sameness. It is a mechanical solution. The act-type that we call larceny could, by virtue of additional trivial descriptive elements, be held to be several different offenses. This seems wrong. If "offense" is a substantive concept, which it is in criminal law, it is a mystery why courts and commentators rely on mechanical tests to measure the double jeopardy sameness of different statutory offenses. Why not rely on a test of substantive sameness? Moreover, why not use the same analysis that helps sort out how many violations of a single larceny statute have occurred?

There is more work to be done. I must offer a way to determine what parts of a statutory crime are act-types; statutes often include circumstances and results, which must be kept separate from act-types when constructing the likely statutory blameworthiness. If all parts of a statute are blameworthy act-types, then my account would be indistinguishable from that in *Blockburger*. The next section offers a method of distinguishing act-types from circumstances and results.

Statutory Act-Types

Michael Moore develops a comprehensive theory of action in his excellent book, *Act and Crime*. Part of his insight is that act singularity is the best account of same offense. In my view, Moore's approach takes insufficient note of harm singularity, a point that I develop later in this chapter, but Moore is otherwise very helpful.

The difficulties in applying act singularity, while real, are manageable. Consider, for example, the aggravated first-degree murder offense of killing a police officer, which entails (1) an act (2) done with murder mens rea, (3) which results in the death (4) of someone who is a police officer. What is the proscribed act-type in this offense? The death can be described as a result, and the victim's status can be described as a circumstance. On the other hand, it is plausible to say that the act is killing a human being (murder is defined that way) and, from there, not incoherent to say that the proscribed statutory act is killing a human being who is a police officer.

The Model Penal Code distinguishes between conduct and what it calls "attendant circumstances" but offers no definition of either concept. Paul Robinson and Jane Grall criticize the Code for this omission and propose a narrow reading of "conduct" and thus a correspondingly broader definition of "result" and "circumstance." Under the Robinson-Grall approach, conduct is limited to "actual physical movement." The effect of this narrow formulation, as they recognize, is to make conduct "a relatively unspecific and unimportant aspect of an offense." Indeed, many acts are non-blameworthy, or much less blameworthy, when taken out of context of their circumstances or results.

For my purpose in measuring legislatively proscribed blameworthiness, I need a broader measure than "physical movement." Fortunately, I do not need to draw a precise line between acts and the context that makes the acts blameworthy. Rather, I need simply to identify which elements are arguably acts and then determine whether those elements create or add to blameworthiness. My goal is to distinguish between blameworthy act-types proscribed by statutes and other elements that (1) are clearly not act-types or (2) have little or nothing to do with blameworthiness.

We can apply this methodology to the aggravated murder statute as follows.[15] First, ask whether the status element is even arguably an act-type. If the answer is yes, the next question is whether it is a blameworthy act-type. Mens rea elements do not constitute act-types and can be disregarded at the first stage. To say that X does act A intentionally is to describe not A but X. It seems unlikely that the status of a victim is an act-type; the standard account of act excludes all properties that cannot be brought about by the actor. When X kills Y, X can do nothing by an act to bring about the property that Y is a police officer.

Assuming, arguendo, a nonstandard account of act that includes the victim's status, the next inquiry is whether status adds measurably to the blameworthiness that would be present without the element.[16] Any element that does not add to the blameworthiness is unlikely to have been considered blameworthy by the legislature. Removing the victim's status would leave killing a human being with murder mens rea. A useful way to approach the question of whether an element adds measurably to the proscribed blameworthiness is to apply Feinberg's harm principle. In a homicide, the wrongful setback to a person's interests occurs by being killed, not by being a police officer who is killed.

To be sure, the legislature created aggravated murder by naming a particular victim status, but the legislative purpose is presumably to deter this form of murder, or enhance the incapacitative effect, by increasing the penalty. It requires an unusual morality, or an unusual status, to find significantly more harm on the basis of the job classification of the victim.[17] Thus, the blameworthy act-type in the aggravated murder statute seems likely to be the killing of a human being, without regard to the status of the victim.

This produces the satisfying result that aggravated murder and nonaggravated murder proscribe the same blameworthy act-type (and thus the same offense); the victim's status as a police officer is not an act-type and, if it were, is not necessary to the blameworthiness. Tracking Blackstone, all homicide statutes proscribe the same blameworthy act-type.[18] This result is satisfying because, otherwise, we would be forced to say that killing a police officer entails two blameworthy act-types: killing and killing a police officer.

Michael Moore agrees that courts should disregard act-types that are not, in his words, "morally salient" when comparing act-types for double jeopardy identity. To use Moore's example, drunk driving, driving without a license, and driving an overweight vehicle all share the act-type of driving. As there is nothing about driving qua driving that is morally salient, there is no sameness of morally salient act-types in drunk driving, driving without a license, and so on.[19]

For a more difficult example, consider forcible rape and statutory rape. Forcible rape is typically defined as intercourse "against the will and without the consent" of the victim. Statutory rape is sex with a person younger than a certain age. A useful way of isolating the issues when comparing act-types is to subtract the blameworthy act-type that the two offenses have in common and then to look at each left-over element to see if it (1) is an act-type that (2) defines a Feinberg harm distinct from the common act-type.

The threshold problem in this example is deciding whether the offense descriptions have a blameworthy act-type in common. They obviously have sex in common, but sex qua sex is not blameworthy. Considered in the abstract, it is not a wrongful setback to anyone's interest. These offenses share the act-type of *wrongful* sex, which is presumably blameworthy but too general to be useful. In constructing the blameworthy act-type from the statutory language, the act-type must be made sufficiently precise to manifest the particular blameworthiness against which the statute is directed. In rape, the relevant blameworthiness is sex against the will of the victim; in statutory rape, the relevant blameworthiness is sex with an underage person. Using these descriptions as the blameworthy act-type, the two offenses have no blameworthy act-type in common and must be different offenses.

It can be argued that the age element in statutory rape is a proxy for lack of consent.[20] On this view, the blameworthy act-type is sex without consent in both statutory rape and forcible rape. While the argument is not without merit, it forfeits the benefits of using the legislative language to construct the act-type. Just as we should reject broadly defining the act-type as wrongful sex, we should also reject rewriting the statutory language in constructing the act-type. The legislative justification for statutory rape might be lack of capacity to consent, but what the legislature chose to proscribe is sex with an underage victim.

Treating rape and statutory rape as different act-types and thus different offenses seems right, viewed though the lens of probable legislative intent of the relevant harms. The actor who has forcible sex against the will and without the consent of an underage person has committed two harms simultaneously. The act-types should be construed to reflect these different harms.

A useful contrast is the *Blockburger* pair of offenses: selling narcotics not in or from the original package and selling narcotics not pursuant to a written order of the purchaser. If we could say that selling narcotics is an innocent activity, then the *Blockburger* offenses would be just like Moore's various driving offenses and my example about sex offenses. We would have to add to the innocent act-type the element that creates blameworthiness, which would in this case be the two circumstance elements (selling not from the original package and selling without a written order of the purchaser). Once we do that, of course, neither act-type is included in the other, which would endorse the Court's view that the offenses are different.

To support this interpretation, we might note that selling narcotics is not a mala in se offense and is not always prohibited by statute. Narcotics are sold every day in hospitals and pharmacies. But selling narcotics is qualitatively different from driving or having sex. The last two activities are lawful unless proscribed because of a dangerous or harmful way of doing the act-type. Selling narcotics, whatever its deontological moral status, has been unlawful in this country for decades unless expressly permitted. The difference is between lawful unless proscribed because of a circumstance and unlawful unless permitted because of a circumstance. This difference locates the blameworthiness in the act-type of selling narcotics, rather than in the circumstances attending the act-type, as was the case with the driving and sex offenses. On this reading, the blameworthy act-type is selling narcotics without statutory permission.

Moreover, the *Blockburger* narcotics offenses are unlike the driving or sex offenses because the additional elements in the narcotics offenses are not themselves blameworthy, as they are in Moore's driving example and my rape example. If selling narcotics is an innocent activity, it is difficult to conceive why it would be criminally blameworthy to sell narcotics not in the original package. It is not typically criminal to buy a package of items and sell the individual items from the package or to sell the package without a written order of the purchaser. In the driving offenses and the rape offenses, the additional elements are what create the blameworthiness. Not so in the *Blockburger* offenses.

Subtracting the blameworthy act-type of selling narcotics from each *Blockburger* offense leaves "not in or from the original stamped package" and "not pursuant to a written order." Neither of these residues is an act-type, nor are they blameworthy. There was, then, a single blameworthy act-type in *Blockburger*, which makes it less likely that Congress intended cumulative punishments.

On the account developed here, blameworthiness is singular when the criminal statutes define a single blameworthy act-type. One obvious and uncontroversial way that statutes can define a single blameworthy act-type is for a series of offenses to be arranged in a hierarchical manner depending on variations in mental state, result, or the scope of the act-type. This can be called "alternative" forms of blameworthiness—giving the prosecutor, judge, and jury a range of choices for a single conviction—rather than distinct blameworthiness that can be punished or prosecuted separately. The next section begins with these hierarchies and then expands the analysis to other, less obvious examples of when blameworthiness is alternative rather than distinct.

Alternative versus Distinct Blameworthiness

First-degree murder, second-degree murder, and manslaughter are usually defined so that the salient difference is the actor's mens rea. Adapting Model Penal Code terminology to the common-law homicide offenses and oversimplifying for ease of explanation, first-degree murder could require purpose, second-degree could require a knowing state of mind, and manslaughter only recklessness as to the risk. This sort of hierarchy naturally produces *Blockburger* included offenses—at least if one assumes, as the Model Penal Code does, that proof of a higher culpable state always proves the lesser.

As Scalia has noted, this kind of inclusion naturally gives rise to the same offense. Though Scalia seems to attribute this to the plain meaning of "same offense," my claim is different: in a mens rea hierarchy, the legislature is creating a set of alternatives for the prosecutor and the jury. The blameworthiness of first-degree murder is greater than that of manslaughter, creating a choice between these offenses without also creating distinct and cumulatively punishable offenses.

A hierarchical pattern can also be created by changing the result element. A legislature could proscribe assault, assault causing injury, assault causing severe injury, and assault causing death. Again assuming that proof of the more severe injury always proves all the less severe injuries, this is a hierarchical pattern.

Another inquiry awaits us. To say that murder is the same blameworthy act-type as manslaughter or that assault with intent to kill is the same blameworthy act-type as assault does not tell us whether robbery is the same blameworthy act-type as larceny. The question here is how to analyze act-type inclusion. This is a form of hierarchical blameworthiness in which what varies is the act-type itself, rather than mens rea or result elements.

The answer, again, is found in the best inference about legislative intent. Though Moore seeks to state a metaphysical account, rather than one based on legislative intent, he argues that "partial identity" of morally salient act-types makes offenses the same.[23] Partial identity of act-types presupposes conjunctive act-types. For example, the conjunctive act-type of robbery includes the act-type of larceny and the act-type of assault.[24] The principle can thus be stated as one of act-type inclusion rather than partial identity.

The philosophical difficulties with the notion of partial identity can be put to one side[25] because my project is not about metaphysical act identity. Thus, I do not need to defend the proposition that acts that are partially identical are nonetheless the same. But Moore's act-type inclusion states a good presumption about legislative intent. It is unlikely that the legislature meant to create distinct blameworthiness when a conjunctive act-type always includes two or more act-types. Robbery is a form of aggravated larceny, aggravated by the conjoined act-type of assault, a relationship that suggests that the legislature did not create distinct blameworthiness when it prohibited both robbery and larceny.[26]

As I discussed in chapter 2, the Court held in *Grady v. Corbin*[27] that the inclusion of act-types should be decided not as the statutes were written (the *Blockburger* approach) but as they are prosecuted (the *Grady* approach). Which approach is to be preferred on my legislative intent account? As Justice Holmes once said about a double jeopardy question, it is a short point.[28] The *Grady* approach probably achieves a fairer result in some cases. A friend who is a federal public defender steadfastly maintains it is unfair to allow the government to convict of both conspiracy and the planned substantive offense.[29] Surely, he argues, the liability for a serious substantive offense should include that for the planning stages.

Perhaps, but this is a criticism of conspiracy law,[30] rather than a prescription for same offense. The reason it seems unfair to punish both the conspiracy and the substantive offense, perhaps, is that it is unfair to punish the mere making of plans to commit crime in the future. We gloss over that unfairness when the conspiracy is the only harm the defendant commits, but it assumes more glaring import when the defendant proceeds to commit the planned harm.

More important, it is legal realism of the first magnitude to use unfairness as a synonym for double jeopardy. While a concern for fairness may partially explain the long history of double jeopardy prohibitions, the only way fairness manifests itself in a hard-edged view of double jeopardy is to prevent more than one jeopardy for the same offense.

In deciding the *Grady* inclusion question, we once again seek the best presumption about legislative intent. A legislature that criminalizes conspiracy almost certainly wants it punished separately from crimes committed pursuant to the conspiracy. The whole purpose of a conspiracy offense is to punish earlier stages of criminal activity. Why assume that this desire to punish somehow disappears when the criminal goes on to commit other crimes?

More generally, a legislature that proscribes distinct blameworthy acts in different offenses would intend these to be separately punishable. That the facts establishing an element in one offense could be used in some cases to prove the other offense is merely a coincidence. On the facts of *Grady*, the use of drunk driving to prove reckless manslaughter is a coincidence that does not affect the legislative intent to make these offenses cumulatively punishable. The actor has, after all, caused two harms: the risk creation associated with drunk driving and the realization of that risk in manslaughter. That they can be proved on the same evidence does not make them the same offense.

If the legislature wishes offenses to merge when they are proved by the same evidence, it can, of course, provide for that outcome. A vehicular homicide statute, for example, could provide that driving offenses merge into the homicide if used to prove it. A conspiracy statute could provide the same about planned substantive offenses. Lacking that evidence of intent, there is no merger, and the Court was thus right to reject *Grady*'s fine-grained act-type inclusion.

So far, I have identified three types of hierarchical relationships among offenses—they may vary by gravity of the mens rea, the severity of the harm caused, or the scope of the act-type proscribed. Blockburger treats hierarchical overlaps as creating a single offense. It is not a bad starting place for a definition of same offense, because it captures an important truth about distinct blameworthiness: if proving one offense always proves another, it is unlikely that the legislature meant to authorize both penalties. It is more likely, in the hierarchical context, that the legislative intent was to create a choice of offenses to allow a single conviction commensurate with the gravity of the blameworthiness shown in the particular case.

But hierarchical patterns are not the only way to infer that the legislature intended to create alternative, rather than distinct, blameworthiness. For example, the legislature might use different but nonincluded circumstance elements to create alternative ways of aggravating a basic offense. Consider larceny, an offense of ancient origin. If the legislature wished to create aggravated larceny offenses, it could do that by adding different aggravating circumstances—for example, larceny at night, larceny from the person, and grand larceny. It is unlikely that the legislature means each of these forms of aggravated larceny to be different from the others so that three convictions could result from a single larceny of valuable property at night from a person. (There is some question about grand larceny, which I take up later.) No natural hierarchy exists here, but the offenses share the larceny core and seem to be alternative ways of aggravating the basic offense of larceny.

In effect, this kind of alternative blameworthiness varies by the particular mode of how the offense is committed, rather than by the hierarchical gravity of offense (by mens rea or result). That blameworthiness can attain alternative status by mode of commission as well as by varying gravity explains why Blockburger produces counterintuitive results in some overlapping nonhierarchical offenses. Judge Rutledge saw this problem and rejected Blockburger as the only means of inquiry:

> [I]n some instances legislative refinement has defined generically identical offenses with narrow differences in intent or in the means or methods of perpetration, e.g., assault with various specific intents and with variously specified weapons. Some of these differences are substantial, others too slender for, in effect, nullifying the constitutional protection against double jeopardy. When they are so or the question is doubtful, the [same-offense analytical] step should be taken consciously and deliberately, not ignored or taken automatically as is done when the process stops with applying the [Blockburger] test.[31]

For one example of "slender" differences, the offense of diverting electric current is a different *Blockburger* offense from larceny because the former does not require intent permanently to deprive the owner of possession (and the latter obviously does not require that electricity be diverted).[32] But the best proof of *Blockburger*'s inadequacy is that sufficiently different ways of describing a single homicide are different offenses. The proposition is flawless if *Blockburger* tells us all we need to know about what makes offenses different. Felony murder, for example, requires proof of an underlying felony; premeditated murder requires proof of premeditation. Several state courts have rejected the *Blockburger* outcome in this context.[33] Others have mindlessly followed *Blockburger* and upheld two convictions for one killing. And why not? When the Supreme Court tells us confidently that *Blockburger* is the sole test of same offense, prosecutors can be excused for believing that the Court means it.

The courts that reject the *Blockburger* outcome are without an analytical tool and thus resort to fairness or common sense. The Colorado Supreme Court justified vacating one of the convictions because "[i]t would be a strange system of justice that would permit the defendant to be sentenced to two concurrent life sentences for the killing of one person."[34] The court cited an Alaska Supreme Court opinion in which the Alaska court said, "It would indeed be a strange system of justice that would allow . . . two life sentences for the killing of one person."[35] Two state courts solved the analytical problem by not offering any justification, instead flatly stating that a single death could not support two homicide convictions.[36] The Iowa Supreme Court reached the same conclusion, justified only by a citation to two legal encyclopedias.[37] One court seemed to rely on an implicit "same-act" kind of analysis, stating: "It is manifestly impossible to kill or slay one person twice."[38] Another court explicitly found a "same-act" limitation on murder convictions: "A defendant cannot be convicted of more than one murder arising out of the same physical act."[39] Several courts used a "surplusage" argument to avoid the issue—as long as the sentences are concurrent, the defendant has not been harmed, and no double punishment issue is presented.[40] The Supreme Court rejected this "concurrent-sentence" theory in 1985, and at least two state courts have also rejected the surplusage theory to hold that only one conviction can attend one killing.[41]

One court resorted to a due process analysis to avoid the *Blockburger* result: "conviction of both charges, arising from the slaying of the same person amounts to piling punishment upon punishment. Fundamental fairness precludes such a practice."[42] Later, the court limply said, "We think that point so obvious as not to need further comment."[43] The jurisprudential theory from these cases seems to be a rule that strange *Blockburger* results, those that are obviously wrong, are not acceptable. Needless to say, this is not a very ringing endorsement of *Blockburger*. How much easier, and more satisfying, to include this protection within double jeopardy by defining "offense" so that a single killing can lead to but one conviction.[44]

In the larceny hypothetical, it is highly doubtful that the legislature would intend larceny from a person to be punished in addition to larceny at night when a single act-token of larceny occurred, but *Blockburger* produces this result. A blameworthy act-type account, with its embedded harm singularity principle, gets it right here: the owner's interests are not wrongfully set back any differently because the property was taken at night than because it was taken from her person. Grand larceny is a harder question because the owner's interest suffers a greater setback when $500 is stolen that when five cents is stolen.

Of course, to say that the owner who loses $500 suffers a greater setback than one who loses five cents is not to say that the harm is *distinct*, only that it is *greater*. Understanding the difference between distinct blameworthiness and alternative blameworthiness is the point of this chapter. A sensible presumption would be that elements differing in quantity (of goods stolen, of drugs sold) are intended to create alternative blameworthiness, rather than distinct blameworthiness. Elements that differ in quantity seem to do the work of hierarchical grading, as in the laws of Aethelberht (ca. A.D. 600), when a single blow that pierced both cheeks was punished at twice the rate of the blow that pierced one cheek.[45]

To the extent there is doubt about whether the amount of money stolen creates alternative blameworthiness, two other analytical moves are available. First, an element must do more than manifest blameworthiness to count as part of the blameworthy act-type under my double jeopardy principle. It must also be an act-type. The amount of money taken by a single act-token of larceny is not likely to be included as part of the act-type. The act-type is taking property, with the value of that property a circumstance existing in the universe. If the actor takes a watch or a ring or a stack of bills, the dollar value is not part of what the actor is seeking to bring about, except in the most general sense that thieves want to steal property with greater, rather than lesser, value.

This, too, is not completely free from doubt. It is, after all, sometimes possible for the actor to bring about the property of how much is stolen (by taking a larger stack of bills, for example). Thus, a second analytical move resorts to a global presumption that the Court uses sporadically, called the "rule of lenity."[46] As the Court's terminology suggests, if doubt exists about whether the legislature meant to create distinct blameworthiness, courts should presume singular blameworthiness. If error is made, it should be made in the direction of finding fewer "units" of blameworthiness. At a minimum, the grand larceny value element raises doubt about whether it is a blameworthy act-type, and that doubt should be resolved in favor of singular blameworthiness.

If grand larceny and larceny at night define a single blameworthy act-type, and thus singular blameworthiness, then the narcotics offenses in *Blockburger* also define only a singular blameworthiness. This is not, of course, to say that the legislature somehow lacks the power to punish both narcotics offenses cumulatively (or the larceny offenses). Chapters 1 and 2 made clear my view on that question. Rather, it is to argue that when the legislature creates the same blameworthy act-type in more than one offense description, a single act-token of that blameworthy act-type should be presumed to manifest singular blameworthiness.

Defining Act-Token Separateness

Having offered a method of isolating statutory blameworthy act-types and comparing them for sameness, I must now offer an account of when act-tokens (discrete acts in the world) are separate. A little-noted part of *Blockburger* addressed the act-token issue with more success than the Court had with the issue of whether prohibiting one sale of narcotics with different attendant circumstances was two offenses of selling narcotics. Blockburger was convicted of two different narcotics offenses and also of two counts of one of those offenses. The two counts arose from the sale of two quantities of narcotics; when one transaction was done, the purchaser paid for another quantity, to be delivered the next day. The Court used Wharton's "impulse" test to decide that there were two offenses of selling: "when the impulse is single, but one indictment lies, no matter how long the action may continue. If successive impulses are separately given, even though all unite in swelling a common stream of action, separate indictments lie."[ ] While this basic notion is consistent with legislative intent, separating "impulses" is a difficult inquiry.

How many theft offenses did the legislature authorize when a thief steals two horses standing side by side? Does it matter if they have different owners? Does it matter if the horses are roped together so that the thief can steal them with one motion? If stealing two horses is two thefts, what about stealing a purse that contains one hundred different items? The act-token question turns in part on the question of how many harms have occurred. This requires an account of harm singularity, which the next section introduces.

Harm Singularity

Usually, when A acts to harm B, a single act-token causes a single harm. A murders B or robs B or steals B's wallet. It would be an easily stated rule if we could say that each act-token is a distinct double jeopardy harm and thus a separate offense. Michael Moore develops and defends this proposition. The defense is not without difficulties, however.

There are two basic sets of problems. First, a single act-token can cause multiple harms. If D strikes fifty persons with a single shot from a shotgun loaded with peas, Bishop found only one offense of battery, because occasioned by one volition (drawing a distinction between "one volition" and "one transaction").[ ] But Bishop acknowledged contrary authority, and a crude harm analysis would contend that because fifty persons are harmed, fifty batteries have occurred. In the Oklahoma City bombing, a single act-token of detonating a bomb killed 167 people. To insist that this is one murder offense because it is one "act" of murder seems wrong. Perhaps, then, courts should consider the distinctiveness of harms in a yet unspecified way when counting the number of offenses.

The other set of problems for action theory comes when multiple act-tokens occur. When act-tokens are distinct, the harms are often distinct as well. For an easy example, the robbery of six people sitting around a table is six offenses of robbery.[ ] Robbery is, of course, the same offense as robbery, but six act-tokens of robbery are six different offenses. Killing four victims with four separate shots is four offenses of homicide.[ ] Another example is larceny and burglary. Hale noted that they are "several offenses, tho committed at the same time. And burglary may be where there is no larceny, and larceny may be where there is no burglary."[ ] The act-token of larceny is distinct from that of burglary, and, by the same reasoning, the harm of the larceny is different from that of the burglary.

But multiple act-tokens sometimes seem to cause a singular harm as measured by Feinberg's harm principle. Taking two items from the top of a dresser with separate motions may be two act-tokens of taking but only one Feinberg harm. The owner's interests are wrongfully set back when the thief takes one item from the dresser; the second taking (or the tenth) seems cumulative rather than distinctive. Using a roughly similar theory, the Supreme Court held that multiple violations of the Fair Labor Standards Act are only a single offense (harm) for each type of violation.[ ]

Feinberg defines harm to include mens rea—A does not wrongfully harm B unless A is at least negligent with respect to the consequences threatened by his act. Notice, though, that mens rea has nothing to do with distinctiveness of the harm. The harm (as a noun) is the same whether A has one or several mental states concerning his act as he wrongs B. A may watch B eat poisoned food intending B's death, then expecting it, then hoping for it, then hoping against it (but knowing that it is likely), then hoping against it (and believing it unlikely). Multiple mental states do not multiply the harm. B's death or sickness from the poison is one death, one sickness, one harm.

In what follows, the "harm singularity" principle draws from Feinberg's definition of harm and thus focuses on the real-world effect of the act, circumstance, and mens rea. The harm singularity principle is that, unless the legislature speaks clearly to the contrary, the scope of the act-token that proves one (and only one) blameworthy act-type is coextensive with the harm proscribed by the act-type. The next section begins with the Court's most sensitive and sensible analysis of the harm/act-token issue.

The Relationship of Act-Tokens to Harms

Larry Simon is right that counting act-tokens in the world is unlikely to provide much guidance on the same-offense question. Shaving is one act-token or several act-tokens or many act-tokens, depending on how coarsely one defines the relevant act-type. But a double jeopardy account merely needs to be able to tell how many tokens of the statutory act-type have occurred. This can be done by careful reference to the statutory language, applying my harm singularity principle.

How many joyriding offenses is it to keep a car for nine days and drive it many times, as in *Brown v. Ohio*? Martin Friedland states that "[m]ost courts" uphold multiple convictions when each violation "is brought about by a different physical act."[53] But his authority for that statement is a case holding that a separate sentence may be imposed "where each offence charged in each count is separate and distinct."[54] Of course. What we need is a test for deciding when each offense is separate and distinct. The answer to that question in *Brown* is the number of times Brown committed the statutory act-type of joyriding. To answer that question requires understanding as precisely as possible the scope of the blameworthy act-type and the way act-tokens instantiate act-types.

The Scope of Act-Types

Brown v. Ohio not only raises and resolves in an appealing way many facets of the same offense problem but also provides hints of a profound conceptual double jeopardy universe. To begin, it seems right to say that a single taking and operation of a single car is a single offense. The same rule holds in England.[55] Yet Justice Blackmun dissented on the ground that Brown must have committed more than one driving episode during the nine days he kept the car. In effect, Justice Blackmun argued that regardless of the relationship between the act-types of auto theft and joyriding, Brown's liability for each act-type could be made to fasten on a different act-token.

Justice Blackmun's view that Brown's driving episodes were different act-tokens seems, at first blush, to make sense. The first and last episodes were probably separated by nine days. If Brown had stolen property on two separate days, we would have two act-tokens of larceny. Why would two driving episodes separated by nine days not be two act-tokens of joyriding?

The answer is that any distinction between act-tokens cannot be calculated until the scope of the statutory act-type is understood. The criminal taking of property from X is a different act-token (of whatever act-type) than a taking from Z. But taking Y's property and keeping it nine days would be only one act-token of larceny. Indirectly making this point, the Court in *Brown* noted that a different case would be presented if the statute made each day of joyriding a separate offense.[56] In the Court's hypothetical case, each day of possession is a separate statutory act-type, and each day of Brown's nine-day possession is a token of one of the act-types.

The act-type question is necessarily antecedent to the act-token question.[57] Justice Blackmun's common-sense view about driving episodes is commonsensical only if a single taking of a car instantiates more than one statutory act-type. Brown's taking is, on standard action theory, more than one act-type in the universe: starting the car, putting it in gear, driving it away, getting out, getting back in, driving, stopping, getting out, getting back in, driving, and so on. But, as I have been at pains to note, the double jeopardy same-offense question has nothing to do with metaphysical action theory and everything to do with the scope of the proscribed act-type. Thus, the crucial question is whether the *Brown* majority was right to find that both joyriding and auto theft proscribed a single act-type of taking a car. It is a more difficult question than the majority acknowledged, which is probably what drew Blackmun's dissent.

Counting Act-Tokens: The Act-Type Scope Issue

The joyriding statute in *Brown* used the verbs "take, operate, or keep" while the auto theft statute used "steal."[58] "Steal" implies that a single act-token of that act-type occurred, regardless of how long Brown had the car. Thus, for purposes of theft liability, only one act-token occurred.

"Take" and "keep" in the joyriding statute have the same scope as "steal." Once an actor has taken, kept, or stolen, there is no future act-token in continued possession or use of the property. "Operate" is murkier, perhaps lending itself to Blackmun's interpretation that each driving episode could be a separately punishable act-token. Since the joyriding act-type is stated in the alternative, "operate" could justify finding more than one act-token on the basis of separate operations. But the Court's rule of lenity might presume that when the legislature uses more than one act-type word to describe what is forbidden, the words should be understood, for purposes of counting act-tokens, as creating a conjunctive act-type.

The Court has long applied a rule of lenity in double jeopardy cases.[59] If a statute is somehow unclear how to count violations (the Court has never specified how this threshold lack of clarity is established), then the Court places a burden of clarity on Congress.[60] In the Court's words, there is a "policy of not attributing to Congress, in the enactment of criminal statutes, an intention to punish more severely than the language of its laws clearly imports in the light of pertinent legislative history."[61] When the statute proscribes alternative act-types, we can be sure we are not punishing in excess of legislative intent if we count only act-tokens of the conjunctive act-type, rather than act-tokens of any of the alternative act-types.

It is an old idea. In an early same-offense case in this country, the Court relied on a 1777 English case in which the court refused to count four sales of bread on Sunday as four violations of a statute that provided that "no tradesman or other person shall do or exercise any worldly labor, business, or work of their ordinary calling upon the Lord's day."[62] Each sale of bread could be an "exercise" of business, but the King's Bench indulged a more lenient construction, finding that the intent of Parliament was to penalize "exercising his ordinary trade on the Lord's day." On this construction of the scope of the act-type, the English court held that selling baked goods on Sunday could be committed only once per Sunday, regardless of how many sales occurred that one day. Otherwise, the court observed, "if a tailor sews on the Lord's day, every stitch he takes is a separate offence." Judges in 1777 appreciated the extraordinary number of act-tokens that can exist if the act-type is defined narrowly enough.

A skeptic might ask why the legislature bothered to define the act-type in the alternative if courts and scholars are going to collapse it into a conjunctive act-type. The answer, of course, requires paying attention to the context in which the question arises. Presumably the legislature created the act-type of "take, operate, or keep" to make certain that actors who did any one of them would be guilty of one count of joyriding. Obviously, Brown could not be convicted of three counts of joyriding on a charge that he took a car, or he operated it, or he kept it. Only one conviction can be entered here because of the nature of alternative act-types. More important, there is no reason to believe that the legislature wanted an actor convicted of three counts of joyriding if he took a car *and* he operated it *and* he kept it.

If that is the right way to read legislative intent, then it seems equally likely that the legislature did not intend to authorize multiple convictions if Brown operated the car more than once during the period he kept it. This demonstrates an important point for my account: counting act-tokens is different from asking if a single act-token has been committed. Whether an offense has been committed is different from when that offense ends and another begins. Though the relationship has never been stated this way, I think it uncontroversial to say that a single act-token can be proved on any of the alternative criminal act-types, but counting act-tokens requires that statutory alternative act-types be considered a conjunctive act-type.

On a conjunctive reading of the joyriding statute for purposes of counting act-tokens, the proscribed act-type is "take, operate, and keep." Brown committed only a single act-token of that act-type, supporting the majority's conclusion that the prosecution had attempted to "divid[e] a single crime into a series of temporal or spatial units." The legislature can make that division, the Court stated, but not the prosecutor. That, of course, is precisely my theory from chapters 1 and 2.

The value of a lenient approach to act-type construction can be seen in *Brown*. Blackmun's view of driving episodes as multiple joyriding offenses means that a defendant could be punished more severely for the misdemeanor of joyriding than for the felony of auto theft. A single taking could never be more than one token of theft as it is normally defined, but a defendant could receive many consecutive sentences for multiple driving episodes based on a single taking. This could not be what the Ohio legislature intended when it relegated joyriding to misdemeanor status.

Crimes that separate the act from the result, such as murder, are a special case of act-type/token relationship. The best example is *Diaz v. United States*,[95] where Diaz was convicted of assault, the victim died, and the government then prosecuted for homicide. Normally, the scope of the act-type of homicide includes the act-type of the assault that caused the killing, regardless of how long afterwards the victim dies. The question in *Diaz* is whether the verdict for assault somehow legally ended the part of the homicide act-type that included assault, in effect making the homicide a different act-token from assault.

Philosophers are split on whether killing is identical to the act that causes the death. Moore defends the coarse-grained view that the act of killing includes the result that the victim died.[96] This leads to problems: how can we say that V's death occurred several hours (or days) after V was killed? In the legal context, however, we can avoid philosophical difficulties. The legal liability for any act-token ends when it is manifested in a verdict, and future occurrences causally related to the earlier act must be a new legal act-token. As *Diaz* put it: "At the time of the trial for the [assault] the death had not ensued, and not until it did ensue was the homicide committed."[97] The Court thus affirmed the homicide conviction.

The last, and in many ways the most difficult, issue is how to count statutory violations when we unquestionably have multiple act-tokens of the statutory act-type but when one act-token may have "consumed" the blameworthiness of the act-type. One solution is to consider multiple act-tokens of the statutory act-type always to be multiple offenses, but this can produce counterintuitive results. For example, a prosecutor once filed 1,800 different informations for sales of beer in a single day; the statutory violation was selling beer without a certificate of inspection.[68] Though the beer seller has clearly committed 1,800 act-tokens of the act-type of "selling beer," it is not inevitably true that he has committed 1,800 violations of the *criminal offense of selling beer without a certificate*. That, after all, is the issue; when to presume that the legislature intended multiple, duplicative act-tokens to be counted as more than one violation.

Thus, the question is whether the legislature meant 1,800 act-tokens to count as 1,800 violations of the blameworthy act-type proscribed by statute.

Counting Act-Tokens: Consuming Blameworthiness

In 1937 Frank Horack wrote, "Carefully analyzed, there appears no obstacle, as a matter of substantive law, to the prosecution of each consequence of a criminal act."[69] If he meant that courts can, by looking hard enough, find a theory to support a conviction for each consequence, he is clearly right. But if he meant that the substantive law always contemplates a separate conviction for each consequence, then Horack is wrong. It seems beyond question that the Missouri legislature did not mean to authorize 1,800 convictions for sales of beer without a license if those sales took place in one day.

There are two questions about the relationship between act-type and act-token, and courts make a mistake when they do not see the difference in the questions. The first question, which is more familiar to courts, is whether at least one act-token of a particular act-type is made out on the state's evidence. If not, of course, no conviction can be entered or sustained. But the question of whether one act-token is made out on the facts proved is not the same as the question of how many act-tokens should be counted as violations of the statutory act-type. The first question is a minimum, sufficiency-of-the-evidence question. The second question is a counting question: yes, we have more than one act-token on these facts, but should we count all the act-tokens as statutory violations?

Courts have struggled with the counting question. In *Ebeling v. Morgan*,[70] the statute made it a crime to "tear, cut, or otherwise injure any mail bag . . . with intent to rob or steal any such mail."[71] Ebeling had cut into six mailbags in a single transaction. Unlike Brown's ongoing posession of the car, Ebeling's first act-token was complete when his knife reached the second mailbag. That the statutory act-token occurred six times does not, however, necessarily mean the legislature authorized counting all six act-tokens.

Insight into *Ebeling* can be gained by asking the question first posed by a student note in the 1907 Harvard Law Review: how many separate injuries has the state suffered?[72] This is a particularly insightful way to ask how many act-tokens the legislature meant to count. The student note applied the "injury-to-state" test to argue that only one theft occurs when someone steals goods belong to several different owners. "[I]t is clear that the state has been injured but once; and where there is only one transaction and one injury to the state, the offenses are identical."[73]

Suppose *J* plays seventy-five hands of poker in a state where it is a crime to "play a game in which money is bet." Convicted on the basis of playing one hand, he raises a double jeopardy objection to a new trial based on a different hand. These are different act-tokens of the act-type of playing a game in which money is bet, but it strains credulity to believe that the state is injured seventy-five times when consecutive games are played. Surely this is, as one commentator noted, a single "continuing injury."[74]

Stealing, from the same room, a purse and a watch that belong to different owners is a single larceny.[75] Bishop concluded that the better rule was that stealing any number of objects in one transaction was only one offense, regardless of the number of owners.[76] Now suppose *B* breaks and enters a mansion and then makes six trips into and out of the burgled structure as she steals goods from inside. *B* is obviously guilty of both larceny and burglary, but is she guilty of six burglaries? Any entry would constitute an act-token of burglary, but the additional entries do not add significantly to the blameworthiness manifested in the act-type of burglary and then consumed by the first entry. Stating it in Feinberg's terms, the second trip across the threshold does not constitute a separate wrongful setback to the victim's interests. The six trips do not appear to be separate "injuries" to the state. Stealing many goods from a mansion is grand larceny, but six convictions for burglary overshoot the blameworthiness mark.

The Court made precisely that mistake in *Ebeling*, assuming that the question of what constituted the first act-token is no different from the question of how best to count statutory violations. On that superficial understanding, Ebeling committed six statutory violations. The Supreme Court accordingly affirmed the six convictions and five consecutive maximum sentences imposed by the trial court, thus permitting a sentence five times longer than could have resulted from a single conviction.

Ebeling noted that congressional intent was "to protect each and every mail bag from felonious injury and mutilation," but this, too, misses the point of whether Congress intended multiple injuries in one transaction to be multiple offenses. Once the Court's category mistake is put to one side, a question still remains regarding Congress' intent. Phrasing the issue suggests the obvious: Congress surely had no intent at all about how many convictions should attend cutting six mailbags during a single transaction. So the real question is, What would Congress have answered had the question been put to it?

The rule of lenity is not particularly helpful in these cases because, even when recharacterized as a burden of clarity, it offers no useful principle of construction. In *Ebeling*, for example, can it be said that the "language" of the mailbag law "clearly imports" six penalties for six cuttings? Well, yes, on one reading. It is, as the Court noted, a crime to injure "any mail bag." But, on the other hand, Congress said nothing about how many penalties should attend multiple cuttings of mailbags in one location. So, on another reading, the language does not clearly import six penalties.

Without some principle to guide the rule of lenity, it is thus nothing more than an ad hoc rationalization for a decision reached on other grounds. The Court upheld the six penalties in *Ebeling*. The chance of upholding one hundred penalties under the same statute is very small. In this case, the Court would trot out the rule of lenity as the basis for its decision, but the real basis would be some rough intuition that one hundred penalties is just too harsh. What is needed to avoid ad hoc analysis is a principle that better gives voice to the intuition about the relationship between blameworthiness and the number of violations.

The best answer will reflect an understanding of how tokens manifest the blameworthiness created by the act-type. It will require an inventory of interests that are subject to wrongful setback. That task is beyond the scope of my present project—it would take a volume itself—but some tentative thoughts can advance the double jeopardy inquiry.

Consider a stack of one hundred one-dollar bills. How many larcenies occur when those bills are stolen by one hundred takings in rapid succession? Is the blameworthiness in this case different from that in stealing one hundred bills in a single taking? In a metaphysical sense, the multiplicity of takings (or blows given in a fight) multiplies the number of act-tokens and moral wrongs committed.

To conclude that each morally wrong act-token should always be counted as a separate criminal violation is to conclude that act-token individuation tells us all we need to know about same offense. But it does not, as Moore seems to concede.[80] The number of bills taken may make no difference. The legislature may think in terms of cohesion of result rather than fragmentation into separate act-tokens when the very same act-token is repeated, with the same goal in mind, within a short time span. Taking one hundred one-dollar bills in a single motion is indistinguishable from taking one one-hundred-dollar bill. Why should the blameworthiness differ if the actor takes the one hundred one-dollar bills in two motions? In ten? In one hundred?[81]

If stealing one hundred bills can be counted as a single larceny regardless of the number of takings, the number of mail bags *Ebeling* cut may not tell us how many offenses he committed. His intent may be more important than the number of act-tokens. The actor's objective is one way of gauging the singularity of harm. The actor who intends to take all one hundred bills has done as much harm with one taking as with one hundred.

The thefts of X's horse from one pasture and of Z's horse from a pasture ten miles away are two larcenies, at least in part because we infer an intent to deprive two owners of their property. But stealing a saddled horse is one larceny, not one larceny of a horse and one of a saddle, at least in part because the intent was to steal a saddled horse. Similarly, stealing a purse is one larceny, not a different larceny for each object in the purse.[82] Moore rejects individuating offenses by intent, but, in these cases, his action theory reaches the same result. "This is because defendants often do just the wrongs they intend to do, in which case the same intent test individuates identically with wrong-relative individuation."[83]

But consider stealing two of X's horses standing a few feet apart. Though there are two act-tokens of larceny here, it could be counted a single larceny as long as the thief had the "single intent" to steal X's horses.[84] This is similar to the Court's "single impulse" analysis from *Blockburger*.[85] Action theory is an unsatisfying way to approach these unusual cases. Stealing a gym bag with the intent to deprive two people of their property would be two larcenies, in my view, despite the single taking.[86] Stealing one hundred one-dollar bills by one hundred takings would, on the other hand, be a single larceny if the thief had formed the intent to steal all one hundred prior to taking the first one.

The offense gravamen of the mail bag statute in *Ebeling* was not merely cutting mailbags, but cutting mailbags "with intent to rob or steal any such mail." One may thus infer that Congress' principal concern was to protect the contents of the mailbags, rather than the canvas bags themselves. If this is right, then why does it make a difference in blameworthiness that six mailbags were cut? Stealing the contents of six mailbags would be one larceny. If it is, then why should it matter that the statute forbade cutting as well as stealing? Ebeling would be guilty of only one offense if he cut into a giant mailbag that contained as much mail as six regular bags. Again, it is unclear why the result should be different just because he made six cutting motions.[87]

Justice Holmes came to see the issue in this light. In an earlier case, he had followed *Ebeling* in holding that each act of putting a letter in the mail was a separate fraud violation, even though only a single scheme was involved.[88] In that case, Holmes commented, "[T]here is no doubt that the law may make each putting of a letter into the postoffice a separate offense."[89] Of course, but that merely restates the issue: did Congress intend that each letter put into the mail, as part of a single scheme, be counted as a separate violation? Holmes, following *Ebeling*, did not seem to think that these were different questions.

More than a decade later, in *United States v. Adams*,[90] Holmes saw the difference. Adams had made two false entries in bank books, both relating to a single deposit and credit. The government prosecuted the false entries successively, as separate violations of the offense of making a false entry with intent to injure or defraud the bank. "It is a short point," Holmes commented.

> The Government contends for the most literal reading of the words, and that every such entry is a separate offense to be separately punishable. But we think that it cannot have been contemplated that the mere multiplication of entries, all to the same point and with a single intent, should multiply the punishment in proportion to the complexity of the bookkeeping.[91]

To ask whether the literal reading was "contemplated" is to seek congressional intent. Holmes's rejection of "multiply[ing] the punishment in proportion to the complexity of the bookkeeping" shows that his benchmark for inferring legislative intent was the blameworthiness of the sequence of act-tokens. Holmes thus stated a version of my principle of consuming blameworthiness. The first false entry, in effect, consumed the blameworthiness of the second entry done with the same intent and with respect to the same deposit.

Using intent to help individuate double jeopardy offense explains why it is a single offense to take two women across state lines in a single vehicle in violation of the Mann Act.[92] On Moore's account, this would be two act-types of violating the Mann Act, one for each victim. Individuation by intent explains why the Court held thirty-two counts under the Fair Labor Standards Act to state but three offenses; the Court treated "as one offense all violations that arise from that singleness of thought, purpose or action, which may be deemed a single 'impulse.'"[93] At a minimum, Moore's action theory suggests eleven violations because eleven employee-victims were named; perhaps he would find thirty-two violations because of the thirty-two act-tokens of the various act-types involving minimum wage, overtime, and record-keeping.

To this point, the harm singularity principle has supplemented action theory as a way of gleaning legislative intent (1) on what constitutes one act-token of a statutory act-type and (2) in cases in which the legislature may intend to authorize only a single criminal violation even though multiple act-tokens of the statutory act-type have occurred.

The last act-token issue arises when there is only one act-token but multiple harms. The harm singularity principle is useful here as well.

Single Act-Token Blameworthiness

Moore claims that the results of the state cases involving single act-tokens and multiple harms are a "checkerboard" that reveal "conceptual confusion."[94] As an example, Moore identifies the following set of results that are the majority rule. First, two murders result when Smith kills Jones and Long with one shot from a powerful gun; Moore posits that Smith intends to kill Jones and is silent about Smith's mens rea with respect to Long. Second, only one homicide offense occurs when Smith kills both Jones and Long while possessing a negligent mens rea as to Jones and no criminal mens rea as to Long. Third, only one larceny is committed when Smith steals a bag containing property belonging to both Jones and Long.

Moore is right, given his premises. These results are conceptually confusing if one seeks to find the answers in act metaphysics, as Moore does. If one individuates act-tokens by the number of victims, each of these examples is two offenses; if, on the other hand, one believes that the act of killing includes the result that the victim dies—as Moore does—then each of these examples is but one act-token and can be only one offense using traditional action theory.[95] What act metaphysics does not permit is the result that courts reach: sometimes there are two offenses and sometimes one.

Moore's coarse-grained individuation defines act-token by what the actor does and not by the consequences, "no matter how numerous the bad consequences."[96] Without another principle, he would be compelled to say that only one offense occurs in each of his sample cases because there is only one act-token. If murder is a single act-type, this would lead Moore to conclude that only a single homicide occurred in each case where there was a single token, and the same with the larceny hypothetical.[97] But, Moore argues that morality here is victim-relative as well as agent-relative. Thus, the act-type of killing Jones must be understood as different from the act-type of killing Long; indeed, an act-type of killing exists for every human who lives in the jurisdiction. On this view, the killing of two people by one act would be not two separate act-tokens but two separate act-types.[98]

While this seems right, it creates problems of its own because it commits Moore to say that eighty-four homicides occur whenever eighty-four victims are killed as a result of a single negligent act-token.[99] Would this be the right answer if the actor was reasonably unaware of the presence of eighty-three of those eighty-four victims? Rejecting act metaphysics in the context of multiple-consequence cases makes it possible to consider what Moore expressly puts aside: "culpability measurement in double jeopardy contexts."[100]

If we reject act metaphysics as the sole guide to individuating offenses, we are free to consider the actor's mens rea as to the unintended victims. So, for example, where Smith intends to kill Jones and also kills Long, we would need to know Smith's mens rea as to Long. In all likelihood, Smith would be acting either knowingly or recklessly with depraved indifference concerning Long. Firing a powerful gun with other people in the vicinity seems at least reckless, and depraved indifference is implicit in Smith's intent to kill Jones. Thus, those courts that find two counts of murder here are right, but not because there are two act-types of murder (the act-type of murdering Jones and the act-type of murdering Long), which is Moore's solution. Nor is it true that the presence of two dead bodies (two consequences) justifies this outcome. There are two bad consequences, to be sure, but Smith is criminally liable only for those outcomes that he causes with the requisite mens rea.

The real reason two murders occur here is that the violations of the act-type of murder should be individuated by Smith's mens rea. If Smith has murderous intent toward both Jones and Long, there are two murders. This seems right. Why should bringing about two deaths with murderous mens rea be treated differently depending on whether it took two shots or only one? On the other hand, if Smith is reasonably unaware of the presence of other humans when he shoots Jones, there is only one murder because only one killing with criminal mens rea.

In the second homicide case, Moore expressly posits that Smith is negligent with respect to Jones but not to Long.[101] On my account, courts are right to consider this only one homicide offense because Smith violated the homicide statute but once. Though Smith is not negligent with respect to Long, by definition, Moore nonetheless claims that Smith "negligently or recklessly kills" Long.[102] How can this be? Moore would convict Smith of the act-type of Long's manslaughter when he did not have the mens rea required for manslaughter. This result, by itself, is good reason to eschew action theory in these unusual cases.

A mens rea solution seems implicit in the notion of legality and statutory construction. The question is how many times Smith has violated the murder statute. To answer this question, we simply apply the homicide statute to Jones' death and then to Long's death. If Smith had no mens rea as to the death of Long, he would have violated the terms of the homicide statute only once. Indeed, Moore's assertion that Smith has done more wrong here is puzzling. More harm has occurred, but how is Smith criminally liable for it? If Smith is liable for Long's death because the bullet passed through Jones, presumably Smith would be liable when his bullet passed through a target. But as long as Smith lacks mens rea in the target case, he is not criminally liable. Why should this result change when the bullet passes through Jones rather than a target? Moore offers no reason to treat these cases differently.

The only problem with the way courts analyze these cases is the assumption that each dead body is a separate harm. Moore is right that this analytic manuever, in effect, introduces a third measure of wrongdoing—the number of harmful consequences—in addition to counting the number of wrongful act-types and the number of times each act type occurred (the act-token question). Moore argues that this manuever is incoherent because the degree of wrongfulness of Smith's action is "fixed once we admit he did one wrong of a certain significance, once."[103] Courts are sometimes guilty of this incoherence.[104]

Despite our agreements on some points, Moore will likely think me guilty of bad metaphysics for mixing harm, action theory, and mens rea to individuate blameworthiness. But I remain convinced that this approach is the only one that treats the statutory language with the respect that it must have—harms are multiple only when the actor had the requisite statutory mens rea as to each consequence. Once we clarify the harm category, by adopting Feinberg's terminology and individuating by intent, the harm manuever is both coherent and compelled by my legislative prerogative account of double jeopardy.

The answer to the larceny case follows from the homicide cases. If Smith does not know that the bag contains the property of two people—the typical case in which courts apply the "single larceny" rule—he has committed one larceny. But if Smith knows who owns the property in the bag and intends to take the property of two people, he has committed two larcenies. The legislature made the taking of the property of another a crime when the actor intends to deprive the owner permanently of possession; two offenses occur when Smith takes property with that intent as to two owners.

Moore's victim-relative morality and coarse-grained individuation of act-tokens lead him to say that two thefts always occur when a thief steals a gym bag containing the property of two persons.[105] This seems counterintuitive; Bishop argued that the "better legal reason" supports finding only one offense when property belonging to two owners is stolen at one time,[106] and I think Bishop is right when the actor lacks intent to steal from two owners. The history of larceny, defined as a crime rather than a tort, has focused on punishing the infringement of ownership and not on restitution of a particular owner.[107] If infringement on individual ownership were crucial to the legislative scheme for defining larceny, as Moore's victim-relative morality requires, restitution would be a crucial remedy; it is not. Moore's view commits him to find one million larcenies in the theft of a truck carrying one million checks, each made payable to a different person.[108]

But courts who treat all "single larceny" cases the same way, irrespective of Smith's knowledge of the multiple ownership, are also missing the point. Why treat a single taking where Smith knows of the multiple ownership differently from one in which Smith opens the locker of Jones and then the locker of Long to steal their property? Why should the singularity of act make a difference when the intent is so clearly multiple? Act metaphysics are not helpful in these cases.

To be sure, individuating act-types by moral wrongs usually mirrors legislative thought on the singularity of offenses. Moore deserves credit for this powerful insight. But on a legislative-intent account of same offense, it is a mistake to ignore the mens rea of the individual offender. When a single act-token of one proscribed act-type causes multiple consequences, the best solution is to individuate by the defendant's culpability. As long as this is understood to mean comparing the defendant's mens rea to that of the statute,[109] it is exactly right. Courts go off the track when they look for answers in the metaphysics of culpability—for example, trying to determine when more than one statutory violation is incident to a "single objective."[110]

Moore properly rejects the "single intent" test when applied as a substitute for act-individuation.[111] A series of shots is not a single act because motivated by a single intent.[112] Three sales of narcotics to three different buyers on three different days is not a single act because made pursuant to a single intent.[113] On the account offered here, mens rea is relevant only after act-individuation has produced the equation "single blameworthy act caused multiple consequences." At that stage, carefully applying the statutory mens rea sometimes produces the answer that the actor has violated the statute once and sometimes that he has violated it more than once.

On this understanding, the distinctiveness of harm provides the answer both to the single-act-token/multiple-harm question and to the multiple-act-token/consuming-blameworthiness question. This seems right. When writing criminal statutes, legislatures consider the nature and distinctiveness of the harm done. That is why joyriding and cohabitation are defined to include a broad time period, while crimes of violence focus on the narrow act causing harm—rape requires penetration, murder requires killing, and battery requires touching.

The distinctiveness of harm caused by the defendant's act-token is, therefore, the best principle to use when seeking legislative intent about how many act-tokens to count as criminal violations or how many criminal violations to ascribe to a single act-token.

A Procedural Defense of Chapter 5

Determining whether one blameworthy act-type is included in another provides the best presumption about legislative intent to create singular blameworthiness in the difficult category of cases when there is no natural hierarchy of mens rea or results. I cannot catalog every conceivable pair of act-types to demonstrate the intuitive force of my argument. Moreover, the account of presumed legislative intent that counts only one violation despite multiple act-tokens of the statutory act-type leaves much room for courts to decide cases as they please. Lacking a comprehensive substantive defense of my concept of singular blameworthiness, I offer instead a procedural defense that follows from chapters 1 and 2.

The blameworthiness principle is nothing more than an inference about legislative intent, and it can always be rebutted by clear intent. If a court applied a blameworthy-act principle to find two statutory offenses to be the same, for example, and the legislature did not intend that result, clarifying legislation could easily be passed to replace the inference of intent with actual intent. Congress did precisely that in 1984 in reaction to the Supreme Court's lenient interpretation of congressional intent concerning the application of the federal felony-firearm statute.[114]

6

Bringing Coherence to
Same-Offense Doctrine

So far I have developed an account that draws an equivalence between same-offense and singular criminal law blameworthiness. The argument is that, for purposes of the Double Jeopardy Clause, offense means the unit of blameworthiness the legislature intends to receive a single criminal ("life or limb") penalty. This singularity can be manifested in a single act-type description that is violated once (with one violation sometimes including more than one act-token) or as the same blameworthy act-type described in more than one statute.

Act-types can thus be the same in two ways: literally the same (which leads to a violation counting problem) or constructively the same (which requires a court to decide, for example, that auto theft and joyriding proscribe the same blameworthy act-type). In constructing a blameworthy act-type, Feinberg's harm principle provides guidance in determining when an act-type element is part of the proscribed blameworthiness. Counting act-tokens is more difficult, but it, too, can be understood by comparing the proscribed blameworthiness to the Feinberg harm caused by the actor.

A blameworthy-act presumption of sameness is a relatively hard-edged rule. When the edges are "soft" compared to *Blockburger*, it is because the blameworthy act-type or act-token question requires courts to think about what the legislature meant to proscribe as a criminal offense. But this is a useful form of indeterminacy. After all, the most determinate rule for same offense is also the most objectionable: first-degree premeditated murder is the same offense as first-degree premeditated murder, and nothing else.

Moreover, as this chapter demonstrates, a blameworthy-act presumption provides a set of outcomes that is closely linked with double jeopardy policies. A place to start is an overview of the doctrinal complexities that have bedeviled the Court's attempt to bring coherence to the same offense question.

A Summary of Blockburger's Failure

Blockburger is the only test that is a plausible alternative to one based somehow on blameworthy acts.[1] *Blockburger* is similar to a blameworthy act test in three ways. First, it compares offense elements, rather than the conduct used to prove offenses. Second, it finds offenses the same if the relevant elements of one are identical to, or included in, the elements of another. Third, at least when applied to the multiple punishment (single-trial) issue, *Blockburger* states a presumption about legislative intent that can be (and in some cases has been) rebutted by contrary legislative intent.

Blockburger is different from my proposed test in two ways. First, the presumption created by a legislative-prerogative test applies equally to single trials and successive prosecutions, while the Court has never hinted that *Blockburger* can be rebutted when successive prosecutions are involved.[2] Second, *Blockburger* reads the relevant offense broadly to include all statutory elements, rather than just blameworthy act-types.

The conceptual difficulty inherent in the *Blockburger* solution has already been explored. In sum, it is that any element (the attendant circumstance of whether the actus reus took place at night, for example) can suffice to create different substantive criminal offenses. But it is unlikely that the legislature meant burglary in the first degree (burglary at night) to be punished in addition to burglary in the second degree (burglary of a commercial building) when a single burglary violates both statutes.

As an early commentator aptly noted, under a *Blockburger*-style test, "an overzealous prosecuting attorney can, by assiduously using his Thesaurus and statute-book and continually redefining the crime, each time requiring slightly different criminal elements, secure repeated convictions for the same offense."[3] Many commentators have recognized that trivial differences in statutes should not create different double jeopardy offenses.[4] Where these efforts have been unavailing is in developing some way to distinguish what differences should count. Some early courts, and later commentators, adopted a "gravamen of offense" test, seeking to identify the core or gist of the offense and to compare those core definitions.[5] William Haddad and David Mullock, for example, argued that the "relevant inquiry should not be whether an additional fact is required in the second prosecution but whether a *materially* different fact, enough to make a truly different offense, must be shown."[6] Otto Kirchheimer argued that the proper question was whether each statute was directed at the same harm or evil.[7] At least two law student writers argued that same offense required only "substantial identity" between offenses.[8] While these verbal formulations are not wrong, they are too soft-edged to be doctrinally helpful.

If these commentators and early courts are right that some elements are to be disregarded in comparing statutory elements for double jeopardy "sameness," two satisfying divisions can be made. First, one can distinguish between elements that are act-types and those that are not act-types; differences in the former but not in the latter imply legislative intent to create distinct criminal blameworthiness. Premeditated murder is a different *Blockburger* offense from felony murder because each requires a different way of proving mens rea, but mens rea is not part of the act-type. Ignoring that difference produces the Blackstone result that a single killing is a single offense of homicide. On the other hand, rape is a different act-type from murder, suggesting (as I show later) that the Court was wrong to hold that they can be the same offense.[9]

The second satisfying distinction that can be made is between elements that manifest criminal blameworthiness and those that do not. Assaulting a federal officer would be a different *Blockburger* offense from assault with intent to kill. If the federal-officer element is a means of asserting jurisdiction, it would not be an element that manifested blameworthiness. Ignoring that element, along with the mens rea in the assault with intent to kill, produces identity between the act-type of assault and the act-type of assault. That result corresponds with my intuition about likely legislative intent.

To signal both of these distinctions, the test proposed here distinguishes between "blameworthy act-types" proscribed by statutes and the other elements that make up offenses but are either not blameworthy or not act-types. Limiting the included-element test to blameworthy act-types produces results that are intuitively appealing and more in accord with likely legislative intent.

Chapter 1 argued that there is value in having a hard-edged rule, and *Blockburger* is a relatively hard-edged rule. It does not require potentially complex decisions about whether a statutory element is an act-type or whether it is blameworthy. Of course, a hard-edged rule is only as good as the set of results it produces, and *Blockburger* is defective on that score.

Surprisingly, *Blockburger* is not as easy to apply to modern criminal statutes as the examples so far may indicate. Courts sometimes fail to realize or correctly apply what may be called the *Blockburger* "double distinction"—*each* statute must require an element that the other does not. If only one statute requires a distinct element, then of course the other statute is a necessarily-included offense. While this seems simple enough, courts do make mistakes in dealing with complex statutes.

In *American Tobacco Company v. United States*,[10] for example, the Court noted only one *Blockburger* distinction when holding that conspiracy to monopolize defined a different offense, under the Sherman Act, from conspiracy in restraint of trade. The Court noted that a conspiracy in restraint of trade "may stop short of monopoly, and the other conspiracy to monopolize . . . may not be content with restraint short of monopoly."[11] While this might have seemed to the Court to state a *Blockburger* double distinction, a moment's reflection discloses that the Court merely says twice that monopoly requires more than restraint. The Court never commented on how restraint of trade requires anything different from monopoly. If it does not, then the goal of restraint of trade is included within the goal of monopoly, and these conspiracies would be the same under *Blockburger*.

An example of the complexity of applying *Blockburger* to a series of state crimes is *State v. Preciose*. The prosecutor charged twenty-three counts arising out of a break-in, the robbery of four occupants, and the sexual assault of one.[12] On this summary of the facts, we would be entitled to think that Preciose committed six crimes: burglary, four counts of robbery, and one count of sexual assault. Given the possibility that the occupants were restrained beyond the time necessary for the commission of the robbery and the sexual assault, we might contemplate one count (perhaps four counts) of false imprisonment. But that is a total of seven, perhaps ten, counts. How did the state manage to turn this criminal episode into twenty-three counts? The answer: offense inflation. The proliferation of ever narrower and more specific criminal offenses gives prosecutors more charging discretion. There is nothing wrong with narrowly defined specific crimes or charging discretion as long as the Double Jeopardy Clause provides a meaningful limit on the number of convictions. But *Blockburger* does not function well on the facts of *Preciose*.

The first two counts were theft and receiving stolen property;[13] the Supreme Court has held that similar federal statutes are the same offense if based on the same act-token of taking/receiving,[14] and the result would likely be the same under the New Jersey statutes. Count three was burglary, which has long been held different from any crime committed inside the structure, a result reached under both *Blockburger* and a blameworthiness account (the blameworthy act-type of burglary—entering— is different from any proscribed act-type that the burglar does inside the structure).

Count four was unlawful possession of a weapon, and count five was possession of a weapon for an unlawful purpose. Though it is an irresistible conclusion that the legislature did not mean these almost-identical offenses to give rise to two convictions for the same possession, *Blockburger* permits two convictions. Unlawful possession requires possession "under circumstances not manifestly appropriate for such lawful uses as it may have," while possession for an unlawful purpose requires possession with a purpose to use the weapon unlawfully. It is possible to possess a gun with intent to use it (later) unlawfully, without possessing it "under circumstances not manifestly appropriate for such lawful uses as it may have." One might have a hunting rifle over one's fireplace and intend later to use it unlawfully, which appears to violate only the unlawful purpose statute. Thus, it seems that counts four and five pass muster under *Blockburger*.

Counts six through nine are criminal restraint. Criminal restraint is clearly a different offense under *Blockburger* from any of the previous five offenses. It might seem, superficially, that a potential counting problem exists here. It is easy to see that robbing four victims is four act-tokens of robbery, but is it four counts of criminal restraint to restrain four people? It might be only a single violation because a single act-token can constitute restraint of more than one person, while different robberies usually require different act-tokens.

But different robberies do not always require different act-tokens. Suppose the poker-game robbery in *Ashe v. Swenson*[15] involved taking the pot of money in the center of the table, which contained the money of all five players. Is this one robbery or five? On my account, the answer is the same as that in the single larceny cases: we must individuate by mens rea in cases where a single act-token causes harm to multiple victims. If the robber intends to rob all five players, the single act-token of taking the money in the center of the table will support five robbery convictions. Nice questions may arise about what the robber did or should infer about the ownership of the money in the center of the table, but these are questions of application and not theory.

If a single act-token of taking property can be multiple robberies, then a single act-token of locking the door can be multiple counts of criminal restraint. The question is one of mens rea. If Preciose intended to restrain all four victims, he is guilty of four counts. If he intended to restrain only one of the people and, for example, did not know the others were in the room, he should be guilty of only one act-token of criminal restraint. In all likelihood, he intended to restain all of the victims as part of the robberies or the sexual assault. Even if he restrained three of the people to enable him sexually to assault the fourth, he still intended their restraint.

Counts ten through twelve were "terroristic threats," an offense that proscribes threatening a crime of violence "with purpose to terrorize another." This, too, is clearly a different *Blockburger* offense from anything charged so far. Counts thirteen through fifteen were armed robbery. Count sixteen was attempted armed robbery. Armed robbery as defined in New Jersey requires theft, plus being armed with a deadly weapon, plus an aggravating element. Six aggravating elements are set out in the statute: the actor (1) inflicts bodily injury, (2) uses force upon another, (3) threatens bodily injury, (4) purposely puts another in fear of bodily injury, (5) commits any crime of the first or second degree and (6) threatens immediately to commit any crime of the first or second degree.

Three counts of armed robbery and one of attempted armed robbery can stand under generally accepted counting principles because each count involves a different victim. But some of the offenses discussed earlier begin to drop out here. Presumably armed robbery (which requires being armed with a deadly weapon) includes possession of a weapon with the purpose to use it unlawfully, as well as possession of a weapon under "circumstances not manifestly appropriate for such lawful uses as it may have." Thus, the robbery convictions appear to knock out both weapons possession convictions, even under *Blockburger*.

But not criminal restraint. Because criminal restraint requires restraint, which robbery does not, and robbery can be committed by theft with injury, neither is included in the other. A person is guilty of robbery in New Jersey if he picks the victim's pocket and, in so doing, inadvertently injures the victim. No restraint need be shown. Thus, the four charges of criminal restraint are different from the robbery charges. The same analysis obviously governs attempted armed robbery. Nor do the convictions for making "terroristic threats" constitute the same offense under *Blockburger* as armed robbery. Armed robbery does not require a threat. Making terroristic threats does not require a theft.

Counts seventeen through nineteen were for aggravated assault, which might logically seem to follow the relationship between common-law assault and common-law robbery and thus be included in the armed robbery. But it is not. Aggravated assault requires an element not required for armed robbery—that serious bodily injury be attempted or caused.[16] Armed robbery is satisfied if bodily injury is threatened or caused and, indeed, does not require bodily injury at all; the mere use of force can prove armed robbery. Thus, three convictions of aggravated assault could stand along with the armed robbery and criminal restraint.

Count twenty was aggravated assault with a deadly weapon. It, too, is separate from robbery. But consider an even more bizarre possibility: as defined in New Jersey, aggravated assault with a deadly weapon is a different *Blockburger* offense from aggravated assault. The former requires proof of harm attempted or caused by a deadly weapon, which the latter does not require, while the basic aggravated assault requires that the harm attempted or caused be *serious* bodily harm. A prosecutor who really wanted to overcharge could have charged four counts of aggravated assault and four counts of aggravated assault with a deadly weapon. If the jury found that the defendant caused serious bodily harm with a dangerous weapon, it could find him guilty on all eight counts.

Counts twenty-one and twenty-two were two descriptions of aggravated sexual assault. In the first, the aggravating factor is that the act was committed during commission of another serious crime (which makes this type of sexual assault an analog to felony murder); in the second description, the aggravating factor was that the actor was armed with a weapon. Because the crimes that trigger count twenty-one sexual assault are not limited to crimes requiring a weapon, these two descriptions of aggravated sexual assault are different under *Blockburger*. Proof of the count twenty-one sexual assault requires proof of a crime, which could be burglary, while the count twenty-two sexual assault requires proof that the actor was armed with a weapon.

Finally, count twenty-three was aggravated criminal sexual contact. Sexual contact is the touching of the victim's intimate parts, which include inner thigh, groin, and breast. Sexual assault requires sexual penetration (vaginal or anal intercourse, cunnilingus, fellatio, or the insertion of the hand, finger, or object into the anus or vagina). Sexual contact thus requires an element that sexual assault does not require (touching of intimate parts is defined more broadly than vagina, anus, and mouth), and sexual assault requires an element not required by sexual contact (penetration). The conviction of aggravated criminal sexual contact can, therefore, stand alongside the two convictions of aggravated sexual assault even if all three are based on a single act-token (e.g., vaginal penetration).

In case the reader has lost count, the score under *Blockburger* is twenty of twenty-three convictions sustained (the two weapons offenses are eliminated as included within the robbery counts, and receiving stolen property is included in theft). These twenty convictions are based on entering the structure, sexual assault, four act-tokens of the act-type of armed robbery, and four counts of the act-type of criminal restraint. Twenty convictions based on this conduct is pretty impressive evidence of offense inflation.

It is unlikely that the prosecutor in *Preciose* intended to stack convictions in this manner. The creative charging was probably to cover all contingencies or to create an incentive for Preciose to plea bargain. If the latter, it appears to have worked; Preciose accepted a guilty plea that had a forty-year sentence, with parole ineligibility for seventeen and one-half years.[17] But we need a better account of same offense than one that requires deferring to prosecutorial good faith in difficult cases.

It is very unlikely that the legislature intended to authorize twenty convictions on these facts. There is little doubt that the legislature intended a single sexual assault/contact to result in one conviction, even if it could be described in three (or more) ways. There is little doubt that the legislature wanted armed robbery to encompass aggravated assault; the former is a more serious offense for purposes of grading than any version of the latter. There is little doubt that the legislature saw robbery as including criminal restraint. There is little doubt that the legislature wanted the making of terroristic threats punished as part of robbery if the threat was what made theft into robbery.

Consider how a blameworthy act account manifests the likely legislative intent here and how easy it is to apply, compared to the maze of statutory analysis required to reach what is often an unsupportable result under *Blockburger*. There are six act-tokens of different proscribed blameworthy act-types. The act-type of burglary is different from all the other act-types, as is the act-type that constitutes both sexual assault and sexual contact. There is one act-token of robbery for each of the four victims. The act-types of aggravated assault, terroristic threats, and criminal restraint are included within the act-type of armed robbery. Armed robbery based on threatening bodily injury contains within it the act-type of threatening to commit a crime of violence, the act-type of attempting to cause bodily injury, and the act-type of restraining another under circumstances exposing the other to risk of bodily injury.[18] The mens rea requirement that the threat have the purpose of terrorizing is not part of the act-type, nor is the circumstance requirement that the injury threatened be serious.

The act-types included in robbery would be the same offense under a blameworthiness account. This corresponds with what I believe the legislature intended. And the analysis is far easier than using *Blockburger*. Using my blameworthy-act account, six offenses were committed, not twenty. The plea bargain resulted in convictions of burglary and armed robbery, perhaps reflecting the prosecutor's view that only a few offenses occurred.

Preciose is good evidence that while a blameworthy-act test is not always easy to apply, neither is *Blockburger*. *Preciose* also confirms that *Blockburger* outcomes are often counterintuitive. Though I will continue to reference *Blockburger*, the focus in the rest of this chapter will be on the blameworthy-act alternative.

A Legislative-Prerogative, Blameworthy-Act Alternative to Blockburger

This section begins by restating the principle that underlines the book: the legislature creates criminal blameworthiness and the procedure for rendering judgments about that blameworthiness. As Justice Washington indicated in 1820, the legislature can have as many penalties as it wants (and can define verdict in any way it wishes). Because the legislature almost never states its intent on whether any two of the thousands of criminal offenses create distinct or overlapping blameworthiness, the most important task is to develop a methodology for presuming that intent. This section identifies several presumptions that naturally arise from a blameworthy-act test. The next two sections discuss the related problem of how to evaluate manifestations of intent to rebut the presumptions.

Act-Type Rule of Lenity

United States v. Woodward[19] presents a difficult issue about act-type inclusion. It also shows, once again, the wooden nature of the *Blockburger* test. The Court of Appeals held that making a false statement defined the same offense as a currency-reporting violation. The currency violation was failure to report bringing into the country more than $5,000; the false statement violation was "conceal[ing] . . . by any trick, scheme, or device a material fact."[20] Both violations were proved by checking the "no" box on the customs form to the question about whether one is bringing more than $5,000 in currency into the country. The Court of Appeals reached the common-sense conclusion that every failure to report a relevant currency transportation was necessarily a concealment of a material fact (the currency transportation).

Blockburger is driven, however, by its mechanical nature, rather than common sense. As the Supreme Court pointed out in a per curiam opinion reversing the Court of Appeals, not every concealment of a material fact is a false statement violation; only those concealments by "trick, scheme, or device" qualify. This language makes the concealment offense theoretically distinct from the currency violation. Congress presumably added it for some reason, and thus it must be true that some concealments are not by trick, scheme, or device. On this understanding, not every currency reporting concealment is a false-statement concealment.

But is this the kind of question we should be asking to infer congressional intent to make cumulatively punishable offenses? Better results attend a more substantive question: is concealment of currency transportation the same act-type as concealment of a material fact by trick, scheme, or device? Rather than mechanically comparing offense descriptions, judges would ask whether "trick, scheme, or device" is part of the act-type description and, if so, whether the requirement adds materially to the blameworthiness of willful concealment. This question forces judges to confront the question of whether the offenses are substantively the same.

Unfortunately, it is not always an easy question. It is not easy in *Woodward*. "Trick, scheme, or device" does not seem to describe a circumstance or result. Those words could imply a mens rea, but Congress expressly required the mens rea of "knowingly and willfully," which makes any additional mens rea requirement surplusage. A process of elimination thus suggests that "trick, scheme, or device" is part of the act-type description.

That seems right on the ground that concealment by trick, scheme, or device suggests some form of action connected with the concealment.[21]

The next question is whether the act-type adds to the blameworthiness. This question is no easier. The comparison is between all knowing and willful concealments and all knowing and willful concealments by "trick, scheme, or device." It is not clear what "trick, scheme, or device" adds to blameworthiness when the harm is the concealment and the mens rea is knowing and willful in both cases. It is in cases like *Woodward* that the rule of lenity is helpful. As noted in chapter 5, the Court has long held that if doubt exists as to whether blameworthiness is distinct, that doubt should be resolved in favor of singular blameworthiness. The Court first applied this presumption when the issue was counting violations—for example, how many violations of the Mann Act occurred in taking two women across state lines in a single vehicle.[22] Later, however, the Court applied the rule of lenity when the application of *Blockburger* was either uncertain or produced unacceptable results.[23] To my mind, doubt exists whether Congress intended knowing and wilful concealments of material facts by trick, scheme, or device to be materially more blameworthy than knowing and wilfull concealments of material facts by other means. Though the *Woodward* Court ignored the rule of lenity, I would apply it and reject the *Blockburger* result.

The Court did precisely that in *Prince v. United States*.[24] The federal bank robbery offenses of entry with intent to commit a felony and aggravated bank robbery are different *Blockburger* offenses; it is theoretically possible for someone to enter the bank before forming the intent to commit a felony. Because of this theoretical double distinction, the typical robber who planned the robbery for months could be convicted of both entry with intent to rob and aggravated bank robbery. But the Court refused to follow *Blockburger*'s idiotic result here. Obviously seeking a common-sense outcome, the Court pored over the history of the Act, including a letter the attorney general had written to Congress prior to passage of the entry provision. Leavening this history with the rule of lenity, the Court held that entry and bank robbery were the same offense.

On a blameworthy-act account, no rule of lenity is necessary to solve *Prince*. The act-type of entry is always included in bank robbery because it does not matter whether the entry is accompanied by any mens rea.[25] But the Court later expanded *Prince* to cases in which there is doubt about whether one act-type includes another, thus giving the rule of lenity a substantive role to play even on a blameworthy-act account. For example, in *United States v. Gaddis*, the Court held that a single bank robbery could be only one offense even when charged as bank robbery and assault with a dangerous weapon during a bank robbery.[26] Because bank robbery does not require use of a dangerous weapon, these offenses are different under *Blockburger*. The act-type question is more difficult—does bank robbery include the act-type of assault with a dangerous weapon? The answer is yes only if "with a dangerous weapon" is a circumstance and not part of the complex act-type of robbing. While these are nice action theory questions, I don't have to answer them. Merely showing that it is plausible to view what the robber has in his hand as a circumstance is ground enough to apply the rule of lenity and hold that bank robbery includes assault with a dangerous weapon, precisely as *Gaddis* did.

A similar question was presented in *Simpson v. United States*.[27] The defendants were convicted of bank robbery and given an enhanced sentence for the "use of a dangerous weapon or device." They were also convicted of using a firearm to commit a felony. *Blockburger* finds these offenses to be different: robbing a bank with an icepick would not violate the felony-firearm statute, and stealing money from an unoccupied bank while armed would violate the felony-firearm statute but not the bank robbery statute.[28] Act-type analysis would agree with the *Blockburger* result if the "use of a dangerous weapon" and "use of a firearm" are considered part of the statutory act-types. If not, the act-type of bank robbery would be included in the act-type of committing a felony.

The Court applied the rule of lenity in *Simpson* to conclude that, *Blockburger* notwithstanding, only one double jeopardy offense had been committed. For a blameworthy act account, *Gaddis* and *Simpson* suggest that if doubt exists about whether an element is an act-type, that doubt should be resolved in favor of its not being an act-type. This suggests that *Woodward* was wrongly decided.

Compound-Predicate Offenses

A compound-predicate offense scheme uses one crime, the predicate, to aggravate another crime, the compound. Felony murder is a classic example; the commission of a felony that causes a death serves to aggravate the homicide offense to first- or second-degree murder. Felony murder can be expressed in the following form: FM = [(F1 or F2 or F3 . . . Fn) + (K)], where K is a killing committed during the perpetration of any F.

Moore discusses the related concept of constituent offenses. Robbery, for example, is the combination of assault and larceny. It can be expressed $R = (A + L)$. Moore argues that $R = (A + L)$ means $R = A$ and $R = L$, but he would likely reject the equation $FM = F_1$ because F_1 is not a moral wrong common with FM when F_2 (or any F) would suffice along with K to prove FM.[29] Thus, Moore would hold that felony murder is not the same offense as rape used to prove felony murder.

The Supreme Court addressed this issue in *Whalen v. United States*,[30] holding that a defendant cannot be convicted of both felony murder and rape when the felony murder required proof of the rape. The Court had previously decided a similar felony murder issue in *Harris v. Oklahoma*,[31] a per curiam opinion that provides almost no analysis. The *Whalen-Harris* issue is difficult for *Blockburger*. Justice Rehnquist noted that applying *Blockburger* to a felony murder statute, when compared to "statutes that define greater and lesser included offenses in the traditional sense, is less satisfactory, and perhaps even misdirected."[32] Does the underlying specific felony, rape, require proof of a different element from the felony murder statute? Yes, if one views felony murder as potentially satisfied by any of the predicate crimes. No, if one views felony murder-rape as a separate crime from felony murder-robbery. The latter is a more specific way of applying *Blockburger*, in effect forcing the state to identity the particular way it will prove an offense when the statute creates alternative ways of proving the offense.

The specific application prevailed in *Whalen*. The Court conceptualized felony murder as if it constituted six separate offenses: felony-murder-rape, felony-murder-robbery, and so on. This seems the right way to approach a statute written in the alternative. In effect, Congress had created six offenses in a single statutory provision.[33] It could have created six statutes, as the Court noted, and the difference in drafting should not be held to create a substantive difference.

The question of whether to force the government to elect a particular alternative divided the fragile *Blockburger* majority in *United States v. Dixon*.[34] The issue in *Dixon* was whether contempt was the same offense as the crime that proved the contempt. Because any crime can prove contempt in the abstract, *Dixon* is a nice analogy to felony murder. Chief Justice Rehnquist, joined by Justices O'Connor and Thomas, preferred to treat the contempt statute as a whole, rather than asking whether a particular contempt order that forbade assault would be the same offense as assault. Treating the contempt statute as a whole, it does not define the same offense as a substantive criminal law offense because it does not mention *any* criminal offenses. Justices Scalia and Kennedy applied *Blockburger* to the specific contempt order, drawing an analogy to this use in the felony murder context.

The specific application seems the best inference about legislative intent in the context of felony murder, but it is less clear in *Dixon*. Why wouldn't Congress want a defendant sentenced for violating a court order and for the crime as well? The violation of the court order is an affront to the judiciary; the crime, of course, is an affront to society as a whole. It might be possible to find enough doubt about congressional intent to apply the rule of lenity to a *Dixon* situation. But *Dixon* is a very unusual case. The Court had never before even addressed the issue of whether violating a court order is a criminal offense. There is no reason to build a double jeopardy structure to accommodate the freakish case. In the typical, run-of-the-mill case involving statutory alternatives, *Whalen* suggests that we should doubt whether the legislature meant each alternative to be treated as a separate offenses for purposes of analyzing the inclusion issue, thus permitting invocation of the rule of lenity as a way to hold that the alternative includes the particular act-type used to prove it. If armed robbery can be proven in six different ways, we should analyze the act-type inclusion issue on the basis of the specific way the state charges the armed robbery.

But the specific approach does not produce a satisfying outcome when applied to felony murder. The notion that the legislature meant a conviction of rape to preempt a conviction of felony murder, or vice versa, strikes me as unlikely. Someone who rapes a woman and then kills her has committed two very different harms, for which the legislature probably intended separate penalties.[35] My intuition here is widely shared. Writing in 1959, two decades before *Whalen*, one commentator noted that "the courts have nearly unanimously held the underlying felony to be a separate and distinct crime."[36] Following *Missouri v. Hunter*,[37] which made clear that legislative intent controls the single-trial same-offense issue, most courts to decide the question have held that felony murder is not the same offense as the underlying felony. In *State v. Blackburn*, for example, the Tennessee Supreme Court noted that the two statutes "are directed at separate evils" and concluded that the legislature "intended multiple punishments."[38]

Given this widely shared intuition, the question is whether a blameworthy-act theory can produce that result without rejecting *Whalen*'s common-sense construction of statutes written in the alternative. The answer is yes, though we must clarify the function of the underlying felony in felony murder. Proof of that felony is required not as part of the blameworthy act-type of murder but as a substitute for mens rea. On that view, which is both historically and functionally justified, rape and felony murder-rape have no blameworthy act-type in common; the only element they share is rape, which does not function as an act-type in felony murder.

Without viewing the underlying felony as a substitute for mens rea, felony murder statutes otherwise require no mens rea at all. It seems unlikely that the legislature meant to create in felony murder a strict-liability first-degree murder offense. Moreover, the structure of felony murder suggests that the underlying felony does not function as an act-type; any of a list of underlying felonies will do, a list the legislature can expand or contract without worry about the resulting conjunctive act-type because they are not creating a conjunctive act-type. The felony murder offense under consideration in *Whalen* is typical:

> Whoever, being of sound memory and discretion, kills another purposely, either of deliberate and premeditated malice or by means of poison, or in perpetrating or attempting to perpetrate any offense punishable by imprisonment in the penitentiary, *or without purpose so to do kills another in perpetrating or in attempting to perpetrate any arson, . . . rape, mayhem, robbery, or kidnapping,* or in perpetrating or attempting to perpetrate any housebreaking while armed with or using a dangerous weapon, is guilty of murder in the first degree.[39]

The structure of this statute suggests that the perpetration of arson, rape, mayhem, robbery, or kidnapping is intended to replace the purposeful mens rea that attends the descriptions of first-degree murder in the part of the statute preceding the italics. This supports the view that the legislature added the felony to the killing not as a conjunctive act-type but, instead, as a mens rea substitute. So viewed, rape and felony murder-rape have no act-type in common, permitting a judge to use *Whalen*'s construction of statutes written in the alternative and still find felony murder distinct from its predicates because each requires a different act-type.[40]

Indeed, a plurality of the Court has told us that the actus reus of the felony functions in felony murder as a "mere means of satisfying a *mens rea* element of high culpability."[41] Using the terminology of this book, the

Court wrote that "the mental states of premeditated murder and felony murder [are] species of the blameworthy state of mind required to proof a single offense of first-degree murder."[42] If proof of the felony establishes a blameworthy "state of mind," then felony murder-rape does not include the act-type of rape, and they are different offenses.

At least two modern compound-predicates statutes share the mens rea feature of felony murder. It is a crime under federal law to engage in a "continuing criminal enterprise" (CCE). CCE is defined without explicit reference to mens rea. A person is guilty of CCE if he (1) violates any felony provision of specified subchapters, (2) the violation is "part of a continuing series of violations" of those subchapters, and (3) the person occupies a supervisory role over five or more persons and obtains substantial income from the organization.[43]

Mens rea is, of course, required with respect to supervising the enterprise. But making money from supervising five or more people is not criminal. The activity engaged in must be a criminal enterprise. The only proof the statute requires of intent to engage in a criminal enterprise is the existence of prior criminal violations. The point to requiring proof of those violations is not to punish the actor again but to infer intent to engage in CCE. The predicates thus function here, as in felony murder, as a stand-in for mens rea in the compound offense.

On this account, the predicate of, for example, importing narcotics has no act-type in common with CCE even if the narcotics charge is part of the CCE proof. On a blameworthy-act account, the lack of a common act-type means that the offenses are presumed to be different. The Court reached the same result, using a stilted analysis that took many pages.[44] Waiting in the wings is the issue of whether RICO (Racketeer Influenced and Corrupt Organizations Act)[45] and its predicate offenses define the same offense. Without belaboring the point, the structure of RICO is functionally the same as CCE. No specific mens rea is required to prove engaging in a pattern of racketeering activity; the predicates supply the intent to engage in racketeering.

I argued in 1984 that the offense-specific *Whalen* version of *Blockburger* would make RICO the same as the predicate felonies used to show a pattern of racketeering activity.[46] Anne Bowen Poulin elaborated that argument in 1992, relying also on *Grady*.[47] Today, of course, *Grady* is no longer among the living. While Poulin and I are right that the *Whalen-Harris* application of *Blockburger* would make RICO the same as its predicates, this observation misses the blameworthiness point, as did the

Court in *Whalen* and *Harris*. What makes RICO blameworthiness different from that of any one of the predicate acts is that RICO and its predicates have no element in common that functions as an act-type. The
Court should overrule *Whalen* and *Harris*.

The next section presents issues that *Blockburger* makes no pretense of
resolving—the conduct dimension of the same-offense issue. How many
"units of prosecution" does the Double Jeopardy Clause permit?

Unit-of-Prosecution Cases

One advantage of a blameworthy-act test is that it simultaneously
solves both the conduct and the definitional dimensions of the same-offense issue. A prerequisite of the *Blockburger* analysis is that the conduct
be the same. As the Court implicitly recognized in *Ashe v. Swenson*,[48] the
Blockburger test has nothing to say about whether the robbery of six
poker players in a single transaction is the same offense. But, as I showed
in chapter 5, a blameworthiness account implies principles about the
scope of the act-type and the consumption of blameworthiness that resolve these cases as part of the larger project.

In cases involving a single statute, the so-called unit-of-prosecution
cases, the same-conduct issue is the only issue. Some courts have used
Blockburger in this context, essentially asking whether each charge requires proof of a fact that the other does not, despite the Court's articulated test, which requires different statutory provisions. Even the
Supreme Court has fallen prey to this confusion. In *Brown*, the Court
noted that collateral estoppel offers a protection beyond *Blockburger*,
using the facts of *Ashe v. Swenson* as an example.[49] While this is, of course,
right (and is the subject of chapter 7), the particular example manifested
confusion about *Blockburger*. The Court noted that each of six robberies
that occurred at the same place and time in *Ashe* was a different offense.
Again, the Court is right, but not for the reason given. These are different
offenses because six victims were harmed, and we should therefore assume that the legislature intended each act-token to manifest distinct
blameworthiness. But *Brown* stated that *Blockburger* could be applied to
the multiple-victim case and would have permitted multiple convictions
because "separate convictions of the robbery of each victim would have
required proof in each case that a different individual had been robbed."
Chief Justice Burger explicitly stated, in his *Ashe* dissent, that *Blockburger*
would deem the offenses different because each indictment would name

a different victim.[50] This is reminiscent of *Vandercomb*, which in 1796 explicitly phrased one test in terms of the contents of the indictments.[51]

Courts are likely to resort to *Blockburger* in the single-statute context for three reasons. Judges do not read the *Blockburger* formulation carefully; they have no other mechanical test to use and do not find helpful the Court's mushy reliance on legislative intent in the unit-of-prosecution cases; and the *Blockburger* test often gives plausible answers when applied to each charge, as in the case of six robberies.

But *Blockburger* can produce absurd results when applied to each charge as written. What if the prosecutor brought multiple larceny charges arising out of the theft of a single purse by describing a different item in the purse for each charge? A defendant is guilty of as many counts of larceny as there were differently describable items in the purse if *Blockburger* is our guide. And what items are differently describable? We would need a principle to answer that question, too.

The Court implicitly rejected using factual differences in the way the charges are written in its first same-offense case, *In re Snow*.[52] As we saw in chapter 3, the issue was whether Snow could be prosecuted for three counts of cohabitation based on different periods of cohabitation with the same women. If factual differences in the indictments could make offenses different under a *Vandercomb* application of *Blockburger*, then the three counts in *Snow* would be different offenses. But the Court did not apply a different-proof test to the indictment in *Snow* and, indeed, has never applied *Blockburger* to the contents of the indictments.

To its credit, *Snow* appreciated that the issue was the scope of the act-type created by the statute: "There can be but one offence between such earliest day [of cohabitation] and the end of the continuous time embraced by all of the indictments."[53] What we learned in chapter 5 is helpful here. The scope of the act-type is clearly ongoing as long as the same parties are cohabiting.

Though the Court got the unit of prosecution issue right in *Snow*, it has not applied the *Snow* blameworthiness principle to cases involving two statutes. In *Albernaz v. United States*,[54] the Court had to decide whether conspiracy to import marijuana was the same offense as conspiracy to distribute marijuana, when a separate statute proscribed each type of conspiracy. The answer, under *Blockburger* is simple: each statute requires proof of a different element. But the Court was forced in *Albernaz* to distinguish another conspiracy case, *Braverman v. United States*,[55] which held that a single conspiracy with multiple goals could support only a single conviction under the basic federal conspiracy statute. Why is it, Albernaz wanted to know, that a single conspiracy with multiple goals is one offense if charged under a single statute but two offenses if charged under two statutes?

It is a good question, and the Court was unable to provide much in the way of a response. The Court's answer was the brute assertion that the existence of two statutes makes a difference. But it makes a difference only if it permits us to infer some relatively clear fact about legislative intent. What kind of presumption should be indulged about the existence of two statutes, each of which proscribes similar conduct? Is that procedural fact really good evidence of intent to create more than one punishable unit of blameworthiness? As the Court later perceptively observed in *Garrett*, to conclude that Congress intended separate offenses does not also mean that it intended cumulative punishments.[56] If Congress wanted conspiracy to import marijuana to be punished in addition to conspiracy to distribute the same marijuana, would Congress have not also wanted any conspiracy with discrete criminal goals to be more than a single punishable unit of conduct?

If this is the best reading of congressional intent, *Braverman* cannot be distinguished from *Albernaz*. One of them must be reasoned incorrectly. On a blameworthiness theory, it is *Braverman* and not *Albernaz* that is badly reasoned. The defendants argued in *Braverman* that the government proved only a single agreement with various goals—for example, to transport distilled spirits, to possess unregistered stills, and to make and ferment mash on unauthorized premises.[57] But how can it be one agreement to agree to do different things? Consider a case in which this point is easier to see: *R* and *S* conspire to rape *X*, to counterfeit money, and to rob a liquor store. It makes nonsense of the concept "one agreement" to say that *R* and *S* had one agreement. On any coherent theory of action, they had three agreements: to rape, to counterfeit, and to rob. They could have agreed to rape and stopped there. When they also agreed to counterfeit, they made a new agreement. And so on.

What makes *Braverman* a harder case is that the prosecutor charged overlapping goals, each of which violated a separate statutory provision—to possess distilled spirits as one goal and to transport them as another; to carry on the business of liquor dealers without the special occupational stamp and to carry on that business without giving bond as required by law. The problem here is a dubious assumption of conspiracy law. It seems unlikely that conspirators who agree to engage in a criminal enterprise also agree to every act that might be committed as part of being in that business.

The Court was faced with two dubious outcomes in *Braverman*. It could have indulged the philosophically dubious view that agreeing to do different things is only one agreement, or it could have indulged the legally dubious view that criminals who agree about overarching goals also agree to every act that is committed along the way. There must be a way to avoid that dilemma.

A more satisfying approach is to redefine what it means for a conspiracy to have separate goals. An agreement, Perkins and Boyce tell us, "constitutes only one conspiracy even if it contemplates the commission of several offenses."[58] In this formulation, "contemplates" serves to provide a negative answer to the question: was it two conspiracies to agree to distill whiskey and to carry on the business of distillers without having given bond?

The end result of limiting the number of counts is good; the analysis is poor. How can an agreement to do different things be only one agreement? We can avoid this awkwardness by simply turning the proposition around. An agreement has only as many criminal purposes as it has explicit goals that are distinct blameworthy act-types. Thus, an agreement "to carry on the business of wholesale and retail liquor dealers without having the special occupational tax stamps required by statute" has, as its explicit goal, the complex act-type of carrying on a liquor business. The narrower goals charged in *Braverman*—for example, transporting distilled spirits—would not be blameworthy acts distinct from that of carrying on a liquor business because they would be included within it.

Now we get the *Braverman* result without the analytic sloppiness: agreeing to achieve different goals results in different agreements, but goals are different only if each requires a distinct blameworthy act. *Braverman* committed a single conspiracy using an act-type definition of conspiracy; though the Court used double jeopardy to limit the number of counts, the better analysis is to define conspiracy more narrowly. The hypothetical defendants *R* and *S* committed three conspiracies (to rape, to counterfeit, and to rob), and *Albernaz* committed two conspiracies (to import marijuana and to distribute marijuana). But if the crimes that are the goal of the conspiracy are the same crime or very similar, as Professor William Theis argues, it is "highly probable" that the conspiracy is singular.[59]

A second claim by Theis is less supportive of the view developed here: he argues that a single agreement is only one conspiracy even if it extends over years and includes different parties (as long as one party is constant). In his words, "[T]here is a presumption that once a defendant enters into a conspiracy, his offense continues, and he does not form new conspiracies each time he breaks the law, even though his accomplices change."[60] Whatever the value of that presumption under the *Braverman* doctrine, it makes nonsense of the notion of the act of agreeing. It cannot be the same act when X and Y agree and when X and Z agree, even if X has the same goal in both agreements.

I have argued that, when trying to determine how many conspiracies exist, there is no difference between conspiracies charged under single statutes and those charged under more than one statute.[61] Indeed, the account developed here never finds any difference between cases involving unit of prosecution (one statute) and those involving multiple statutory act-types. Both kinds of cases present the same issue—how to determine the singularity of blameworthiness. Possession cases are good examples of this unity.

Possession Cases

So-called "continuous offenses" require analyzing the scope of the act-type. The most common of these offenses proscribe possession. Justice Brandeis concluded for a unanimous Court in *Albrecht v. United States* that "possessing and selling are distinct offenses" that can be punished separately.[62] In Brandeis's view, the possession at the moment of sale is evidence of earlier possession. A defendant who is punished for both possession and sale is punished for the sale and for the possession that existed prior to the sale.

While it is clearly within the power of the legislature to divide the act-types in this manner, the Brandeis analysis misses the point of whether Congress intended that result. It seems unlikely that a statute prohibiting possession manifests legislative intent to punish the possession that existed prior to the sale. Why would the legislature divide a continuous possession? Putting the principle in *Snow* terms, possession is a single act-token as long as it is uninterrupted. Similarly, the joyriding is a single act-token as long as the actor keeps the car, as the Court held in *Brown*.

Possession is included in sale just as joyriding is included in auto theft. The seller must have possession (actual or constructive) of what he sells.

Brandeis was wrong in *Albrecht*. The better presumption is that a generic offense of possession is included in the offense of sale.

The Court followed *Albrecht* to hold that making a counterfeit plate is a different offense from possessing it.[63] This is even more difficult to justify. Here, making and possession begin at the same time. But the Court started getting this issue right in the 1950s, first holding that robbery is the same offense as receiving proceeds taken in the robbery.[64] A harder case followed: larceny, and receiving and concealing the stolen property days later by a defendant who did not directly participate in the theft. The Court adhered to its view that theft liability, however imposed, entails possession of the proceeds, and the act-type of receiving and concealing the stolen property is thus included in the act-type of stealing.[65]

If *Snow* and *Brown* are right, possession is a single act-token as long as it continues. Thus, the Court's recent treatment of this issue is to be preferred over the Brandeis view. The account offered in this book is only a presumption about legislative intent, however, and the legislature is free to state that possession and sale are different offenses.

Dual-Sovereignty Same-Offense Presumptions

Given the United States federal system, the same-offense question sometimes arises when offenses are enacted by different legislative bodies. This is referred to as "dual sovereignty." The Court has a flat rule here: "dual-sovereignty" prosecutions are exempt from the Double Jeopardy Clause. When more than one sovereign prosecutes, the defendant loses even though he would win if a single sovereign were to prosecute the two offenses. This policy privileges federalism over double jeopardy.

Dissenting from the Court's 1820 decision in *Houston v. Moore*,[66] Justice Story noted two possible outcomes when a defendant was convicted or acquitted under a state law that proscribed the same offense as a federal law. Either the federal authorities were thereby deprived "of their authority to try the same case, in violation of the jurisdiction confided to them by Congress," or the defendant is "liable to be twice tried and punished for the same offense, against the manifest intent of the act of Congress, the principles of our common law, and the genius of our free government."[67]

Justice Washington, delivering the Court's judgment in *Houston*, agreed with Story that federal and state statutes could not both be given effect when they proscribed the same offense. It is not clear whether Washington saw this result in terms of double jeopardy or in terms of general principles of federalism, but he did see the problem as one of ascertaining legislative intent. If the two legislative wills "correspond in every respect, then the latter is idle and inoperative; if they differ, they must, in the nature of things, oppose each other, so far as they do differ."[68] Washington inferred that neither legislature would have intended these outcomes—that is, would not have intended to create an "inoperative" criminal provision, or one that opposed the legislature of the other sovereign.

Justice Johnson's concurring opinion in *Houston* stated the contrary, formalist dual-sovereignty theory: "Why may not the same offence be made punishable both under the laws of the States and of the United States? Every citizen of a State owes a double allegiance; he enjoys the protection and participates in the government of both the State and the United States."[69] By 1847 the dual-sovereignty view commanded a clear majority of the Court, though only in dicta.[70]

This same-offense analysis is different from what we have seen so far because a single formalistic principle can answer all state-federal same-offense questions—one size fits all. Even statutes identical in every word are different double jeopardy offenses on Justice Johnson's view. The Court has followed Johnson's formalist view: statutes are not the same offense when passed by different legislatures because legislatures operate independently of each other and have distinct interests to protect by their criminal law. Thus, a conviction of conspiracy in state court does not prevent a federal prosecution of the same conspiracy.[71] Nor does collateral estoppel or issue preclusion fare any better; an acquittal of bank robbery in federal court does not forbid a state prosecution of the same bank robbery regardless of the facts found in the defendant's favor in the first proceeding.[72]

Moreover, on the principle of legislative independence, each state is a sovereign separate from the other forty-nine states; a murder conviction in Georgia does not bar a murder prosecution in Alabama of the same defendant for the same killing.[73] The same analysis governs Indian tribal courts; a conviction in an Indian tribal court does not bar a federal prosecution.[74] But the principle of legislative independence does not justify dual prosecutions for state and municipal offenses.[75] As subdivisions of states, municipalities have no legislative independence.

Martin Friedland wrote, "It is a strange breed of federalism which demands such results. The accused is subjected to prosecution by the combined resources of two jurisdictions."[76] Most commentators agree, though some would permit exceptions for particular kinds of reprosecutions.[77] One commentator attacks the dual-sovereignty doctrine on the ground that it is the people, not the formal government, who are sovereign, and the people who sit on federal juries are the same people who sit on state juries.[78] This view would, of course, permit state-state prosecutions because those people are different.

Rather than apply formalistic federalism or argue about who is really sovereign, we can solve the double jeopardy problem by applying legislative intent, making the question whether each sovereign intended the proscribed blameworthy act-type to be prosecuted in addition to the same blameworthy act-type proscribed by the other sovereign. Justice Washington's opinion suggests this analysis. He noted that a single legislature could "impose upon the same person, for the same offense, different and cumulative punishments" because that would be "the will of the same body to do so" and there can be "no opposition of wills."[79]

From this notion that legislative wills should be construed to operate in harmony, Washington stated a presumption of singular blameworthiness—if one sovereign imposes a punishment for a certain offense, "the presumption is, that this was deemed sufficient, and, under all circumstances the only proper one."[80] On this view, a single legislature can create as many different penalties as it wants for the same offense, but the penalty imposed by one sovereign estops the other sovereign from imposing a different penalty for the same offense.

Washington seemed to infer that a single legislature would intend all its penalties to apply. But Washington was not willing to infer that different legislatures were aware of what the other was doing. This explains his concern with opposing wills. An unintended opposition of wills meant, for Washington, that the defendant was being punished twice even though the legislature of the second sovereign to prosecute did not intend a second penalty.

One can question Washington's assumption that a single legislature always intends cumulative penalties when it passes more than one statute proscribing the same blameworthy act-type, at least when that assumption is applied to the modern era and the seven thousand crimes that are on the books.[81] Skepticism on that point explains my reliance on a blame-worthy act-type presumption that only a single offense per blameworthy act is intended. But Washington's other assumption seems plausible, at least when applied to the state-federal issue.

Congress is unlikely to check the statute books of the fifty states when it enacts federal criminal statutes. Though it would be easier for a state to check federal law, there is a centuries-old tradition that criminal law is a state responsibility. That tradition has eroded somewhat in the past three decades, but the erosion expanded federal jurisdiction, rather than limiting state jurisdiction. Thus, state legislatures probably assume that their enactment of criminal laws is privileged. Perhaps, then, we should presume that neither legislature intended to authorize a prosecution for the same blameworthy act-type that the other sovereign has already prosecuted. The common law of Blackstone's era supports this presumption, though American federalism was not, of course, present in the common law. The closest analogy is that a foreign trial barred an English prosecution.[82]

The presumption of singularity also operates in the Canadian system, where criminal laws were initially assigned exclusively to the federal government. Though that model did not last in a pure form, it at least made clear that the criminal law of the provinces exists at the sufferance of the federal government. One way of analyzing the dual-sovereignty question in Canada, Friedland notes, is to ask whether the federal government has occupied the field with the intent to exclude the provinces.[83] If so, only a single prosecution is permitted. This is consistent with asking whether the second sovereign to prosecute intended to authorize that trial in addition to the first sovereign's prosecution.

The plausibility of an intent account can be seen when two other dual sovereignty applications are contrasted to the state-federal issue. The Court has held that municipal offenses are not different from state crimes because municipalities derive their authority from the states and thus are the same sovereign.[84] On a legislative-intent account, nothing in the relationship between municipal and state governments rebuts a presumption in favor of the state government "occupying the field" and thus intending only singular blameworthiness.

The outcome is different, however, when federal and Indian crimes overlap. Here the dual-sovereignty analysis at least makes sense; some Indian tribes were still at war with the federal government in the late nineteenth century. But the analysis is more satisfying if phrased in terms of likely congressional intent. It seems quite unlikely that Congress intended an Indian trial to bar a federal prosecution for the same act or offense. Thus, the Court reaches the right result here,[85] but only because the historic differences between Indian tribes and the federal government give us good reason to rebut a presumption of singular blameworthiness.

In one early case, the Court refused to rely on dual-sovereignty theory, holding in 1878 that the criminal courts of the state of Tennessee had no jurisdiction to try a federal soldier who was part of the post–Civil War occupying army.[86] The Court explicitly based its decision on the grounds of jurisdiction rather than same offense,[87] in effect holding that the existence of a warlike state between two sovereigns deprived the occupied sovereign of the power to create blameworthiness for acts committed by members of the occupying army. The dual sovereignty doctrine would, of course, have produced the opposite outcome; the state of Tennessee had been defeated in the Civil War, but it was still a sovereign state that had been readmitted to the Union.

Similarly, the federal statute making crimes of certain civil rights violations was enacted shortly after the Civil War when Congress reasonably feared that state courts, particularly in the South, would not be capable of always providing justice to minority citizens. Given this background, it seems almost certain that Congress intended the civil rights criminal statute to provide a remedy in addition to state law. This common-sense view permits federal civil rights trials to proceed after state verdicts, without also making available the whole weight of federal criminal law (unless Congress makes clear its intent to make available other criminal statutes). A legislative-prerogative view of dual sovereignty, in short, permits what may be the best of all worlds: a remedy for state trials that fail in a flagrant way to remedy civil rights violations[88] and a bar on general federal reprosecutions.

Dual-sovereignty issues posed by overlap in jurisdiction between Indian and federal courts, between federal and former Confederate states, and between federal civil rights statutes and state law seem qualitatively different from state-state issues or general Congress-state issues. If this is right, a virtue of an intent account is that it allows a different resolution of these questions, rather than requiring all dual-sovereignty issues to be decided by a wooden application of a structural, abstract federalism principle.

Choosing one presumption over the other makes little practical difference on the state-federal or state-state dual sovereignty issue. Either presumption is easily overcome by a single, global expression of legislative intent. As the Court favors the structural federalism principle, the burden is currently on states to give up the right to prosecute following a federal trial. More than half the state legislatures have adopted global statutory bars that reverse the Supreme Court's federalism presumption in favor of forbidding two trials for the same criminal conduct.[89]

The state statutes vary in their definitional approach to same offense; some use tests that are broader than anything the Court has ever used, such as same conduct or same act.[90] What they have in common, however, is more important than how they differ: all bar certain state trials that follow federal prosecutions and thus reject the grant of absolute power to prosecute state crimes that the Court bestowed in *Bartkus v. Illinois*.[91]

At the federal level, Congress has never reversed the Court's presumption, but the Department of Justice has operated for decades under a self-imposed limitation that is, in some ways, broader than a blameworthy-act test. Though subject to a series of exceptions for cases in which the state prosecution leaves substantial federal interests "demonstrably unvindicated,"[92] the policy is otherwise broader than any same-offense test the Court has used—indeed, in line with the broadest state statutory bars and Justice Brennan's same transaction test. Federal prosecutions must pass the substantial-interest standard if based on the "same act(s) or transaction(s)" as the state case.[93] Otherwise, the Department of Justice will not permit the federal prosecution to proceed.

This federal policy was announced by the attorney general who was a Republican, less than two weeks after the Court made clear that the federal government was not limited in its power to reprosecute state crimes.[94] It is significant that a Republican attorney general gave up the total freedom to reprosecute granted by the Court. That the policy remained intact during the presidencies of Nixon, Reagan, and Bush, with attorneys general such as John Mitchell and Ed Meese, is little short of remarkable.

This action at the state and federal level during an era of increasing American anger over crime rates and criminals is substantial evidence that most policymakers privilege double jeopardy protection over federalism. A skeptic might attack both items of evidence as less than meets the eye. Sandra Guerra notes that the state statutes are often narrowly construed.[95] The vague language of the federal policy invites abuse, and the administrative nature of the policy does not permit judicial review.

Moreover, the Department of Justice values its independence on this point. When an ad hoc task force of the American Bar Association Criminal Justice Section considered recommending the codification of the administrative policy, the response of the Clinton Department of Justice was quite negative.[96]

But these skeptical attacks do not detract from the overarching point, which is to focus on the very existence of the state statutes and the federal policy. These are self-imposed limitations. Regardless of interpretation, each sovereign gave up the complete, unfettered power to prosecute its own criminal laws provided under the guise of federalism. It seems that federalism is viewed with less favor than the protection against double jeopardy.

However the dual sovereignty presumption is structured or rebutted, the double jeopardy analysis should turn on legislative intent. If the legislature intends to punish the same blameworthy act-type more than once in the dual-sovereignty context, it need only say so. On this view, the blameworthy-act question in the criminal law of a single jurisdiction is just a subset of the larger question about how to read legislative intent on the separate applications of penalties generally. And the question of how to rebut the relevant presumptions is also the same.

Rebutting Same-Offense Presumptions

Because *Blockburger* is such a bad presumption, courts strain to find ways to bypass *Blockburger* entirely. One way to minimize the role of *Blockburger* is to look for another presumption that might provide a more satisfying result. So, for example, *Iannelli v. United States*[97] considered the application of Wharton's Rule to offenses that are separate under *Blockburger*. The offenses were conspiracy to violate and violation of a federal gambling statute that required joint participation of five or more persons.[98] These are different offenses under *Blockburger*—conspiracy requires agreement, which gambling does not, and gambling requires proof of gambling, which a general conspiracy obviously does not. But Wharton's Rule is an exception to the general rule that conspiracy is separate from the crimes contemplated: if one of the offenses "necessarily require[s] the participation of two persons for its commission,"[99] whether or not it requires agreement, Wharton's Rule produces substantive merger.

Because the federal gambling statute required participation of five or more persons, it fits Wharton's Rule. The Court in *Iannelli* discussed Wharton's Rule at length, apparently willing to apply its presumption to rebut the *Blockburger* presumption. Ultimately, however, the Court found sufficient indicia of legislative intent to punish both offenses, thus rebutting Wharton's presumptive rebuttal of *Blockburger*. Nonetheless, that the Court seemed willing to discard *Blockburger* for a rather arcane and narrow presumption perhaps suggests a lack of commitment to *Blockburger*'s methodology.[100]

Another way the Court minimizes *Blockburger* is by exaggerating the quality of legislative intent rebutting a bad *Blockburger* presumption. In *Simpson v. United States*,[101] for example, the Court avoided use of *Blockburger* by essentially relying on the remarks of a single member of Congress—the sponsor of the felony firearm statute—and on the rule of lenity.[102] A blameworthy-act account reaches the same lenient result.[103]

But an act account, just like the Court's multiple-punishment doctrine and its rule of lenity, merely state a presumption. As is true under the Australian Crimes Act, a legislature in this country merely has to "specifically intend" double punishment to rebut the presumption in favor of one punishment for one act.[104] Six years after *Simpson*, Congress revised the felony-firearm statute to make clear that it wanted the felony-firearm conviction in addition to any enhanced sentencing under another crime of violence.[105] That, of course, ends the matter on a legislative-prerogative account, for successive trials as well as multiple punishment; it ends the matter on the Court's account if the issue is multiple punishment.[106]

When *Blockburger* produces a particularly idiotic result, the Court finds it rebutted without any explicit legislative intent at all. One example is the application of *Blockburger* to continuing criminal enterprise (CCE). Using the *Whalen* offense-specific felony-murder application of *Blockburger*, CCE defines the same offense as any of its predicates. The Court recognized this in *Garrett v. United States*, noting that "the predicate offense does not require proof of any fact not necessary to the CCE offense."[107] In a labyrinthine analysis, the Court struggled to find indicia of congressional intent to rebut *Blockburger*.[108]

As little direct evidence existed, the Court drew inferences from the statute. For example, a CCE offense necessarily spans a longer period of time than most predicate felonies. Relating this point to Garrett's case, the Court observed: "Whenever it was during the 5 1/2-year period alleged in the indictment that Garrett committed the first of the three predicate offenses required to form the basis for a CCE prosecution, it could not then have been said with any certainty that he would necessarily go ahead and commit the other violations required to render him liable on a CCE charge."[109] The Court's point was that "multilayered conduct, both as to time and to place" may not lend itself to *Blockburger* analysis.[110] Yes, true enough, but this is simply another way to say that *Blockburger* is not a good presumption.

A blameworthy-act account reaches the *Garrett* result.[111] It is better to apply a presumption in which one has confidence than attempt to reconstruct legislative intent by drawing murky inferences. A good example of the latter is *Gore v. United States*.[112] Two of the offenses in *Gore* were the *Blockburger* offenses: sale of narcotics not in or from the original stamped package and sale of narcotics not pursuant to a written order. We concluded in chapter 5 that these offenses describe the same blameworthy act-type. The third offense was sale of the same narcotics knowing them to have been unlawfully imported. If we subtract the common act-type from these offenses, the left-over element in the third offense is "knowledge of unlawful importation." Is this a blameworthy act-type? No, it is not an act-type at all. Thus, a blameworthy-act test presumes that the third *Gore* offense is the same as the first two.

What kind of evidence was available to rebut this finding? Though *Gore* sought evidence to support the *Blockburger* presumption, rather than to rebut it, the Court's discussion is useful. Five members of the Court found evidence of intent to authorize cumulative penalties in the "three different enactments, each relating to a separate way of closing in on illicit distribution of narcotics, passed at three different periods, for each of which a separate punishment was declared by Congress."[113]

This analysis is less compelling than it seems at first glance. Legislatures usually place different offense descriptions in different enactments—auto theft and joyriding, for example, or murder and manslaughter. Of course a separate punishment for each offense was declared; this is inevitable with different offense descriptions. When has a legislature ever described a crime without authorizing a punishment?

So the evidence in *Gore* that Congress meant the same blameworthy act-type to be punished three times is that the statutes were passed at different times. While this fact is at least responsive to the question of whether Congress intended to cumulate penalties, it cannot be dispositive. One can imagine any number of reasons Congress may later pass a statute proscribing the same act-type without intending it to be punishable in addition to the earlier statute.

Two of the offenses in *Gore* were defined by Internal Revenue Code statutes designed to close off different ways of selling narcotics without paying the excise tax—selling without a written order of the purchaser and selling not in the original stamped package.[114] The third offense, sale with knowledge of unlawful importation, is in the dangerous drug part of the federal criminal code, designed to punish persons who encourage the importation of narcotics.[115] It is easy to envision Congress, at different times, seeking to encourage tax compliance and to discourage narcotics importation, without intending the penalties to be cumulated.

While many find Chief Justice Warren's dissent in *Gore* persuasive— Warren argued that Congress had not authorized cumulative punishments[116]—*Gore* remains inscrutable on the merits. Who knows what Congress was thinking on the issue of cumulative punishments? The evidence is sufficiently in equipoise that any same-offense presumption in which we have confidence should prevail. It is critical, then, which presumption a court uses. *Blockburger* presumes that all three offenses are distinct; there is surely insufficient evidence to rebut that presumption.

On my blameworthy-act account, the three statutes proscribe the single blameworthy act-type of selling narcotics, thus presuming a singular blameworthiness. A presumption that closely tracks legislative intent should be difficult to rebut. This book has argued that a blameworthy-act account is a better proxy for legislative intent than *Blockburger*. If this is right, rebutting a presumption from an act account should require legislative intent that is very clear.[117]

Though the presence of different statutes passed at different times is evidence of intent to cumulate penalties, it falls far short of clear. Indeed, the murky inferences the Court drew in *Gore* failed to persuade the four dissenters even to accept the *Blockburger* presumption. The better view, then, is that only a single double jeopardy offense was created by the three statutes and that only a single conviction should have been permitted.

Missouri v. Hunter[118] went far toward correcting the Court's *Blockburger* confusion. Reference to *Blockburger* is unnecessary, the Court noted, when "a legislature specifically authorizes cumulative punishments under two statutes."[119] When the legislative intent is clear enough, the Court recognized, "a court's task of statutory construction is at an end and the prosecutor may seek and the trial court or jury may impose cumulative punishment under such statutes in a single trial."[120] This is so because "[w]ith respect to cumulative sentences imposed in a single trial, the Double Jeopardy Clause does no more than prevent the sentencing court from prescribing greater punishment than the legislature intended."[121]

The only confusion remaining is implicit in the preceding quotation. Again and again, *Hunter* was careful to limit its holding and analysis to the single-trial setting. This implies, as Justice Marshall charged in dissent, that the Court was interpreting same offense "to mean one thing for purposes of the prohibition against multiple prosecutions and something else for purposes of the prohibition against multiple punishments."[122] Justice Marshall's opinion is quite astute on this overarching point: a protection against double jeopardy is a protection against repetitious and overlapping charges, regardless of whether they are brought in one proceeding or in successive trials. Marshall is right that these two protections *should* be interpreted in the same fashion.

But Marshall did not recognize that the only coherent and stable test of when charges overlap is whether the legislature intended to create singular or distinct blameworthiness. That was the contribution of the *Hunter* majority. If one combines Marshall's dissenting view about the stability of same offense in different procedural contexts with the majority's view about how to determine same offense, one winds up with a legislative-intent conception of the Double Jeopardy Clause. In short, one winds up with the conception urged in this book.

This is a satisfying outcome. It gives the legislature ultimate power to define singular blameworthiness, while using act/harm theory to solve all cases in which the legislature has not spoken clearly. Act/harm theory is a better presumption than *Blockburger* because it is linked with our intuitions about what makes criminal law offenses different.

Same-Offense Presumptions Summarized

The entire same-offense landscape can be viewed most usefully as a map of (probable) legislative intent. This book's premise is that the legislature can have as many double jeopardy offenses as it wants. The easy part of the map, then, is honoring clear legislative intent to create distinct (or singular) blameworthiness. It is unnecessary to engage in further analysis if the legislature is clear enough about its intent to create distinct blameworthiness (or to authorize only one penalty). Similarly, as we saw in chapter 4, the historic distinction between the functions of civil damages and criminal sanctions creates a heavy presumption that the legislature means civil remedies to be imposed in addition to any criminal sanction. As long as the sanctions imposed are clearly authorized, it does not matter for my double jeopardy account whether the prosecutor seeks authorized sanctions in one proceeding or two or whether the sanctions are denominated "civil" or "criminal."

Where the map discloses no clear indication of intent and there is no ready-made civil/criminal presumption—the vast majority of cases—a second presumption comes into play: the same blameworthy act-type is only a single offense. Blameworthy act-types are the same when they are identical or when one includes the other. Diverting electric current is identical to larceny (the only act-type in both is taking property without consent); larceny is included in robbery but larceny is not included in burglary because they share no blameworthy act-type.

As the act-type presumption can be rebutted only by clear intent to the contrary, the presumption is effectively irrebuttable at this stage of the analysis. If there is clear legislative intent to create distinct or singular blameworthiness, the case is resolved by the deference paid to intent without regard to act-types. Once the act-type analysis is reached, there is, by definition, no clear legislative intent.

Keeping the focus on blameworthy acts also illuminates the act-token puzzle. The inquiry comes in two forms. One, typified by *Brown*, is the determination of how many act-tokens of the criminal act-type have occurred. Here the Court's rule of lenity suggests presuming the broadest plausible reading of the statutory act-type for the purposes of counting act-tokens. The Court's treatment of this issue in *Brown* was thoughtful and persuasive.

The second act-token inquiry is the *Ebeling v. Morgan* issue of how many act-tokens to count as statutory violations when several occur at the same time and place. Drawing again on the Court's rule of lenity presumes that the legislature meant courts to count only once when repetitive act-tokens manifest the statutory harm in the same way. This harm analysis sometimes requires examining the mens rea of the statute as well as the act-type. Cutting into six mailbags with intent to steal the contents of all six should be counted only as one offense, as should the larceny of one hundred items from a large table. The Court's treatment of the counting issue in *Ebeling* was wooden and unpersuasive.

In sum, the venerable *Blockburger* test should be amended to apply only to blameworthy act-types and should be made subordinate to clear legislative intent regardless of whether the charges are brought in one trial or two. A legislative-prerogative, blameworthy-act account provides an answer to unit-of-prosecution-cases, as well as to cases that involve different statutes; it is more discriminating than *Blockburger*; its results are better when they differ from *Blockburger*; and the link between the proposed test and blameworthiness give us confidence to apply it to the vast majority of cases that lack explicit legislative intent. Picking the right presumption is important because the lack of explicit intent in virtually all cases means that the presumption comes close to stating a substantive double jeopardy rule.

7

Unifying Same-Offense Theory
A Blameworthiness Test of Collateral Estoppel

As we have seen, a daunting challenge for a same-offense theory is to explain the disparate ways in which two offenses can be the same offense. In chapter 6 I argued that a blameworthiness account unifies the same-offense question, whether it arises in multiple violations of a single statute or in violations of different statutes and whether it arises in one trial or two trials. The next task is to explain the collateral estoppel dimension of the same-offense problem. No one has attempted to unify collateral estoppel with the traditional same-offense issues. That is my goal in this chapter.

The issues are superficially different: double jeopardy collateral estoppel, like its civil-law sibling, is narrowly focused on issue preclusion. A comparison of offense descriptions or an analysis of the scope of the prohibited act-type is quite beside the point. Indeed, if the defendant prevails on a same-offense claim, collateral estoppel is literally beside the point. Because collateral estoppel is a separate, supplemental protection, it could be located in the Due Process Clause, as Amar and Marcus contend.[1] But collateral estoppel is conceptually part of a blameworthiness account of double jeopardy. It is a way of showing singular blameworthiness and thus can be viewed as implicit in the same-offense language of the Double Jeopardy Clause.

The collateral estoppel claim is that an earlier proceeding has resolved in the defendant's favor an issue that is necessary for the second prosecution. Although offense 1 and offense 2 do not share the quality of offense sameness, an acquittal of offense 1 has resolved an issue that makes the defendant not guilty of offense 2. The parallel to *autrefois acquit* is obvious. Indeed, Friedland has noted that issue preclusion is often implicit in the way *autrefois acquit* is defined.[2]

Res judicata has been part of English law at least since the twelfth century, when it appeared in Glanville's *Treatise*: "A concord . . . is called final because it puts an end to the matter, so that neither litigant may in future depart from it."[3] Imprisonment was one penalty for disregarding a "final concord" in that era.[4] The procedure by which a party could claim "former concord" in Glanville's England focused on the record of the first proceeding: "When the justices have come to court and are in full agreement as to the record, it is necessary, as was said above, to abide by their record, and neither party may object to it."[5]

Issue preclusion is an implication of res judicata, one that focuses on issues settled by the earlier judgment. In criminal law, it is a one-way street, benefiting the defendant but not the state. Though some commentators and at least one English court have suggested that a conviction can be used as conclusive evidence against the accused in a later case,[6] it is generally accepted that issue preclusion does not operate against criminal defendants in this country. Part of the reason is that defendants have the right to confront witnesses and the right to a jury trial.[7]

While issue preclusion is unrelated to same offense in a formal sense, it is related to blameworthiness. Assume R claims alibi and mistaken identity in defending against the charge of robbing V. The state then indicts R for robbing Z, who was standing next to V. There is no question that robbery of Z is a different offense from robbing V. Nonetheless, on the facts of R's particular case, the second robbery is the same offense as the first, in the sense that proof of innocence of one automatically proves innocence of the other.

Collateral estoppel can, therefore, be conceptualized as a case-sensitive same-offense claim. If the jury finding as to offense 1 necessarily means the defendant cannot be guilty of offense 2, then 1 and 2 must come out the same way whether or not the offenses share a definitional identity. The matter is different, of course, if R's defense to the robbery was that the money he took from V belonged to him. In that case, the acquittal cannot be used to prove innocence of robbing Z, and they are not effectively the same offense.

This understanding of collateral estoppel is implied by a blameworthiness conception of same offense. The legislature creates statutory blameworthiness, some of it criminal and some of it civil. But the legislature does not authorize criminal penalties or civil sanctions in the absence of a finding that the actor was the one who brought about the blameworthy state of affairs. A finding that the actor did not bring about the blameworthy state of affairs means that he should suffer no penalty, civil or criminal.

But there are doctrinal problems. When the border is crossed and re-crossed between civil and criminal, as we saw in chapter 4, the comparisons are often difficult. For example, the same parties are inevitably involved when traditional double jeopardy is invoked—the same criminal defendant[8] and the same state or federal government. A same-party requirement partly animates the Court's dual sovereignty doctrine.[9] One reason to permit different governments to prosecute the same offense is the fear that the interests of one sovereign will not be vigorously advanced by the other. This is a concern in civil res judicata as well. Should criminal collateral estoppel generally require the same parties?

Requirement of Same Parties

In the 1766 case of *Rex v. Duchess of Kingston*,[10] the issue was whether the finding of an ecclesiastical court that the duchess was not married was conclusive evidence, in the king's court, that the duchess was not guilty of bigamy. The Lord Chief Justice of the Court of Common Pleas, Sir William De Grey, noted that the judgment of a court "directly upon the point" was binding on all other courts before whom the same parties raised the same matter, even if raised for a different purpose.[11] But the king was not a party to the ecclesiastical proceeding, and the duchess lost her collateral estoppel claim. Supporting its judgment, the court noted that the king had responsibility for protecting the public peace, and ecclesiastical courts lacked jurisdiction in any matter not "altogether spiritual."

An early Supreme Court opinion was not so concerned with the identity of parties. In *Gelston v. Hoyt*,[12] the Court dealt with the preclusive effect of an acquittal in an in rem forfeiture case. An in rem proceeding is one begun against an object itself, in this case a ship, rather than a person. There is no necessity to have jurisdiction over the owner of the object because the suit is against the object itself. The in rem action against the ship had resulted in an acquittal, and the owners of the ship were suing the seizing officers for tort damages. The *Gelston* issue was whether the defendants (the seizing officers) could litigate the question of whether the ship had been properly seized.

Perhaps the wrongfulness of the seizure had been settled by the acquittal of the ship in the original forfeiture action. Because the ship was acquitted, the seizure must have been wrongful. The other possibility is that

204 | *Unifying Same-Offense Theory*

the original acquittal might not be binding, for one reason or another, on the defendants in the new tort action. After all, they were not parties to the original forfeiture action, and they had never themselves litigated the question of the ship's seizure. Should a court bind them to the earlier judgment even though they did not participate in it?

Yes, the Court held in *Gelston*. How were the interests of the seizing officers represented in the original action? The officer "virtually identifies himself with the government itself, whose agent he is, from the moment of the seizure up to the termination of the suit."[13] The Court went further, noting in dicta that even if the seizing officer "were a mere stranger, he would still be bound by such sentence, because the decree of a court of competent jurisdiction in rem is, as to the points directly in judgment, conclusive upon the whole world."[14]

The English court in *Kingston* did not have a similarly expansive view of collateral estoppel. In one way, the initial proceeding in the ecclesiastical courts was similar to an in rem proceeding. The duchess initially brought suit against a man who claimed to be her husband, asking the ecclesiastical court to determine that she was "free from all matrimonial contracts or espousals."[15] The court held in her favor. As the issue was the validity of the marriage—a determination of legal status—it might seem indistinguishable from an in rem proceeding, which seeks to determine the legal status of property. On this view, the judgment in favor of the duchess in the ecclesiastical courts would be "conclusive upon the whole world."

An analogous claim would be insanity. In *Hotema v. United States*,[16] the defendant killed three people on the same day. Two of the three indictments were consolidated for trial, Hotema defended on the ground of insanity, and the jury acquitted. The same defense was presented to the third indictment, but the second jury could not agree on a verdict, and a mistrial was granted. A new jury was impaneled, and this time Hotema was convicted.[17]

As to collateral estoppel, all three killings took place on the same day, creating a plausible collateral estoppel argument that the first jury had determined Hotema's status as someone who lacked capacity to commit a crime. It is unlikely that Hotema could have been alternately sane and insane during the same day. The Supreme Court rejected Hotema's appeal but not the collateral estoppel claim, which Hotema apparently did not raise. He instead argued that the trial for the first two killings was a same-offense bar to the third indictment. This argument is obviously flawed, as we have seen; three killings are three different offenses in all but the most unusual circumstances.

Properly presented, Hotema's collateral estoppel claim should have won. His claim can be distinguished from the marital status question on which the duchess lost because in Hotema's case the same parties litigated the same issue in both trials. The king in *Kingston* was not a party to the first suit, nor was the king on constructive notice of the litigation of the marital status of the duchess, which would be true in an in rem proceeding.

The same-parties issue puts two principles directly in conflict. The first, argued by the duchess in *Kingston*, is that once an issue is determined by a court of competent jurisdiction, the matter is at an end. No reason exists to prefer the finding of a subsequent court to the initial court. Thus, the initial finding can be accepted as the truth and, therefore, as binding on the whole world. The second principle, inherent in the requirement of same parties, is that fairness should give every person who has standing to raise an issue the opportunity to litigate it. The in rem proceeding in *Gelston* is arguably a substitute for same parties; the requirement that the property be served with notice presumably puts on notice everyone with standing to defend the claim.

The English court followed the second principle. As a matter of double jeopardy, rather than fairness, the *Kingston* result is suspect. Perhaps it is only because bigamy is not a criminal offense that deeply disturbs the modern conscience; perhaps it is that the reliance of the duchess on the ecclesiastical judgment seems justified on the facts of the particular case—what court could better determine what was a matter of church law? Whatever the reason, a determination by a court that specializes in questions of marriage that the duchess was not married should have been an end to the matter.

A few years after *Hotema*, the Supreme Court accepted a version of the duchess's argument. In *United States v. Mason*,[18] the defendants were charged with a federal conspiracy that provided enhanced punishment if state crimes were committed during the course of the conspiracy. Because the defendants had been acquitted of the murder that the government wanted to use for enhanced sentencing, the Court upheld the defendant's plea in bar with an analysis that could have been used by the duchess:

> The murder in question, if committed at all, was, as a distinct offense, a crime only against the state; and after the defendants were acquitted of that

crime by the only tribunal that had jurisdiction of it as an offense against the state, it is to be taken that no such crime of murder as charged in the indictment was in fact committed by them.[19]

To be sure, *Mason* can be distinguished on the technical ground that the king's court had concurrent jurisdiction over determining marital status, at least where bigamy was the issue, while the federal court had no jurisdiction to determine whether state crimes had been committed. This is a formalistic response to the question of whether "same parties" is always a prerequisite to a valid collateral estoppel claim. The same parties were not involved in *Mason*, and the Court upheld what is in essence a collateral estoppel claim.

Kingston could happen today. Suppose *W* sues *H* for alimony in a state where alimony can be awarded only if marriage is proven, and a civil court determines that *W* and *H* were never married. Then the state charges *H* with the criminal offense of bigamy, based on a claim that *H* was married to *W*. This is, again, a status determination, which is somewhat similar to the in rem proceeding in *Gelston*. Modern collateral estoppel would not protect *H*, though it is difficult to see why the state should have a chance to prove a different legal status than *W* was able to prove.

There is, of course, the fear that *H* and *W* will collude to obtain a judgment that is a fraud upon the court. This fear raises an accuracy concern about the first finding and would be a reason to prefer another principle if the fear were well founded. The king argued in *Kingston* that the duchess might be guilty of collusion concerning the judgment in the ecclesiastical court. Should we deny preclusive effect to all judgments because a small percent might be flawed?

One problem with any attempt to extend the *Gelston* in rem principle to status judgments is that it threatens to abolish entirely the same-parties requirement. Suppose the parents of *V* sue *X* for the tort of contributing to the delinquency of *V*, a minor. In the tort case, *X* defends by seeking to prove that, when the relevant events occurred, *V* was no longer a minor. The jury returns a verdict for *X*. This verdict determines *V*'s legal status at the critical point in time and, on the analysis just given, could be seen as a bar to any future effort to determine that particular legal status by a criminal charge. But what if *X* defended on the grounds that, though *V* was a minor, his acts did not constitute contributing to the delinquency of a minor? If the jury acquits, it is not a determination of a legal status but purely a finding of fact in *X*'s favor.

Why should we distinguish between determining a legal status, which requires findings of fact, and a pure finding of fact? As no reason suggests itself, we must either reject any attempt to extend *Gelston*, or reject the same-parties requirement generally. We return to this question after examining the other collateral estoppel issues. One issue is whether a civil judgment can be used in a criminal case.

Collateral Estoppel Civil/Criminal Blameworthiness

There is no double jeopardy harm, indeed there is no double jeopardy, in the absence of two jeopardies of life or limb or two convictions of life or limb offenses. Double jeopardy guarantees a single blameworthiness determination for a single offense. Thus, on the chapter 4 argument, if either of two offenses is not a "life or limb" offense, the state may seek a judgment in both.

The collateral estoppel aspect of double jeopardy is a specialized application of that blameworthiness principle. Here, the protection centers not on same offense but on the process as a whole. On a robust view of this blameworthiness principle, a defendant may offer res judicata from a civil proceeding to bar a criminal trial. From a blameworthiness perspective, a finding in the defendant's favor on an issue required for "life or limb" blameworthiness necessarily determines that issue for all time, whether or not that determination arose in a "life or limb" proceeding.

This means, of course, that a civil res judicata claim can pose a double jeopardy bar to a criminal prosecution that seeks to reexamine that issue (at least as long as the same-parties requirement is satisfied). The equation does not, however, work the other way. Though other res judicata doctrines may apply, nothing about double jeopardy bars a civil suit unless the "life or limb" threshold is met. An acquittal in a criminal case is irrelevant to a civil trial that falls below the "life or limb" threshold, not because, as the Court has held, the standards of persuasion are different,[20] but because there is nothing at risk in the second trial that requires double jeopardy protection. On this "life or limb" account, *Gelston* would have been wrong to apply a double jeopardy collateral estoppel bar because the second proceeding was a tort suit, which is not a "life or limb" action. (The actual basis for *Gelston* seems to be more civil res judicata than criminal collateral estoppel.)

As long as the "life or limb" case follows the civil case, however, collateral estoppel is potentially involved. The Court has never addressed this precise issue, but *United States v. Oppenheimer*[21] can be stretched to fit. *Oppenheimer* contains the famous statement by Holmes that offers a rationale for applying collateral estoppel to a criminal case: "It cannot be that the safeguards of the person, so often and so rightly mentioned with solemn reverence, are less than those that protect from a liability in debt."[22]

The *Oppenheimer* issue was whether a pretrial dismissal on statute of limitations grounds barred another trial. Under the Court's twice-in-jeopardy doctrine, the second trial can proceed because, as we see in the next chapter, pretrial dismissals occur outside the jeopardy framework and thus cannot constitute a jeopardy outcome. As the case was thus outside the Fifth Amendment, the government argued that collateral estoppel "does not exist for criminal cases except in the modified form of the 5th Amendment."[23] Holmes seemed to concede the premise that the Double Jeopardy Clause would not bar a second trial on the facts of the case and then wrote, "But the 5th Amendment was not intended to do away with what in the civil law is a fundamental principle of justice in order, when a man once has been acquitted on the merits, to enable the government to prosecute him a second time."[24]

To be sure, *Oppenheimer* involved two criminal cases, and it is therefore not authority for the proposition that a civil judgment in favor of a defendant could bar a criminal prosecution. Nonetheless, Holmes referred to collateral estoppel as a "fundamental principle of justice" in "the civil law" and then used it in a context when double jeopardy would not otherwise apply. This suggests that Holmes accepted its cross-over nature between civil and criminal. If a principle of civil justice would bar a criminal trial when jeopardy had not attached in the earlier proceeding because of a timing problem, it should bar a criminal trial when double jeopardy did not "attach" because the prior proceeding was civil in nature.

This reading of *Oppenheimer* is inconsistent with *Hoag v. New Jersey*, in which the Court later "entertain[ed] grave doubts whether collateral estoppel can be regarded as a constitutional requirement."[25] But *Hoag* did not survive *Ashe v. Swenson*, where the Court held that collateral estoppel was "embodied in the Fifth Amendment guarantee against double jeopardy."[26] In *Ashe*, the state charged six counts of robbery based on the robbing of six victims. This is a classic example of six act-tokens that manifest six separate Feinberg harms. Even on a lenient act-token view (see chapter 5), there is no same-offense bar to six trials and six convictions for robbery. But the state tried one count first, and the jury acquitted Ashe. The Court held that the state could not try him for any of the other robberies.

As *Ashe* overruled *Hoag*, *Oppenheimer* can be read expansively to permit offering a civil verdict as a collateral estoppel bar in a criminal case. The next section explores whether the different standards of persuasion in civil and criminal cases have any implication for collateral estoppel.

Standards of Persuasion

The ability of collateral estoppel to cross over between civil and criminal law raises an issue about different standards of persuasion that does not, of course, exist when two criminal prosecutions (or two civil trials) form the basis of the issue preclusion claim. If the civil case goes first, as we saw in the preceding section, the defendant should be able to offer a collateral estoppel claim against a subsequent criminal prosecution that seeks to reexamine the same blameworthiness (always assuming that the relevant same-parties requirement is met). The civil verdict has established that less than a preponderance of the evidence supported finding blameworthiness, which means that the proof was far below the criminal standard of beyond a reasonable doubt.

But the standard of persuasion suggests the opposite rule if the criminal case goes first. A defendant is entitled to an acquittal if the state's proof exceeded a preponderance but was less than beyond a reasonable doubt. The acquittal thus does not necessarily establish that the civil plaintiff would have failed and the Court has held that the civil case can proceed.[27]

This issue rarely arises. Civil offenses do not authorize incarceration and thus are not "life or limb" offenses. In chapter 4 I acknowledged that a prosecutor can abuse a civil offense in a way that transforms it into a "life or limb" proceeding, as in *Halper*,[28] but these are exceedingly rare occurrences. When the second proceeding is civil in form and mode, defendants cannot assert a collateral estoppel claim on the account offered in this book, because of the "life or limb" requirement, and on the Court's doctrine, because of the differing standards of persuasion.

For the truly rare case in which the civil trial is a "life or limb" proceeding, the Court's standard of persuasion bar should be ignored. The precision that justifies this bar is ephemeral. Yes, the acquittal in the criminal case could have been based on evidence greater than a preponderance but less than proof beyond a reasonable doubt. The acquittal was roughly as likely, however, to have been based on evidence less than preponderance.[29] In the latter case, the defendant is denied the issue preclusion to which he would have been entitled had the Court known the precise nature of the initial acquittal.

The Court's current view of this issue implicitly rejects *Gelston*'s holding that the acquittal in the in rem forfeiture is binding in the subsequent civil case. The Court has also overruled *Coffey v. United States*,[30] which had explicitly rejected the standard of persuasion argument. Coffey was acquitted of the criminal charge of operating an illegal distillery. The Court acknowledged the persuasion argument but held that the civil forfeiture of the distillery apparatus could not follow because it was "substantially the same thing" as a criminal case.[31] The Court held, in effect, that the fact of whether *Coffey* operated an illegal distillery had been determined for all time and for all purposes.

A blameworthiness account is fully consistent with *Coffey* on those rare occasions when the civil proceeding rises to the level of a "life or limb" proceeding. It is too bad that the Court abandoned *Coffey*, presumably to reduce the scope of double jeopardy protection, rather than take the more textually justified position that a civil forfeiture is not a "life or limb" offense. Now that the Court has essentially adopted the latter position,[32] perhaps it is not too late to resurrect *Coffey* for those rare cases when the civil proceeding involves a "life or limb" offense.

Rethinking Collateral Estoppel

My account of double jeopardy matches singular blameworthiness with single outcomes. Collateral estoppel depends on (assumes) the accuracy of the first proceeding, but determinations of blameworthiness are at best rough approximations. The Court made this clear in *Harris v. Washington*.[33] The state court held that the failure of the trial court to permit the jury to hear admissible evidence in the first trial should allow the state a second chance; the theory here is that the first acquittal is somehow not accurate enough if the state's case has not been fully presented through no fault of the state. The Court reversed, holding a second trial to be barred "irrespective of whether the jury considered all relevant evidence [in the first prosecution] and irrespective of the good faith of the State in bringing successive prosecutions."[34]

Similarly, there is no "reverse collateral estoppel" that resurrects an earlier outcome that was unfavorable to the defendant. Consider the following scenario: a defendant is convicted, retried after appeal and acquitted, and tried a third time and convicted. The state argued that collateral estoppel should not operate because the first trial ended in a conviction. The Court rejected the state's argument; the key point in time is the acquittal. Once acquitted, the defendant can rely on collateral estoppel regardless of what preceded the acquittal.[35]

These cases manifest a sort of "rough" justice: if the defendant gets a favorable ruling, the Court will apply it broadly, without regard to whether it is precisely accurate. This common-sense approach suggests that we should not permit formal differences in the standard of persuasion to permit reprosecution of an issue determined in the defendant's favor, but that issue comes up so rarely on a "life or limb" understanding of jeopardy that its resolution hardly matters.

Another common-sense outcome is to reject collateral estoppel in single trials, as the Court has done. The jury in *United States v. Powell*,[36] for example, found the defendant not guilty of the predicate drug crime but guilty of the compound offense that required proof of the predicate crime. Though this outcome is logically impossible, the Court refused to reverse the conviction on the ground of collateral estoppel. To conclude that collateral estoppel should arise from the acquittal "assumes that the acquittal on the predicate was proper—the one the jury 'really meant.'"[37]

This issue has come out differently in England, though Friedland contends that "the better interpretation of these cases is that the conviction was quashed because it was unreasonable [based on insufficient evidence] and not because it was not possible as a matter of issue estoppel."[38] If the government introduces sufficient evidence, nothing in a blameworthiness account suggests reversing a conviction because it was joined with a logically inconsistent acquittal.[39] Anne Bowen Poulin argues that in some cases the acquittal is not logically inconsistent with the conviction and that it should be held to bar later trials requiring proof of an issue foreclosed by the acquittal (though it would not result in reversal of the companion conviction).[40] This accords with my blameworthiness account; the logically consistent acquittal should end the defendant's blameworthiness for all issues foreclosed by the acquittal.

The same-parties requirement is also grounded in a common-sense view of the legal process. If a private citizen goes first, a realistic fear of fraud exists, the same concern that led Henry II to limit acquittals by the water ordeal.[41] The civil litigants could strike their own bargain, leading to a verdict for the defendant that did not accurately reflect his blameworthiness. This was the argument the king made to reject the verdict in favor of the Duchess of Kingston in the ecclesiastical court.

Moreover, there is the quite separate concern about fairness to civil litigants. In the absence of a same-parties requirement, the government could go first and sometimes deprive the citizen of her chance to prevail in a proceeding with a less onerous standard of persuasion. This is the issue that led to the "year-and-a-day" rule. The common law required the king to wait a year and a day before indictment to give the private suit time to proceed.[42] Finding this rule too restrictive, Henry VII promulgated a statute in 1487 that permitted both the king's indictment and the private suit to proceed in murder cases.[43]

The separation of the sovereign and the tort system was a good compromise in 1487 and is still a good compromise today. The compromise creates a certain conceptual dissonance when the same issue is reexamined in a second proceeding, which is most clearly seen when the judgment of a speciality court is reexamined in a court of general jurisdiction (*Kingston* and, by analogy, *Mason*). Nonetheless, the 1487 compromise can be justified on the grounds of fairness to civil litigants, on the notion that the harm to the private citizen is somehow distinct from the harm manifested by criminal law, and on the fear of fraudulent use of the civil process to avoid criminal liability.[44]

A related question is whether the same governmental entity has to be bringing the criminal charge in both proceedings—whether there is a dual sovereignty exception to collateral estoppel. Friedland argues that the Canadian federal system should not recognize an exception for dual sovereignty in collateral estoppel issues,[45] but the Canadian system is different from ours. In Canada, "there is only one system of criminal courts and generally only one body, the province, charged with administering the criminal law."[46]

In the United States, different courts and prosecutors are involved. The concern about fraud arises again, although it is surely less likely that prosecutors and courts will participate in fraud to protect defendants from criminal liability in other jurisdictions. But the resolution of this issue is simple: it should track the resolution of the same-offense issue between sovereigns. If a legislature intended its criminal law to create blameworthiness distinct from that of the other sovereign, then it surely did not intend collateral estoppel to bar its prosecutors. Without reaching the legislative-intent issue that underlies my blameworthiness account, the Supreme Court has held that neither sovereign has to recognize collateral estoppel implications from an acquittal in the courts of the other sovereign.[47]

The account in chapter 6 presumes that states do not intend to reprosecute the same blameworthiness already prosecuted by the federal government, and vice versa. On that presumption, a collateral estoppel bar against the other sovereign would also arise in acquittals. By rebutting this presumption and making its intent clear to reprosecute the same blameworthiness, a legislature would simultaneously make extra-sovereign collateral inapplicable to its prosecutions. Failing explicit rebuttal, an acquittal should give rise both to a same-offense and collateral estoppel claim against other sovereigns.

My blameworthiness account of collateral estoppel can be summarized as follows: no government can proceed against a defendant in a "life or limb" proceeding if it depends on proof of an act-token found not to have occurred in an earlier proceeding in the courts of the same, or another, government. This is but a variant of the basic same-offense account: a defendant cannot be tried or punished twice for a single commission of the same "life or limb" blameworthy act-type. I have thus attempted to show a unity between collateral estoppel and double jeopardy that Amar and Marcus deny is possible.[48]

8

Second Jeopardies
A Fresh Look at Blackstone's Solution

We can now say good-bye to same offense. The focus in this chapter is on trial procedure and outcome, rather than on the substantive question of when offenses are the same. The question is whether a second jeopardy is threatened or has occurred. This question is important, of course, only if the second jeopardy concerns the same offense; for purposes of this chapter and the next, we simply assume that the relevant offenses are the same offense. In most second-jeopardy cases, the charge at the second trial is identical to the first one, which satisfies all same-offense tests.

This chapter examines the Court's approach to the twice-in-jeopardy problem and offers a case-by-case blameworthiness account as an alternative. For example, I argue that a hung jury based on insufficient evidence bars a new trial because the defendant's lack of blameworthiness has been determined. The Court disagrees. In chapter 9 I offer a more global legislative-prerogative account of second jeopardies, focusing on the extent to which explicit legislative action can change traditional concepts of verdict and appeal.

Madison's original language prohibited more than one trial for the same offense. This language presumably prohibits more than one exposure to verdict, and the reason for terminating the exposure is unimportant. But the Clause as adopted and ratified does not forbid more than one trial or exposure to verdict. It forbids more than one jeopardy. Until we know when one jeopardy is over, we do not know when the bar arises.

Blackstone encountered no difficulties here because the eighteenth-century rule about terminations of jeopardy was elegant: the pleas in bar arose only after a prior acquittal or conviction.[1] This elegant rule worked in Blackstone's day because juries were required to deliberate until they reached a verdict in capital cases and could be discharged in noncapital cases only if both parties consented.[2] Blackstone's rule is manifested in several state constitutions.[3] Our more permissive modern procedure about jury deliberation demands a rule about early terminations. But the rule could still be Blackstone's, which is that early terminations are just not jeopardy outcomes. What is wrong with returning to Blackstone's formulation?

The answer is: (almost) nothing. The task of this chapter is to justify, and explain, that answer. In chapter 3 I argued that the conventional wisdom was wrong about Justice Story's famous mistrial opinion in *United States v. Perez*.[4] Story did not state a rule for reviewing trial court mistrials. Instead, Story stated that defendants cannot prevail on a double jeopardy claim unless they can show an acquittal or conviction for the same offense.

Verdicts end jeopardy because verdicts are the blameworthiness outcome the process is designed to produce. At that point, a rational system would have no interest in redetermining blameworthiness. In individual cases, the state's interest in redetermining blameworthiness might be rational, even compelling, but the system has a whole would collapse under its own weight if some principle did not generally constrain redeterminations. That principle, embodied in the Code of Hammurabi, is a broadly stated res judicata rule.

As a general matter, there is no reason to believe that fact-finder #2 will render a more accurate judgment about blameworthiness than fact-finder #1 and thus no reason to permit #2 to proceed, at least when the question is a systemic one. In effect, the double jeopardy rule merely embodies in the Constitution that rational system of res judicata, presumably to prevent individual instances of behavior inconsistent with the rational systemic model.

But a second determination of blameworthiness is impossible without a first determination. Two easy examples exist of this principle, both of which have been part of the common law since 1200: conviction and acquittal.

Formal Verdicts as the End of Jeopardy

Verdicts are the end of jeopardy, as they were in the king's courts in the thirteenth century and five hundred years later when Blackstone wrote his *Commentaries*, but only if they remain undisturbed. If a defendant elects to attack a conviction and if the conviction is vacated, no verdict remains to serve as a Blackstonian plea in bar of another trial. The question of an acquittal remaining undisturbed is more complex than it first seems, and the next section begins with that issue.

Acquittals

Defendants do not, of course, appeal acquittals, and the federal government and most states do not permit a prosecution appeal. A largely ignored issue is whether double jeopardy prevents a prosecution appeal. The Court held, near the beginning of the twentieth century and over Holmes's dissent, that the Double Jeopardy Clause bars a federal appeal of an acquittal.[5] In a state case in 1986, the Court rather casually stated that double jeopardy also barred a state appeal of an acquittal if a reversal would "lead to proceedings that violate the Double Jeopardy Clause."[6]

James Strazzella questions whether it is double jeopardy or the procedural law that prohibits the appeal of an acquittal.[7] As he correctly notes, the acquitted defendant is not exposed to a second jeopardy by virtue of an appeal. A double jeopardy issue arises only if the acquittal is vacated and the defendant is forced to trial a second time. One way to conceptualize the issue is that double jeopardy bars a second trial in the face of an acquittal, and the procedural law bars a futile appeal.

The distinction is important in two kinds of cases. In the first kind, about which Professor Strazzella wrote, a few states permit the prosecution to appeal, typically to obtain "advisory rulings limited to future cases."[8] It is important for that category of cases to understand that the Court has never held that the Double Jeopardy Clause bars prosecution appeal when the only effect would be an advisory opinion. In the second category of cases, a legislature might permit a prosecutor to appeal trial court rulings that led to an acquittal and, if the trial judge were overruled, to retry the acquitted defendant with a correct set of legal rulings. Would the Double Jeopardy Clause permit this system? The next chapter considers this fundamental question.

But in describing the current state of the law, it is safe to say that an acquittal bars a second trial for the same offense, and the only real issue is to determine which outcomes are acquittals. Two kinds of questions arise. First, perhaps an acquittal obtained by fraud is not really an acquittal. Second, perhaps an acquittal is not really an acquittal if the trial judge acts arbitrarily or erroneously and deprives the state of its chance to obtain a conviction.

The most obvious way in which an acquittal may not be an acquittal is if the defendant bribes the judge to return a not-guilty verdict as trier of fact.[9] Ann Bowen Poulin argues that courts should ignore the acquittal and permit a second trial "if the prosecution establishes, beyond a reasonable doubt, that the acquittal was a product of a corrupt [judicial] process."[10] In these cases, the defendant has relinquished "any claim to a protected interest in the finality of the fact finder's verdict or in the termination of the stress and anxiety of the trial."[11] Professor Poulin argues that a similar exception should not be recognized when a defendant corrupts members of the jury; here, the corruption of the process is less profound because, presumably, some or most of the jury are not corrupted.

David Rudstein recognizes that an acquittal obtained by fraud is a corruption of the process but argues that it happens so infrequently that "the game hardly seems worth the candle."[12] The "candle," as Professor Rudstein sees it, is the potential for harassment of acquitted defendants and the loss of finality of acquittals. The state could come forward years later, allege fraud, and force an acquitted defendant, at a minimum, to defend the charge of fraud.

As I noted in chapter 1, it seems unlikely that the legislature would want to give finality to an acquittal in the limited set of circumstances carved out by Poulin: when the state can prove beyond a reasonable doubt that the defendant corrupted the judge. Moreover, I can draw support from Blackstone here, as Rudstein acknowledges. In one statement of *autrefois acquit*, Blackstone limits it to cases "when a man is once fairly found not guilty upon any indictment."[13] Though these cases arise too infrequently to make much difference, the better rule for a legislative-intent account is Poulin's.

In *Sanabria v. United States*,[14] the trial judge excluded evidence on the erroneous belief that the indictment did not cover the proferred evidence. An alternative to excluding evidence because it was improperly alleged in the indictment would have been to dismiss the indictment because it improperly alleged one of the elements. Had the judge taken that option, the dismissal would not have been the end of jeopardy.[15] But *Sanabria* held that an acquittal was an acquittal and could not be appealed.[16]

Westen and Drubel criticize this distinction, arguing that the two errors are "functionally identical."[17] That is the problem with legal-realist policy analysis; a clever advocate can make almost any two things appear functionally the same. In this case, Westen and Drubel focus on the procedural similarity: both cases involve defects in the charging document and consequent dismissal at the defendant's behest. But the only function that should determine the end of jeopardy is substantive: if the judge merely dismissed the indictment for a procedural flaw, he would not have resolved the elements of the offense in the defendant's favor. Once we free ourselves from interest balancing and policy analysis, it is sheer sophistry to equate a dismissal where the trier of fact has found the case unproven[18] with a case in which the judge has found an element improperly alleged in the indictment.

Sanabria can be fully defended, however, only if we can explain why acquittals, but not convictions, are an absolute bar to further proceedings. Westen suggests that acquittals are an absolute bar because acquitted defendants enjoy a unique type of "relief and desire for repose" and because double jeopardy protects jury nullification.[19] Another explanation is that acquitted defendants do not appeal their verdicts. On this Blackstonian view, convictions and acquittals are identical double jeopardy events when rendered. They acquire a different procedural status when a defendant chooses to appeal a conviction. If the conviction is vacated, the state is permitted to begin again, unless something about the reversal determines the blameworthiness issue in the defendant's favor.

In effect, Blackstone's verdict rule works as follows: when a defendant offers a double jeopardy defense to a trial, the court determines whether there is an extant verdict for the same offense (an acquittal, an undisturbed conviction, or a conviction overturned in a way that makes it substantively an acquittal). Looking at the end of the appeal process to see whether a verdict exists to bar another jeopardy provides a better explanation of the disparate treatment of acquittals and convictions than Westen's views about nullification and repose. As to repose, it is not clear why double jeopardy should protect particular expectations about future proceedings. As to nullification, it is not clear why double jeopardy, and not the Sixth Amendment right to a jury trial, is the protector of nullification.

What is clear is that Blackstone would have insisted on an extant verdict to bar a second jeopardy. That still seems the best explanation for why convictions are today treated differently from acquittals. Some trial outcomes that are not formal verdicts can be "acquittal equivalents," but I defer the discussion of these outcomes until we have disposed of formal verdicts. Acquittals pose no problem, at least outside the corrupted-judge context. Whether rendered by judge or jury, whether based on a fair interpretation of the evidence or a raw exercise in jury nullification, an uncorrupted acquittal is the end of any "life or limb" proceedings by the state against the defendant for the same offense. (As the world saw, with some misgivings, in the O. J. Simpson civil case, and as chapter 4 made plain, an acquittal in a criminal case does not bar a civil suit.) Of the two kinds of formal verdicts, only convictions present issues yet to be resolved.

Undisturbed Convictions

Criminal procedure was far simpler in Blackstone's day. If a defendant made a double jeopardy plea in bar, a judge merely had to determine whether a prior trial had ended in an acquittal, a conviction with a judgment, or a conviction without a judgment. If so, the defendant could successfully plead *autrefois acquit, autrefois attaint,* or *autrefois convict.*[20] If no verdict existed, the plea was no good.

If one ignores the modern procedural pertubations (the conditional guilty plea, appeal, motion for a new trial following conviction, and dismissal after a conviction), convictions produce the same result today. When Nathaniel Brown was faced with an auto theft charge based on the same taking for which he had already served thirty days in jail, he raised a plea of former conviction. And, as we have seen, the Supreme Court held that double jeopardy barred Ohio from prosecuting Brown for the same offense.

This part of double jeopardy has not changed for eight hundred years (even longer if we include Greek and Roman law) because it is the core of double jeopardy. Infused with notions of res judicata, the idea that one verdict on an issue ends the defendant's jeopardy is both fair and procedurally necessary. As noted earlier, any system that determines outcomes must have a limit on the number of times the same question can be considered. And "one" is the only fair limit when "life or limb" is at risk.

Thus, the only double jeopardy issue that arises when a defendant relies on an undisturbed conviction (or acquittal, for that matter) is whether the new proceeding is for the same offense as the one that produced the verdict. But, once a conviction is disturbed, new issues arise.

Convictions Reversed on Appeal

In Blackstone's day, a convicted defendant could seek to have the judgment "falsified, reversed, or avoided" by showing that the original judgment was rendered in some way that made it voidable. The example Blackstone gives is a judgment entered by those who lacked the authority to do so.[21] A convicted defendant could also petition the king's courts from the inferior courts by a writ of error that showed "notorious mistakes in the judgment or other parts of the record," such as a misdescription of the accused, the sheriff, or the court.[22] Leaving aside the technical (and outmoded) judgment of outlawry, the effect of reversing or falsifying the judgment of conviction was that "all former proceedings are absolutely set aside, and the party stands as if he had never been at all accused."[23] In Blackstone's day, as in my account, the accused "still remains liable to another prosecution for the same offence; for the first being erroneous, he never was in jeopardy thereby."[24]

This follows logically from Blackstone's notion that a verdict is a plea in bar. Remove the verdict, and you remove the plea in bar. While this is not the modern English rule,[25] it is the modern rule in the United States. In *United States v. Tateo*[26] the Court reaffirmed an earlier precedent and held that a reversal clears the way for a new trial. The *Tateo* Court acknowledged the contrary modern English rule but rejected it largely on policy grounds. The Court wrote: "It would be a high price indeed for society to pay were every accused granted immunity from punishment because of any defect sufficient to constitute reversible error in the proceedings leading to conviction."[27]

A more Blackstone-like explanation can be found in the case on which *Tateo* relied. This 1896 case is also useful in drawing a distinction between convictions and acquittals as verdict bars. Two defendants in *Ball v. United States*[28] had been convicted in an earlier trial, and their convictions had been set aside on appeal because of a defect in the indictment. At the new trial, the trial judge overruled the plea of former jeopardy. The defendants were convicted and sentenced to death. Their claim in the Supreme Court was that a verdict ended jeopardy, whether or not it is overturned on appeal for error.

In deciding that question the *Ball* Court made a distinction that has rarely been noted. Westen and Drubel urge a different rationale, one drawn from the Court's later explanation of *Ball*: "Given the difficulty of affording a defendant a completely error-free trial the first time around, the State is 'excused' for committing the error and allowed to assert its interest in law enforcement over the defendant's interest in finality."[29] If one uses this rationale, one gets the right answer in *Ball* on the conviction issue—the indictment error can be excused and the government permitted to assert its interest in law enforcement. The government can disregard the outcome of the flawed proceeding and begin again. The problem with this characterization is that it cannot explain the acquittal issue also raised by *Ball*.

There was a third defendant in *Ball*, Miliard Filmore Ball,[30] who was found not guilty by the jury in the initial trial. Since he was charged and tried under the same indictment as the other two defendants, the excusal-of-error rationale means that the government could disregard the outcome of his flawed proceeding—the acquittal—and begin again with respect to him, too. In *Ball*, we do not have to argue about whether one error is more excusable than the other: it was precisely the same error in the same indictment that infected both the convictions and the acquittal. If the error justified overriding the convicted defendants' finality interest in the first outcome, it also, without an additional parameter, overrides Miliard Filmore Ball's interest in the first outcome.

But the Court held in *Ball*, after a rather lengthy and somewhat defensive analysis distinguishing English authorities, that Miliard Filmore Ball could not be reprosecuted. Thus, another parameter is needed. Westen and Drubel read the *Ball* opinion as suggesting that the most significant interest in the double jeopardy hierarchy of (legal realist) values is a defendant's interest in jury nullification. On this reading of *Ball*, the additional parameter is that acquittals by a jury are categorically different from any other outcome.

Asserting a jury nullification parameter, as a brute fact, does harmonize the results in *Ball*, but it is historically and conceptually unsatisfactory. The historical flaw is that neither Blackstone nor any of the other English authorities ever favored the finality of acquittals over the finality of convictions.[31] Moreover, support for this distinction in the *Ball* opinion results from a modernist misreading. Although the *Ball* Court stressed the jury finding of factual innocence, its purpose was to distinguish the English rule that a void indictment never gave rise to a jeopardy bar. The *Ball* Court asserted that the English doctrine of void indictments applied only to outcomes not based on factual innocence.

The distinction *Ball* made between the convictions and the acquittal is not based on acquittals being categorically different, or even on some abstract view of Miliard Filmore Ball's factual innocence; the distinction is based on what Miliard Filmore Ball did following the outcome—nothing. The Court noted several times that what rendered the convicted defendants subject to reprosecution was that they had chosen to erase the conviction. For example, "[I]t is quite clear that a defendant who procures a judgment against him upon an indictment to be set aside may be tried anew."[32] In an even more instructive passage, the Court distinguished three situations: [1] the English void verdict rule; [2] the convicted defendant; and [3] the acquitted defendant. The point to distinguishing [1] is to reject the English rule that an acquittal on a void indictment cannot be used as a jeopardy bar:

> [1] But, although the indictment was fatally defective, yet, if the court had jurisdiction of the cause and of the party, its judgment is not void, but only voidable by writ of error, and until so avoided cannot be collaterally impeached. [2] If the judgment is upon a verdict of guilty, and unreversed, it stands good, and warrants the punishment of the defendant accordingly, and he could not be discharged by writ of habeas corpus. [3] If the judgment is upon an acquittal, the defendant, indeed, will not seek to have it reversed, and the government cannot.[33]

A clearer statement of the relevant principle is difficult to imagine. It has nothing to do with jury nullification and everything to do with the defendant's election to stand on or to reverse the initial outcome. The defendants in *Ball* were treated differently simply because Miliard Filmore Ball took no action to upset his acquittal, while the other defendants sought and obtained reversals of their verdicts. I have previously used "verdict election" to describe this principle,[34] which is consistent with the Court's explanation of *Ball*.[35]

Not only is the *Ball* Court's description clear; the concept of verdict election is self-derivable from the way the criminal process treats verdicts. Defendants X and Y appeal their convictions and obtain a reversal. No verdict now exists that manifests the first jeopardy. No barrier exists to a reprosecution. Blackstone's common law produces the same result. But defendant Miliard Filmore Ball does not appeal his verdict. An extant verdict manifests the first jeopardy; it matters not whether that verdict is an acquittal or a conviction. An extant verdict is an insurmountable barrier to a new trial. On this view, no double jeopardy issue arises in a mistrial case where no determination of guilt or innocence can be found in the outcome. Using blameworthiness to explain the second jeopardy aspect permits a return to Blackstone, to Story's *Commentaries*, and to Story's reading of Story's opinion in *Perez*.[36]

By contrast, Westen and Drubel's legal realism requires that their hierarchy of double jeopardy values be accepted and then balanced in a complex process that is more an ad hoc rationalization of the Court's doctrine than a helpful analytical tool.[37] Westen and Drubel confuse matters further when they seek to harmonize the mistrial and the appeal cases by use of their jury nullification value. They argue that the same rationale explains both categories of cases—whether the prosecution was manipulating error in the first trial to avoid an acquittal. Manipulation is one explanation of the mistrial doctrine, as we see later,[38] but it has nothing to do with appeals. It does not explain why Miliard Filmore Ball was treated differently from his codefendants. More important, it is a question that need not be answered. If one takes the Blackstonian view that mistrials have nothing to do with cases involving verdicts, one is not forced on the Procrustean bed of trying to harmonize two very different lines of cases.

Once again, a careful look at what the earlier courts and commentators thought about double jeopardy provides a more satisfactory explanation of doctrine than a set of vague policies and values. Defendants who successfully appeal their convictions can be reprosecuted because no verdict exists as barrier. That rule does not apply to defendants who do not appeal their verdicts, which includes many convicted defendants as well as acquitted defendants. The double jeopardy world was still simple when *Ball* was decided in 1896, and it made a lot more sense than the Westen and Drubel world of 1978.

Guilty Pleas

There are two double jeopardy questions involved with guilty pleas. First, how does double jeopardy doctrine operate as a framework within which prosecutors and defense counsel bargain for repose and finality? Stated differently, how do the various double jeopardy rules and exceptions—for example, dual sovereignty—affect the process by which guilty pleas are negotiated? This intensely pragmatic and important question is beyond the scope of the present book, but Daniel Richman's examination is both thorough and thoughtful.[39]

The second question is theoretical: are the consequences of a guilty plea conviction different from those of a conviction after a trial? The answer is no and yes. For the typical guilty plea conviction, the procedural process by which it is obtained is irrelevant. If the defendant does not succeed in disturbing the conviction, it stands as a bar to another proceeding to the same offense.

But what happens when the guilty plea follows an earlier verdict for the same offense? If the defendant is permitted to appeal his guilty plea, the underlying conviction must be vacated. But the rule for appealing guilty plea convictions is very strict—about the only errors that can be raised on appeal are errors in the voluntariness of the guilty plea or in the procedure that led up to the plea.[40] So the issue is whether a defendant can appeal on the ground that the guilty plea conviction violated the Double Jeopardy Clause.

The Court permits this kind of appeal.[41] Double jeopardy violations are one of a very small subset of errors unrelated to the plea itself that can be raised on appeal.[42] The reason for this exception, according to the Court, is that the double jeopardy violation deprives the state of the authority to bring a second proceeding. If the state lacked authority even to file charges, the entire process is tainted, and no reason exists to give preclusive effect to the guilty plea. This comports with Blackstone's view of *autrefois attaint* (a common law plea now merged into the doctrine of former conviction): all proceedings after an accused had been attainted were superfluous. Similarly, with an extant verdict: all proceedings based on the same offense are superfluous and may be disregarded.[43]

A second procedural wrinkle involved with guilty-plea convictions is that defendants can promise to do certain things in the future in exchange for a guilty plea to a lesser offense. If the defendant fails to live up to the contractual agreement, what are the double jeopardy consequences? Again, if one examines this issue in the abstract, without worrying about fairness to a particular defendant, the answer seems pretty clear. Assuming that guilty pleas can be made conditional—which is not a double jeopardy issue—and assuming that the defendant failed to do what he promised, the contract would give the state the authority to vacate the underlying conviction. Once the underlying conviction has been vacated, the defendant is in the same position as if the conviction had been reversed on appeal.

The Court reached this result in *Ricketts v. Adamson*.[44] The agreement stated that in the event of breach, "the parties shall be returned to the positions they were in before this agreement."[45] Adamson pleaded guilty to second-degree murder in return for his promise to testify against others involved in the murder. When he refused to testify in a retrial of the others, the state court vacated the second-degree murder conviction and re-instated the original charges. He was subsequently convicted of first-degree murder and sentenced to death. The Supreme Court upheld the conviction and sentence.

One might draw a distinction between Adamson and the typical defendant who appeals his conviction and obtains a reversal. This distinction would make something of the typical defendant who exercises the appellate procedure to disturb his conviction, while Adamson did nothing. He did not seek legal action to disturb his conviction; indeed, he stood on the conviction as a jeopardy bar.[46] But ultimately this distinction does not hold. Adamson did do something to upset his conviction. His refusal to execute the agreement was a legal action for which he could be held accountable.[47] He chose a path, with legal consequences, just as the typical defendant who successfully appealed his conviction.

The final wrinkle in guilty-plea convictions intersects the acquittal doctrine. An acquittal is a manifestation of lack of blameworthiness, and a conviction can sometimes function as a partial acquittal. If, for example, a defendant is charged with first-degree murder and convicted of second-degree murder (the facts of *Green v. United States*),[48] the fact-finder has implicitly acquitted the defendant of first-degree murder. Should the defendant obtain a reversal of the second-degree murder conviction, retrial is permitted for that charge but not for the higher charge of which he has been implicitly acquitted. So held in *Green*.

One might seek to expand the *Green* doctrine to guilty-plea convictions, but the analogy is inapt. When the prosecutor accepts a guilty plea to a lesser offense, there is no fact-finding about the blameworthiness of the defendant for the greater charge. Thus, as the Court has held, a guilty-plea conviction does not implicitly acquit of any other offense.[49]

Sentencing Problems

When trial judges enter more than one conviction, defendants can raise a double jeopardy issue on appeal by claiming that two or more of these convictions are for the same offense. If the defendant is wrong, that's the end of the story. If the defendant is right, appellate courts must decide which convictions to vacate. This issue turns out to be mostly about sentencing.

We should begin with what may be obvious but was not decided until 1985. More than one conviction for the same offense is a violation of double jeopardy without regard to the sentences imposed on the multiple convictions (or whether any sentence at all was imposed). The only possible remedy for a violation of the double jeopardy multiple-punishment doctrine is to vacate the offending convictions.[50]

The issue arose because courts adopted strategies to avoid vacating convictions (probably from a desire not to have to retry a defendant if one conviction was subsequently overturned). Courts sometimes left the offending convictions intact and ordered all but one sentence to be vacated. Alternatively, courts sometimes left the convictions intact and ordered the sentences to be served concurrently.[51] But, in 1985, the Supreme Court held that the offending legal event was not the existence of multiple sentences but the existence of more than one conviction for the same offense.[52]

This is right on a Blackstone view because even a conviction *without judgment* permitted a defendant to claim the plea of former conviction in 1764. If one accepts the analogy between multiple convictions in one trial and multiple trials,[53] then the existence of more than one conviction must offend double jeopardy in every context. Unfortunately, this recognition does not solve all the problems about how to remedy multiple convictions when the error is discovered on appeal.

While a full discussion of this highly technical issue is beyond the scope of the current work,[54] the problem can be sketched here. Suppose the trial judge enters convictions for offense *A*, offense *B*, and offense *C*. The judge imposes five-year sentences for all convictions and orders the sentences for *A* and *B* to be served concurrently, with the sentence for *C* to be served consecutively. The net effect of this sentencing package is that the defendant faces a ten-year sentence, with a concurrent term of five years for the first part of the sentence. Now assume that the appellate court determines that the conviction for *C* violates the double jeopardy multiple-punishment doctrine. What is to be done?[55]

If the appellate court mechanically vacates the conviction for *C* and affirms the other two, the result is that the defendant faces two concurrent sentences of five years each, half as long as the sentence the trial judge meant to impose. As appellate courts lack the authority to resentence, the only remedy that permits the total sentence to be what the trial judge intended is to vacate all convictions and remand for resentencing. But assuming the defendant asked only for conviction *C* to be reversed, it is not clear that appellate courts possess the authority to reverse the others. And there are potential due process problems that are not discussed here.[56]

The Supreme Court has never spoken to this issue. It may depend more on notions of procedural finality in appellate review than on double jeopardy. Judges can avoid the problem by making sure that one conviction carries a sentence that reflects the judge's view of the defendant's blameworthiness. If this is not possible, because no one offense permits a sentence of that length, judges can order each sentence consecutive with each other (and the pairs concurrent with other pairs) to ensure that the sentencing package cannot be changed by an appellate reversal of one sentence. In the hypothetical, for example, the judge could have ordered A served consecutively with B, and B served consecutively with C, and A served consecutively with C, and all three pairs to be served concurrently.

The sentencing issues discussed so far arise only when more than one conviction is entered. Are there double jeopardy sentencing problems when only a single conviction is entered? Not in Blackstone's day, but recent modern complexities in sentencing, particularly the federal sentencing guidelines, have opened up potential double jeopardy claims. So far, consistent with Blackstone, the Supreme Court has failed to find any double jeopardy problems associated with sentencing as long as there is only one conviction per same offense.

Some simple matters first. There are no double jeopardy problems in resentencing under a single conviction after an earlier conviction has been reversed on appeal and the defendant reconvicted. The sentencing judge must give the defendant credit for time already served but may otherwise impose any sentence permitted by law.[57] Though there are potential due process problems here,[58] there is no double jeopardy problem, the Court has told us, because the "slate has been wiped clean. The conviction has been set aside and the unexpired portion of the original sentence will never be served."[59] This manifests a Blackstonian view of second jeopardies.

So double jeopardy permits judges to resentence at will after a conviction that follows an appellate reversal. But what if the relevant sentencing guidelines require the prosecutor to disclose, and the judge to consider, uncharged conduct that constitutes a crime? If that uncharged conduct results in a sentence enhancement, can the prosecution later bring a prosecution based on the uncharged conduct? Yes, the Court held in *Witte v. United States*.[60] Sentencing enhancements "do not punish a defendant for crimes of which he was not convicted, but rather increase his sentence because of the manner in which he committed the crime of conviction."[61]

This perhaps abstract distinction follows from the Court's century-long treatment of habitual-offender crimes. Habitual-offender crimes punish a defendant more severely if he has been previously convicted of other crimes. In a way, the defendant is being punished again for the past crimes, but the Court has consistently held that the legislature may view the past crimes as evidence suggesting that the defendant is more dangerous, more in need of reform, and thus a better candidate for a longer sentence. In the Court's words, the increased penalty "is a stiffened penalty for the latest crime, which is considered to be an aggravated offense because a repetitive one."[62]

The Court's treatment of sentence enhancment fits nicely with the legislative-prerogative view of double jeopardy developed in this book. As long as the legislature is clear that it wants the additional penalty, which is clear in the habitual-offender laws, there is no double jeopardy reason to oppose the additional penalty. Indeed, a legislative-prerogative theory would also permit the government to use uncharged conduct for which the defendant had been tried and acquitted as long as the legislature made clear that it authorized this outcome. There is nothing magic about an acquittal that overrides the legislature's ability to configure a procedural system that uses conduct to determine blameworthiness, as long as the prosecutor has to prove the conduct in the new proceeding. This, of course, follows from my Blackstonian view that only verdicts have jeopardy status. The Supreme Court agreed, in *United States v. Watts*,[63] holding that the conduct underlying an acquittal may be used to enhance a sentence under the federal sentencing guidelines.

To be sure, there are difficult sentencing issues involving due process and construction of sentencing guidelines, but the only Model 3 double jeopardy sentencing requirement is that a trial judge cannot impose more than one conviction for the same offense. Because Congress has denominated enhancement as something other than a verdict, it does not matter that the enhancement is based on conduct for which the defendant was convicted or acquitted. On this issue, the Court has closely paralleled the Blackstone blameworthiness account of double jeopardy. Other nuances appear when we consider the concept of "acquittal equivalence" in the next three sections.

Overview of Acquittal Equivalence

There are two categories of outcomes that lack the status of a formal verdict: mistrial and dismissal. The procedural distinction, roughly, is that a mistrial keeps the original indictment or other charging instrument in place and thus contemplates a retrial. A dismissal, as its name suggests, dismisses the indictment or charging document and is indifferent as to retrial. For a few years, the Court seemed to intimate that a substantive jeopardy distinction might exist between these outcomes. But the only distinction the Court has made so far is that dismissals, but not mistrials, can be viewed as equivalent to an acquittal.[64] A jeopardy bar arises, for example, if a judge dismisses an indictment because the state has failed to prove that the defendant was sane at the time the crime was committed.

In chapter 2 I argued that jeopardy policy has nothing to do with preventing harassment and everything to do with preventing unauthorized judgments, which include convictions and dismissals of defendants who are entitled to acquittals.[65] *Ireland's Case*[66] shows why this "acquittal equivalence" must be accepted as a jeopardy policy, whatever else may also be included. Five defendants were charged with conspiracy to murder the king. The year was 1678, and the previous century had seen the bitter Reformation, the residue of which lingers to this day. Only a few years prior to *Ireland's Case*, the authorities had thwarted the famous Gunpowder Plot to blow up Parliament that is still memorialized as Guy Fawkes Day. The prosecutor in *Ireland's Case* sought to show that the plot against King James was motivated by the same English "papists" who, "being moved and seduced by the instigation of the devil,"[67] had sought to "introduce the popish religion, and to destroy the established Protestant religion in England."[68]

At the close of the evidence, the judge summarized the case for the jury. He noted the requirement that the crime be proved by two witnesses and stated that, with respect to two of the defendants, Whitebread and Fenwick, the requirement had not been met. The prosecution had proved the existence of a plot to kill the king, according to the judge, but not against these defendants. The judge concluded, "[S]o that though the testimony be so full, as to satisfy a private conscience, yet we must go according to law, too." Thus, "it is a great evidence that is against them [Whitebread and Fenwick]; but it not being sufficient in point of law, we discharge you of them; it is not a legal proof to convict them by, whatsoever it may be to satisfy your consciences. Therefore remove Mr. Fenwick and Mr. Whitebread from the Bar." The judge ordered Fenwick and Whitebread returned to prison "until more proof may come in."[69] Both were later retried, convicted, and executed,[70] their plea of former jeopardy rejected because no formal verdict existed.[71]

It is unlikely that our system, with independent judges, would ever produce a travesty of justice on the order of *Ireland's Case*. Nonetheless, the possibility of prosecutorial manipulation of the process argues for a mistrial doctrine that discourages prosecutors from using early trial termination as acquittal avoidance. Drawing on *Ireland's Case*, an early termination should not prevent an analysis of the evidence to see whether an acquittal would have occurred.

The result in *Ireland's Case* is wrong, on this view, not because the trial ended prior to verdict but because there is no reason to distinguish between defendants who are acquitted and those who would have been acquitted had the jury been permitted to return a verdict.[72] Deciding which defendants belong in the latter category is obviously difficult. If we hypothetically had foreknowledge of the evidence that would be admitted, we could construct a universe of defendants against whom the state will present a legally insufficient case. A double jeopardy account sensitive to substance rather than procedure would not permit this class to be subdivided into those who are acquitted and those whose trial is ended by the prosecutor's motion.

We do not have the ability to predict the future, of course. But that does not mean we should ignore the problem of acquittal avoidance. Some amendment to Blackstone's pleas in bar is thus necessary. The nature of the amendment is implicit in the concept of blameworthiness. The entire double jeopardy principle underlying this book can be restated as a prohibition of treating singular blameworthiness as anything other than singular blameworthiness. In the first seven chapters, this principle allowed me to simplify the same-offense doctrine and to unify it with collateral estoppel. In the second jeopardy context, this principle means that no possible double jeopardy issue can arise unless the first trial has produced a finding as to blameworthiness.

We can relax Blackstone's reliance on formal verdicts by recognizing that lack of blameworthiness can be manifested in outcomes other than formal verdicts. Other endings can be "acquittal equivalents," by which I mean an ending that resolves the blameworthiness issue in favor of the defendant. An example is a dismissal granted on the ground of insufficient evidence.

At this point, the argument is vulnerable to the legal-realist claim that something as vague as acquittal equivalence opens the way, at best, to interpretational difficulties and, at worst, to the infinite regress to the bargain basement of legal realism where each case requires its own rule. It is a fair criticism, but some soft-edged principle cannot be avoided if we wish to give courts the authority to prevent or rectify *Ireland's Case*. Acquittal equivalence requires courts to look at the record in each nonverdict jeopardy case, but that is what courts do when defendants appeal convictions on the ground of insufficient evidence. Moreover, it is possible to limit acquittal equivalence to keep it from consuming the entire mistrial doctrine.

Verdicts end jeopardy. But verdicts can occur in ways other than a formal entry of judgment. Acquittal equivalents occur in three procedural settings: at the end of trial, on appeal, and (rarely) in mistrials. The issues at the end of trial and on appeal are conceptually linked and can usefully be considered as paradigm cases of acquittal equivalence.

Paradigm Acquittal Equivalence: Dismissals and Appellate Reversals That Resolve Blameworthiness

An outcome that resolves the facts of the case in the defendant's favor is an acquittal, whether or not it is called by that name. *Green v. United States*[73] is the classic example. Green was found guilty of second-degree murder following a trial on a charge of first-degree murder. The Court held that the effect of the formal verdict was to acquit Green of first-degree murder,[74] a rule that Bishop had recognized early in the twentieth century.[75] As odd as it may sound, even a conviction can be an acquittal. The Court showed how seriously it took the analogy to acquittal when it later held that the mere prosecution of the "acquitted" offense was a violation of double jeopardy, even though the defendant was convicted of the same lesser-included offense as in the first trial (so, in one sense, defendant was not harmed by the second trial).[76] This is precisely how a formal acquittal works, and the Court held that an implicit acquittal works the same way.

The Court refused to extend *Green* to routine sentencing. In *United States v. DiFrancesco*,[77] the government appealed a sentence on the ground that it was "clearly erroneous"—too lenient—under the relevant dangerous-special-offender sentencing provisions, which permitted government appeal. The defendant claimed that the government was forbidden to appeal his favorable sentence because it was tantamount to an implicit acquittal of a harsher sentence. The Supreme Court rejected this claim, noting a "distinction between acquittals and sentences" that "does not require that a sentence be given a degree of finality that prevents its later increase."[78]

The Court was right to reject this analogy. Double jeopardy blameworthiness is an either/or proposition. Either Green is guilty of first-degree murder or he is not. If not, either he is guilty of second-degree murder or not. Judgments that a defendant is not guilty of X crime is a judgment that the defendant is blameless for X crime.

By contrast, the "acquittal" of longer sentences does not entail a finding that the defendant is blameless. It manifests, instead, a judicial notion about proportionality of the penalty to the demonstrated blameworthiness. But, as we saw in chapter 1, double jeopardy has nothing to say about proportionality, deferring that question to the Cruel and Unusual Punishment Clause or to the Due Process Clause.[79]

The Court made an exception to *DiFrancesco* for death penalty sentencing. A finding against the death penalty by the judge or jury "acquits" the defendant of the death penalty, and the state cannot seek that penalty if a new sentencing hearing is later required.[80] Again, the Court's result follows by analogy to verdict blameworthiness. The two-tier procedure in death cases requires a separate sentencing hearing at which new evidence is admitted under relaxed rules of evidence, and the only issue is whether to apply the death penalty. The process of hearing new evidence and making an either-or decision on the death penalty very much resembles the either-or decision on guilt. Indeed, if one views the death penalty as different from all others, the analogy is striking. A defendant is either "guilty" in the sense of deserving this unique penalty or he is not.

Dismissals as Acquittals

The Court muddied the jeopardy waters for a time by introducing a concern with finality or harassment rather than acquittal equivalence in dismissal cases. *United States v. Jenkins* held that a dismissal barred further proceedings "devoted to the resolution of factual issues going to the elements of the offense charged."[81] Even if these factual issues were not resolved in the defendant's favor in the first trial, that they remain unresolved was enough to convert the dismissal into a jeopardy bar.

The unanimous opinion, written by Justice Rehnquist, relied on Justice Black's oft-quoted language from *Green* about the double jeopardy limit on the power of the state "to make repeated attempts to convict an individual for an alleged offense, thereby subjecting him to embarrassment, expense and ordeal and compelling him to live in a continuing state of anxiety and insecurity, as well as enhancing the possibility that even though innocent he may be found guilty."[82] But, as already noted, Justice Black's eloquent language is not analytically helpful. Yes, it is more costly for defendants to undergo two trials, but the costs of a second trial are unacceptable only when the first trial has produced an outcome that we recognize as the end of jeopardy for a single offense. Drawing on Michael Moore, I attempted in chapter 2 to dispel the confusion that some magical quality exists about second prosecutions that changes the same-offense analysis.

Similarly, the threat of a second prosecution does not magically transform dismissals into verdicts. The costs to the defendant of two proceedings are severe regardless of the reason for having a second proceeding, but these costs are cognizable in double jeopardy policy only when there is a reason to treat the first outcome as the end of jeopardy. Is a dismissal the end of one jeopardy just because it would require a new proceeding if reversed on appeal? *Jenkins* held yes, but the outcome is in no way predetermined by Justice Black's quote.

Three years later, in *Scott v. United States*, the Court admitted that "we pressed too far in *Jenkins* the concept of the 'defendant's valued right to have his trial completed by a particular tribunal.'"[83] In an opinion by Justice Rehnquist, the author of *Jenkins*, the Court overruled *Jenkins* by a vote of 5-4, candidly admitting that "vastly increased exposure to the various facets of the Double Jeopardy Clause" had led it to conclude that *Jenkins* was "wrongly decided."[84] It may well be the only time a Justice has authored an opinion overruling a case in which he wrote the Court's opinion.

Rehnquist acknowledged in *Scott* that Black's quote is not helpful: "These historical purposes are necessarily general in nature, and their application has come to abound in often subtle distinctions which cannot by any means all be traced to the original three common-law pleas."[85] Rehnquist is half right in this observation. Yes, Black's quote is more oratory than analytic. But most of the subtle distinctions that have developed in defining second jeopardy can be traced to Blackstone's common-law pleas. The ones that cannot be traced to Blackstone should be abandoned. Specifically, *Scott*, but not *Jenkins*, can be traced to the plea of *autrefois acquit*.

Indeed, *Scott* noted that Justice Black's quote is fully honored if the government is forbidden to reprosecute when Blackstone's common-law pleas would forbid a retrial.[86] The Court followed this insight by recognizing that the label "acquittal" does not necessarily answer the question of whether a dismissal operates as an acquittal. *Scott* held that a dismissal requested by the defendant was a bar to retrial only when "the ruling of the judge, whatever its label, actually represents a resolution [in the defendant's favor], correct or not, of some or all of the factual elements of the offense charged."[87] This is what I mean by "acquittal equivalence." Thus, with more agonizing than necessary, *Scott* held exactly what Blackstone would have predicted: an acquittal bars a new trial, and a midtrial dismissal that is not an acquittal does not bar a new trial or an appeal.

Nonacquittal dismissals simply have no double jeopardy effect. Thus, *United States v. Wilson*[88] held that a nonacquittal dismissal after conviction does not bar an appeal. The Court's rationale was that no new trial would be required. Either the trial judge will be upheld or the jury verdict of guilt will be reinstated. But an unresolved issue is posed in those (surely rare) cases when the judge grants an acquittal notwithstanding the jury's verdict based on the judge's view that the evidence was insufficient.[89] The problem here is not that we do not have a verdict in form or substance, which is the problem in most dismissal and mistrial cases; rather, it is that we have too many verdicts, both formally and substantively. The jury concluded that the defendant was guilty. The judge, hearing the same evidence, concluded that he was not guilty. Is there any reason to prefer the judge's conclusion to that of the jury?

The *Wilson* rationale seems robust enough to permit an appeal here.[90] Double jeopardy protection operates against a second verdict for the same offense. As James Strazzella recognizes, the bar of an appeal following a jury acquittal is merely an ancillary rule designed to protect the defendant against having to defend a meaningless appeal.[91] When the trial judge overrules a jury conviction, the appeal is not meaningless because the jury verdict can be reinstated and no new trial need occur. *Wilson* should permit an appeal here, as at least one state court has held.[92] The decision on blameworthiness was, after all, a split decision.

Dismissals that determine the lack of legislatively decreed blameworthiness, usually on the ground of insufficient evidence, are acquittal equivalents that should be treated exactly like acquittals. Dismissals after conviction permit appeal by the prosecution, because a new trial is never necessary. Other forms of dismissals can be appealed by the state, and, if the appeal is successful, a new trial can be held.

Defendants can appeal convictions, of course. Sometimes defense appeals will produce an acquittal equivalent.

Appeals as Acquittals

We saw earlier that defense appeals that produce a reversal leave no extant formal verdict to operate as a jeopardy bar. But could not an appellate reversal leave an acquittal equivalent? *Scott* recognized that a resolution of facts in the defendant's favor is an acquittal equivalent. The same concept should apply in appeals. The defendant in *Burks v. United States*[93] won his appeal on the grounds that the conviction was not supported by sufficient evidence. The Court held that this was equivalent to an acquittal, thus barring a new trial.

Ball v. United States,[94] which permitted a new trial after reversal, did not have to be overruled. As *Burks* noted, the *Ball* reversal was based on a flawed indictment, not on insufficient evidence. Verdict election makes sense in the former situation but not the latter. The latter outcome means that the trial jury should never have been permitted to deliberate. Had the trial judge done his job, or had the jury done its job, *Burks* would have received an acquittal at the trial level.

Burks is merely an application of the basic principle that jeopardy ends when a defendant is found substantively not guilty. Findings of not guilty at the trial court level—either by judge or by jury—end the matter forever,[95] but findings of legally insufficient evidence by appellate courts are a little more complicated. In *Forman v. United States*,[96] a panel of the Court of Appeals reversed the defendant's conviction with instructions to enter a judgment of acquittal on the ground that, as the case had been tried, no other verdict was possible. Upon rehearing, however, the Court of Appeals changed its mind, noting a theory that would have permitted a conviction, and ordered a new trial. The defendant appealed the second judgment, arguing that the first Court of Appeals judgment operated as an acquittal.

The Supreme Court affirmed the second judgment. Though this case predated *Burks*, the issue should come out the same way today. Once a defendant puts into play the question of whether his conviction is supported by legally sufficient evidence, the issue is not resolved until the review is complete. Evidence is not legally insufficient until there is a final, unreviewable order holding that it is legally insufficient.

The post-*Burks* Court was willing to engage in quite fine distinctions about what constitutes an insufficient-evidence reversal. The Court ultimately drew a distinction between reversals when evidence is insufficient as a matter of law and reversals when evidence is against the weight of the evidence.[97] Though Justice White may be right that the effect of this fine distinction is to undermine *Burks*,[98] the Court's theory is right: no jeopardy bar should arise unless the reversal effectively finds the defendant not guilty.

The Court has also held that the *Burks* determination must be based on the evidence the trial court actually admitted, even if some of it should have been suppressed and thus not available to the jury.[99] The defendant argued that he was entitled to a review of sufficiency based only on the evidence that should have been presented. The Court disagreed. Again, the theory is right. The reason to treat reversal for insufficient evidence as an acquittal equivalent is that no rational jury could have convicted on that evidence. The reviewing court thus must put itself in the position of the jury. Moreover, as a practical matter, if the trial court had refused to admit certain state evidence, the prosecution might have been able to find other, similar evidence that was admissible.[100]

Burks, like *Scott*, applies only to outcomes that resolve blameworthiness. An example of a case that might or might not be an acquittal equivalent is the one in which the prosecutor knowingly withheld exculpatory evidence. The Pennsylvania Supreme Court tackled this issue in *Commonwealth v. Smith*,[101] and Anne Bowen Poulin has written an excellent article on the double jeopardy implications of this violation.[102]

Both *Smith* and Poulin focus on the misconduct of the prosecutor and view the Double Jeopardy Clause as harmed by the covert undermining of the fairness of the first trial. On this view, the second trial is a double jeopardy harm of the harassment variety that we saw in chapter 2. As my double jeopardy construct has no place for harms that result from generalized due process unfairness, the focus is on whether the first trial would have resolved the defendant's blameworthiness in his favor. This requires a counterfactual determination: had the exculpatory evidence been admitted, would the defendant have been acquitted?

Details of the counterfactual inquiry remain to be developed; admittedly, this test is no easier to satisfy than the amorphous "harassment" inquiry required by traditional double jeopardy policy. But counterfactual analysis at least asks the right question—did the first trial constitute a verdict equivalent? Because the state is at fault for the failure to disclose in *Smith*, the mechanism for sorting out the counterfactual claims should be reasonably easy for the defendant to satisfy in this category. With that in mind, I would apply a version of the harmless error rule: considering the exculpatory evidence together with the evidence that was admitted, would the state have had overwhelming evidence of guilt? If so, the defendant has suffered no cognizable double jeopardy harm. If not, the first outcome should be treated as an acquittal.

One advantage of this approach is that it should temper the anger and surprise that greet decisions like *Smith*.[103] Rather than viewing double jeopardy as a reward to defendants who have been treated unfairly or as a punishment for prosecutors who have misbehaved, a bar of a second trial should be less controversial if the outcome is seen as equivalent to an acquittal. Viewing an acquittal as a likely outcome of the first trial had it been fair makes a double jeopardy bar logically appropriate. This is, of course, the rationale of *Burks*, made more difficult here by the counterfactual inquiry.

Acquittal Equivalence in Mistrials

The argument to this point is that the Court's second jeopardy doctrine is informed by acquittal equivalence—the *Green* implicit acquittal doctrine, the *Scott* dismissal rule, and the *Burks* insufficient-evidence exception to the *Ball* general rule that a successful appeal permits a new trial. Acquittal equivalance can be extended to some mistrials, like *Ireland's Case*. But can it be extended to more typical mistrials?

Judicial manipulation as in *Ireland's Case* has not appeared in the reported cases in this country. Moreover, whatever the extent of prosecutorial manipulation, defendants almost never win jeopardy claims based on mistrials. Of sixteen mistrial cases in the Supreme Court, the defendant gained a majority vote in only one, *Downum v. United States*,[104] and that by a 5-4 margin. The question is whether the acquittal equivalence concept can do any work in this category of cases.

Bishop in 1923 drew a distinction between the double jeopardy effect of discharging a jury on the ground that the jurors were later found to be disqualified and discharging juries for other reasons.[105] The former category permitted retrial, but not the latter. It seems likely from Bishop's analysis that he viewed the typical jury discharge as equivalent to an acquittal.

> Whenever, after the jury is sworn, it is found that the evidence is not sufficient to convict; or that a material witness for the prosecution is absent; or that such witness is unacquainted with the nature of an oath, and so requires instruction before testifying; or that the witness is suddenly taken too ill to proceed,—no second trial can be had.[106]

The first example (evidence not sufficient) is clearly an acquittal equivalent, and the others could be if Bishop envisioned the trial continuing without a key witness for the prosecution. This reading of Bishop is supported by an earlier reference to the effect of a prosecutor discontinuing an indictment during trial. Bishop states, without explanation, that "the legal effect is an acquittal."[107] If my reading of Bishop is right, the idea of acquittal equivalence in mistrial cases is an old one.

Prosecution-Requested Mistrials

When the prosecutor requests a mistrial, two concerns arise: the unfairness of forcing the defendant to gear up for another trial and the *Ireland's Case* unfairness of permitting the state to avoid an acquittal. The first kind of unfairness can be obviated by getting the defendant's consent to the mistrial; it is less clear that the *Ireland's Case* concern is completely addressed by the defendant's consent to the mistrial. Focusing on the first kind of unfairness for the moment, in chapter 2 I identified the general unfairness of facing a second trial as harassment and concluded that it is a soft-edged policy that does not give courts much guidance in resolving individual cases.

Implicitly accepting the soft-edged characterization, the Court has adopted a legal realist approach to mistrials requested by the prosecution, as we saw in detail in chapter 3. The Court purports to balance the relevant interests, the fulcrum being the "manifest necessity" phrase taken from Justice Story. This balance involves finality, the weakest of the values in the Westen and Drubel heirarchy. On this reading of the Court's doctrine, a no-verdict outcome forced on the defendant violates the weak finality interest and becomes a weak presumption that no new trial can begin. But because this is a weak interest, and a weak presumption, the state can rebut the presumption by showing "manifest necessity," whatever that means.

A fuller quotation from Story's opinion observes that the trial court may discharge the jury without a verdict upon finding "a manifest necessity for the act, or the ends of public justice would otherwise be defeated."[108] One analysis has demonstrated that this statement is susceptible to three interpretations: (1) either manifest necessity or the ends of public justice may justify a mistrial, (2) manifest necessity justifies a mistrial and the ends of public justice justify permitting a new trial, and (3) manifest necessity must exist and the ends of public justice must be served before a mistrial can be declared.[109] The "ends of public justice" is as vague as "manifest necessity," thus magnifying the difficulty of using this standard.

The vagueness of the concepts, and the inevitable tendency of judges to permit the state to have one full shot at defendants, has produced a jurisprudence that recognizes almost any governmental excuse as "manifest necessity."[110] The mistrial cases involving the right to a verdict typically explain the facts, quote the "manifest necessity" language, and then either conclude that manifest necessity was present, as a ritualistic incantation, or defer to the judgment of the trial court. It is difficult to quarrel with Stephen Schulhofer's conclusion that the manifest necessity standard is a "thoroughly deceptive misnomer, perhaps not rivaled even by the Holy Roman Empire."[111]

The defendant won *Downum v. United States*,[112] however, and this case may provide a clue about what really counts in the mistrial analysis. The prosecution moved for mistrial before any witnesses testified, on the ground that the key prosecution witness on two counts was unavailable. The judge granted this motion over defense objection, and the Supreme Court held that double jeopardy prohibited a retrial. One way to explain *Downum* is to say that prosecutors are simply stuck with their mistakes. If a prosecution-requested mistrial resulted from prosecutorial error, an unfairness that rises to the level of a jeopardy bar has occurred. That reading does not, however, survive *Illinois v. Somerville*,[113] where the prosecutor negligently drafted the indictment but prevailed against a jeopardy challenge to the prosecution-requested mistrial.

Justice Rehnquist, who wrote the majority opinion in *Somerville*, offered an explanation for *Downum* that did not focus on the prosecutor's mistakes. The key for Rehnquist was whether the mistrial "operated as a post-jeopardy continuance to allow the prosecution an opportunity to strengthen its case."[114] If, as in *Downum*, the prosecutor will likely strengthen its case following the mistrial, courts should not find manifest necessity. If no reason exists to think that the state's case will look different at the next trial, as in *Somerville*,[115] then no jeopardy bar arises.

Rehnquist is on the right track. Focusing on the prosecutor's chance to strengthen the state's case raises the second kind of unfairness, the kind that my blameworthiness theory recognizes: the possibility that defendants will be denied acquittals to which they were entitled. This chapter amplifies Rehnquist's standard by seeking to make it more precise and by linking it with my blameworthiness theory. Before doing that, I examine the other category of mistrials: those requested by defendants.

Defense-Requested Mistrials

The Court applies a different mistrial standard when the defendant moves for a mistrial. At first glance, it might seem that a defense motion for a mistrial should have no jeopardy implications at all. After all, the defendant is getting what she wants; why should she be allowed to complain later? But as the Court has recognized, if a defendant-requested mistrial could never be grounds for barring retrial, the state might seek to insulate the prosecutor's conduct from the scrutiny that attends a prosecution-initiated mistrial by forcing the defense to make the motion. Moreover, if the defendant is *entitled* to an acquittal, perhaps her ill-advised motion for a mistrial should be ignored.

Oregon v. Kennedy[116] is the seminal case on defense-requested mistrials. Defense counsel attempted to establish bias on the part of a prosecution witness by questioning him about a criminal complaint that he had filed against the defendant. The prosecutor then sought to rehabilitate the witness by eliciting the reasons why he had filed the complaint. The trial court sustained a series of objections to this line of questioning, rulings that the Oregon Court of Appeals later characterized as "probably wrong."[117]

Faced with substantial impeachment of one of her witnesses and an inability to rehabilitate the witness because of probably erroneous evidentiary rulings, the prosecutor then asked if the witness had ever done business with the defendant. When the witness said no, the prosecutor asked, "Is that because he is a crook?"[118] Not surprisingly, the judge granted the defense motion for a mistrial. Should this mistrial be the end of jeopardy?

The state appellate court "accepted the trial court's finding that it was not the intent of the prosecutor to cause a mistrial" but held reprosecution barred in any event because the prosecutor was guilty of "overreaching."[119] The Supreme Court reversed, in an opinion by Justice Rehnquist that adopted as a standard whether the prosecutor "intended to 'goad' the defendant into moving for a mistrial."[120] But, as Justice Stevens pointed out in a separate opinion, it is "almost inconceivable" that the defendant could show "intent to provoke a mistrial instead of an intent simply to prejudice the defendant."[121]

The Rehnquist standard (in fact if not in theory) permits prosecutors free rein to introduce prejudicial elements into a trial that is not going well. The worst that can happen is that the defendant obtains a mistrial, and the state can begin again. If the defendant does not obtain a mistrial, the jury will have seen or heard the prejudicial evidence. These options must seem appealing to a prosecutor whose case is not going well.

Unfortunately, the test proposed by Stevens (writing for three other members of the Court as well as himself) is also flawed. It is whether "egregious prosecutorial misconduct has rendered unmeaningful the defendant's choice to continue or to abort the proceeding."[122] How would a reviewing court know when the defendant's choice to continue the trial had become "unmeaningful"? This is pure legal realism that seeks a unique right outcome for each case. But how could this standard help anyone decide an actual case?[123]

The dilemma, then, is that the Rehnquist standard has relatively hard edges but is virtually impossible to meet, and the Stevens standard is possible to meet but has hopelessly soft edges. There must be a better way. Perhaps a focus on blameworthiness can provide a better test for mistrials than the Court's twin tests—"manifest necessity" for prosecution-requested mistrials and "intent to goad" for defense-requested mistrials.

Counterfactual Acquittal Equivalence

Acquittal equivalence in the mistrial context is obviously more speculative than a reversal of a conviction on grounds of legally insufficient evidence that follows a review of the record of a full trial. The record is incomplete in most mistrial cases, and the question must be answered as a counterfactual: would the defendant have been entitled to an acquittal, as a matter of law, had the trial judge denied the motion for a mistrial? Something close to this kind of counterfactual inquiry underlies Justice Rehnquist's comment that the *Downum* mistrial "operated as a post-jeopardy continuance to allow the prosecution an opportunity to strengthen its case."[124] The prosecution's concession that its key witness on two counts was not available created an inference that the defendant might have won at least those counts had the case gone forward.

Indeed, *Downum* quoted with approval from a Ninth Circuit case that used an analysis very much like counterfactual acquittal equivalence:

> [T]he district attorney entered upon the trial of the case without sufficient evidence to convict. . . . There is no difference in principle between a discovery by the district attorney immediately after the jury was impaneled that his evidence was insufficient and a discovery after he had called some or all of his witnesses.[125]

It is not quite as simple as the Ninth Circuit makes it seem. Deciding that the evidence would have been insufficient requires conjecture. One way of making the test less speculative is to put the burden of proof on the defendant and to weigh the evidence at the point of the mistrial motion unless there is a basis to predict the rest of the state's case. The defendant will lose if no plausible acquittal claim suggests itself. If a defendant makes a plausible counterfactual acquittal claim, however, one could indulge a bias in favor of finding a jeopardy bar. This bias can be defended as a way of discouraging prosecutors from begininng trial with weak cases and as a way of incorporating part of the finality interest that can be more directly addressed as a due process claim.[126]

Incorporating this bias into the counterfactual inquiry merely requires softening the standard. Rather than ask whether the defendant would have been entitled to an acquittal as a matter of law if the motion had been denied, we could ask whether there was a realistic possibility that the state's case would have been legally insufficient had the trial gone forward. Even on this softer standard, defendants will not win very many of these cases, but they win very few under the current doctrine. At least on the counterfactual test, we know and can state clearly why defendants lose—they cannot demonstrate a realistic possibility of a legally insufficient case had the judge denied the mistrial motion.

Sometimes the counterfactual inquiry is quite simple. In *Somerville,* the basis for the mistrial was a fatal defect in the indictment. The Court permitted a retrial on the ground that the error did not suggest manipulation, and it made little sense to force the state to proceed with a trial that contained automatic reversible error. On the counterfactual account, defendants have the burden of demonstrating that an acquittal was a realistic possibility; as the record contained no evidence, *Somerville* cannot make a plausible claim to acquittal equivalence. (I assume here, as did the Court, that state law permitted a conviction despite the flawed indictment.)

The defendant in *United States v. Jorn*[127] was prosecuted for assisting the preparation of fraudulent income tax returns. The government subpoenaed five taxpayer witnesses to testify against Jorn. The judge warned the first of these witnesses of his privilege against self-incrimination and then refused to allow him to testify, despite his expressed willingness, until he had consulted a lawyer.[128] The judge ascertained from the prosecutor that the remaining witnesses were "similarly situated" and discharged the jury "so abruptly"[129] that there was no opportunity for the prosecutor to "suggest a continuance" or the defendant "to object to the discharge of the jury."[130]

A plurality of the Court held that the mistrial was a jeopardy bar, focusing on the defendant's right to a particular jury. But *Jorn* is best explained as acquittal equivalence. The judge terminated the trial before evidence of guilt was introduced and in a way that suggested the government's case was going to be insufficient had the trial continued. Without any of its taxpayer witnesses, the government's case was unlikely to be sufficient. While defendants normally lose if the record is bare of evidence, because the burden is on the defendant to show a realistic likelihood of an acquittal, the judge's actions in *Jorn* permit the defendant to carry that burden.

Justices Black and Brennan would have decided *Jorn* on the ground that the "action of the trial judge amounted to an acquittal."[131] The plurality rejected this resolution because the record did not show that the trial judge relied "on facts relating to the general issue of the case."[132] Had the trial judge relied on the facts, Jorn would have been acquitted in the strong, *Scott* sense of a finding of evidence insufficiency. But a blameworthiness account suggests that counterfactual acquittal equivalence should also be treated as the end to jeopardy.

Jorn should not be tried again, in the view of Black and Brennan, because "the action of the trial judge amounted to an acquittal." Precisely right. It was *not* an acquittal, as is a dismissal for insufficient evidence, but it *amounted* to an acquittal because Jorn was deprived of a realistic possibility of acquittal had the case gone forward. What the plurality's "right to go to a particular tribunal"[133] means, on this view, is the right to have the particular government's case evaluated *as if it had gone to the jury.*

The counterfactual acquittal equivalence in *Downum* is not quite as obvious as in *Jorn.* The only "evidence" in the *Downum* record was the content of the prosecutor's mistrial motion that cited a missing key witness on two counts. As to those two counts, the prosecutor's assertion that he lacked a key witness should satisfy the counterfactual test for acquittal. The difficulty with *Downum* is that the Court barred retrial on all counts. Perhaps this is justifiable as a sort of penalty on the prosecution for dismissing the uninvolved counts along with the weak counts or as a blanket inference of insufficiency infecting all counts. But the jeopardy bar on the other counts is much more difficult to justify as a counterfactual acquittal equivalent.

The defendant in *Brock v. North Carolina*[134] had a compelling acquittal equivalence claim but lost because the Court analyzed the claim under the Due Process Clause. Two of the state's witnesses refused to testify on self-incrimination grounds. The prosecutor then told the court that the testimony of those witnesses "was necessary for the State to present its case fully before the jury" and moved for a mistrial, which the trial judge granted.[135] *Brock* was decided prior to incorporation of the Double Jeopardy Clause into the Fourteenth Amendment, and the Court explicitly noted that it was not reaching the double jeopardy issue.[136] Under the Due Process Clause, as we see in chapter 9, the test was: "Is that kind of double jeopardy to which the state has subjected [the defendant] a hardship so acute and shocking that our polity will not endure it?"[137]

The statement of the test implies that an outcome can be double jeopardy without simultaneously violating due process. Using the very high due process threshold, the Court found no violation. In dissent, Justice Douglas put the issue in acquittal equivalence terms, claiming that both double jeopardy and due process should prevent prosecutors from being able to "call a halt in the middle of a trial in order to await a more favorable time, or to find new evidence, or to make up the deficiencies in the testimony of its witnesses."[138]

Whatever the right outcome under the Due Process Clause, Douglas's view endorses my blameworthiness account of the Double Jeopardy Clause. The blameworthiness question is the counterfactual—would the case have proceeded favorably to the accused?—not whether the prosecutor was at fault for the lack of evidence. The state's concession in *Brock* that the missing testimony was "necessary for the State to present its case fully" is more than enough to meet the counterfactual test. If *Brock* occurred today, with the Double Jeopardy Clause fully enforceable against the states, the defendant should win on the implicit acquittal equivalence rationale in *Downum.*

Acquittal equivalence in mistrial cases also illuminates the defense-requested mistrial category. As noted earlier, the Court's standard in *Oregon v. Kennedy* was whether the prosecution intended to goad the defendant into moving for a mistrial, while the Stevens alternative standard was whether the defendant's choice to continue the trial was rendered "unmeaningful."

On a blameworthiness account of double jeopardy, there is only one question in cases that end short of verdict: would the defendant have had a realistic chance at an acquittal if the judge had denied the mistrial motion? There is no reason to treat the identity of the party who moves for a mistrial as anything other than an evidentiary fact in judging the defendant's chance of an acquittal. We do not need to worry about "overreaching" or "goading" or "egregious prosecutorial misconduct" that "has rendered unmeaningful the defendant's choice to continue or to abort the proceeding." We need only ask the blameworthiness question: can this defendant show a realistic possibility of an acquittal had the judge denied a mistrial?

If the mistrial occurs during the state's case, as in *Kennedy*, an acquittal equivalence test would be almost impossible for the defendant to satisfy unless the record manifested a weak case.[139] Assuming a case of typical strength, the transcript would disclose only the prosecution witnesses and their cross-examination. That would be not be enough, in a typical case, to allow the defendant to meet the burden of showing that he would have had a realistic chance of an acquittal at the point of mistrial. When the mistrial is granted well into the defense case, the reviewing court is better able to judge whether there was a realistic possiblity that the state's case would be legally insufficient. When this judgment favors the defendant, the mistrial should bar a second trial even though granted on the defendant's motion.

The policy justification for an acquittal equivalence mistrial rule inheres in the actual harm done (or not done) to the defendant. If the defendant had a realistic chance at an acquittal, the prosecutor has violated the defendant's double jeopardy rights in a very real sense. If not, the only harm that is done, and it is not a cognizable double jeopardy harm, is that the defendant has to endure a second trial to remedy the flaw in the first trial. What we would like to know before deciding whether a defendant should face a second trial is whether real double jeopardy harm was done, so why not ask it directly and have the jeopardy question turn exclusively on the answer?

A thought experiment demonstrates the wisdom of a mistrial doctrine based solely on acquittal equivalence.[140] Combine the facts of *Downum* and *Somerville*: the prosecutor wants a mistrial because her key witness cannot be found, but she coincidentally discovers a fatal defect in the indictment (that cannot be cured by amendment). She candidly discloses both grounds for mistrial to the judge. Because *Somerville* held that this indictment defect is manifest necessity that justifies a mistrial, the prosecutor's acquittal-avoidance motive is presumably irrelevant. But this is just the kind of mistrial that double jeopardy should count as a bar. On an acquittal equivalence account, a second trial is barred because the focus is on the chance for acquittal, not on the state's grounds for a mistrial or the likelihood that a conviction would be automatically reversed on appeal.

Hung-Jury Acquittal Equivalence

The next category is the no-verdict termination imposed by the judge after the jury fails to reach a verdict, commonly called a "hung" jury. To begin with the obvious, the Court has held that a jeopardy bar arises when the jury cannot return a verdict and the judge grants the defendant's motion for acquittal.[141] This, of course, is an acquittal, rather than a no-verdict outcome.

It should not be surprising that a judge might grant a motion for acquittal following a hung jury. Although hung juries can be caused by other factors, the most likely cause is that some of the jury find the evidence insufficient to convict. The overlap between hung juries and acquittals appears in *Hotema v. United States*,[142] discussed in chapter 7 for its collateral estoppel implications. Hotema was charged with three murders; he was tried for two murders in a single trial and acquitted on the ground of insanity. The jury hearing the last murder case could not agree on a verdict, and the government reprosecuted. Hotema was convicted when a new jury heard the government present its case for the third time. That one jury acquitted strongly suggests the hung jury resulted from juror doubts about Hotema's sanity.

A defendant in Hotema's situation can make a motion for acquittal following the jury's failure to reach a verdict. The difficult issue is whether the Double Jeopardy Clause requires appellate courts to entertain an appeal when the trial judge overrules the motion for acquittal following a hung jury.[143] It might seem obvious that defendants should have this right. After all, it is no more difficult to evaluate the evidence underlying a hung jury than that underlying a conviction, and appellate courts regularly perform the latter analysis.

The Court had, for a century and a half, routinely permitted retrial following discharge of a hung jury,[144] but, in 1985, for the first time, it addressed a claim specifically based on the failure of the trial judge to recognize evidence insufficiency. The argument is powerful: if the jury and trial judge have made a mistake, if the defendant is legally entitled to an acquittal, why should he not be given the benefit of a jeopardy bar? Moreover, as the defendant in *Richardson v. United States*[145] recognized, a hung jury resulting from legally insufficient evidence is no different from a conviction based on insufficient evidence. When the Court held in *Burks* that a conviction based on insufficient evidence was an acquittal equivalent,[146] it opened the door to the argument that a hung jury based on insufficient evidence should be treated the same way. Moreover, the venerable *Perez* case is not precedent to reject Richardson's argument; there was no motion for an acquittal following the hung jury in *Perez*. One can distinguish a defendant who offers a hung jury as a jeopardy bar and one, like Richardson, who offers the failure of the trial judge to grant a motion for acquittal as a potential jeopardy bar.

Probably only a few hung juries result from evidence that an appellate court would find legally insufficient. A jury can be hung (in most states) by only one holdout juror, who may have an idiosyncratic view of the evidence. The due process standard for legally sufficient evidence is a low one—whether any rational trier of fact could have found the essential elements of the crime beyond a reasonable doubt.[147] There are many cases in which the evidence is weak but legally sufficient under this test; only egregiously defective cases warrant reversal.

Any case that fails to meet the Court's evidence sufficiency standard is woefully weak. The jury should have acquitted, and the trial judge should have granted the postdismissal motion for acquittal. The appellate court can remedy this double failure of the process in the same way the Court now requires appellate courts to remedy convictions based on insufficient evidence. As the Court implicitly recognized in *Richardson*, an insufficient-evidence hung jury is substantively the same as a formal acquittal. Why not treat it the same way?[148]

The defendant in *Richardson* was simply asking the Court to elaborate the mistrial rule in the same way that the Court in *Burks* elaborated the appellate reversal rule. Richardson was not arguing that all mistrials constitute the end to jeopardy; he was not even arguing that all hung jury mistrials constitute ended jeopardies; he asked only that appellate courts judge whether a hung jury mistrial is based on legally insufficient evidence and, in that small category of cases, declare that acquittal equivalence bars a new trial.

The Court did not seize the opportunity to make the mistrial rule symmetrical with the appellate reversal rule. Instead, Justice Rehnquist wrote for the Court that the mistrial rule "has its own sources and logic"[149] and held that a retrial following a hung-jury mistrial is always permissible, relying on Story's opinion in *Perez*. Perhaps unconvinced that even the internal logic of the mistrial rule demanded this result, Rehnquist also noted that "Justice Holmes' aphorism that 'a page of history is worth a volume of logic' sensibly applies here."[150] In effect, the Court held that precedent, and not logic, justified its refusal to recognize the *Burks* symmetry.

Justice Brennan noted in dissent that, under the majority's rule, "a defendant who is constitutionally entitled to an acquittal but who fails to receive one—because he happens to be tried before an irrational or lawless factfinder or because his jury cannot agree on a verdict—is worse off than a defendant tried before a factfinder who demands constitutionally sufficient evidence."[151] True enough, but the majority's rule is even more bizzare than Brennan's argument implies. Assuming legally insufficient evidence, the defendant who receives a hung jury is not only worse off than the defendant who is acquitted; he is also (in theory) worse off than the defendant who is *convicted*.[152] The latter defendant can appeal and receive an appellate reversal that is a bar to a new trial; the hung jury defendant has to suffer a new trial, during which the government has a chance to hone its case.

The implications of the majority's position are startling. Consider a situation in which the evidence is demonstrably insufficient, and eleven members of the jury vote to acquit but one juror votes to convict. If the eleven cannot convince the one to change his mind, the defendant would be better off (again, in theory) if the eleven switched their votes to conviction. Then the defendant could test the sufficiency of the evidence without giving the government another chance to present its case.

Perhaps the Court was concerned about the additional burden on appellate courts if it recognized Richardson's argument. But that is inadequate reason to ignore the logic of *Burks*. Either *Burks* or *Richardson* must be wrong, and, on a blameworthiness account, it is *Richardson*. Only two members of the Court dissented from the decision in *Richardson* to treat a hung-jury mistrial less favorably than a conviction based on insufficient evidence.[153] This suggests how conceptually barren is the Court's double jeopardy universe.

If a future Court is willing to rethink this problem, it need only recognize the distinction drawn earlier between the defendant who offers a hung-jury mistrial as a bar to retrial and a defendant who seeks review of the trial court's denial of the motion for acquittal. As to the former defendant, no procedure exists to decide whether the hung jury resulted from legally insufficient evidence, and one could defer to the historical argument that a hung jury never constitutes a jeopardy bar. As to the latter defendant, however, the existence of a procedure for appealing the trial court's denial of the motion for acquittal suggests that the proper course is to treat this situation like any other appeal and reach the merits of the claim.

Oddly, eight members of the Court in *Richardson* agreed that the federal statute governing appeal permitted "review of the sufficiency of the evidence . . . as a necessary component" of a double jeopardy claim,[154] only to hold that a hung-jury claim could *never* be meritorious. After holding that Richardson had a "colorable double jeopardy claim appealable under 28 U.S.C. § 1291,"[155] the Court dropped an Alice-in-Wonderland foonote, which says in its entirety:

> It follows logically from our holding today that claims of double jeopardy such as petitioner's are no longer "colorable" double jeopardy claims which may be appealed before final judgment. A colorable claim, of course, presupposes that there is some possible validity to a claim. Since no set of facts will support the assertion of a claim of double jeopardy like petitioner's in the future, there is no possibility that a defendant's

double jeopardy rights will be violated by a new trial, and there is little need to interpose the delay of appellate review before a second trial can begin.[156]

Thus, Richardson had a colorable claim, appealable under 28 § U.S.C. 1291, but, once the Court reached the merits of his appeal, there could never be a colorable claim in the future, and thus no future defendant would have a colorable claim. It may be, as the Court asserts, that the hung-jury doctrine "has its own sources and logic,"[157] but it is very bad logic indeed if it supports the Court's view that defendants have (had?) a colorable claim that is not now (never was?) a colorable claim.

When a defendant seeks appellate review of the order denying the motion for acquittal, *Perez* is technically inapplicable, and *Richardson* holds that this claim is procedurally appealable. All that is necessary to restore coherence to this corner of double jeopardy is to permit the hung-jury appeal to be heard substantively, as a type of *Burks* claim.

Though *Richardson* based its procedural appealablity ruling on a federal statute, the requirement of procedural review is also embedded in the Double Jeopardy Clause. The Court noted in *Abney v. United States* that "if a criminal defendant is to avoid exposure to double jeopardy and thereby enjoy the full protection of the Clause, his double jeopardy challenge to the indictment must be reviewable before that subsequent exposure occurs."[158] If the conceptual incoherence of *Richardson* can be rectified, the solution recommended here can be imposed on states that permit motions for acquittal following a hung jury. If a state does not permit such motions, there would be no procedural predicate upon which a substantive blameworthiness argument could work. But as long as a procedural predicate exists, the Double Jeopardy Clause should require appellate review of orders that overrule motions for acquittal, whether they follow convictions or mistrials.

Attachment of Jeopardy

If jeopardy does not end until verdict—formal verdict or acquittal equivalence—it does not matter when it begins. In Blackstone's day, the beginning of jeopardy was the same as the end of jeopardy. No procedural mechanism existed to terminate a trial prior to verdict, and it would have made no sense to speak of a beginning or ending of jeopardy.

Today, our criminal procedure permits preverdict terminations out of a concern for defendants. In Blackstone's day, the rules permitted more certainty and less fairness on this issue. Defendants knew that they would get a verdict and that no new trial could follow as long as the verdict stood. The difficulty, of course, is that defendants could not get a mistrial if they wanted one, regardless of how many errors had infected the trial.

In the Court's doctrine, a gap exists between the beginning of jeopardy and the end of jeopardy. The beginning of jeopardy is important in the Court's doctrine because it signals when a mistrial must be tested for manifest necessity and a dismissal must be tested for acquittal equivalence. Prior to the beginning of jeopardy, a termination has no jeopardy implications. Suppose a judge grants a mistrial because the jury is hung; the government reschedules a trial, and the judge grants a pretrial motion for acquittal. The judge's action is explicitly based on the ground that he has already heard the government's case and is now persuaded that the government has insufficient evidence to convict. As we have seen, a judicial finding of insufficient evidence counts as an acquittal and thus is a bar to a new trial for that offense.

But not on the Court's view of the "attachment" of jeopardy. The second dismissal is not a verdict, regardless of its grounds, because it does not end a jeopardy. It does not end a jeopardy because no jeopardy on the second attempt to convict had begun. What has not begun cannot end. While this seems unduly formalistic, it was the holding in *United States v. Sanford*.[159]

Two years later, in *Crist v. Bretz*, the Court held that the Double Jeopardy Clause requires jeopardy to attach when the jury is sworn, striking down Montana's provision that jeopardy attached when the first witness was sworn.[160] The Court stated, in dicta, that the Montana rule was appropriate for a trial without a jury but constitutionally defective for trials with juries. Since the difference between the time the jury is sworn and the time the first witness is sworn is a short period that includes only opening arguments, one is left to wonder what is so crucial about this period that it necessitated invalidating Montana's rule that both kinds of jeopardy begin when the first witness is sworn.

No coherent policy reason has been offered for the distinction, as Justice Powell pointed out in his dissent in *Crist*.[161] The Court quoted the platitude that the Double Jeopardy Clause protects "the defendant's valued right to have his trial completed by a particular tribunal"[162] and further articulated the genuine (but necessarily general) concern that the

Double Jeopardy Clause is designed to minimize "harassing exposure to the harrowing experience of a criminal trial."[163] These platitudes do not, however, require the attachment of jeopardy at any particular point. As Justice Blackmun remarked, these interests could just as easily "support a conclusion that jeopardy attaches at the very beginning of the jury selection process."[164]

The Court noted several possible lines for attachment—for example, jury selection and the prima facie case. The government recommended a "sliding scale" that would have abolished a fixed line. On this view, "the further the trial has proceeded the more justification is required for a mid-trial termination."[165] Stephen Schulhofer, in his usual thoughtful style, defended a variety of jeopardy lines in a way roughly consistent with the government's position (and one year earlier).[166] On a legal-realist view that exalts individual solutions for individual cases, no other approach seems defensible. Westen and Drubel are true to their legal realism when they note that the choice of a single line from among many is arbitrary "if by arbitrary one means that the decision is essentially 'an exercise in line drawing.'"[167] Though the Court has been heavily influenced by legal realism in double jeopardy analysis, it rejected the individual-case approach to the attachment of jeopardy. We are thus left with a "bright line" that has no convincing rationale beyond the perceived need to have a point of demarcation.

A blameworthiness account rejects the Court's bright-line attachment doctrine, not in favor of a sliding scale as favored by the legal realists but in favor of returning to Blackstone's notion that jeopardy begins and ends at verdict. It does not matter whether a judge resolves the facts in the defendant's favor before or after the process has crossed some imaginary line. Once the facts are resolved in the defendant's favor, by dismissal or as a counterfactual mistrial inquiry, jeopardy both begins and ends. Blackstone turns out to be right again.

The Court's solution is, at best, arbitrary. At worst, it is nonsensical. The outcome of the pretrial dismissal case, *Sanford*, depended completely on the fortuity of whether the judge decided the motion for acquittal before or after the trial began. The Court was wrong to reject Sanford's jeopardy claim. To be sure, virtually all pretrial dismissals do not represent a judgment on the merits of the government's case,[168] but when they do, as in *Sanford*, the acquittal equivalence of the outcome should be recognized, not submerged beneath a formalistic doctrine about the attachment of jeopardy.

Mistrials That Are Not Acquittal Equivalents

In this chapter I have argued that the no-verdict cases are best understood as requiring the defendant to demonstrate that the outcome is some form of acquittal equivalent. Acquittal equivalents come in two forms: dismissals that actually resolve the factual elements in the defendant's favor and the counterfactual determination that, on the basis of the record, the defendant can show a realistic possibility that the state's case would have been legally insufficient had it gone forward.

As noted throughout this chapter, several Supreme Court opinions contain dicta suggesting a broader purpose behind the double jeopardy mistrial rule—to protect a defendant's "valued right" to a particular jury.[169] These statements never explain the origin of this "valued right" beyond a generalized fear of repetitive trials. The origin of this right is a finality interest, which exists even in cases where an early outcome would not qualify as an acquittal equivalent.

Although precisely predicting how acquittal equivalent claims will be decided is impossible, we can say precisely what interest of the defendant is at stake: defendants should not be deprived of their right to go to verdict when they have a realistic chance of an acquittal. That defendant has already demonstrated lack of blameworthiness, at least in a counterfactual sense, and should receive the shield of an acquittal.

The finality interest, on the other hand, is much more amorphous. Why does a defendant have an interest in a particular jury? However the interest is defined, it winds up being a fairness interest. Even the standard for determining when that interest is violated, derived from *Perez*, sounds in fairness: a defendant has a right to a particular jury unless the prosecution can show a "manifest necessity for the [mistrial], or the ends of public justice would otherwise be defeated."[170]

I once argued that the finality interest in going to verdict sounds in due process, not double jeopardy.[171] If mistrial claims premised on finality are qualitatively different from acquittal equivalent claims, as my argument presupposed, one might ask why the Supreme Court began analyzing these finality claims under the Double Jeopardy Clause. A careful look at the cases demonstrates that the Court drifted into the practice, first pointing out that no claim could be made at all (*Perez*), then maintaining that no claim could be made but, if one could, this would not be one,[172] and finally discussing the merits of the claim as if they mattered.[173] After that, it was a short trip to recognizing the claim.[174] The reason the Court fell down this slippery slope is that the two categories of mistrial claims look procedurally alike. The only difference is the substance of the claim, and sloppy analysis could see this difference as one of degree rather than kind.

But a difference in kind does exist. Acquittal equivalence mistrial claims are about verdicts, and other mistrial claims are about fairness. If fairness is the issue, courts must balance the defendant's finality interest against the need for the mistrial in light of the "ends of public justice." What will this balance look like? What kinds of cases justify mistrials outside of acquittal equivalence? Nothing in double jeopardy theory is helpful; there is no verdict, and no analogy to a verdict.

The focus on fairness suggests locating this part of the mistrial doctrine in the Due Process Clause, which traditionally uses a balancing test to decide whether a right has been denied on the facts of a particular case.[175] The relocation project is merely a change in labels. Mistrial finality claims have always been analyzed differently from other double jeopardy questions, reflecting implicit judicial recognition that finality claims are conceptually different from other double jeopardy claims. Double jeopardy analysis in other areas depends on a binary analytical structure: same offense, different offense; same sovereign, different sovereign; civil remedy, criminal punishment; one conviction, more than one conviction.[176] The Court's use of interest balancing to resolve mistrial finality cases suggests that they are generically different from the rest of double jeopardy. As James Shellenberger and James Strazzella put it: "The Supreme Court has maintained a strict double jeopardy bar in those circumstances in which the common law rules imposed a finality on judgments when it came to successive prosecutions. However, where the Court has moved beyond these common law situations, its results appear to represent a majority assessment of a basically pragmatic balancing of interests."[177] My acquittal equivalance theory is an explicit recognition of the difference between verdict finality and pragmatic balancing of interests.

To the extent that a coherent doctrine can be distilled from (or imposed upon) these mistrial finality cases, it is difficult to improve on Stephen Schulhofer's two-tier standard.[178] Late mistrials would receive strict scrutiny because of the defendant's greater interest in completing the trial and the greater potential harm in a new trial. The later the mistrial, the stricter the scrutiny.

Mistrials declared early in the trial are less harmful. Schulhofer concludes that early mistrials should be evaluated under a more flexible "sound judicial adminstration" standard. Under this standard, "the defendant is entitled to some protection against the burden of reprosecution, but the nature of the burden ordinarily will not be sufficient to justify awkward or expensive alternatives to mistrial, and the trial judge normally will be in a position to render a fair and trustworthy judgment on the need to abort the proceedings."[179] The test is whether the trial court's judgment is "responsible" and whether appellate review of that judgment should be deferential.[180] This standard is essentially what the Court later adopted in *Arizona v. Washington*,[181] which is appropriate for the finality subset of mistrial claims but not, as I have argued in this chapter, for the acquittal equivalence claims.

By subtracting the finality mistrial claims from the second jeopardy doctrine, while adding the *Ireland* class of acquittal equivalents, we wind up with a second jeopardy doctrine based on blameworthiness. Defendants who have not elected to void a criminal judgment have a good double jeopardy claim when the first trial has ended in a formal verdict, in an outcome that is functionally the same as an acquittal, or in an outcome that suggests an acquittal would have followed had the trial not terminated early. Any other bar to a second trial must be found in the Due Process Clause or in a due-process style double jeopardy analysis that is consciously distinct from the acquittal equivalence analysis.

That this approach can be traced directly to Blackstone is not reason enough to accept it. But I am not alone in recognizing the virtue of returning to something like Blackstone's pleas in bar. Jay Sigler has argued that returning to the English final-judgment rule, with added procedural limitations to make it difficult to withdraw a case, is fairer both to the accused and to the prosecution. Requiring a final judgment would "insur[e] a full hearing for both the state and the accused."[182]

I agree.

9

The Role of Legislative Intent in Determining the End of Jeopardy

We saw in chapters 2–6 that "same offense" is what the legislature means singular blameworthiness to be. In the second jeopardy part of the analysis, the legislative intent question goes to what the legislature means to count as a verdict. Unlike the same-offense context, where the legislature rarely speaks directly to the question of what constitutes singular blameworthiness, the legislature always tells us what constitutes a verdict. Either in statutes or rules of criminal procedure, the legislature specifies the form of a verdict, how it may be appealed or corrected, and when it becomes final if no action is taken to upset it. Rarely does a legislative definition of verdict depart from the Blackstonian model. In Blackstone's day, and in ours for the most part, a verdict is delivered by a judge or jury; a conviction may be appealed but not an acquittal; the appeal of a conviction is based on the record of the original trial.

When a legislature provides for verdict models that do not fit this verdict paradigm, difficult jeopardy questions arise. For example, the Court had a chance to consider in 1937 whether a state could appeal an acquittal.

Appeal Asymmetry

In *Palko v. Connecticut*,[1] a statute authorized the state to appeal trial court rulings when three conditions were met: (1) the ruling was one of law, (2) the presiding judge gave permission for the appeal, and (3) the appeal was one that the accused could have made against a ruling in the state's favor.[2] In effect, the statute created partial symmetry between defendants and the state regarding appeals; the state would be permitted to appeal in some situations in which the accused could have appealed.

Connecticut was one of only five states without a state constitutional double jeopardy provision,[3] and Palko was restricted to arguing the Double Jeopardy Clause and the common law plea of *autrefois acquit*. The latter argument was technically flawed because *autrefois acquit* was a plea in bar of a new trial rather than an appeal. Appeals of convictions were relatively rare in Blackstone's day, and there is doubt whether the common law even recognized appeals by the prosecutor.[4]

Though the Supreme Court bars appeals of federal acquittals on the grounds of superfluity—there is no point to an appeal if a second trial cannot proceed in any event[5]—the Connecticut statute made a substantive change in the common law when it permitted acquittals to be reversed. In this situation, Palko's argument against the appeal was outside the scope of the common-law pleas. If the appeal was successful, the acquittal would no longer be in existence, and *autrefois acquit* could not bar a second trial. Palko's real argument, then, was against the statute permitting acquittals to be reversed. The state court upheld the statute, finding that the societal interest in an error-free procedure outweighed the defendant's interest in the initial verdict.[6]

The initial verdict was second-degree murder. The state appealed, seeking permission to retry the defendant on first-degree murder on the ground that the judge had erroneously charged the jury and had erroneously excluded a confession.[7] The Connecticut Supreme Court reversed the conviction and gave the state the right to retry Palko for first-degree murder. On retrial, with the legal errors corrected, Palko was convicted of first-degree murder and sentenced to be executed.[8] The result of Palko's retrial suggests that the errors had prevented the state from getting the verdict to which it was entitled at the first trial. The difficulty with retrials, however, is that one never knows the precise effect of correcting legal errors. The prosecutor obviously has incentive in the second trial to "re-examine the weaknesses in his first presentation in order to strengthen the second."[9]

The Supreme Court reviewed Palko's case in an opinion written by Justice Cardozo and joined by all but one member of the Court.[10] The Court refused to incorporate the Double Jeopardy Clause into the Due Process Clause and thus analyzed the appeal statute under due process standards.[11] The Court found that the statute's goal of ensuring the accuracy of acquittals justified any limitation on the due process liberty interest. The statute did not "violate those 'fundamental principles of liberty and justice which lie at the base of all our civil and political institutions."[12] As the Court put it, Connecticut's system of state appeals

> is not cruelty at all or even vexation in any immoderate degree. If the trial had been infected with error adverse to the accused, there might have been review at his instance, and as often as necessary to purge the vicious taint. A reciprocal privilege, subject at all times to the discretion of the presiding judge, has now been granted to the state. There is here no seismic innovation. The edifice of justice stands, its symmetry, to many, greater than before.[13]

The due process standard of review was very deferential. Was "the kind of double jeopardy to which the statute has subjected [Palko] a hardship so acute and shocking that our polity will not endure it?"[14] Stated more succinctly, the question was whether the state practice "was repugnant to the conscience of mankind."[15] Before a statute authorizing a prosecution appeal would violate due process, on the Court's view, it must shake the very "edifice of justice,"[16] violate the "conscience of mankind," and prove unendurable to our polity.[17] Palko had little chance with that standard.

How does *Palko* come out on a double jeopardy analysis when the state would not benefit from the extremely deferential due process standard of review that Cardozo used? Specifically, what would be the outcome in *Palko* if the state statute were analyzed under a blameworthiness account of double jeopardy that recognizes the primacy of legislative intent?

Blameworthiness and State Appeals

Under a legislative intent account of double jeopardy, the legislature can limit the finality of a verdict however it wishes. It is difficult to avoid this conclusion even if one does not directly privilege legislative intent. In chapter 8 I defended a "verdict election" view of double jeopardy that makes extant verdicts a bar to another trial, just as they were in Blackstone's day.[18] We give defendants the right to appeal convictions, presumably because of concern about unfair or inaccurate outcomes. When an appeal is successful, no conviction remains to bar a new trial. Similarly, several states permit appeals of rulings that occur before the trial begins.[19]

This account, of course, says nothing about whether acquittals could be made subject to appeal if a legislature wished. Verdict election does not create a privileged status for acquittals; if an acquittal is reversed on appeal, no verdict remains to bar a new trial (as in *Palko*). Unless a way of privileging acquittals can be found, verdict election permits a legislature to authorize appeals of acquittals.

Consider two thought experiments: (1) the legislature abolishes appeals entirely; (2) the legislature abolishes defense appeals but permits state appeals. In the first case, it is difficult to see a double jeopardy violation. The lack of an appeal process might be a due process violation on the ground that it creates an unacceptable risk of erroneous conviction. But it is unclear what the chance of a wrongful determination in any given case has to do with preventing wrongful *multiple* determinations, which is all that double jeopardy prohibits. Abolishing appeals seems to pose no double jeopardy problem.[20]

If this is right, no other way of arranging the appellate process violates double jeopardy. The second thought experiment—abolishing only defense appeals— surely violates due process, but it, too, has nothing to do with preventing wrongful multiple determinations of blameworthiness. A system that does not permit defense appeals never has more than one extant verdict for the same offense; if the state appeals an acquittal, either the appeal will be rejected, in which cases the acquittal stands, or the acquittal will be reversed, in which case no verdict exists to bar a second trial.

The only way Palko can win a double jeopardy claim (as opposed to the due process claim that we know he lost) is if double jeopardy somehow requires the state to treat acquittals with more deference than convictions. Indulging this premise means that the very appeal from an acquittal is a double jeopardy violation. But how is this principle inherent in double jeopardy? It might be a good idea in a system where the state has many built-in advantages. Some bias in favor of acquittals is probably inherent in due process. The Westen-Drubel account incorporates aspects of the right to a jury trial into double jeopardy and thus privileges jury nullification as the preeminent double jeopardy value.[21] On this view, the *Palko* statute would presumably be unconstitutional because it would limit jury nullification. But the work in this account is done by jury nullification, which is logically located in the right to a jury trial. No particular reason exists to call this a double jeopardy protection.

A blameworthiness account of double jeopardy supports the view of the Connecticut legislature: there is no reason to find demonstrated lack of wrongdoing if the acquittal is infected by an error of law that prevented the state from presenting its case against the defendant. On my account, the legislature determines what counts as blameworthiness and when that determination is final. If the legislature decides that an acquittal is not final until after all appeals have been exhausted, that determines the "what" and the "when" about criminal blameworthiness. As a law review writer concluded prior to *Palko*, "[T]he question of the acquittal or immunity of one charged with crime, like the question of his guilt, should not be regarded as settled until it has been ascertained through the just and fair application through the Courts of the rules and principles of law."[22]

As a double jeopardy event, an acquittal is no different from a conviction. Acquittals, to be sure, create the potential for a different double jeopardy outcome because of the prospect of a collateral estoppel bar. But if collateral estoppel does not apply—and it would not if the acquittal has been reversed—a defendant who is relying on *autrefois acquit* is in the same position as one who is relying on *autrefois convict*.[23]

The next question is whether the legislative-prerogative view of appealing acquittals departs in any significant way from double jeopardy history and doctrine.

Pre-*Palko* Treatment of Acquittals

Appeals from verdicts were, of course, unknown in ancient legal systems that used the ordeal as a mechanism to determine guilt. The Hebrew system used human judges to render judgment from the time of Moses.[24] Early Jewish law drew a distinction between correcting erroneous convictions and erroneous acquittals. An acquittal was a final outcome, but convictions could be reversed on several grounds.[25]

The Talmud makes clear the extent to which the initial verdict bound the state but not the defendant. Even newly discovered evidence would not disturb an acquittal. "If the culprit was found guilty by the court, and thereafter one of the judges said: 'I have something to say in his defense,' the culprit is to be granted a new trial. . . . If, however, the culprit was found innocent, and thereafter one of the judges said: 'I have incriminating arguments against him,' the culprit is not to be brought back for a new trial."[26] Mendelsohn has concluded that a verdict of acquittal could not be reversed, though the defendant's "guilt might now be established on new and conclusive evidence."[27]

This kind of protection is not inconsistent with *Palko*. Redetermining the facts underlying an acquittal is quite different from reversing an acquittal for errors of law. Though appellate review of fact-finding does not seem to create a double jeopardy problem, it would trench too harshly on the right to a jury trial.[28] What is the value of a jury trial if the fact-finding can be reversed on appeal?[29]

But early Jewish law also forbade reversal of acquittals on the grounds of legal errors. On Mendelsohn's account, "[E]ven when the judges themselves discover that their verdict of acquittal was founded on a mistake of law, that verdict cannot be revoked."[30] This historical view cannot coexist with *Palko*. Like its review-of-facts sibling, however, the bar on review of legal errors may have its conceptual home in a doctrine other than double jeopardy, perhaps an expanded notion of presumption of innocence.[31]

The question for this chapter is whether a good reason exists to locate an anti-*Palko* doctrine in double jeopardy. Blackstone drew no distinction between acquittals and convictions as pleas in bar. Neither did Coke, Hawkins, or Hale. The only time the common law drew even a partial distinction, it was in favor of *convictions*, not acquittals. This was the doctrine of variance. The strictness of the common-law pleading rules led quite often to variance acquittals, a technical verdict that courts were loathe to recognize as a jeopardy bar. An acquittal of robbery in the county of *B*, Hale told us, does not bar a trial for a robbery in county *C*.[32] This could be, of course, because the robberies are physically different, or it could be that the first indictment misdescribed the place of the robbery.

Hale gives a clearer example of misdescription variance: the acquittal of the robbery of John Stiles on proof that the victim was John Nokes.[33] The king could not amend the indictment to correct for this misdescription, thus leading to an acquittal despite evidence that the robbery occurred. To bar a retrial here would be a miscarriage of justice, and courts developed the doctrine of variance to avoid that result. If the proof that led to acquittal on the first indictment would sustain the second indictment, the acquittal was due to variance and could be ignored.

This standard might sound familiar; it is the standard the King's Bench adopted in *King v. Vandercomb*, the case Scalia has cited as historical support for *Blockburger*.[34] But *Vandercomb* is a variance case, rather than a case that applied a general rule about same offense. In the first trial, the crown charged the singular conjunctive offense of burglary and larceny.[35] An acquittal resulted when the crown proved burglary but failed to prove larceny.[36] The King's Bench permitted the second trial for burglary based on intent to steal, rather than actual theft, stating that these burglary offenses are different. These facts tenuously fit the *Blockburger* test: each burglary offense requires an element different from the other (actual theft in the first case, intent to steal short of actual theft in the second).

But it is more satisfying to view *Vandercomb* as a variance case. The phrasing of the *Vandercomb* test, limiting its scope to acquittals, manifests a concern with variance: "unless the first indictment were such as the prisoner might have been convicted upon by proof of the facts contained in the second indictment, an acquittal on the first indictment can be no bar to the second."[37] When the acquittal was caused by variance, proof of the second indictment would not prove the first, thus establishing that a misdescription was at the heart of the problem. In these cases, but not when the first trial ended in a conviction, a new trial is good social policy.

In 1854 the Supreme Court analyzed a case as if it were prepared to recognize a variance exception to double jeopardy.[38] The government argued that the evidence necessary to convict on the second indictment could not have been admitted under the first indictment and, therefore, that the later charges could not have been proved in the first trial. On a *Vandercomb* view of variance, this would make the later offenses different from those that resulted in an acquittal in the first trial. The Supreme Court took the argument seriously but held that the later charges could have been made out on the first indictment, thus rendering moot the government's variance argument.[39]

As late as 1889, the Court reserved the option to adopt a less expansive test in the context of former acquittal than former conviction, presumably to handle the variance situation the Court had recognized in 1854. Though *In re Nielsen* is much discussed in the double jeopardy literature, commentators have for the most part failed to notice the Court's comments about the effect of acquittals.[40] After holding that the prior conviction barred a new trial, the Court said: "Whether an acquittal would have had the same effect to bar the second indictment is a different question, on which we express no opinion."[41] The Court has never returned to the issue of variance. Given modern pleading rules, which permit liberal amendments to indictments, it is much more difficult for a variance acquittal to occur today.

Whatever the right outcome on variance, the common law did not privilege acquittals over convictions, and the Supreme Court has since 1889 assumed that the two verdicts are equivalent (again ignoring collateral estoppel). If there is no reason to treat an acquittal with more deference than a conviction, there is no double jeopardy reason to prohibit a state appeal of an acquittal. Frank Palko, it turns out, had neither a good due process nor a good double jeopardy claim.

Two additional arguments supplement the conclusion that *Palko* did not present a good double jeopardy claim. One is that Justice Holmes shared this view, something that Justice Cardozo noted with respect in *Palko*. In 1904, in *Kepner v. United States*, Holmes rejected quite angrily the majority's conclusion that an appeal of an acquittal always violates the Double Jeopardy Clause.[42] Cardozo remarked that Holmes's dissent "show[s] how much was to be said in favor of a different ruling," that is, one that would permit a state to appeal in some situations.[43]

As usual with Holmes, the logic is flawless, even if the premises are open to question: "If a statute should give the right to take exceptions to the government, I believe it would be impossible to maintain that the prisoner would be protected by the Constitution from being tried again. He no more would be put in jeopardy a second time when retried because of a mistake of law in his favor, than he would be when retried for a mistake that did him harm."[44] The premise here is that there is no reason to privilege acquittals.

The other argument in favor of *Palko* is related to the Holmes argument. If the legislature has carte blanche to create and define criminal blameworthiness, it must also have the double jeopardy authority to design a system for producing judgments about that blameworthiness. In *United States v. Sanges*, the Court drew a distinction between judgments "upon a verdict of acquittal" and judgments "upon a determination by the court of an issue of law."[45] The Court continued: "In either case, the defendant, having been once put upon his trial and discharged by the court, is not to be again vexed for the same cause, unless the legislature, acting within its constitutional authority, has made express provision for a review of the judgment at the instance of the government."[46]

Sanges did not explain the distinction between acquittals and appeals based on errors of law. As noted earlier, a jury acquittal presents Sixth Amendment jury trial issues. Considering only double jeopardy, however, the legislature has carte blanche to ascribe "verdict status" to almost all trial outcomes. The only double jeopardy limit is the extremely unlikely possibility that the legislature would expressly authorize more than one verdict for the same offense.

In *Palko*, the Court explicitly left open this question, reserving what "the answer would have to be if the state were permitted after a trial free from error to try the accused over again or to bring another case against him."[47] If a state were to authorize a scheme that permitted the prosecutor to follow an acquittal with a new trial for the same offense, on the Henry II ground that too many defendants were escaping justice, this would violate double jeopardy. The problem with this scheme is that it treats the first verdict as if it were not a blameworthiness determination. The double jeopardy principle does not permit legislatures that kind of freedom.

Current Status of the Legislative Role

In 1969 the Court overruled part of the *Palko* holding. *Benton v. Maryland* held that double jeopardy is a fundamental protection[48] and thus part of the Fourteenth Amendment Due Process Clause. Although *Benton* noted that "*Palko*'s roots had . . . been cut away years ago,"[49] the Court stopped short of explicitly overruling *Palko*. As the dissent noted, *Benton* had a stronger due process case than *Palko* and thus could have won under the *Palko* standard.[50]

Benton was charged with larceny and burglary in a two-count indictment. He was convicted of burglary and acquitted of larceny. Because an intervening Maryland Court of Appeals case rendered the indictment invalid due to an error in the selection of the grand jury, Benton's case was remanded to the trial court, which gave him the option to demand a new indictment. When he chose that option, however, the state reindicted on both counts, and Benton was tried and convicted of both larceny and burglary.

The state's theory was analogous to the early English cases that held that an acquittal on a void indictment did not bar a new trial because a verdict obtained on a void charging document was itself void. As the *Benton* Court correctly pointed out, the English "void indictment" theory was rejected by the Court the first time it appeared, in the 1896 case of *Ball v. United States*.[51] Of course, *Palko*'s refusal to incorporate double jeopardy into the Due Process Clause gave states the option not to follow the double jeopardy rule of *Ball*.[52] Nonetheless, consider the question purely as a matter of due process understood to require fundamental fairness. The error that led to reversal was in the indictment, not in the trial. In the words of the author of *Benton*, Justice Harlan, "[T]he defect in the composition of the grand jury could not have affected [*Benton*'s] subsequent acquittal at trial." Continuing to quote Harlan: "The State has no more interest in compelling [Benton] to stand trial again for larceny, of which he had been acquitted, than in retrying any other person declared innocent after an error-free trial."[53] This understanding of what Maryland did leaves little doubt that it was a violation of due process, considered as fundamental fairness and without regard to *Ball*'s double jeopardy rule. Thus, *Benton* could have been decided in the defendant's favor under the *Palko* due process standard.

The Connecticut procedure approved in *Palko* might therefore still withstand scrutiny. At a minimum, we can say that *Benton*'s rejection of the Maryland procedure does not reject Connecticut's statute, which remains in force (though no reported post-*Palko* cases involve implicit acquittals).[54] There is, of course, another difference between *Palko* and *Benton* that is crucial to a legislative-prerogative account of double jeopardy: the Connecticut legislature spoke clearly on what counted as a final verdict of acquittal. The new trial in Maryland resulted from the prosecutor's efforts to manipulate judicial doctrine.[55] In a pre-*Benton* case, Chief Justice Vinson drew the same distinction between *Palko* and another double jeopardy/due process case: "We often have said that the considered action by a state legislature or the Congress of the United States places the issue of constitutionality in a different posture in respect of due process of law."[56]

On the theory offered in this book, if the legislature defines what constitutes a final verdict, that is what constitutes a final verdict. Prosecutors are not permitted to decide what outcomes count as final, which is the teaching of *Benton*, nor are judges when they act other than to determine the issue of blameworthiness, which, as we shall see, is the teaching of *Ohio v. Johnson*.[57] The legislature, however, is not only permitted but expected to decide this question. The Connecticut statute is more than merely distinguishable from the situation in *Benton*; it should be upheld.

In *Trono v. United States*,[58] the Court discussed with approval two situations in which states changed their law to authorize outcomes that had previously been held to violate double jeopardy. Both had to do with the *Green* doctrine that a conviction of a lesser offense implicitly acquits of the greater.[59] The New York high court had held, many years before *Green*, that conviction of a lesser offense when the greater is charged prohibits a trial for the greater following a reversal of the lesser on appeal.[60] A later statute, however, sought to deprive defendants of implicit acquittals: "When a new trial is ordered it shall proceed in all respects as if no trial had been had."[61] The New York Court of Appeals held the statute constitutional, even though it overturned what that court had previously held to be guaranteed by the state constitutional double jeopardy provision.

Trono also discussed *Kring v. Missouri*,[62] which, though technically an ex post facto case, has a double jeopardy predicate. The law in Missouri at the time of the homicide was that of *Green* and the early New York law: a reversal of a second-degree murder conviction on appeal did not permit the state to recharge first-degree murder. Prior to Kring's retrial, the Missouri legislature changed the rule to permit retrial on the greater offense, as New York had done. Though the Supreme Court held the change to be ex post facto to Kring, it went out of its way to note that there was "no question of the right of the state of Missouri, either by her fundamental law or by an ordinary act of legislation, to abolish this rule."[63]

Both of these cases predate the application of the Double Jeopardy Clause to the states. Neither, therefore, is authority for the proposition that these changes are permissible under the Double Jeopardy Clause. But they show at a minimum that some state courts accepted the power of the state legislatures to change fundamental, constitutional state law. *Trono's* endorsement of these cases perhaps signals the Court's acceptance of the proposition that legislatures can change what counts as a blameworthiness determination.

In sum, the legislature determines what procedural outcomes are verdicts. But neither judges nor prosecutors can create a verdict if there has been no finding about blameworthiness. This limitation on the power of judges and prosecutors explains some of the Court's difficult cases.

When Outcomes Are Verdicts

The clearest example of permissible legislative carte blanche is the juvenile procedure in *Swisher v. Brady*[64] that we examined in chapter 3.[65] The Court held, consistent with a legislative-prerogative principle, that Maryland could define "verdict" in juvenile court to be what a judge does after reviewing favorable findings made by a magistrate. If the judge accepts those findings, the juvenile has been acquitted. If the judge rejects the magistrate's findings, the juvenile has been convicted. But the verdict does not occur, procedurally, until the judge acts.

Keeping the focus on the procedural context of "verdict" explains *Ohio v. Johnson*.[66] The trial court accepted the defendant's guilty plea to involuntary manslaughter and theft, which were lesser included offenses under state law, respectively, of murder and robbery. The judge then dismissed the greater offenses over the prosecutor's objections. Recognizing that multiple punishment problems would arise if Johnson wound up with four convictions, the Supreme Court nonetheless held that the dismissed charges could be reinstated. After all, as the Court implied, one option open to the judge if the defendant was later convicted on the greater charges was to dismiss the lesser charges, leaving only two convictions in place (one for murder and one for robbery).[67]

I once argued that *Johnson* was wrongly decided based on my view that the preeminent double jeopardy interest was finality.[68] Once the judge accepted the guilty pleas, I argued, Johnson had guilty verdicts that he could use as a Blackstone plea in bar against a new trial. But I was privileging the wrong double jeopardy policy. Double jeopardy does not exist to guarantee finality. Though it achieves finality in almost all cases, its purpose is to guarantee that singular blameworthiness receives a singular penalty.

On this view, the question is not whether Johnson could point to any verdict but whether his blameworthiness on the greater charges had been determined. And it had not. The trial judge dismissed the greater charges; he did not enter an acquittal. An acquittal bars a new trial when the judge formally enters that verdict, even when the prosecution has not rested and the judge has no statutory authority to do what he did.[69] Similarly, an acquittal is final when a judge grants a posttrial motion for acquittal following a hung jury.[70] But in *Johnson*, the blameworthiness was undetermined on the greater charges, and the Court was right that no double jeopardy bar on trial of those charges existed.

The matter is different if the state initially chooses to seek a verdict only on the lesser charges; the defendant can then rely on the conviction as a jeopardy bar.[71] The outcome is also different if a defendant is tried to the judge as fact-finder, and the judge finds him guilty of lesser charges without mentioning the greater charges. This is *Green*. But, as the Court noted, Johnson had "not been exposed to conviction on the charges to which he pleaded not guilty" and thus could not invoke the *Green* doctrine.[72]

Johnson simply holds that judges cannot create a verdict without reaching the merits of blameworthiness.[73] This explains why the act of pronouncing sentence on one count has no jeopardy implications for other counts.[74] Similarly, if a judge sentences on two counts and suspends sentence on 110 counts, the act of suspending sentence does not create a verdict. The judge can later sentence on one of the 110 counts as long as the result is no more than one conviction for the same offense.[75] If a judge sentences the defendant to less than the maximum and the conviction is reversed, nothing in double jeopardy forbids the judge from imposing a greater sentence.[76] And, obviously, a botched execution does not constitute a verdict that bars a second attempt at execution.[77]

Nor does sentence enhancement create a second verdict. If the legislature has authorized sentence enhancement on the basis of prior conduct, the most logical inference is that it did not intend the enhancement to operate as a blameworthiness determination in addition to the conviction being entered. The Court has repeatedly upheld these sentencing schemes against arguments based on double punishment.[78] Sentencing judges often take prior conduct into account in the absence of legislative authorization, but this exercise of sentencing discretion is even more clearly lacking verdict status.[79]

The legislature retains the power to create verdicts. In *Spaziano v. Florida*,[80] the Court noted a line of cases holding that a nondeath sentence in a death penalty case has the status of a verdict for double jeopardy purposes. In *Spaziano*, however, the jury verdict was advisory in nature. The key to the Court's opinion was that state law explicitly reserved the decision point on death or nondeath to the judge. But this is just another way of saying that the state procedure made the initial "verdict" less than a verdict.[81]

A somewhat similar system is the two-tier system some states have for minor crimes. Defendants can void a conviction obtained in the first tier by simply appealing to the second-tier court. In this kind of system, the legislature has made the first verdict voidable at the option of the defendant. A defendant cannot interpose an insufficient-evidence jeopardy bar following a first-tier conviction, the Court held in *Justices of Boston Municipal Court v. Lydon*.[82] Though the Court used a different theory, on my account the legislature has prescribed the only way a conviction can be reversed, and the judiciary cannot create other ways of undoing a blameworthiness determination.

Lydon is not subject to the *Burks* rule that an appellate reversal on insufficient evidence is a jeopardy bar.[83] *Burks* is based on the jeopardy consequences of a procedure authorizing appeals. *Lydon* could prevail on a *Burks* analogy only if *Burks* had held that defendants are entitled to a review of evidence sufficiency when the system does not provide for review of convictions.

The argument here requires revisiting *Richardson v. United States*.[84] In chapter 8 I argued that courts should treat a motion for acquittal following a hung jury as an appealable outcome, thus permitting a jeopardy bar to arise when the state's case was legally insufficient. But this, too, can be contrasted to Lydon's argument. Motions for acquittal are recognized in every jurisdiction. Though they normally follow a conviction, there is no reason to assume that the legislature meant to forbid appeal of a motion for acquittal following a mistrial if the claim is legally insufficient evidence. Once that equivalence is accepted, the *Richardson* claim gets funneled into the normal appeal process. Lydon, on the other hand, asked the Court to create a new system for evaluating the outcomes in the first tier of a two-tier system.

The *Richardson* argument (see chapter 8) is based on an inference about likely legislative intent. Just like the same-offense presumptions (see chapter 6), this inference can be rebutted by clear legislative intent. If a court read the relevant appeal procedure to permit *Richardson* claims and the legislature did not want that outcome, the legislature would merely have to amend the rules to forbid an appeal following a hung jury and, on a legislative-prerogative view of the matter, that would be the end of *Richardson* claims. Without that clear intent, however, *Richardson* claims belong in the normal process for appealing motions for acquittal.

Judges decide blameworthiness when they act as fact-finder, but they cannot change the procedure the legislature has established to determine blameworthiness. They cannot accept a guilty plea to a lesser offense and thus relieve the defendant of liability for the greater offense. When the defendant has been convicted more than once for the same offense, trial or appellate judges cannot solve the multiple punishment problem by suspending sentence on all but one conviction.[85] The legislature has determined that a conviction is a blameworthiness determination, and suspending sentence on a conviction does not change its characterization as a conviction.

Judges are similarly forbidden to treat multiple convictions as part of a single "package" to escape double jeopardy review.[86] Nothing about a sentencing pattern can create or change the quality of "verdict."[87] Some outcomes are verdicts and some are not, but no procedural act of a judge can change this essential quality.

When State Appeals Are Authorized

As noted earlier, the jury trial right forbids giving appellate courts the power to reverse an acquittal and enter a conviction. But if the state were to authorize reversal of an acquittal because infected by legal errors, the appellate court action would not contradict any finding of blameworthiness; instead, it would permit a new jury to render a judgment that is more accurate. Justice Cardozo and Justice Holmes both believed that state appeals of acquittals for legal error should be permitted when authorized by the legislature. These are not lightweight minds. As no historical or conceptual basis appears to privilege acquittals as double jeopardy events, the judgment of Cardozo and Holmes that state appeals are not automatically forbidden should be accepted.

The authorization of state appeals, like the legislative authorization of distinct blameworthiness for the same blameworthy act, must be both express and clear. The nineteenth-century Court put it this way in *Sanges*: "[I]n the absence of any statute expressly giving the right to the state, a writ of error cannot be sued out in a criminal case after a final judgment in favor of the defendant."[88] Since 1971, the federal statute governing appeals permits the government to appeal an order of a district court "dismissing an indictment or information as to any one or more counts, except that no appeal shall lie where the double jeopardy clause of the United States Constitution prohibits further prosecution."[89] The Court has explicitly held that acquittals cannot be appealed under this statute, regardless of how erroneous the acquittal might be and even if based on an error of law.[90]

A blameworthiness account agrees. A general authorization of appeals except where a new trial violates double jeopardy does not authorize the appeal of acquittals. Quite the contrary. Anglo-American law since at least the twelfth century has been that an acquittal bars a new trial, and the statutory authorization would therefore incorporate that prohibition as part of what is not allowed. As *Sanges* noted over a century ago about an earlier statute permitting appeal, it "says nothing as to the party by whom the writ of error may be brought, and cannot, therefore, be presumed to have been intended to confer upon the government the right to bring it."[91]

A modern Blackstonian view of second jeopardy, with a dash of Holmes and Cardozo, produces a satisfying account. A second trial for the same offense is forbidden only when the defendant can point to a verdict that is recognized as a final outcome by the procedural law. This verdict is a conviction (which also implicitly acquits of a greater offense if it was charged), an acquittal, a dismissal that resolves the factual elements in favor of the defendant, or a mistrial granted under circumstances that imply that the defendant had a realistic chance for an acquittal. In all of these categories, if the procedural law of the jurisdiction permits an appeal, the verdict is final only if the verdict is unappealed or appealed and affirmed. While other constitutional rights forbid the appeal of the jury's fact-finding that underlies an acquittal—notably the right to a jury trial—nothing in the Constitution forbids the state from authorizing an appeal on grounds of legal errors.

Justice Holmes, in my view, was right on this point.

10

A Final Defense
A Bill of Particulars and an Answer

When all is said and done, my idea in this book is simple: the Double Jeopardy Clause incorporates legislative judgments about substantive and procedural blameworthiness. The legislature creates substantive blameworthiness when it enacts criminal statutes. Determining when blameworthiness is singular or distinct (the same offense or different offenses) requires a set of presumptions about legislative intent in the vast majority of cases that lack explicit evidence of that intent. The most important presumption is that a single blameworthy act-type is a single offense, subject to an exception for multiple harms with requisite mens rea as to more than one harm. If the legislature speaks clearly to the issue of distinct blameworthiness, however, it can have as many offenses as it wants from one act-type.

When the legislature fails to authorize incarceration for a particular offense, the Double Jeopardy Clause "life or limb" requirement is not met, and there is no requirement that the legislature expressly authorize more than one sanction per act-type. The legislature might create a civil remedy, impose a regulatory sanction, and authorize incarceration for the same act-type, but nothing in the Double Jeopardy Clause prevents a defendant suffering all three sanctions for a single act-token of that act-type. Historically, this makes sense; double jeopardy was reserved for serious crimes at common law, and the Framers' use of "life or limb" signals that jeopardy requires serious criminal consequences. Conceptually, it makes sense as well: compensation and regulation are different enterprises from the criminal law's concern with retribution and incapacitation.

The legislature defines procedural blameworthiness when it decides what events count as the end to the first jeopardy. The end of jeopardy is a blameworthiness determination, which a formal verdict always manifests. Because the legislature could not be assumed to want defendants to be deprived of an acquittal, courts must recognize when terminations that lack formal verdict status must nonetheless count as acquittals. I have referred to these outcomes as "acquittal equivalents." They include appeals and dismissals that resolve the factual elements in the defendant's favor as well as mistrials under circumstances that create an inference that the state's evidence would have been insufficient to convict had the case gone forward.

On this account, no need exists to demarcate the "attachment" of jeopardy, which is the point the Court uses to require analysis of the reasons for early termination. The Court has fixed this line at the swearing of the jury. Only in the rarest of cases would a defendant be able to show acquittal equivalence at an earlier point, but defendants should receive a jeopardy bar whenever they can demonstrate acquittal equivalence.[1]

In sum, a defendant demonstrates double jeopardy only if she can show more "life or limb" trials or punishments than the legislature intended. She can do this by showing a former acquittal for the same offense or that a second trial depends on proof of an act-token that was found, in an earlier trial, not to have occurred (collateral estoppel). Alternatively, she can create a presumption that two convictions are for the same offense by showing two charges based on the same act-token of the same blameworthy act-type description, causing a single harm; unless rebutted by clear legislative intent, this presumption will prevail. It does not matter, for this second claim, whether the state brings the charges in one trial or in successive prosecutions.

Because the legislature determines both substantive and procedural blameworthiness, it can, if it wishes, decree successive prosecutions for the very same act-type. Some will say (some have said) that it is crazy to permit the legislature to authorize successive prosecutions by declaring its intent to create separate offenses. One of the ways my oddness has been pointed out to me is with the hushed remark, "Not even Scalia makes this argument." Like most academics, I am willing to make a new argument. I also think I am right. In addition, while Michael Moore does not locate his same-offense account in legislative intent, his recognition that offenses that can be punished cumulatively can be prosecuted successively[2] keeps me from feeling hopelessly isolated.

To the charge that I would allow the legislature to overrule the Double Jeopardy Clause, I plead not guilty. My claim is that the scope of the Double Jeopardy Clause is determined by legislative intent on substantive and procedural blameworthiness. If I am right, the legislature can never act in a way inconsistent with the Double Jeopardy Clause. If I am wrong, it is not because the legislature has nothing to say about blameworthiness but because there is a better conception of the Double Jeopardy Clause.

To the charge that my proposal vitiates some clear understanding of same offense having nothing to do with legislative intent, I plead not guilty. There is no such understanding. *Blockburger* itself is nothing more than a presumption about legislative intent—a flawed presumption, in my view, but a presumption in any event. Once the Court abandoned the *Grady* equivalence between offense and the way an offense was proved,[3] there was nothing left but comparisons of offense elements.

Because the legislature has complete control over the way offense elements are written, no test of offense elements can be anything other than subject to the legislature's control. If Scalia is right that *Blockburger* is a constitutional barrier to successive prosecutions, legislatures can easily avoid that barrier by adding a distinct element to lesser offenses. Had the Ohio legislature wanted, in the wake of *Brown v. Ohio*,[4] to make joyriding separately punishable and prosecutable from auto theft, it had merely to require in the joyriding statute that the car be kept from the owner for more than a certain amount of time (an hour, a minute). Though that element would be met in fact by almost all cases of theft, theft does not require that the stolen item be kept for any length of time. If the legislature can avoid *Blockburger* this easily, why not permit direct avoidance, as by a statement of intent that the prosecutor has the option to prosecute separately (and thus punish separately) joyriding and auto theft?

To the charge that my proposal permits the legislature mindlessly to multiply penalties and prosecutions, I plead not guilty. On my account, there are strong presumptions against multiple convictions, which require explicit legislative intent to overcome. When my presumptions are compared to the current doctrine, as I did in this book, defendants win as many or more cases under my scheme as under the Court's tortured, confusing case law, which recognizes legislative intent as only one part of the analysis.

To the charge that my proposal permits the legislature to have the definition of offense and verdict that it wants, I plead guilty. But who else is institutionally capable of defining these terms? The Court has held that the legislature can have as many penalties as it wants for the same offense,[5] fulfilling Justice Washington's prophecy from 1820.[6] Once a legislature can authorize as many penalties as it wants, why not permit the prosecutor to obtain those penalties in any way permitted by the joinder law of the jurisdiction?

In sum, I think I am guilty of only what is historically true and institutionally required about double jeopardy.

Notes

NOTES TO THE INTRODUCTION

1. U.S. Const. amend. V. Henceforth, I will use the modern spelling, "offense," except when quoting early sources.

2. In re Vitale, 375 N.E.2d 87 (Ill. 1978).

3. Illinois v. Vitale, 447 U.S. 410, 419–20 (1980) (noting "substantial" claim of double jeopardy if state follows traffic conviction with homicide prosecution based on same conduct).

4. United States v. Ursery, 518 U.S. 267 (1996).

5. Bartkus v. Illinois, 359 U.S. 121 (1959).

6. Downun v. United States, 372 U.S. 734 (1963).

7. The mistrial doctrine is discussed in detail in chapter 8.

8. See the discussion of Richardson v. United States, 468 U.S. 317 (1984), in chapter 8.

9. Id. at 325–26.

10. Burks v. United States, 437 U.S. 1 (1978), discussed in chapter 1 & chapter 8.

11. The example is Justice Souter's. United States v. Dixon, 113 S.Ct. 2849, 2883 (1993) (Souter, J., dissenting).

12. Grady v. Corbin, 495 U.S. 508 (1990).

13. United States v. Dixon, 509 U.S. 688 (1993). I discuss *Grady* and *Dixon* in more detail in chapter 2.

14. Id. at 713 (Rehnquist, C.J, concurring in part and dissenting in part) (joined by O'Connor & Thomas, JJ.). The difference in the two versions is not important to my point here. For a discussion of the difference, see chapter 5.

15. Id. at 720 (White, J., concurring in the judgment in part and dissenting in part) (joined by Stevens, J., and Souter, J., as to Part I); id. at 741 (Blackmun, J., concurring in the judgment in part and dissenting in part); id. at 743 (Souter, J., concurring in the judgment in part and dissenting in part) (joined by Stevens, J.).

16. George C. Thomas III, An Elegant Theory of Double Jeopardy, 1988 U. Ill. L. Rev. 827.

17. 1 Annals of Congress 753 (statement of Roger Sherman).

NOTES TO CHAPTER 1

1. Benton v. Maryland, 395 U.S. 784, 795 (1969).

2. Note, 65 Yale L.J. 339, 342 n.14 (citing 2 Pollock & Maitland, 470).

3. This is Michael Moore's modern count of total state and federal crimes. Moore, 4. Double jeopardy applied only to felonies in Blackstone's day, but today applies much more broadly, as I detail in chapter 4.

4. Distinguishing a criminal from a civil violation is a knotty problem (see chapter 4), but, to keep the argument as simple as possible, I deal here with a violation that is undeniably criminal.

5. Kant, 198.

6. Edmund v. Florida, 458 U.S. 782 (1982) (holding that the Eighth Amendment did not permit imposition of the death penalty on a getaway driver who did not participate in the murders).

7. 459 U.S. 359 (1983).

8. Whalen v. United States, 445 U.S. 684, 701 (1980) (Rehnquist, J., dissenting) (quoting Westen & Drubel, 113).

9. See Montana Department of Revenue v. Kurth Ranch, 511 U.S. 767, 769, n.1 (1994).

10. 432 U.S. 161, 165 (1977). Very few commentators have argued that legislative intent to punish or try twice avoids the double jeopardy problem. The few exceptions include King, Excessive Penalties; Mead; and Thomas, Blameworthy Acts.

11. I plead guilty to the charge of putting the emphasis on successive prosecution theory rather than where (I now see) it belongs: the either/or sentencing decision affecting judges. For my earlier view, see Thomas, Successive Prosecutions.

12. 432 U.S. 161, 166 (1977).

13. Id. at 165 (quoting United States v. Jorn, 400 U.S. 470 (1971) (plurality opinion)).

14. Actually, I do not have to imagine that skeptic. Many of my Rutgers colleagues played the skeptic's role with a great deal of relish when I presented this theory at a law school colloquium in the fall of 1995. See also McElroy, 399.

15. See, e.g., Olson, 40 (noting that this antipositivism jurisprudence is "alternatively labeled as historicism, usage and custom, and Burkeanism").

16. Olson, 44.

17. The double jeopardy and criminal law sense of "offense" are, on the argument offered in this book, precisely the same sense.

18. Friedland, 3–4. See also Sigler, 39.

19. See chapter 2.

20. See Harmelin v. Michigan, 501 U.S. 957 (1991) (endorsing, at best, an extremely narrow proportionality principle in noncapital cases).

21. The Court's partial answer is that the death penalty cannot be imposed

for any crime that did not itself cause a death. See Coker v. Georgia, 433 U.S. 584 (1977). This approach, of course, is firmly grounded in Kantian (and biblical) principles.

22. Harmelin v. Michigan, 501 U.S. 957 (1991).

23. See Prince v. United States, 352 U.S. 322 (1957) (holding Congress did not intend both penalties to apply).

24. Moore, 339.

25. LaFave & Scott, 605 (noting that the common-law judges had "some help from the legislature" on this task).

26. Comment, 33 Am. Crim. L. Rev. 123, 149. Australia apparently continues to use the *Vandercomb* rule for measuring the protection offered against successive prosecutions. Id. at 141–42. For a discussion of *Vandercomb*, see chapter 9.

27. 432 U.S. 197 (1977).

28. 501 U.S. 624 (1991).

29. Id. at 630–31.

30. Id. at 637 (citation omitted).

31. Id. at 637–38.

32. Id. at 638.

33. 467 U.S. 493 (1984).

34. 432 U.S. 161 (1977).

35. *Johnson*, 467 U.S. at 493.

36. 471 U.S. 773 (1985).

37. The included-offense inquiry is admittedly not as simple as it first appears. While CCE always requires proof of some felonies from a very long list, it does not always require proof of importing marijuana (other felonies will do). These so-called compound-predicate offenses require a decision about how narrowly to read the requirement of "necessarily-included." But the Court has held that the compound-predicate offense of felony murder is the same offense as the underlying predicate felony. Harris v. Oklahoma, 433 U.S. 682 (1977) (per curiam). I discuss the issue of how best to apply the included-offense test in chapter 6.

38. Id. at 784.

39. See Note, 49 Ohio St. L.J. 773, 811–12 (criticizing this reading).

40. 471 U.S. at 806 (Stevens, J., dissenting). See also Thomas, Successive Prosecutions, 364–69.

41. 471 U.S. at 790.

42. 471 U.S. 773, 788–89.

43. Id. at 804–5 (Stevens, J., dissenting) (joined by Brennan & Marshall, JJ.).

44. 4 Blackstone's Commentaries *335–36.

45. 1 Britton, 104 & 112.

46. For an excellent analysis of one state's still-extant "private prosecution" law, see New Jersey Developments, 44 Rutgers L. Rev. 205.

47. 4 Blackstone's Commentaries *336.

48. Batchelder cites early state cases in his 1883 law review article for the proposition that conviction of a lesser offense bars prosecution of the greater. Batchelder, 738–53. He notes, and disapproves of, a few cases holding to the contrary (most of these cases involve unusual facts or jurisdictional issues). From 1887 to Brown, the line of cases is as follows: In re Nielsen, 131 U.S. 176 (1889) (adultery included within unlawful cohabitation); Grafton v. United States, 206 U.S. 333 (1907) (homicide included within assassination); Prince v. United States, 352 U.S. 322 (1957) (unlawful entry of bank included within bank robbery). See McElroy, 388 (noting "settled" law from Nielsen to 1969, the date of McElroy's article). The early law review literature confirms the prevalence of the included-offense model of same offense as at least one test to be applied. See, e.g., Note, 45 Harv. L. Rev. 535, 539 (published shortly after Blockburger); Comment, 33 Harv. L. Rev. 110, 111; Note, 11 Ky. L.J. 221, 221; Comment, 40 Yale L.J. 462, 469. Bishop's Ninth Edition, published in 1923, noted that a jeopardy for the highest or lowest degree of included offenses should bar a second jeopardy. 1 Bishop, 780–82, §§ 1054–57.

49. Amar & Marcus.

50. The omitted exception to former attainder is that an attainted principal can be forced to a second trial to permit the accessories to be convicted, a rule of substantive criminal law that has no relevance today.

51. 4 Blackstone's Commentaries *336–37.

52. 4 Blackstone's Commentaries *337.

53. Batchelder, 753. He went on, in point 4, to condemn the exception for crimes that become more serious when the assaulted party dies after the conviction of assault. The Supreme Court later endorsed this exception. Diaz v. United States, 223 U.S. 442 (1912). Otherwise, Batchelder stated rules for same offense that the Supreme Court would recognize today.

54. Sigler, 100.

55. Comment, 45 J. Urban L. 405.

56. 2 Hale, 241–250.

57. For commentary on these cases, see Horack; see also Note, 32 Mich. L. Rev. 512 (1932); Note, 24 Minn. L. Rev. 522 (1940).

58. Comment, 75 Yale L.J. 262, 276.

59. In this context, the critique is devastating. Some states have statutory bars against more than one punishment or trial for the same act. Courts have tended to seek a metaphysical definition of "act," with no success. See, e.g., Johnson, Reflections on the Neal Doctrine (recounting California courts' experience); Comment, 32 S. Cal. L. Rev. 50 (same); Note, 56 Minn. L. Rev. 646 (Minnesota experience).

60. Chapter 5 discusses the "rule of lenity" in detail. As the name implies, it is a rule that resolves doubts about the scope of the proscribed act in favor of a le-

nient construction. If the question is how many violations of the Mann Act occur when a defendant takes two women across a state line at the same time, the answer is that the scope of the proscribed act is crossing the state line (with however many women) unless Congress has made clear its intent that the number of women determine the number of violations. See Bell v. United States, 349 U.S. 81 (1955).

61. See Gore v. United States, 357 U.S. 386 (1958).

62. Whalen v. United States, 445 U.S. 684 (1980).

63. United States v. Scott, 437 U.S. 82 (1978).

64. Rudstein, 620–35. Professor Rudstein rejects the treatise view in favor of a bright line rule that an acquittal is an acquittal, thus saving courts from having to delve into allegations of fraud months or years later. "Given the relatively few cases in which a defendant obtains her acquittal through fraud, the game hardly seems worth the candle." Id. at 651. For a more detailed discussion of the acquittal-by-fraud issue, see chapter 8.

65. 1 Bishop 747, § 1009.

66. Burks v. United States, 437 U.S. 1 (1978).

67. Ashe v. Swenson, 397 U.S. 436 (1970).

68. Schulhofer, 491.

69. Crist v. Bretz, 437 U.S. 28 (1978).

70. Downum v. United States, 372 U.S. 734 (1963).

71. Richardson v. United States, 468 U.S. 317 (1984).

72. Id. at 323.

73. Id. at 325–26.

74. Witte v. United States, 515 U.S. 389 (1995).

75. The Court simply read its precedents broadly to hold that enhancement "does not constitute punishment for that conduct within the meaning of the Double Jeopardy Clause." 515 U.S. at 399. Professor Peter Henning would draw a distinction between sentencing guidelines' "relevant conduct" that "relates to the quality of the first offense" and conduct that is "external to the criminal activity that is the subject of the charges used in sentencing." Henning, 42. The latter kind of enhancement would require expanding the original charge to include the elements of the external criminal activity and thus would make the first offense include the later one via a lesser-included-offense analysis. On my account, neither enhancement would be a verdict unless Congress meant it to be, and thus double jeopardy would not be a bar to a later trial based on "relevant conduct." For a commentator who agrees that legislative authorization answers all double jeopardy questions under the sentencing guidelines, see Supreme Court Review, 86 J. Crim. L. & Criminology 1539.

76. See United States v. Watts, 117 S.Ct. 633, 644 (1997) (Kennedy, J., dissenting) (noting that this procedure raises "concerns about undercutting the verdict of acquittal").

77. United States v. Watts, 117 S.Ct. 633 (1997) (per curiam), relied on the difference in proof required to convict and that required to enhance. Because the government had to prove the relevant conduct beyond a reasonable doubt to convict but only by a preponderance of the evidence to enhance, it was possible that the jury acquittal did not resolve those facts in the defendant's favor—the jury might have found a preponderance but less than beyond a reasonable doubt. While that is correct, it misses the larger point that sentencing is not a verdict.

78. Tateo v. United States, 377 U.S. 463 (1964); Ball v. United States, 163 U.S. 662 (1896).

79. North Carolina v. Pearce, 395 U.S. 711 (1969).

80. Id. at 721.

81. *Pearce* created a due process right in some circumstances not to be sentenced to a longer term following appeal and reconviction. See also Alabama v. Smith, 490 U.S. 794 (1989).

82. Ricketts v. Adamson, 483 U.S. 1 (1987).

83. United States v. Halper, 490 U.S. 435 (1989).

84. Id.

85. Department of Revenue of Montana v. Kurth Ranch, 511 U.S. 767 (1994).

86. See Hudson v. United States, 118 S.Ct. 488 (1997).

87. See chapter 6.

88. Houston v. Moore, 18 U.S. (5 Wheat.) 1 (1820).

89. Cassell, 708–15.

90. 432 U.S. 161 (1977).

91. Id. at 165.

92. David Schuman is less charitable, commenting on the "incoherence, confusion, and intellectual dishonesty" of the Court's search and seizure jurisprudence. Schuman, 591.

93. Cohen, 833.

94. Kafka, In the Penal Colony, 224.

95. Peller, 1174. There have been many skeptical responses to this robust claim of indeterminacy. See, e.g., Hegland; Posner; Solum; Thomas, Gravitational Effect.

96. See, e.g., Kelman; Williams.

97. Fiss, 741. Fiss did not subscribe to the account but was merely summarizing it.

98. For an analysis of Justice O'Connor's penchant for balancing tests in the double jeopardy area, see Thomas, Elegant Theory, 832–34.

99. Posner, 862.

100. This would qualify as an "exigent-circumstance" exception to the general requirement that police must have a warrant to search a house. See Warden v. Hayden, 387 U.S. 294 (1967) (by implication).

101. 434 U.S. 497 (1978).
102. Ronald Dworkin, Law's Empire.

NOTES TO CHAPTER 2

1. See, e.g., 1 Select Pleas of the Crown 33 & 79–80.
2. Ashe v. Swenson, 397 U.S. 436, 447 (1970). *Ashe* is not a paradigm double jeopardy case because the two trials did not involve the same robbery. Six men were robbed at the same time, and each trial charged robbery of a different victim. Technically, the second trial was thus not for the same offense, but the Court held that the state was estopped from proceeding because the first verdict necessarily meant that the defendant was not one of the robbers. See chapter 7. My point for the present discussion is that the prosecutor in this case saw nothing wrong with asking a second jury to reexamine the crucial fact already found in the defendant's favor. To file a second charge for the exact same offense after an acquittal is no more invasive of the repose and finality inherent in a double jeopardy protection. Prosecutors do not violate the paradigm application of double jeopardy, however, because the double jeopardy rule is clear on that set of facts.
3. See Ashcraft v. Tennessee, 322 U.S. 143 (1944) (holding a confession produced after thirty-six hours of relentless question to be involuntary and thus a violation of due process).
4. See United States v. Jenkins, 420 U.S. 358 (1975), overruled by United States v. Scott, 437 U.S. 82 (1978), discussed chapter 2.
5. See Amar & Marcus.
6. 355 U.S. 184, 187–88 (1957).
7. See chapter 2.
8. See United States v. Scott, 437 U.S. 82, 100–1 (1978); Illinois v. Somerville, 410 U.S. 458, 466 (1973); United States v. Jorn, 400 U.S. 470, 484 (1971); Wade v. Hunter, 336 U.S. 684, 689 (1949).
9. Schulhofer, Jeopardy and Mistrials.
10. Id. at 473.
11. Id. at 514–19.
12. See chapter 2.
13. Compare Model Penal Code § 1.07 (1) & (2). The text oversimplifies these provisions, but the technical nuances are not important for my point, which is that the MPC provides a greater limitation on trials than on convictions. Because I cite Bishop when he agrees with me, I should note that, on this point, Bishop seems to agree with the two-tier approach, though his statement of the rule is less than clear. 1 Bishop 785, § 1060.
14. Sigler, 97–98.
15. Model Penal Code §§ 1.07–1.09.

16. Moore, 353.

17. 131 U.S. 176 (1889).

18. I made this argument in Thomas, Successive Prosecutions.

19. 432 U.S. 161 (1977).

20. Brown v. Ohio, 432 U.S. 161, 166–67 n.6 (1977).

21. Id. at 168 (quoting *Nielsen*, 131 U.S. at 188.)

22. Id. at 166–67 n.6.

23. Illinois v. Vitale, 447 U.S. 410 (1980). For an early discussion of *Vitale*, see Thomas, RICO Prosecutions, 1389–1404.

24. 495 U.S. 508 (1990).

25. Anne Bowen Poulin observes that *Grady* "appears to adopt precisely the '*Vitale* two-tiered test' advocated by Professor Thomas." Poulin, Muddy Waters, 903–4, quoting Thomas, Successive Prosecutions, at 382. This is now somewhat embarrassing because, as the rest of the chapter makes plain, I no longer believe that the two-tier test is a plausible interpretation of the Double Jeopardy Clause.

26. I simplify *Grady* in the text. The Court actually held that convictions for drunk driving and failure to keep to the right of the median barred a later trial for reckless manslaughter, criminally negligent homicide, and third-degree reckless assault. For a more detailed examination, and critique, of *Grady*, see Thomas, Modest Proposal.

27. Poulin, Muddy Waters. Another defense is to draw on dicta in *Brown v. Ohio* and other cases. See Note, 79 Ky. L.J. 847. Indeed, I used this method to predict *Grady*. Thomas, Successive Prosecutions.

28. Poulin, Muddy Waters at 910–14.

29. Id. at 914.

30. I should be both fair and candid. I once defended *Grady* by drawing an equivalence between "offense" and culpability proved by conduct. See Thomas, Modest Proposal. What I failed to see then was that culpability is more than the conduct used to prove the offense; it must begin and end with the offense elements themselves. So while I was correct to draw an equivalence between offense and culpability, I now believe the further reliance on conduct as showing culpability was mistaken.

31. Friedland, 161.

32. See Thomas, Successive Prosecutions, 332 n.52 (collecting authorities). For an excellent discussion and comparison of the mandatory joinder approaches taken by the states, see Vestal & Gilbert, 19–22.

33. Friedland draws the same distinction in English law between offense and transaction. Friedland, 93 (concluding that *autrefois convict*, *autrefois acquit*, and issue estoppel should be narrowly construed, with the "rule against unreasonably splitting a case [to] be the main barrier against unwarranted harassment of the accused").

34. 123 U.S. 372 (1887).

35. Id. at 375. See also Ex parte De Bara, 179 U.S. 316 (1900) (following *Henry* and reiterating, id. at 322, that the issue of the "ultimate punishment" had been left to the court).

36. Ashe v. Swenson, 397 U.S. 436, 469 (1970) (Burger, C.J., dissenting).

37. Richardson, 158. Richardson agrees that the Double Jeopardy Clause does not bar harassing prosecutions, identifying the Due Process Clause as the home of that protection. Id. at 159–68.

38. See Poulin, Complex Criminal Cases, 124 (noting that *Grady* "leaves a gap in double jeopardy protection" because it permits the government to craft the relevant transaction and thus often avoid the *Grady* inclusion).

39. 509 U.S. 688 (1993).

40. As we shall see, *Blockburger*'s test can be rebutted in the context of a single trial by contrary legislative intent. Still, it is fair to say that the included-offense test is the only general, all-purpose same-offense test.

41. For some thoughts on what *Dixon* might mean, see Henning, 23–43; Richardson, 135–39; Rudstein, Summary Contempt, 705–14.

42. 509 U.S. at 720 (White, J., concurring in the judgment in part and dissenting in part) (joined by Souter J., as to Part I, and Stevens, J.) (agreeing with Scalia on the two charges which precipitated the dissenting votes from Rehnquist, O'Connor, and Thomas; disagreeing with Scalia on the other two charges); id. at 741 (Blackmun, J., concurring in the judgment in part and dissenting in part) (refusing to reach the double jeopardy issue on the facts of *Dixon* but stating that he agreed with White's and Souter's resolution of the issue); id. at 743 (Souter, J., concurring in the judgment in part and dissenting in part) (joined by Stevens, J.) (agreeing with White on outcome but defending an even more expansive view of the Double Jeopardy Clause).

43. Id. at 713 (Rehnquist, C.J., concurring in part and dissenting in part) (joined by O'Connor & Thomas, JJ.) (disagreeing with Scalia's application of Blockburger to two of the four charges).

44. Amar & Marcus, 38.

45. Chapter 6.

46. Moore, 353.

47. Moore, 353.

48. Susan Klein cites my early work to support the idea that the Double Jeopardy Clause prohibits vexatious multiple trials. Klein, 243 n.243. I plead guilty to having claimed that double jeopardy barred successive prosecutions and only derivatively limited the number of convictions. By 1988, however, I began to see that the matter was more complex. For example, I saw that double jeopardy theory could be unified by defining its mission as limiting the number of blameworthiness determinations. See, Thomas, Elegant Theory, at 850 ("The double jeopardy clause functions to protect verdicts. Verdicts, of course, determine criminal culpability based on particular conduct and its consequences.") From that under-

standing, it was a short move to my legislative-prerogative thesis, presented in this book, which rejects all harassment theories (including my own 1984 version; see Thomas, Successive Prosecutions). A sample of other commentators supporting a two-tier definition of same offense includes Kirchheimer; Remington & Joseph; Note, 11 Stan. L. Rev. 735; Note 52 U. Cin. L. Rev. 467.

49. See, e.g., Ronner, at 776 (unclear whether Ronner envisions that protection in the Double Jeopardy Clause itself or in the Eighth Amendment).

50. Id.

51. King, Excessive Penalties, 115.

52. Richardson, 151.

53. The government was not overreaching in *Green* as much as it might appear from the text. It would have been flagrant overreaching if the government had sought a first-degree indictment in addition to the second-degree conviction, but this was not the case. Green had secured an appellate reversal of the second-degree murder conviction. With no conviction to bar a second trial, the government could proceed with a murder indictment, and the only issue was whether it could begin again with a first-degree murder indictment.

54. Difficult questions sometimes arise about which conviction is erroneous if more than one is imposed when only one is authorized. But for the present, I need only the general principle.

55. Whalen v. United States, 445 U.S. 684, 688 (1980).

56. Some states permit prosecution appeal of certain legal questions following an acquittal. See Note, 43 Wash. and Lee L. Rev. 295; Palko v. Connecticut, 302 U.S. 319 (1937) (upholding Connecticut statute of this general type). *Palko* is discussed in detail in chapter 9.

57. United States v. Jenkins, 420 U.S. 358 (1975).

58. Id. at 390, quoting *Green*, 355 U.S. at 187.

59. United States v. Scott, 437 U.S. 82 (1978).

60. 432 U.S. 161 (1977).

61. Some difficulties in application arise when dealing with compound-predicate offenses. In this category, one offense (the compound) requires proof of another (the predicate)—for example, felony murder. Is robbery a necessarily-included offense of felony murder based on robbery? Yes, on one reading of necessarily included, and no on another reading. See chapter 6.

62. See chapter 5.

63. Westen & Drubel, 159–62.

64. Amar & Marcus, 34–35. See chapter 3.

65. Westen and Drubel would require that the punishment imposed on the first conviction be credited to the defendant if he is convicted in the second trial—thus, on at least one reading of what "punishment" means, he is not punished twice. Amar and Marcus would retain *Blockburger* as a presumption about

legislative intent to punish cumulatively and they too would presumably insist that two sentences could not be imposed.

66. Many states have enacted mandatory joinder statutes. See Thomas, Elegant Theory, 868–69 n.240.

67. 1 Bishop 786, § 1061 (1).

68. 1 Bishop 785, § 1060.

69. This is an elaboration of the "verdict finality" argument I first made in Thomas, Elegant Theory.

70. Palko v. Connecticut, 302 U.S. 319 (1937), discussed chapter 9.

71. Missouri v. Hunter, 459 U.S. 359 (1983), discussed chapter 3.

72. 372 U.S. 734 (1963).

73. *Green* vacated a verdict for first-degree murder. In Price v. Georgia, 398 U.S. 323 (1970), the defendant was convicted of voluntary manslaughter as a lesser-included offense of murder. That conviction was reversed for trial error. The state retried Price for murder; he was again convicted of the lesser offense of manslaughter. The Court reversed the second manslaughter conviction because it had been imposed in a trial that itself violated double jeopardy. Having been acquitted, implicitly or otherwise, of murder, Price could not be tried for that crime regardless of the outcome.

74. Burks v. United States, 437 U.S. 1 (1978).

75. United States v. Scott, 437 U.S. 82 (1978).

76. 432 U.S. at 171 (Blackmun, J., dissenting).

77. Chapter 5 considers the proper scope of the proscribed act in the Ohio joyriding/auto theft statutes.

78. Felony murder requires proof of a felony; premeditated murder requires proof of premeditation. Strictly applied, therefore, the Court's test would permit two convictions, and two prosecutions, for the same killing. This point is developed in more detail in chapter 6.

79. Whalen v. United States, 445 U.S. 684 (1980).

80. I once titled an article "An Elegant Theory of Double Jeopardy." I now regret the youthful enthusiasm that led to this somewhat embarrassing title. To make matters worse, as Lloyd Weinreb pointed out to me in a letter, my account, while more elegant than the mess the Court has created, was not fully elegant. So I refrain from claiming elegance for the present restatement of my 1988 article. I do claim, however, that the book's account solves both the conduct and the definitional dimensions of the "same-offense" problem with a single stroke.

81. Exodus 20.

82. Exodus 18:16 (New English Bible 1970).

83. See Nahum 1:9 (King James).

84. See Bartkus v. Illinois, 359 U.S. 121, 152 n.4 (1959) (Black, J., dissenting), relying on 25 Migne, Patrologia Latina 1238 (1845).

85. 1 Pollock & Maitland 448 (quoting original in Latin).

86. The next verse supports this reading: Nahum 1:10 (stating that God's enemies "shall be devoured as stubble fully dry").

87. See Nahum 1:9 (New English version).

88. 4 Blackstone's Commentaries *336. The use of former attainder to bar prosecution for felonies that were not the same offense, though conceptually sound, did not endure many years after publication of the *Commentaries*. Parliament soon required that the plea of former attainder be limited to the same offense. See 7 and 8 Geo. IV c. 28 s. 4 (1827).

89. The Babylonian Laws 13.

90. Id. at 15.

91. See chapter 7.

92. Demosthenes 20.147 (reprinted in 1 Demosthenes 589).

93. See 1 J.L. Strachan-Davidson, Problems of the Roman Criminal Law 155 (1912).

94. See id. at 127–45.

95. VI Polybius 14.6, quoted in Strachan-Davidson, 127.

96. See The Opinions of Paulus, Title XVII (quoting the Roman jurist Paulus that "after public acquittal a defendant could again be prosecuted by his informer within thirty days, but after that time this cannot be done"); 2 Strachan-Davidson, 177.

97. Theodor Mommsen, Strafrecht 277, quoted in 2 Strachan-Davidson, 177.

98. See Dig. Just. 48.7.2, reprinted in 4 The Digest of Justinian 797 ("the governor must not allow a man to be charged with the same offenses of which he has already been acquitted"); Dig. Just. 49.6, reprinted in id. at 865 (allowing appeal after conviction). The Digest is silent on whether the state can appeal an acquittal, but all the examples of appeals from criminal judgments involve appeals from convictions. See Dig. Just. 49.1.6, 49.1.15, 49.1.18, 49.4.1, 49.4.2.3, 49.5.2, 49.7.1.2 & 3, 49.7.1.5, 49.9.1. reprinted in id. at 865, 866, 867, 869–70, 871, 872, 872–73, 873, 874.

99. 1 Pollock & Maitland, 130.

100. See The Constitutions of Clarendon c. 3 (1164), reprinted in Sources of English Legal and Constitutional History 12.

101. See 1 Pollock & Maitland 448.

102. Id. at 455–56 n.1.

103. See id.

104. 1 Pollock & Maitland, 124, citing 1 Gesta Henrici (Benedictus) 33.

105. Id. at 457.

106. Id.

107. Id. at 455 n.1.

108. Id.

109. Friedland, 7.

110. See 1 Pollock & Maitland, 454–56 (noting that Becket's double punishment argument "had neither been tolerated by the state nor consecrated by the church," id. at 454, and that "Becket's theory about double punishment was condemned by Innocent III" by decree "to this day part of the statute law of the catholic church," id. at 455). See also Barkus v. Illinois, 359 U.S. 121, 152 n.5 (1959) (Black, J., dissenting) (noting that Becket's "assertions that Henry's proposals would result in double punishment for the clerics has been much debated by historians").

111. This position is, of course, highly controversial. For the traditional, contrary view, see Friedland, 7 (stating, as if obvious, that punishment by both the king and the church is double punishment).

112. 4 Blackstone's Commentaries *373.

113. By Blackstone's day, the offender who was granted his clergy could be subject to one or more unpleasant consequences, though Blackstone insisted they were "concomitant conditions" rather than "consequences of receiving this indulgence." Id. at 373. These "concomitant conditions" included being branded, whipped, fined, or imprisoned for up to one year. Id. at 367–73. Even more unpleasant "conditions" were discretionary with the judge: "the court, in their discretion, instead of such burning in the hand or whipping, may direct such offenders to be transported to America (or . . . to any other parts beyond the seas) for seven years. . . ." Id. at 371. While the Supreme Court would surely consider these "concomitant conditions" to be criminal punishments today, see Chapter 4, they were insignificant compared to hanging.

114. I am for the moment using "same act" interchangeably with "same offense," as Becket and Saint Jerome did. Further evidence on this point can be found in the remaining sections in this chapter.

115. It is not clear whether these pleas evolved in some manner from the Becket-Henry confrontation or were simply bubbling up in the secular courts simultaneously. The existence of four different pleas by 1203 suggests the latter origin. Cf. Sigler, 3 (Becket-Henry disagreement may have "foreshadowed the current legal doctrine," or pleas in bar "may have derived from the Continent through canon law, rather than being native to England").

116. 1 Select Pleas Of The Crown 33 (case 76, year 1203) (alternative ground for finding appeal "null") (other ground that prosecutor "made no mention of sight or hearing"); id. at 79–80 (case 124, date uncertain) (letting one of defendants be "quit" of robbery charge because he was previously "discharged" of same offense).

117. See id. at 21–22 (case 47, year 1202) (asking "by what warrant they outlawed the same man twice for the same death", id. at 22); id. at 35 (case 79, year 1203) (finding a former "concord" for the same offense); id. at 38–40 (case 82, year 1200) (finding prosecution against at least one defendant null because of proof of prior compromise between prosecutor and that defendant).

118. See id. at 17 (case 40, year 1202) (postponing resolution of plea, because prosecutor denied withdrawing prosecution, until evidence "be had upon this matter"). Withdrawal was recognized by Britton as a bar to a new prosecution in the late thirteenth century. See 1 Britton 103–4 (drawing parallel between withdrawal and acquittal); id. at 113 (establishing plea of former acquittal as bar to new prosecution); id. at xviii (fixing probable date of publication as 1291–92).

119. See 1 Select Pleas of the Crown, 77–78 (case 121, date uncertain) (other defenses were untimely prosecution and improper motives of prosecutor).

120. 1 Bracton (Woodbine ed.), xlii (Translator's Note).

121. 2 Bracton, 391.

122. Id. at 397, 398, 400.

123. 2 Fleta 82.

124. Mirror Of Justices 175.

125. 1 Britton 113.

126. Wrote v. Wigges, 76 Eng. Rep. 994, 996–97 (1591).

127. 4 Blackstone's Commentaries *336.

128. 2 Bracton, 391.

129. Finklestein, 68 (laws 10 & 11). Hammurabi's Code provided for ordeal of water for sorcery if the accuser was "unable to sustain" the charge. If the accused drowned, the accuser got his house; if the accused survived, the accuser was put to death, and the accused took his house. Code of Hammurabi 2.

130. 4 Blackstone's Commentaries *342.

131. Finklestein, 188; 4 Blackstone's Commentaries *342–43; 2 Pollock & Maitland, 599.

132. Though we lack records as far back as 1176, Maitland found only one case between 1201 to 1219 where the accused was not acquitted by the ordeal. Friedland, 6 (citing 1 Maitland, Select Pleas, xxiv, 75). Moreover, Pollock & Maitland report evidence "from a Hungarian monastery which kept a register of judgments" in the thirteenth century. "This evidence is said to show that it was about an even chance whether the ordeal of hot iron succeeded or failed." 2 Pollock & Maitland, 599 n.1. Further implicit evidence is that in "certain cases" the procedure "gave the appellee [defendant] a choice between bearing the iron and allowing the appellor to bear it. This seems to show that the result could not be predicted with much certainty." Id. Finally, anecdotal evidence indicated lack of confidence in the ordeal. See id. at 599 n.2 (noting an occasion in which fifty defendants "escaped" the ordeal of iron).

133. See Assize Clar. c. 14 (1166), reprinted in Sources of English Legal and Constitutional History 15. Outlawry was, in effect, a declaration that the community would "make war" upon an individual. See 2 Pollock & Maitland, 449.

134. Assize North. c. 1 (1176), reprinted in Sources of English Legal and Constitutional History 16. Here, we can more clearly see an evolving confidence in the judgment of jurors and a growing mistrust of the ordeal. See 2 Pollock &

Maitland, 599. This trend, of course, culminated in this country with the Sixth Amendment right to trial by jury.

135. See Hunter 12 (citing 22 Ed. IV Fitz. Cor 44 (1482)). Prior practice had been that the king could bring an indictment first, but an acquittal on the indictment barred the private appeal. Id.

136. See 3 Hen. VII, c.1 (1487). This statute worked a change in the common law. Sigler is thus wrong to claim that Coke misstated "contemporary doctrine" when he wrote that an acquittal on an indictment is no bar to a private appeal in murder cases. Sigler, 17–18.

137. 2 Bracton, 391.

138. Friedland, 10.

139. 26 Hen. VIII, c.6 (1534). Friedland views this statute as one of the "significant lapses in the rational development of double jeopardy rules." Friedland, 10.

140. Hunter, 12–13.

141. 4 Blackstone's Commentaries *366–67.

142. Id. at *373. The text oversimplifies somewhat. Clerics in orders were entitled to benefit of clergy without punishment of any kind. Lords of parliament and peers of the realm were likewise entitled to benefit of clergy without punishment, but for a first offense only. It was commoners who had to endure a lesser punishment to claim benefit of clergy for their first offenses.

143. 4 Hen. VII, c. 13 (1487).

144. 23 Hen. VIII c.1 (1531).

145. 8 Eliz. c. 4 (1565) & 18 Eliz. c. 7 (1576).

146. 18 Eliz. c. 7 (1576).

147. 4 Blackstone's Commentaries *374.

148. Lisle's Case, 84 Eng. Rep. 1095, 1101 (1697).

149. Coke's Third Institutes, 212.

150. 9 Hen. VII, c.1 (1487).

151. Coke's Third Institutes, 213. Though Coke used the broader "offense," it is clear from the context that he limited double jeopardy pleas to felonies. Hale states the plea more accurately as *auterfoits attaint de mesme felonie*. See 2 Hale, 251.

152. See 2 Hale, 250.

153. Coke's Third Institutes, 213.

154. Id. at 213–14.

155. See Coke's Third Institutes, 213. By the time of Blackstone, the plea of former pardon was considered a separate plea in bar. 4 Blackstone's Commentaries *337. See also 2 Hale, 241 (listing *auterfoits attaint* of another felony as a plea in bar); id. at 252.

156. Coke's Third Institutes, 213.

157. Id.

158. Id.

159. Id.

160. See id. at 214; 2 Hale, 241.

161. Prior to 1565, benefit of clergy barred prosecution for any felony formerly committed, even if the felony did not qualify itself for benefit of clergy. Coke's Third Institutes, 214. A statute of Elizabeth's limited the effect to former felonies for which clergy was permitted. 8 Eliz. c. 4 (1565).

162. Grady v. Corbin, 495 U.S. 510, 530 (1990) (Scalia, J., dissenting).

163. 4 Blackstone's Commentaries *336.

164. Id. at *335.

165. 1 Blackstone's Commentaries on the Laws of England xiv (ed. G. Sharswood 1885) (noting publication date of 1769).

166. 1 Annals Cong. 434 (1789).

167. Presumably, a defendant's election to end the trial prior to verdict would have been viewed as a waiver, thus permitting a second trial.

168. 1 Annals Cong. 753.

169. 4 Blackstone's Commentaries *335.

170. "Jeopardy" derives from the Old French *jeu parti*, "signifying an even, or divided, game, a game in which the chances are even." Webster's New International Dictionary of the English Language 1332 (2d ed. 1957).

171. Kepner v. United States 195 U.S. 100, 134 (1904) (Holmes, J., dissenting).

NOTES TO CHAPTER 3

1. Moore, Act and Crime.

2. In re Snow, 120 U.S. 274 (1887), discussed in chapter 3.

3. 22 U.S. (9 Wheat.) 579 (1824).

4. Id. at 579.

5. Id. at 580.

6. Id.

7. See chapter 1.

8. 22 U.S. at 580.

9. United States v. Haskell, 26 Fed. Cas. 207, 212 (1823) (holding that a discharge of a jury on grounds of lack of verdict is not a valid double jeopardy plea.)

10. 3 Story, § 1781.

11. Story also cited Rawle on the Constitution, ch. 10, pp 132–33. Id.

12. 437 U.S. 28 (1978). For a discussion of *Crist* on the merits, see chapter 8.

13. Id. at 34 n.10.

14. Justice Powell, in dissent, saw "manifest necessity" as an "independent [common law] rule barring needless discharges of the jury," Id. at 44–45 (Powell, J., dissenting).

15. 434 U.S. 497 (1978).

16. Id. at 506 (footnotes omitted).
17. Id. at 511.
18. Id.
19. United States v. Scott, 437 U.S. 82 (1978), discussed in chapter 8.
20. 437 U.S. 1 (1978)
21. Ball v. United States, 163 U.S. 662 (1896).
22. *Burks*, 437 U.S. at 10 (emphasis in original).
23. Indeed, some state rules of procedure recognize a distinction between reversals of convictions that are not supported by legally sufficient evidence and reversals of convictions that are against the weight of the evidence. The latter standard explicitly puts the trial judge (and later the appellate court) in the position of serving as a thirteenth juror. It is not necessary for a judge to find no legally sufficient evidence to reverse a conviction as against the weight of the evidence; the judge might simply decide that the evidence raises a doubt in her mind, even though a rational jury could find guilt beyond a reasonable doubt. These categories of reversals have different double jeopardy consequences. See Tibbs v. Florida, 457 U.S. 31 (1982), discussed in chapter 8.
24. *Burks*, 16 (emphasis in original).
25. 1 Bishop 774, § 1048.
26. Sigler, 101.
27. The common law developed some quite good, but largely ad hoc, answers to these questions. See, e.g., 35 Harv. L. Rev. 615 (robbery of two victims is two robberies); 20 Harv. L. Rev. 642, 643 (theft in one transaction of goods belonging to several owners is a single theft). But the nineteenth-century effort to ground an understanding of offense in act or injury to the state was largely abandoned, leaving the way clear for a mindless counting of offense violations. See, e.g., 12 Ky. L. Rev. 249 (approving of case finding that each hand of stud poker was a separate double jeopardy offense of gambling).
28. 2 Hale, 245.
29. Id.
30. 237 U.S. 632, 640 (1915).
31. 120 U.S. 274 (1887).
32. Id. at 276–77.
33. Id. at 282.
34. Id. at 285.
35. 131 U.S. 176 (1889).
36. Id. at 187. Professor Olson points out that the Court read "sexual intercourse" into the cohabitation statute so that it was not *really* an element to be compared with the elements of adultery. Olson, 48–49. But on this point, I agree with Amar and Marcus: by virtue of statutory interpretation of a federal statute, the net effect of *Nielsen* is to make "sexual intercourse" an element of cohabitation. Amar & Marcus, 42.

37. 220 U.S. 338, 342 (1911).

38. Id. at 343.

39. The state approach is discussed and compared to my blameworthy act approach in chapter 5.

40. 284 U.S. 299 (1932).

41. The assertion that the other elements in the *Blockburger* statutes are not blameworthy acts must be defended, as chapter 5 attempts to do.

42. 284 U.S. at 301.

43. *Grady,* 495 U.S. 529 (Scalia, J., dissenting).

44. 168 Eng. Rep. 455 (K.B. 1796).

45. *Grady,* at 533 (Scalia, J., dissenting).

46. 168 Eng. Rep. at 461.

47. Brown v. Ohio, 432 U.S. 161, 168 (1977).

48. The English usage of this test ignored the doctrine that permits conviction of lesser-included offenses. The test was a mechanical one which asked whether the proof of the facts in the second indictment would convict of the offense charged in the first indictment.

49. Friedland, 98. To be fair to *Vandercomb,* the King's Bench almost certainly intended this test not as an all-purpose same-offense test but, rather, as a test for variance. Id. at 100. Variance occurs when the state proves a different offense than it charged. See chapter 9.

50. *Vandercomb,* 168 Eng. Rep. at 460 (discussing Turner's Case, Kely. 30).

51. Id. No second indictment had been procured in *Turner's Case;* the decision "was merely a direction from the Judges to the officer of the Court how to draw the second indictment for the larceny." Id.

52. Gavieres v. United States, 220 U.S. 338, 343–44 (1911).

53. 202 U.S. 344 (1906).

54. Id. at 381 (quoting 1 Bishop, Criminal Law, § 1051).

55. See Grady v. Corbin, 495 U.S. 508 (1990), discussed in chapter 2.

56. Few courts or commentators have stated this truth explicitly, perhaps because it is obvious, perhaps because it is not. For a welcome exception, see Poulin, Complex Criminal Cases, 118.

57. Friedland, 98–99. Continuing: "For example, unnecessary averments in the second might mean that a special plea would succeed, whereas unnecessary averments in the first might mean that it would not." Id. at 99.

58. See United States v. Dixon, 509 U.S. 688 (1993). To be sure, there is some play in the joints, as five members of the *Dixon* Court were willing to consider the particular contempt order that the defendant was charged with violating. But this is different from examining the indictments to see whether the allegations are distinct. One state court has stated explicitly that *Blockburger* "must stand or fall on the working of the statutes alone, not on the indictment." State v. Close, 623 P.2d 940, 950 (Mont. 1981).

59. 384 U.S. 436 (1966).

60. But not completely. The Court has been divided over the application of *Blockburger* to several complex statutory offenses. See United States v. Dixon, 113 S.Ct. 2849 (1993) (plurality); Garrett v. United States, 471 U.S. 773 (1985); Whalen v. United States, 445 U.S. 684, 688 (1980); Jeffers v. United States, 432 U.S. 137 (1977) (plurality).

61. Perhaps *Miranda* is no better than *Blockburger*. See George C. Thomas III, The Real-World Failure of Miranda: A Plea For More (and Better) Empirical Evidence, 43 U.C.L.A. L. Rev. 821 (1996).

62. Houston v. Moore, 18 U.S. (5 Wheat.) 1 (1820).

63. Id. at 23.

64. See chapter 2.

65. 438 U.S. 204 (1978).

66. See id. at 226–27 & n.8 (Marshall, J., dissenting).

67. Note, 49 Ohio St. L.J. 773, 799. One might ask why recommend functionalism if the resulting balancing test will be difficult to perform. The commentator explains that "a functional approach will enable the Court to realize when actions by the state interfere with the double jeopardy clause's protections." Id. How a balancing test will accomplish this clarity is not explained.

68. Westen has made a similar argument, though he finds the salient distinction between a jury fact-finding and other findings, based on his privileging of jury nullification as the preeminent value protected by double jeopardy. Westen, 1038–39 n.136. The distinction I draw is between a finding accepted by the relevant procedure as final and one that is defined as tentative.

69. They do not. See McKeiver v. Pennsylvania, 403 U.S. 528 (1971).

70. 438 U.S. at 212.

71. Id. at 216 n.14.

72. 273 U.S. 1 (1927).

73. Id. at 11.

74. 432 U.S. 161, 165 (1977).

75. Id. (footnote omitted).

76. Chapter 6 argues that *Brown* also gets exactly right the difficult issues of how to compare statutory descriptions and how to count violations of a single statute.

77. Jeffers v. United States, 432 U.S. 137 (1977).

78. See *Brown*, 432 U.S. 166–67 n.6: "The *Blockburger* test is not the only standard for determining whether successive prosecutions impermissibly involve the same offense. Even if two offenses are sufficiently different to permit the imposition of consecutive sentences, successive prosecutions will be barred in some circumstances where the second prosecution requires the relitigation of factual issues already resolved by the first."

79. Whalen v. United States, 445 U.S. 684, 688 (1980).

80. 450 U.S. 333, 344 (1981).
81. Id. at 345 (Stewart, J., concurring in the judgment).
82. Id. (citation omitted).
83. For a discussion of the "cold war" between the Missouri Supreme Court and the United States Supreme Court, see Thomas, Multiple Punishments After *Missouri v. Hunter.*
84. 459 U.S. 359 (1983).
85. Id. at 362.
86. See Whalen v. United States, 445 U.S. 684 (1980).
87. Justice Stewart had retired by 1983.
88. *Hunter,* 459 U.S. at 365 (quoting State v. Haggard, 619 S.W.2d 44, 51 (Mo. 1981)).
89. Id.
90. 357 U.S. 386 (1958). For more detail on *Gore,* see chapter 6.
91. This was the Court's characterization of the legislative intent in *Hunter.* 459 U.S. at 368.
92. For the contrary view, see Schwartz, 845–46. Of course, if the multiple collateral consequences are not authorized by the legislature, their imposition would violate double jeopardy. See Ball v. United States, 470 U.S. 856 (1985) (holding that multiple convictions constitute multiple punishment whether or not a sentence has been imposed, in part because of the collateral consequences). I discuss the implications of *Ball* in Thomas, Sentencing Problems.
93. 85 U.S. (18 Wall.) 163 (1873).
94. For a more detailed examination of *Lange,* including an analysis of three different theories of multiple punishment raised by the case, see Thomas, Multiple Punishments After *Missouri v. Hunter.*
95. See *Kurth Ranch,* 511 U.S. 767, 799 (1994) (Scalia, J., dissenting).
96. Whalen v. United States, 445 U.S. 684, 690 n.4 (1980). The Court noted that the separation of powers doctrine would similarly forbid federal courts from "imposing multiple punishments not authorized by Congress." Id. at 689.
97. *Lange,* 83 U.S. (18 Wall.) at 173.
98. See the commentators and Supreme Court dicta cited (approvingly) in Thomas, Successive Prosecutions, 340–59.
99. Moore, 353.
100. The *Kurth* majority seemed to agree, implicitly holding that the tax collection proceeding was a second prosecution and thus barred regardless of the legislative intent to punish cumulatively. Scalia argued that a tax collection proceeding is not a criminal prosecution. On my view, as I argue in the text, this debate is pointless.
101. See Thomas, Unified Theory of Multiple Punishment, 25–54.
102. Note, 45 Vand. L. Rev. 273, 307. The author lodges a criticism of *Block-burger*'s dual nature different from my legislative-prerogative critique: If *Block-*

burger is a form of statutory construction, federal courts cannot legitimately apply it to state cases because statutory construction of state statutes is uniquely within the jurisdiction of state courts. Id. at 310. I do not disagree with this view but point out that the Court has applied *Blockburger* only once to reverse a state court same-offense case and in doing so was at pains to insist that it was following the state court construction of the statute. Brown v. Ohio, 432 U.S. 161 (1977).

103. 4 Blackstone's Commentaries *336. The use of former attainder to bar prosecution for felonies that were not the same offense, though conceptually sound, did not endure many years after publication of the *Commentaries*. Parliament soon required that the plea of former attainder be limited to the same offense. See 7 & 8 Geo. IV c. 28 s. 4 (1827).

104. Scalia might respond that the Double Jeopardy Clause did not incorporate the plea of former attainder. Grady v. Corbin, 495 U.S. 508, 530 (1990) (Scalia, J., dissenting). True enough, but the point in the text is contextual and not substantive. The existence of a broad plea of former attainder and a narrow plea of former conviction is significant because it demonstrates that the concern of the common law was punishment and not the number of trials. The contextual understanding that multiple punishment is the same evil as multiple trials was undoubtedly held by the Framers, as *Lange* implies.

105. Friedland, 171–80.

106. Scalia's argument here, of course, is that the change in the language effected by the Framers was intended to change this part of double jeopardy protection. All the evidence about why the Framers changed Madison's language is to the contrary, however. See chapter 2.

107. 83 U.S. (18 Wall.) at 173.

108. 471 U.S. 773 (1985).

109. Chapter 6 discusses the category of "compound-predicate" offenses.

110. For more evidence on this point, see Poulin, Complex Criminal Cases, 108–9, and the authorities she cites.

111. Sigler, 38.

112. Id. at 41.

113. Id. at 67.

114. Id. at 75.

115. Id. at 41.

116. Green v. United States, 355 U.S. 184, 187 (1957).

117. Sigler, 222–23.

118. Comment, 75 Yale L.J. 261, 264.

119. Id. at 266.

120. Simon recommends that mandatory joinder be read into the Double Jeopardy Clause, which technically sets his solution apart from the Model Penal Code's legislative solution. Unfortunately, trying to read mandatory joinder into

the Double Jeopardy Clause is a deeply flawed project, as I seek to demonstrate in chapter 2.

121. See Kirchheimer.

122. Westen & Drubel, 84–85.

123. See McKay, 8–9 (making this criticism of Westen & Drubel).

124. Amar & Marcus, 28–44.

125. Green v. United States, 355 U.S. 184 (1957).

126. 4 Blackstone's Commentaries *336. Amar believes that the theoretical distinctiveness of murder and manslaughter is implicit in Diaz v. United States, 223 U.S. 442 (1912), where the Court allowed a homicide prosecution to follow an assault conviction. Since assault is a necessarily-included offense of homicide, Amar reads Diaz to permit murder to be prosecuted following conviction of the necessarily-included offense of manslaughter, assuming the second prosecution is not vexatious. In Diaz, the victim did not die until after the assault conviction, thus making the second trial nonvexatious. This interpretation of Diaz seems implausible. The killing had not yet occurred when the assault conviction was imposed, thus making these different acts. Indeed, Diaz makes this point: "At the time of the trial for the [assault] the death had not ensued, and not until it did ensue was the homicide committed." Id. at 449 (emphasis added).

127. See Batchelder, 738–53, and the cases cited in n.48, chapter 1.

128. 1 Bishop 775, § 1050.

129. Amar & Marcus, 38 n.190.

130. Nancy King has attempted to give content to the Amar-Marcus "vexatious prosecution" standard, but the improvement is, to my mind, only marginal. See King, Three Dimensional.

131. I made this criticism in Thomas, Blameworthy Acts, and Amar responded by claiming that "life or limb" is a "grimly poetic synecdoche," not meant to be taken literally. To argue otherwise, Amar claims, is to miss the "big difference between plain meaning textualism and tin ear textualism." Amar, Sixth Amendment Principles, 660 n.76. I suggest that "tin ear textualism" is in the ear of the listener.

132. 471 U.S. at 784.

NOTES TO CHAPTER 4

1. 1 Britton xviii.

2. Id. at 104. See also id. at 112 (noting that an acquittal on "our" suit does not bar a private appeal).

3. See LaFave & Israel, § 17.4(a).

4. Kennedy v. Mendoza-Martinez, 372 U.S. 144, 168 (1963).

5. 118 S.Ct. 488 (1997).

6. See Thomas, A Modest Proposal.

7. 490 U.S. 435 (1989).

8. See Hudson v. United States, 118 S.Ct. 488 (1997).

9. 116 U.S. 427 (1886).

10. United States v. McKee, 26 F. Cas. 1116 (C.C.E.D. Mo. 1877) (No. 15,688).

11. 116 U.S. at 445.

12. 1 Bishop 733, § 990

13. See McKechnie, 359–367 (discussing chapter thirty-six of Magna Carta, which provided for a writ to test the adequacy of a homicide charge before twelve recognitors and thus to allow unjustly accused defendants to avoid the trial by battle).

14. See Russell, 135.

15. See McKechnie, 366–67 (noting that trial by battle was nonetheless not officially repealed until 1819).

16. See 2 Pollock & Maitland, 461.

17. See 1 Annals Cong. 754.

18. Sigler states that "threat of death or mutilation" was a necessary element of early double jeopardy doctrine, but offers no evidence. Sigler, 39.

19. See Chapter 2.06.

20. 4 Blackstone's Commentaries *335.

21. 1 Annals of Congress 753.

22. Id.

23. 1 S. Jour. 167. Obviously, a mistake was made in omitting "twice" from the Senate language about being put in jeopardy. "Twice" appeared in an earlier Senate motion to amend the House language. Id. at 154.

24. Sigler has an excellent summary of the drafting and approval of the Double Jeopardy Clause. Sigler, 27–34.

25. 1 S. Jour. 209.

26. 85 U.S. (18 Wall.) 163, 168–73 (1873).

27. Moore, 1.

28. Cox, 1307.

29. Id. at 1238.

30. For law review commentary on state cases raising this issue, see Note, 18 Campbell L. Rev. 391; Comment, 44 U. Kan. L. Rev. 1009; Note, 29 Loy. L.A. L. Rev. 1273; Note, 23 New Eng. J. on Crim. & Civ. Confinement 239.

31. For law review commentary on state cases, see Kravitz, 29 Akron L. Rev. 123; Note, 23 Fordham Urb. L.J. 923; Casenote, 4 Geo. Mason L. Rev. 521; Comment, 65 UMKC L. Rev. 104.

32. See Annual Survey, 5 Widener J. Pub. L. 809.

33. See Pasley, 114 Banking L.J. 4. The Supreme Court has since corrected this corner of *Halper* and sent a signal that *Halper* is essentially dead.

34. See Survey of Recent Developments, 27 Seton Hall L. Rev. 1161.

35. See Comment, 26 Cumb. L. Rev. 231.

36. 511 U.S. 767 (1994).
37. Id. at 784.
38. Id.
39. 1 Bishop 733–734, § 990 (emphasis added). See also Gooch, 22 (relying on Bishop).
40. 372 U.S. 144 (1963).
41. Id. at 168. Compare *Halper*'s definition of a criminal sanction: where the sanction "cannot fairly be said solely to serve a remedial purpose, but rather can be explained only as also serving either retributive or deterrent purposes." 490 U.S. at 448.
42. Id. (citations omitted).
43. See Supreme Court Review, 85 J. Crim. L. & Crim. 936, 957 (arguing that the Montana tax fails only two of the seven tests).
44. See chapters 3 & 6.
45. King, 183–84.
46. Some evidence of the startling nature of the *Halper-Kurth Ranch* doctrine is the quantity of law review commentary and the sometimes forced humor of the titles. For examples of the latter, see Casenote, The Tax Man Cometh, But Fear Not, 28 Creighton L. Rev. 475; Note, The Supreme Court Assaults State Drug Taxes with a Double Jeopardy Dagger: Death Blow, Serious Injury, or Flesh Wound?, 29 Ind. L. Rev. 695; Note and Comment, Is the DUI Defense D.O.A.?, 29 Loy. L.A. L. Rev. 1273; Casenote, *Department of Kurth Ranch*: Double Jeopardy. A: Multiple Punishment Component. Q. What Is Confusion?, 15 N. Ill. U. L. Rev. 433; Note, Up In Smoke, 28 Tex. Tech. 923; Note & Comment, Enlarging the Sargasso Sea of Double Jeopardy, 17 Whittier L. Rev. 477.

Other examples of commentary on the *Halper* doctrine include Hall, 32 Idaho L. Rev. 527; Klein, 82 Iowa L. Rev. 183; Neafsey & Bonanno, 7 Fordham Envtl. L.J. 719; Note, 23 Am. J. Crim. L. 431; Case Comment, 75 B.U. L. Rev. 505 (1995); Casenote, 30 Creighton L. Rev. 235; Case Note, 73 U. Det. Mercy L. Rev. 117; Case Comment 7 U. Fla. J.L. & Pub. Pol'y 385 (1994); Summary, 25 Golden Gate U. L. Rev. 331; Supreme Court Term, 110 Harv. L. Rev. 206; Symposium, 32 Idaho L. Rev. 545; Note, 81 Iowa L. Rev. 775; New Decisions, 83 J. Tax'n 316; Comment, 71 St. John's L. Rev. 153; Casenote, 5 Seton Hall Const. L.J. 1231; Comment, 48 S.C. L. Rev. 405; Note; 4 S. Cal. Interdisciplinary L.J. 323; Comment, 21 S. Ill. U. L.J. 149; Comment, 26 Stetson L. Rev. 373 (1996); Note, 48 Tax Law. 911; Note and Comment, 71 Wash. L. Rev. 489 (1996).

47. Rudstein, Civil Penalties. Susan Klein, among others, insists that *Halper* was correctly decided and thus that no correction is needed. In part, this may be because she values history less than I do. Klein, 257 n.309.
48. Henning, 43–71.
49. Id. at 69. Henning contrasts the inflexible nature of double jeopardy protection with the Excessive Fines Clause in the Eighth Amendment, which, by def-

inition, requires proportionality. It also permits a court to reduce the fine to an acceptable level. If *Halper* had been decided as an Eighth Amendment case, the Court could have remanded for a determination of the appropriate amount of the fine. This approach can satisfy both defendants, who pay only a fine that is proportional to the harm caused, and the government, which is permitted to recover a reasonable amount of damages.

50. One could, of course, analyze cases like *Halper* and *Kurth Ranch* under the Excessive Fines Clause of the Eighth Amendment. See Supreme Court Review, 85 J. Crim. L. & Criminology 936.

51. 118 S.Ct. 488 (1997).

52. Id. at 491.

53. Id. at 497 (Stevens, J., concurring in the judgment).

54. Kansas v. Hendricks, 117 S.Ct. 2072 (1997).

55. *Hudson*, 118 S.Ct. at 497 (Stevens, J., concurring in the judgment).

56. 518 U.S. 267 (1996). Susan Klein does not share my view that *Ursery* is a favorable development. Klein, 233–41.

57. See also Hall, at 542 (noting, prior to *Ursery*, the "unique role of civil forfeiture statutes as a tool for recovery of the proceeds of crime, and for other remedial purposes").

58. The Court also had to distinguish *Austin*, which held that a civil forfeiture is a "punishment" for purposes of the Eighth Amendment prohibition of "cruel and unusual punishment." Austin v. United States, 509 U.S. 602 (1993). The Court's distinction is clever, but thin, and illustrates the difficulty in assuming that all "punishment" is a "life or limb" penalty.

59. Cassella, 594.

60. 490 U.S. at 448. One commentator noted that the best definition of "remedial" may be "not criminal." Comment, 45 U. Miami L. Rev. 911, 947.

61. For a thorough examination of the license revocation issue, see Comment, 46 Emory L.J. 329.

62. Henning, 51. See also Comment, 46 Emory L.J. 329, 355 (concluding that the license revocation issue must be resolved on a case-by-case basis, requiring "each state to look at its laws carefully to determine whether the sanctions imposed by the administrative license revocation statutes are in fact serving a remedial purpose or whether they are a punishment imposed without trial and masked as a civil sanction").

63. 118 S.Ct. at 494.

64. Three members of the *Hudson* Court refused to join the part of Chief Justice Rehnquist's majority opinion requiring "clearest proof," but that requirement commanded a majority of the Court.

65. See 2 Pollock & Maitland, 451.

66. Id.

67. Id. at 462.

68. See id. at 452 (noting that even homicide was emendable at times by payment of money, horses, or oxen) & 456 (noting "signs" that the line between emendable and unemendable "fluctuated from time to time and still fluctuates as we pass from district to district").

69. See Duncan v. Louisiana, 391 U.S. 145, 160 (1968) (quoting District of Columbia v. Clawans, 300 U.S. 617, 628 (1937) (internal citation omitted).

70. See Baldwin v. New York, 399 U.S. 66 (1970) (plurality).

71. 407 U.S. 25 (1972).

72. Scott v. Illinois, 440 U.S. 367, 373 (1979).

73. Abney v. United States, 431 U.S. 651 (1977) (deciding the issue as one of statutory construction of the federal interlocutory appeal statute).

74. For a more general argument that incarceration is generically different from all other consequences of the legal system, see Colb, Freedom from Incarceration.

75. Breed v. Jones, 421 U.S. 519, 529 (1975).

76. *Halper*, 490 U.S. at 449.

77. Moore, 353.

78. See chapter 2 for a discussion of why legislative intent should control in successive prosecutions as well as single trials.

79. *Kurth Ranch*, 511 U.S. at 801 (Scalia, J., dissenting).

80. See Thomas, Elegant Theory, 873–82 (describing a theory of election that works against the prosecutor as well as defendants).

81. See, e.g., Fugate v. New Mexico, 470 U.S. 904 (1985) (equally divided Court affirming lower court's refusal to bar homicide prosecution following traffic convictions) (Powell, J., not participating); Thigpen v. Roberts, 468 U.S. 27 (1984) (holding traffic convictions a due process bar to manslaughter trial; not reaching double jeopardy question); Illinois v. Vitale, 447 U.S. 410, 419–20 (1980) (noting "substantial" claim of double jeopardy if state follows traffic conviction with homicide prosecution based on same conduct).

82. See, e.g., Illinois v. Zegart, 452 U.S. 948 (1981) (Burger, C.J., dissenting from denial of certiorari) (state court had held that traffic conviction barred homicide prosecution).

NOTES TO CHAPTER 5

1. Mead, 874.

2. See Bentham, 71–81 (using somewhat different terminology).

3. Feinberg, Harm to Others; Offenses to Others; Harm to Self; Harmless Wrongdoing.

4. Feinberg, Harm to Others, 105–6.

5. Mead, 874.

6. For an innovative argument that criminal liability does not require a volitional movement, see Husak, 78–111. For the opposite view, see Moore, 18–59.

7. See chapter 1.

8. These requirements are usually referred to, respectively, as actus reus and the principle of legality. See, e.g., Husak, 7–11.

9. See, e.g., Moore, 360 (noting a class of cases in which most courts have rejected the metaphysically correct view because of "a moral insight (that they have not known how to conceptualize in terms of action-identity)").

10. See Thomas, Unified Theory of Multiple Punishment, 15.

11. Model Penal Code § 1.13 (9).

12. Robinson & Grall, 719–25.

13. Robinson & Grall, 719.

14. Id.

15. Moore agrees. Moore, 207.

16. Moore uses a similar method. Moore, 208.

17. Akhil Amar stated to me that a statute limited to killing the president would, in his view, manifest significantly greater blameworthiness than a generic murder statute. I'm not sure I agree but, in any event, police officer status is not similarly unique.

18. 4 Blackstone's Commentaries *336 (noting that murder and manslaughter are the same offense).

19. Moore, 339–40.

20. Thanks to David Griffin, one of my excellent research assistants.

21. See Model Penal Code § 2.02 (5).

22. Grady v. Corbin, 495 U.S. 508, 526 (1990) (Scalia, J., dissenting).

23. Moore, 330–49.

24. Moore, 342.

25. When pressed, Moore finds support in "our practices with regard to double-jeopardy adjudication . . . how we both do and should adjudicate double-jeopardy cases." Id. at 335. This may be a way of conceding defeat on the philosophical point. I note a certain linguistic oddness about partial identity. We would hardly say, "My garage is the same structure as my house" because this entails the more problematic "My house is the same structure as my garage." Rather, we would say, "My garage is part of the structure that is my house." Thus, as a matter of terminology, I prefer act-type inclusion to partial identity.

26. Cf. Prince v. United States, 352 U.S. 322 (1957) (holding bank robbery the same offense as entry of a bank with intent to rob).

27. 495 U.S. 508 (1990).

28. United States v. Adams, 281 U.S. 202, 204 (1930), discussed in chapter 5 Holmes's short points are one paragraph; mine are a little longer.

29. Telephone conversation with Michael Dwyer, Assistant Public Defender,

Eastern District of Missouri and Southern and Central Districts of Illinois. Commentators generally agree. See Mead, 882–83; Remington & Joseph, 546–47; Note, U. Cin. L. Rev. 467, 487 n.135; Comment, U. Cin. L. Rev. 79, 82.

30. See Johnson, Conspiracy.

31. District of Columbia v. Buckley, 128 F.2d 17, 21 (D.C. Cir. 1942) (Rutledge, J., concurring).

32. Selman v. State, 406 P.2d 181 (Alaska 1965).

33. See the cases cited in nn. 34–39 and 41.

34. People v. Lowe, 660 P.2d 1261, 1271 (1983).

35. Gray v. State, 463 P.2d 897, 911–12 (Alaska 1970) (holding that two convictions for first-degree murder, and convictions for first- and second-degree murder, "could not be allowed to stand").

36. Ubelis v. State, 384 So.2d 1294 (Fla. Ct. App. 1980); Franks v. State, 323 N.E.2d 221 (Ind. 1975).

37. State v. Gilroy, 199 N.W.2d 63, 68 (Iowa 1972) (citing 21 Am. Jur. 2d, Criminal Law § 546; C.J.S. Criminal Law § 1567(5)).

38. Loscomb v. State, 416 A.2d 1276, 1285 (Md. App. 1980). See also People v. Sparks, 266 N.W.2d 661, 665 (Mich. App. 1978) ("There was only one murder and hence one crime . . .").

39. People v. Pitsonbarger, 568 N.E.2d 783 (Ill. 1990).

40. Ferguson v. Caldwell, 452 F.2d 1011 (6th Cir. 1971); McFadden v. United States, 395 A.2d 14 (D.C. App. 1978); People v. Miller, 412 N.E.2d 175 (Ill. App. 1980), cert. denied, 454 U.S. 871 (1981); People v. Leonti, 222 N.E.2d 591 (N.Y. Ct. App. 1966), cert. denied, 389 U.S. 1007 (1967).

41. Thacker v. United States, 599 A.2d 52 (D.C. Ct. App. 1991); People v. Mack, 473 N.E.2d 880 (Ill. 1984).

42. *Loscomb*, 416 A.2d at 1285.

43. Id. at 1286.

44. The act-token question is, of course, different from the act-type question, and counting violations is sometimes different from both act-type and act-token questions, as I seek to show. The *Loscomb* result is consistent with finding a single act-type; nonetheless, the court seemed to signal approval of two convictions of either act-type because two victims died in the car accident. Id.

45. Laws of the Earliest English Kings 11 (laws 46 & 47).

46. See chapter 5; chapter 6.

47. 284 U.S. at 302 (quoting Wharton's Criminal Law § 34 (11th ed.)).

48. 1 Bishop 785, § 1061 (1). See also Comment, 7 Minn. L. Rev. 348, 349 (suggesting a "one-act" test that produces one murder when a single shot kills two victims because it "seems to conform to the spirit of the rule as to double jeopardy).

49. See Ashe v. Swenson, 397 U.S. 436 (1970).

50. Ciucci v. Illinois, 356 U.S. 571 (1958).

51. 2 Hale 245.
52. United States v. Universal C.I.T. Credit Corp., 344 U.S. 218 (1952).
53. Friedland, 213.
54. Id. (quoting Blake, 45 Cr. App. R. 292, 295 (1961)).
55. Friedland, 205.
56. *Brown*, 432 U.S. at 169 n.8.
57. Moore agrees, finding "no legally usable answer to the question 'How many acts?', until we know what morally salient *type* of act is involved with a given statutory offense." Moore, 385. Morally salient, on Moore's account, is roughly what I mean by blameworthy. Id. at 385–90.
58. 432 U.S. at 163 nn. 1 & 2.
59. See Thomas, Unified Theory of Multiple Punishment, 15–22 & 37–44.
60. Id. at 41–44 & 90–93.
61. Prince v. United States, 352 U.S. 322, 329 (1957).
62. In re Snow, 120 U.S. 274, 283–85 (1887) (discussing Crepps v. Durden, Cowp. 640 (K.B. 1777)).
63. 432 U.S. at 169.
64. Id. at 169 n.8 (noting that hypothetical statute making each day of joyriding a different offense presents different case). See also Friedland, 217 & n.4 (citing examples of English statutes "which provide specifically for cumulative penalties, such as a certain penalty for each day that the offence continues").
65. 223 U.S. 442 (1912).
66. Moore, 281–301.
67. 223 U.S. at 449 (emphasis added).
68. State v. Broder, 90 Mo. App. 169 (1901) (holding that each sale was a separate offense) (appeal involved only two convictions). Since there were no photocopy machines in 1901, one wonders how even an industrious prosecution produced 1,800 pieces of paper charging the beer sale violation—presumably, the prosecutor had a printer set type and print 1,800 copies.
69. Horack, 822.
70. 237 U.S. 625 (1915).
71. Id. at 629.
72. 20 Harv. L. Rev. 642 (1907).
73. Id. at 643.
74. 37 Harv. L. Rev. 912, 912. But see Johnson v. Commonwealth, 256 S.W. 388 (Ky. Ct. App. 1923) (holding that each hand is a separate double jeopardy offense); Comment, 12 Ky. L. Rev. 249, 250 (approving of *Johnson* and concluding that it is "in accord with the weight of authority").
75. 1 Bishop 779, § 1053 (11).
76. 1 Bishop 789, § 1062.
77. 237 U.S. at 631 & 629.
78. 237 U.S. at 629.

79. Prince v. United States, 352 U.S. 322, 329 (1957).

80. Moore concedes that the individuation of intentions may be relevant to the same offense question but limits his analysis to action theory. Moore, at 305 n.1. Despite his concession that intent may play a role in individuating offenses, Moore later rejects the "same-intent" test as having any philosophical validity or manifesting double jeopardy policies in any useful way. Id. at 381–83 & 388–90.

81. Horack suggests that the cases do not support twelve larceny convictions for stealing a dozen eggs from a sack by twelve muscular contractions. Horack, 810.

82. The hypothetical is Heidi Hurd's. Bishop noted that, whatever the English rule, the American rule is to find only one larceny if multiple items belonging to the same owner are taken at one time. 1 Bishop § 1061 (3). See also Note, 20 Harv. L. Rev. 642, 643 (arguing that the result is the same even if the items had different owners).

83. Moore, 389.

84. By "single intent," I mean the thief formed a plan to steal two of X's horses prior to stealing the first one. It would be different if the thief stole the first one and then decided to steal the second one, a mens rea that would justify finding two larcenies. I put "single intent" in quotations marks because I am aware of the difficulties inherent in dividing or quantifying intent. See Horack, 813 ("The 'number of intents,' both as an evidentiary and as a psychological problem, seems more for the conjurer than for the judges."). See also chapter 5.

85. 284 U.S. at 302 (quoting Wharton's Criminal Law sec. 34 (11th ed.)).

86. It is also seven larcenies on Moore's view. He avoids the singularity of act-token here by finding multiple act-types.

87. If doubt exists that this imputed congressional intent is the way Congress would have answered the question about six mailbags in one spot, the rule of lenity resolves the question in favor of lenity. Because it is plausible to infer the intent to punish Ebeling's conduct just once, and because that inference results in a less harsh treatment, it must be accepted.

88. Badders v. United States, 240 U.S. 391 (1916). See also Ex parte Henry, 123 U.S. 372 (1887) (holding that each mailing was a separate offense).

89. 240 U.S. at 394 (emphasis added).

90. 281 U.S. 202 (1930).

91. Id. at 204.

92. Bell v. United States, 349 U.S. 81 (1955).

93. United States v. Universal C.I.T. Credit Corp., 344 U.S. 218, 224 (1952) (quoting Blockburger v. United States, 284 U.S. at 302, quoting Wharton's Criminal Law §34 (11th ed.)).

94. Moore, 359.

95. See, e.g., Owens (criticizing the Alabama rule that a single act can give rise to only one conviction).

96. Moore, 365.

97. The Court contemplated this outcome in Ladner v. United States, 358 U.S. 169, 178 (1959) (dictum) (suggesting that but a single assault is committed if one shot wounded two federal officers).

98. Moore, 362.

99. See, e.g., State v. Pa. R.R., 9 N.J. 194 (1952).

100. Moore, 363–64 n.13.

101. Moore, 359.

102. Id. at 363. If there was any doubt about Moore's premise in this case, it is dispelled in the next paragraph, where he summarizes the second hypothetical as "the killer who in fact kills two but only negligently risked death to one." Id.

103. Id. at 362.

104. See, e.g., State v. Irvin, 603 S.W.2d 121 (Tenn. 1980) (overruling precedent to adopt rule that each dead body is a different homicide as long as the defendant had the requisite intent as to one of the victims); Vigil v. State, 563 P.2d 1344 (Wyo. 1977) (surveying jurisdictions applying multiple-victim rule).

105. Moore, 364–65.

106. 1 Bishop § 1061 (3). Horack agrees that this should be only one larceny. Horack, 810.

107. See Brickey, 1141 (concluding that, under the ancient law, "[p]roof of guilt was secondary to obtaining specific restitution," while the modern crime of larceny manifests the "interest of the sovereign in suppressing theft and punishing wrongdoers"); id. at 1128 ("Instead of abolishing that ancient institution [of recovery], the crown created an alternative and strictly penal procedure" for the crime of larceny.).

108. I posed this hypothetical to Moore at a criminal law colloquium at the University of Pennsylvania law school in December 1995, and he agreed that it would have to be one million larcenies on his view.

109. See Cooper v. State, 595 P.2d 648 (Alaska 1979) (holding that five shots fired in the direction of three police officers can be three counts of assault only if the defendant intended to injure all three officers); People v. Bigsby, 367 N.E.2d 358 (Ill. App. 1977) (finding an intention to kill two victims and thus upholding multiple prosecutions based on single act); Jackson v. State, 492 A.2d 346 (Md. App. 1985) (multiple prosecutions for shooting at two police officers permissible only if defendant intended to harm each officer); Herron v. State, 805 P.2d 624, 627 (N.M. 1991) (statute did not evince legislative intent to punish each penetration of a single orifice if multiple penetrations occur "within sufficient temporal proximity" to show "a single criminal intent bent on a single assaultive episode"); People v. Warren, 1 Park. Crim. 338 (N.Y. 1832) (single act of poisoning two people will support two prosecutions if defendant intended to poison both).

110. This is the California *Neal* test, which, while on the right track, quickly

sank beneath the troubled sea of metaphysics: what constitutes a "single objective"? See Johnson, Reflections on *Neal.*

111. See Sigler, 107 (single offense if single act and single intent). For a critique of the thoroughgoing single intent test, see Moore, 305 n.1, 381–83, 389 n.50; Philip Johnson, Reflections on *Neal*, 369 (noting the "inconsistencies and ambiguities inherent in" the "single intent and objective formula"). See also Horack, 812; Note, 32 Mich. L. Rev. 512, 516 (1932); Note, Minn. L. Rev. 522, 552 (1940).

112. Moore, 381.

113. United States v. Daughtery, 269 U.S. 360 (1926).

114. See H.R. Rep. No. 98-1030, 98th Cong. 2d Sess., reprinted in 1984 U.S. Code Cong. & Ad. News 3490 (concluding that two of the Court's decisions "negated the section's use" in "precisely the type of extremely dangerous offenses for which a mandatory punishment for the use of a firearm is the most appropriate"). I discuss these cases in chapter 6.

NOTES TO CHAPTER 6

1. The legal-realist view does not use a test at all; the identity required by Amar and Marcus is not a plausible alternative; Scalia is correct that a "same transaction" or "same conduct" definition fails to come close to defining "same offense." Moore's test also uses blameworthy ("morally salient," in his terms) acts to construct a same-offense test. Moore, 385–90.

2. See chapter 3.

3. Note, 7 Brooklyn L. Rev. 79, 82. See also Note, 65 Yale L.J. 339, 349.

4. For a few examples, see Friedland, 110 (*Blockburger* "totally inadequate"); Carroway, 108 ("deficiencies" of *Blockburger* "are manifold"); Fisher, 87 ("mistake" to rely entirely on *Blockburger*); McElroy, 392 (noting the mechanical application of "an abstract formula at the sacrifice of meaningful constitutional and factual analysis"); Note, 10 New Mexico L. Rev. 195, 204 (*Blockburger* "virtually annuls the constitutional guarantee against double jeopardy"); Note, 19 U.C.L.A. L. Rev. 804, 817 (*Blockburger* "entirely inappropriate"); Comment, 75 Yale L.J. 262, 274 ("insensitive to the policies of the double jeopardy clause").

5. Mead, 874.

6. Haddad & Mullock, 533.

7. Kirchheimer, 58 Yale L.J. 513.

8. Comment, 2 De Paul L. Rev. 263, 266; Comment 21 La. L. Rev. 615, 622.

9. See discussion later in this chapter.

10. 328 U.S. 781 (1946).

11. Id. at 788.

12. 609 A.2d 1280 (N.J. 1992).

13. Because the statutes are cited in the *Preciose* opinion, 609 A.2d at

1281–82, I see no need to cite to each statute as I discuss the particular New Jersey offense.

14. Milanovich v. United States, 365 U.S. 551 (1961).

15. 397 U.S. 400 (1970), discussed in chapter 7.

16. Armed robbery, of course, requires a distinct element from any assault offense—theft.

17. 609 A.2d at 1282.

18. The method of act-type inclusion used in this analysis is to examine the way an offense is charged if the statute sets out alternative means of proof. So, for example, armed robbery charged as threatening bodily injury includes aggravated assault (which requires attempted bodily injury), even though armed robbery can be proved in other ways. As we see later in this chapter, the Court has used this "specific" approach to statutes written in the alternative in compound-predicate cases. As a test, I applied a "specific" version of *Blockburger* to the *Preciose* offenses, but only three counts dropped out, leaving seventeen different offenses. The reader is spared the details, which occupy several paragraphs. The apt comparison is, however, the one used in the text—nonspecific *Blockburger* (twenty offenses committed) and specific act-type inclusion (six offenses committed)—because the Court has not made clear whether it will extend the specific approach outside the compound-predicate context while I explicitly adopt use of the "specific" approach to act-type inclusion.

19. 469 U.S. 105 (1985).

20. 18 U.S.C. § 1001.

21. The federal courts have narrowly construed "trick, scheme, or device" to require concealment by affirmative act. 449 U.S. 108 n.5 (citing United States v. London, 550 F.2d 206 (5th Cir. 1977)). This construction supports viewing "trick, scheme, or device" as part of the act-type.

22. Bell v. United States, 349 U.S. 81 (1955). See also United States v. Universal C.I.T. Credit Corp., 344 U.S. 224 (1952).

23. Prince v. United States, 352 U.S. 322 (1957).

24. 352 U.S. 322 (1957).

25. For a more detailed discussion of Prince, see Thomas, Unified Theory of Multiple Punishment, 37–42.

26. 424 U.S. 544 (1976). The Court also held that entering the bank with intent to rob it and possession of the proceeds of the robbery were included offenses of the bank robbery. The first holding follows directly from *Prince*. The second follows from our understanding of "continuous" offenses in chapter 5. The act-type of possession continues indefinitely, and thus it does not matter that the robbers continued to possess the proceeds days, weeks, or months later. Though *Gaddis* was unclear about the precise remedy required when the four convictions carried concurrent sentences, this issue was later resolved by United States v. Ball, 470 U.S. 856 (1985). A single offense can support only a single con-

viction; in a *Gaddis* situation, three of the convictions must be vacated. For a more detailed discussion of this double jeopardy problem, see Thomas, Sentencing Problems.

27. 435 U.S. 6 (1978).

28. For a more detailed discussion of *Simpson*, see Thomas, Unified Theory of Multiple Punishment, 62–65.

29. Actually, I know Moore rejects that equation because he said so during a December 12, 1995, criminal law workshop at the University of Pennsylvania.

30. 445 U.S. 684 (1980).

31. 433 U.S. 682 (1977) (per curiam).

32. 445 U.S. at 708 (Rehnquist, J., dissenting).

33. *Whalen*, 445 U.S. at 694.

34. 509 U.S. 688 (1993); see chapter 2.

35. *Whalen*, 445 U.S. at 713 (Rehnquist, J., dissenting). Rehnquist reached this result by applying *Blockburger* to the felony-murder statute as a whole, rather than to specific ways of committing felony murder. "One can commit felony murder without rape and one can rape without committing felony murder." Id. at 710.

36. Note, 9 Buffalo L. Rev. 378, 380.

37. 459 U.S. 359 (1983).

38. 694 S.W.2d 934, 937 (Tenn. 1985). See also People v. Williams, 195 Cal. App. 3d 398 (1987), cert. denied, 488 U.S. 832 (1988); State v. Greco, 579 A.2d 84 (Conn. 1990); State v. Enmund, 476 So.2d 165 (Fla. 1985); State v. Gonzales, 783 P.2d 1239 (Kan. 1989); State v. Close, 623 P.2d 940 (Mont. 1981); Talancon v. State, 721 P.2d 764 (Nev. 1986); State v. McCovey, 803 P.2d 1234 (Utah 1990); Fitzgerald v. Commonwealth, 292 S.E.2d 798 (Va. 1982). For the opposing view of relevant legislative intent, see Cook v. State, 841 P.2d 1345 (Wyo. 1992).

39. *Whalen*, 445 U.S. at 710 (Rehnquist, J., dissenting) (emphasis added) (quoting D.C. Code §22-2401 (1973)).

40. For the same reason, my account diverges from the earlier case that reached the same result on state charges of robbery and felony murder. Harris v. Oklahoma, 433 U.S. 682 (1977) (per curiam).

41. Schad v. Arizona, 501 U.S. 624, 639 (1991) (plurality). Though only four members of the Court joined this part of the Court's opinion, the other five did not disagree with the plurality's reading of felony murder. Other issues divided the Court. *Schad* is discussed in more detail in chapter 1.

42. Id. at 640.

43. 21 U.S.C. § 848(b)(2).

44. See Garret v. United States, 471 U.S. 773 (1985).

45. 18 U.S.C. § 1962 et seq.

46. Thomas, RICO Prosecutions, 1377–86.

47. Poulin, Complex Criminal Cases.

48. 397 U.S. 436 (1970), discussed in chapter 7.

49. 432 U.S. at 166 n.6 (referring to Ashe v. Swenson, 397 U.S. 436 (1970)).

50. *Ashe*, at 464 (Burger, C.J., dissenting) (arguing that *Blockburger* is satisfied because the second charge required proof of a fact that the first did not—robbery of a different person).

51. See chapter 3.

52. 120 U.S. 274 (1887), discussed in chapter 3.

53. Id. at 285.

54. 450 U.S. 333 (1981).

55. 317 U.S. 49 (1942).

56. 471 U.S. at 784.

57. 317 U.S. at 50 n.1.

58. Perkins & Boyce, 683.

59. Theis, 306.

60. Id. at 303.

61. If two conspiracies define different blameworthiness, it must be true that conspiracy and a substantive offense define different blameworthiness. The Court has long held this to be true. United States v. Bayer, 331 U.S. 532 (1947). A plausible rule-of-lenity challenge did not cause the Court to change its mind on this point. Callanan v. United States, 364 U.S. 587 (1961).

62. 273 U.S. 1, 11 (1927).

63. United States v. Michener, 331 U.S. 789 (1947) (per curiam).

64. Heflin v. United States, 358 U.S. 415 (1959).

65. Milanovich v. United States, 365 U.S. 551 (1961); cf. id. at 558 (Frankfurter, J., dissenting) (while disagreeing that an accomplice should benefit, noting "hornbook law that a thief cannot be charged with committing two offenses— that is, stealing and receiving the goods he has stolen"). United States v. Gaddis, 424 U.S. 544 (1976), was self-evident after *Milanovich*; robbery and possession of proceeds of robbery are the same offense.

66. 5 Wheat. 1 (1820).

67. Id. at 72 (Story, J., dissenting). Story did not include the Double Jeopardy Clause as an offended principle, probably because of his view that the state penalty did not put the defendant's "life or limb" in jeopardy. See chapter 4.

68. *Houston,* 5 Wheat. at 23.

69. Id. at 33. Johnson did not mean that the same offense could be *punished* by both the state and federal governments; he saw that as restrained by the Double Jeopardy Clause in appropriate cases. Id. at 34. Obviously, he did not think the case before the Court was an appropriate case for double jeopardy protection, presumably because the penalty was minor and thus the defendant's "life or limb" was not in jeopardy.

70. See Fox v. Ohio, 5 How. 410 (1847) (holding that the state statute was not unconstitutional because of the possibility that prohibited dual punishment

might arise); see also Moore v. Illinois, 55 U.S. (14 How.) 13 (1852); Wilkes v. Dinsman, 48 U.S. (7 How.) 89 (1849).

71. Abbate v. United States, 359 U.S. 187 (1959). See also United States v. Lanza, 260 U.S. 377 (1922).

72. Bartkus v. Illinois, 359 U.S. 121 (1959). Of course, *Bartkus* was decided before the Court clearly established the collateral estoppel principle in Ashe v. Swenson, 397 U.S. 436 (1970)—see chapter 7—but if the very same crime can be reprosecuted, as it can under *Bartkus*, there would be no reason to treat a collateral estoppel bar differently.

73. Heath v. Alabama, 474 U.S. 82 (1985).

74. United States v. Wheeler, 435 U.S. 313 (1978).

75. Waller v. Florida, 397 U.S. 387 (1970).

76. Friedland, 426.

77. See, e.g., Amar & Marcus; Cassell; Guerra; Herman, Dual Sovereignty; Hoffman; McElroy.

78. Note, 102 Yale L.J. 281.

79. Houston v. Moore, 18 U.S. (5 Wheat.) 1, 23 (1820).

80. Id.

81. See Moore, 4.

82. See 4 Blackstone's Commentaries *335.

83. Friedland, 411. This issue does not appear to arise very often in Australia because federal crimes are largely "conducted in State or Territory courts, using the criminal procedure of the State or Territory." Comment, 33 Am. Crim. L. Rev. 123, 152 (quoting Deborah Sweeney & Neil Williams, Commonwealth Criminal Law 38 (1990)). To the extent it arises when states prosecute first, it may be that the *Vandercomb* common law pleas would bar the second trial. Id.

84. Waller v. Florida, 397 U.S. 387 (1970).

85. United States v. Wheeler, 435 U.S. 313 (1978).

86. Pryor v. Coleman, 97 U.S. (7 Otto) 509 (1878).

87. Id. at 518–19.

88. See Hoffman. Not all scholars want this outcome, of course. Susan Herman steadfastly rejects any form of dual sovereignty exception, but she also rejects legislative intent as having any relevance on the scope of double jeopardy protection. Herman, Triple Play; Herman, Dual Sovereignty. See also Cassell (arguing for an originalist interpretation that would bar all dual sovereign prosecutions).

89. See Note, 102 Yale L.J. 281, 294 n.94 (listing twenty-three state statutes); see also Colo. Rev. Stat. Ann. 18-1-103 (West 1994); Kansas Crim. Code Ann. 21-3108(3) (Vernon 1993); Nevada Rev. Stat. Ann. 171.070 (Michie 1993) (three states not listed in the student note). This is a total of twenty-six states.

90. See, e.g., Alaska Stat. sec. 12.20.010 ("act"); Cal. Penal Code sec. 656 ("act

or omission"); Ind. Code sec. 35-41-4-5 ("same conduct"); Mont. Code Ann. sec. 46-11-504 ("same transaction").

91. 359 U.S. 121 (1959).

92. See United States Attorney's Manual 9-2.142 (IV) (revised December 14, 1994).

93. Id. at I.C.

94. Abbate v. United States, 359 U.S. 187 (1959), decided on March 30, 1959. The federal policy was announced on April 7, 1959. See 27 U.S.L.W. 2509 (April 7, 1959). The first Supreme Court case to address this policy was Petite v. United States, 361 U.S. 529 (1969), dismissing a federal prosecution when the Department of Justice determined it had been brought in violation of the administrative policy, which is now often called the *Petite* policy. See also Rinaldi v. United States, 434 U.S. 22 (1977), holding that a judge could not deny a Department of Justice motion to dismiss a prosecution brought in violation of the *Petite* policy.

95. Guerra, Myth of Dual Sovereignty.

96. Task Force Meeting of April 16, 1994 (attended by Harry Litman, Deputy Assistant Attorney General). The Task Force ultimately called, instead, for tightening the substantive and procedural requirements of the policy. To this recommendation, the Department of Justice responded warmly, as it had already begun a review of the administrative policy. When the revised policy was issued on December 14, 1994, it incorporated many of the recommendations of the Task Force and was an improvement over the vague commands of the previous policy statement. To say that it is improved is not, of course, to say that prosecutorial discretion has been removed or that judicial review has been imposed.

97. 420 U.S. 770 (1975).

98. 18 U.S.C. § 371 and 18 U.S.C. § 1955, respectively.

99. Id. at 773–74 n.5, quoting R. Anderson, Wharton's Criminal Law and Procedure § 89 (1957).

100. For further discussion of *Iannelli* and Wharton's Rule, see Thomas, RICO Prosecutions, 1424–30; Comment, 71 Nw. U.L. Rev. 547.

101. 435 U.S. 6 (1978).

102. The Court also cited adoption of the House version rather than the Senate version. The sponsor of the Senate version had stated that his version would permit imposition of both penalties. Id. at 14. The Court also cited the rule of construction to give "precedence to the terms of the more specific statute where a general statute and a specific statute speak to the same concern, even if the general provision was enacted later." Id. at 15–16. See also Busic v. United States, 446 U.S. 398 (1980) (applying *Simpson* to another offense that had its own enhanced sentencing provisions).

103. See discussion earlier in this chapter.

104. Comment, 33 Am. Crim. L. Rev. 123, 149.

105. H.R. Rep. No. 98-1030, 98th Cong. 2d Sess., reprinted in 1984 U.S. Code Cong. & Ad. News 3490 (concluding that the *Simpson* doctrine "negated the section's use" in "precisely the type of extremely dangerous offenses for which a mandatory punishment for the use of a firearm is the most appropriate").

106. See chapter 2 for a defense of the unity of same offense in different procedural contexts.

107. 471 U.S. 773, 778 (1985).

108. The Court also offered a fact-dependent reason to permit a second trial, holding that Garrett had continued his CCE activity beyond the date of the predicate felony trial, thus engaging the "subsequent-conduct" exception to double jeopardy protection. In a sense, the Court viewed the subsequent conduct as tantamount to waiver.

109. Id. at 788–89.

110. Id. at 789.

111. Reading the predicate as proof of mens rea, there is no common act-type; thus they are not the same offense. My act-type account disagrees with Jeffers v. United States, 432 U.S. 137 (1977). The Court found that Congress did not intend to create cumulatively punishable offenses in CCE and conspiracy to distribute narcotics. The Court could cite to no specific evidence of congressional intent, relying instead on vague notions about the "comprehensive penalty structure" of CCE that allowed "little opportunity for pyramiding of penalties" from other provisions of the same congressional act. Id. at 156.

112. 357 U.S. 386 (1958).

113. Id. at 391. See also Harris v. United States, 359 U.S. 19 (1959) (applying the *Gore* analysis).

114. IRC 4705(a) & 4704(a) (1954), respectively.

115. 21 U.S.C. 174 (1952).

116. 357 U.S. at 394 (Warren, C.J., dissenting).

117. 459 U.S. 359 (1983).

118. 459 U.S. 359 (1983).

119. Id. at 368.

120. Id. at 369.

121. Id. at 366.

122. Id. at 369 (Marshall, J., dissenting).

NOTES TO CHAPTER 7

1. See Amar & Marcus, 31.

2. Friedland, 121 (quoting 1 Chitty, Criminal Law 454). See also McLaren, 203–4.

3. Glanvill 96 (Book VIII, 3). Glanville's Treatise was the earliest English treatise, published around 1187, id. at xi (dating treatise at 1187–89).

4. 2 Pollock & Maitland, 519.

5. Glanvill, 100 (Book VIII, 8–9).

6. See, e.g., Rex v. Duchess of Kingston, 20 How. State Tr. 355, 542 (1766); Kirchheimer, 532; Vestal & Coughenour, 698–99. Friedland cites other sources. Friedland, 154.

7. Id. at 155.

8. Obviously, a defendant cannot assert the double jeopardy or collateral estoppel rights of another defendant. See Standefer v. United States, 447 U.S. 10 (1980).

9. See Paulsen.

10. 20 How. State Tr. 355 (1766).

11. Id. at 538.

12. 16 U.S. (3 Wheat.) 246 (1818).

13. Id. at 319.

14. Id. at 320.

15. 20 Howell's State Tr. at 372.

16. 186 U.S. 413 (1902).

17. Whether Hotema's hung jury should constitute a jeopardy bar is considered in chapter 8.

18. 213 U.S. 115 (1909).

19. Id. at 124 (emphasis in original).

20. See Chapter 7.03.

21. 242 U.S. 85 (1916).

22. Id. at 87.

23. Id.

24. Id. at 88.

25. 356 U.S. 464, 471 (1958).

26. 397 U.S. 436, 445 (1970).

27. See United States v. One Assortment of 89 Firearms, 465 U.S. 354 (1984).

28. See chapter 4.

29. For some speculations about the distribution of criminal verdicts along a spectrum of 0 percent guilty to 100 percent guilty, see Thomas & Pollack, Rethinking Guilt, 21–23. We speculated that the distribution might be normal and centered around a mean between 60 percent and 80 percent. The percentage of acquittals is, of course, inversely related to the guilty percentage. A mean of guilty percentage near 60 percent suggests that almost as many acquittals are below 50 percent as are above 50 percent.

30. 116 U.S. 427 (1886). *Coffey* was decided one year prior to the Court's first same-offense case, In re Snow, 120 U.S. 274 (1887), and both were written by Justice Blatchford. *Snow* is discussed in chapter 3.

31. Id. at 443.

32. See chapter 4.

33. 404 U.S. 55 (1971) (per curiam).

34. Id. at 56–57. See also Turner v. Arkansas, 407 U.S. 366 (1972) (holding that an acquittal for murder barred prosecution for robbery committed during the same episode).

35. Simpson v. Florida, 403 U.S. 384 (1971).

36. 469 U.S. 57 (1984).

37. Id. at 68. To the same effect is Dunn v. United States, 284 U.S. 390, 394 (1931), in which Justice Holmes wrote, "That the verdict may have been the result of compromise, or of a mistake on the part of the jury, is possible. But verdicts cannot be upset by speculation or inquiry into such matters." See also Harris v. Rivera, 454 U.S. 339 (1981) (per curiam) (holding permissible inconsistent verdicts as between two defendants); Friedland, 146–53 (English rule the same).

38. Friedland, 143.

39. For an extended argument that fairness requires an exacting examination of inconsistent verdicts, see Mueller. Even were I to agree with Mueller about fairness, my double jeopardy account is based on blameworthiness. If an outcome is unfair but tells us nothing about the jury's view of blameworthiness, my account would not find any bar to affirming that outcome.

40. Poulin, Collateral Estoppel, 44–48.

41. See chapter 2.

42. Jill Hunter, 12.

43. See chapter 2.

44. For an analysis of res judicata and dual sovereignty that defends the same-parties requirement without the hesitation shown in the text, see Paulsen.

45. Friedland, 416–17.

46. Id. at 417.

47. Bartkus v. Illinois, 359 U.S. 121 (1959). The defendant was acquitted of federal bank robbery and then tried for the same bank robbery in state court. The Court did not mention collateral estoppel, which had not then been held applicable to the states, but the analysis focuses on the separateness of the two systems of law and procedure.

48. Amar & Marcus, 31.

NOTES TO CHAPTER 8

1. Two of the four pleas in bar were former acquittal and former conviction. The other two pleas in bar, former attaint and former pardon, required a conviction as a triggering mechanism.

2. Rex v. Perkins, 90 Eng. Rep. 1122 (K.B. 1698).

3. Sigler, 83–84.

4. 22 U.S. (9 Wheat.) 579 (1824).

5. Kepner v. United States 195 U.S. 100 (1904).

6. Smalis v. Pennsylvania, 476 U.S. 140, 145 (1986).

7. Strazzella, Prosecution Appeals.

8. Strazzella, at 20 (citing Wyoming as a "leading example").

9. For a discussion of a case involving these facts, see Poulin, Judicial Accountability; Rudstein, Fraudulently Obtained Acquittal.

10. Poulin, Judicial Accountability, 990.

11. Id. at 989.

12. Rudstein, Fraudulently Obtained Acquittal, 651.

13. 4 Blackstone's Commentaries *335.

14. 437 U.S. 54 (1978).

15. Lee v. United States, 432 U.S. 23 (1977).

16. See also Fong Foo, 369 U.S. 141 (1962). For an argument that the Court's double jeopardy jurisprudence implicitly accepts even an acquittal produced by fraud as a bar to further proceedings, see Rudstein.

17. Westen & Drubel, 165.

18. In Sanabria v. United States, 437 U.S. 54 (1978), the trial judge directed the verdict of acquittal. In this role, however, the trial judge is operating as the fact finder.

19. Westen, 1008.

20. For a discussion of the differences between former attaint and former conviction, see chapter 2.

21. 4 Blackstone's Commentaries *390.

22. Id. at 391.

23. Id. at 393.

24. Id.

25. Friedland's discussion of this point is excellent, and he recommends adopting the United States rule. Friedland, 221–74.

26. 377 U.S. 463 (1964).

27. Id. at 466.

28. 163 U.S. 662 (1896).

29. Westen & Drubel, 150–51 n.303 (citing United States v. Tateo, 377 U.S. 463, 466 (1964)).

30. To be distinguished from codefendant John C. Ball.

31. If anything, the English authorities favored the finality of convictions over acquittals. See chapter 9.

32. *Ball*, 163 U.S. at 672.

33. Id. at 669–70 (brackets added).

34. Thomas, Elegant Theory.

35. See Murphy v. Massachusetts, 177 U.S. 155, 158 (1900) (discussing *Ball* and noting that Murphy "set the proceedings in question in motion" that led to reversal). See also Montana v. Hall, 481 U.S. 400, 404 (1987) (distinguishing *Brown v. Ohio* from a case in which the defendant obtained an appellate reversal

because *Brown* "did not overturn the first conviction; indeed, he served the prison sentence assessed as punishment for that crime"); Hill v. Texas, 316 U.S. 400, 406 (1942) (noting that a defendant "whose conviction is reversed by this Court need not go free if he is in fact guilty, for Texas may indict and try him again") (reversal for denial of equal protection in selection of grand jury members).

36. Although Bishop states that double jeopardy should bar a new trial after an appellate reversal, he seems to assume that the convicted defendant was "entitled to an acquittal." 1 Bishop, 772, § 1047. Given that assumption, of course, the reversal could be viewed as an acquittal equivalent, as the Court did many years later in *Burks v. United States*, discussed in § 8.03 [D].

37. For a discussion of the Westen-Drubel hierarchy, see chapter 3.

38. See discussion later in this chapter.

39. See Richman, Bargaining About Future Jeopardy.

40. Tollett v. Henderson, 411 U.S. 258 (1973).

41. Menna v. New York, 423 U.S. 61 (1975).

42. The only other similar error admitted to this subset to date is a due process violation based on the prosecutor's motives for initiating a second trial. Blackledge v. Perry, 417 U.S. 21 (1974).

43. The superfluity must be ascertainable from the face of the record—that is, a court must be able to rule from the record whether the offenses in question are the same offense. If the guilty plea defendant's claim requires further proceedings to resolve, the normal rule applies and the guilty plea waives the double jeopardy claim. This exception was recognized in United States v. Broce, 488 U.S. 563 (1989), where the defendants pleaded guilty to two separate conspiracy indictments and then later sought to vacate the convictions and sentences under one indictment on the ground that there was but one conspiracy for double jeopardy purposes. The Court held that the defendants' double jeopardy challenge was foreclosed by their guilty pleas.

44. 483 U.S. 1 (1987).

45. Id. at 9.

46. See Thomas, Elegant Theory, 851–52.

47. I assume here that Adamson was accountable for the breach. The Supreme Court was divided on that issue.

48. 355 U.S. 184 (1957), overruling Trono v. United States, 199 U.S. 521 (1905).

49. Ohio v. Johnson, 467 U.S. 493 (1984).

50. Figuring out which conviction to vacate is not always as easy as it sounds. In most cases, the appellate court vacates the lesser-included offense, which almost always carries a lesser sentence. In this way, the length of the sentence imposed by the trial court is not changed unless the sentences are consecutive. But even when sentences are concurrent, problems arise if the "lesser" offense carries

a greater punishment. See, e.g., Sours v. State, 593 S.W.2d 208, 223 (Mo. 1980) (vacating the "greater" conviction, which carried a lesser sentence).

51. These variations, and others, are discussed in Thomas, Sentencing Problems.

52. Ball v. United States, 470 U.S. 856 (1985). The effect of *Ball* on the multiple punishment sentencing doctrine is considered in more detail in Thomas, Sentencing Problems.

53. See chapter 2.

54. For a full discussion, see Thomas, Sentencing Problems.

55. These facts are a simplified version of the facts in United States v. Henry, 709 F.2d 298 (5th Cir. 1983) (en banc).

56. The due process issue is whether rearranging the concurrent sentences into consecutive sentences on the remaining valid convictions violates the "retaliatory motivation" doctrine of North Carolina v. Pearce, 395 U.S. 711 (1969). The difficulty of this due process/double jeopardy issue is suggested by the division of the Fifth Circuit Court of Appeals in the case that suggested the hypothetical. United States v. Henry, 709 F.2d 298 (5th Cir. 1983) (en banc). The plurality opinion reversing conviction *C*, with a windfall for the defendant, was joined fully by five judges. Two judges filed separate opinions "specially concurring." Six judges joined the dissent, arguing that double jeopardy and due process permitted resentencing.

57. North Carolina v. Pearce, 395 U.S. 711 (1969).

58. *Pearce* held that the Due Process Clause provided a presumption of judicial vindictiveness unless the new sentence is based on "identifiable conduct on the part of the defendant occurring after the time of the original sentencing proceeding." Id. at 726. This due process aspect of *Pearce* was steadily eroded until, in Alabama v. Smith, 490 U.S. 794 (1989), the Court overruled the presumption of vindictiveness, while still allowing for actual proof of vindictiveness.

59. 395 U.S. at 721 (emphasis deleted).

60. 115 S.Ct. 2199 (1995).

61. United States v. Watts, 117 S.Ct. 633, 636 (1997) (characterizing the holding in *Witte*).

62. Gryger v. Burke, 334 U.S. 728, 732 (1948). The earliest case to permit this form of sentence enhancement was Moore v. Missouri, 159 U.S. 673 (1895). See also Graham v. West Virginia, 224 U.S. 616 (1912); McDonald v. Massachusetts, 180 U.S. 311 (1901).

63. 117 S.Ct. 633 (1997).

64. The Court has never held what I say in the text, though it is the only sensible way to put together the mistrial cases and the dismissal cases. The Court did explicitly hold, in United States v. Scott, 437 U.S. 82 (1978), and Lee v. United States, 432 U.S. 23 (1977), that the characterization of the outcome as a dismissal does not, by itself, create a jeopardy bar to another trial. I argue that any substan-

tive distinction between mistrial and dismissal is superficial and should be ignored. Some mistrials can be acquittal equivalents just as surely as some dismissals.

65. See chapter 2.

66. 7 How. St. Tr. 79 (1678).

67. Id. at 82.

68. Id. at 86.

69. Id. at 120.

70. Id. at 585–86.

71. Id. at 316–17 (rejecting the jeopardy plea "because there was no condemnation or acquittal").

72. The trial judge intimated that the evidence was sufficient in quantity, the only defect being the technical requirement of two witnesses. Nonetheless, under the substantive law of England, the only verdict possible was acquittal. Thus, whether Fenwick and Whitebread were factually innocent, they were legally entitled to an acquittal.

73. 355 U.S. 184 (1957), overruling Trono v. United States, 199 U.S. 521 (1905).

74. Brantley v. Georgia, 217 U.S. 284 (1910) (per curiam), had earlier rejected this argument as "absolutely without merit," though the Court did not bother to state why it was meritless. Brantley was decided before the Court extended the Double Jeopardy Clause to the states, and part of the defendant's argument was that the Supreme Court should overrule the state court construction of the Georgia Constitution. Thus, the basis for Brantley may simply have been respect for state courts.

75. 1 Bishop 745, § 1004.

76. Price v. Georgia, 398 U.S. 323 (1970) (defendant convicted of same lesser-included crime at both trials; held, second trial violated double jeopardy because he was in jeopardy of greater offense, of which he had been implicitly acquitted).

77. 449 U.S. 117 (1980).

78. Id. at 137.

79. See chapter 1.

80. Arizona v. Rumsey, 467 U.S. 203 (1984); Bullington v. Missouri, 451 U.S. 430 (1981). Compare Poland v. Arizona, 476 U.S. 147 (1986) (no double jeopardy verdict occurs when appellate court overrules trial court's basis for death penalty and later affirms death penalty on grounds that trial court first rejected).

81. 420 U.S. 358, 370 (1975).

82. 355 U.S. 184, 187–88 (1957).

83. 437 U.S. 82, 100–101 (1978) (quoting Wade v. Hunter, 336 U.S. 684, 689 (1949)).

84. Id. at 86–87. The "vastly increased exposure" to double jeopardy issues resulted from a change in the Act authorizing federal appeals. Congress shifted in

1971 from an intricate statutory formulation to a rule permitting appeal in all cases "except no appeal shall lie where the double jeopardy clause of the United States Constitution prohibits further prosecution." Id. at 85. This development, naturally, "shifted the focus of the debate from issues of statutory construction to issues as to the scope and meaning of the Double Jeopardy Clause." Id.

85. Id. at 87.

86. Id. at 95–96.

87. Id. at 97 (quoting United States v. Martin Linen Supply Co., 430 U.S. 564, 571 (1977) (brackets added by the Court in *Scott*)). Justice Brennan, in dissent, argued that the distinction between acquittal equivalents and other dismissals favorable to the defendant cannot be maintained. While close cases will of course exist, I disagree with Brennan that the distinction is any more difficult to maintain than any of the countless others that exist in law.

88. 420 U.S. 332 (1975). See also United States v. Morrison, 429 U.S. 1 (1976).

89. See Fed. R. Crim. P. 29(c). Dismissals after verdict are rare because the judge will have had an opportunity to rule on the underlying issues prior to verdict. If the judge rules against the defendant at that earlier point, there is little reason to expect a different outcome after the jury has returned a verdict of guilty.

90. The Supreme Court has suggested as much. See United States v. Scott, 437 U.S. 82, 92 n.7 (1978); United States v. Jenkins, 420 U.S. 358, 365 (1975). See also Shellenberger & Strazzella, 157–59.

91. Srazzella, 21–27.

92. State v. Avcollie, 384 A.2d 315 (Conn. 1977), involving the same statute that the Court approved in Palko v. Connecticut, 302 U.S. 319 (1937). See chapter 9.

93. 437 U.S. 1 (1978).

94. 163 U.S. 662 (1896), discussed in chapter 8.

95. The trial judge can return a not guilty verdict in bench trials or, if the rules of procedure permit it, in response to a motion for directed verdict of acquittal.

96. 361 U.S. 416 (1960).

97. Compare Hudson v. Louisiana, 450 U.S. 40 (1981) (legally insufficient evidence constituting a jeopardy bar) with Tibbs v. Florida, 457 U.S. 31 (1982) (finding no jeopardy bar in legally sufficient evidence which is nonetheless against the weight of the evidence).

98. Tibbs v. Florida, 457 U.S. 31, 51 (1982) (White, J., dissenting) (joined by Brennan, Marshall, and Blackmun, JJ.).

99. Lockhart v. Nelson, 488 U.S. 33 (1988). The Court upheld a sentence that required four prior felony convictions even though one of the convictions had been pardoned; the judge considered the pardoned conviction because the defense did not object to it. Once the pardon was proven, however, only three con-

victions could be used under state law, and the defendant raised an insufficient evidence challenge to the sentencing. The Court held that the state could introduce evidence of another conviction on resentencing because *Burks* did not apply to bar further action.

100. Id. at 41–42. There should be an exception to this principle when the prosecutor intentionally introduces tainted evidence, and the error is not discovered until after conviction. Here, I agree with a commentator who argues that double jeopardy should forbid a second trial if, with the tainted evidence excluded, insufficient evidence remains to support the conviction. Note, 94 Mich. L. Rev. 1346, 1363. As the commentator correctly concludes in the cases of intentional prosecutorial misconduct, the "appropriate presumption . . . is that the prosecutor had no equivalent evidence of equivalent value to introduce at trial." Id. at 1366.

101. 615 A.2d 321 (Pa. 1992).

102. Poulin, Limits of Double Jeopardy.

103. Poulin, Limits of Double Jeopardy, 629.

104. 372 U.S. 734 (1963). The defendant also won United States v. Jorn, 400 U.S. 470 (1970) (plurality). The losing mistrial cases are Richardson v. United States, 468 U.S. 317 (1984); Oregon v. Kennedy, 456 U.S. 667 (1982); Arizona v. Washington, 434 U.S. 497 (1978); Dinitz v. United States, 424 U.S. 600 (1976); Illinois v. Somerville, 410 U.S. 458 (1973); Gori v. United States, 367 U.S. 364 (1961); Wade v Hunter, 336 U.S. 684 (1949); Lovato v. New Mexico, 242 U.S. 199 (1916); Keerl v. Montana, 213 U.S. 135 (1909); Dreyer v. Illinois, 187 U.S. 71 (1902); Thompson v. United States, 155 U.S. 271 (1894); Logan v. United States, 144 U.S. 263 (1892); Simmons v. United States, 142 U.S. 148 (1891); United States v. Perez, 22 U.S. (9 Wheat.) 579 (1824).

105. 1 Bishop 768–69, §§ 1037–40.

106. 1 Bishop 768, § 1037.

107. 1 Bishop 753, § 1016.

108. *Perez*, 22 U.S. (9 Wheat.) at 580.

109. See Comment, 69 Nw. U.L.Rev. 887, 893 (1975).

110. See, e.g., Note, 15 Am. Crim. L. Rev. 169, 189 (noting lack of "predictability" of mistrial standard); Note, 49 N.Y.U. L. Rev. 937, 948 (noting that "manifest necessity" standard "does mightily favor the interest of the state in prosecuting criminals when balanced against the rights of the accused"); Comment, 69 Nw. U.L. Rev. 887, 904 (noting that "ambiguity" of "manifest necessity" standard "has permitted the evolution of two distinct standards—standards which may give opposite results when applied to the same situation").

111. Schulhofer, 491.

112. 372 U.S. 734 (1963).

113. 410 U.S. 458 (1973).

114. Id. at 469.

115. The Court's conclusion about the error seems right; why would a prosecutor intentionally create uncorrectable error in the indictment in order to preserve the option to move for a mistrial? If the trial proceeds to the prosecutor's liking, the resulting conviction is still automatically reversible.

116. 456 U.S. 667 (1982).

117. See State v. Kennedy, 619 P.2d 948, 949 (Or. App. 1980)

118. 456 U.S. at 669.

119. Id. at 670.

120. Id. at 676.

121. Id. at 688 (concurring in the judgment). For other criticism of the *Kennedy* test, see Ponsoldt, 94–100.

122. 456 U.S. at 689 (Stevens, J., concurring in the judgment) (joined by Brennan, Marshall, and Blackmun, JJ.). This is similar to the standard articulated in dicta in Dinitz v. United States, 424 U.S. 600, 611 (1976) (whether the prosecutor engaged in tactics in bad faith to goad the defendant into requesting a mistrial or to prejudice his prospects for an acquittal).

123. See 456 U.S. at 680 (Powell, J. concurring) (noting this difficulty and arguing that a reviewing court should "rely primarily upon the objective facts and circumstances of the particular case").

124. Illinois v. Somerville, 410 U.S. 458, 469 (1973).

125. *Downum*, 372 U.S. at 737–38 (quoting Cornero v. United States, 48 F.2d 69, 71 (9th Cir. 1931)).

126. See chapter 8.

127. 400 U.S. 470 (1971) (plurality). See Illinois v. Somerville, 410 U.S. 458, 469 (1973) (characterizing conduct of trial judge in Jorn as "erratic").

128. 400 U.S. at 472–73.

129. Id. at 473.

130. Id. at 487.

131. Id. at 488 (Black, J. & Brennan, J., concurring in the judgment).

132. Id. at 478 n.7.

133. Id. at 485.

134. 344 U.S. 424 (1953).

135. Id. at 425.

136. Id. at 426.

137. Id. at 427, quoting Palko v. Connecticut, 302 U.S. 319, 328 (1937).

138. Id. at 442 (Douglas, J., dissenting).

139. Though the Court was using the two unhelpful standards I detailed in the text, it was unanimously of the view that the "crook" question should not have created a jeopardy bar. Justices Stevens, Brennan, Marshall, and Blackmun concurred in the judgment. See id. at 679 & 680.

140. Thanks to Nick Costantino, one of my excellent research assistants, for this idea.

141. United States v. Martin Linen Supply Co., 430 U.S. 564 (1977).

142. 186 U.S. 413 (1902).

143. If the trial judge grants the motion for acquittal, presumably there can be no appeal because no verdict exists to reinstate if the trial judge is reversed. See discussion earlier in this chapter. So at least in the federal system, and in the states which do not permit appeals from acquittals, the judge's grant of an acquittal following a hung jury operates just like a jury acquittal.

144. See Richardson v. United States, 468 U.S. 317 (1984); Logan v. United States, 144 U.S. 263 (1892); United States v. Perez, 22 U.S. (9 Wheat.) 579 (1824). The hung jury doctrine is critiqued quite effectively in Findlater, Retrial After Hung Jury. See also Schulhofer, 522–24 (arguing that retrials after hung juries should be tested by strictest standard of mistrial review).

145. 468 U.S. 317 (1984).

146. See Burks v. United States, 437 U.S. 1 (1978).

147. Jackson v. Virginia, 443 U.S. 307 (1979).

148. Marsha Wenk argued this point in the context of *Richardson* until I finally saw its merit.

149. 468 U.S. at 323.

150. Id. at 325–26.

151. Id. at 327 (Brennan, J., concurring in part and dissenting in part).

152. I understand that, practically speaking, a defendant would probably prefer a hung jury to a conviction. But, in the world of double jeopardy theory, we can assume that an appellate court will recognize the insufficient evidence leading to the conviction, and this recognition will create a jeopardy bar to a second trial.

153. 468 U.S. at 326 (Brennan, J., concurring in part and dissenting in part) (joined by Marshall, J.).

154. 468 U.S. at 322. Only Justice Stevens dissented from that part of the Court's opinion. Id. at 332.

155. Id. at 322.

156. Id. at 326 n.6 (citations omitted).

157. Id. at 323.

158. 431 U.S. 651, 662 (1977).

159. 429 U.S. 14 (1976) (per curiam).

160. 437 U.S. 28 (1978). The Court had stated that rule in dicta seventy-five years earlier. Kepner v. United States, 195 U.S. 100, 128 (1904).

161. 437 U.S. at 49 (Powell, J., dissenting).

162. Id. at 36 (quoting Wade v. Hunter, 336 U.S. 684, 689 (1949).

163. Id. at 38.

164. Id. at 39 (Blackmun, J., concurring).

165. Id.

166. Schulhofer, 512–24.
167. Westen & Drubel, 99 (quoting Crist v. Bretz, 437 U.S. 28, 37 (1978)).
168. For example, the Court has held that the dismissal of an indictment does not bar the government from bringing a second indictment. Ex parte United States, 287 U.S. 241, 250–51 (1932). While this is consistent with the Court's attachment doctrine, it is also consistent with a blameworthiness conception of double jeopardy. The dismissal of an indictment is not a judgment on the merits of the prosecution's case because the grand jury is a screening mechanism, and the government is not required to present its entire case.
169. See Illinois v. Somerville, 410 U.S. 458, 466 (1973); United States v. Jorn, 400 U.S. 470, 484 (1971); Wade v. Hunter, 336 U.S. 684, 689 (1949).
170. *Perez*, 22 U.S. at 580.
171. Thomas, Elegant Theory.
172. In Keerl v. Montana, 213 U.S. 135, 138 (1909), for example, the Court quoted Justice Story's language about the discretion of the trial judge as the "settled law of the Federal courts." In the next paragraph, however, the Court discussed the facts which gave rise to the mistrial before "finding no error" in that decision.
173. In Lovato v. New Mexico, 242 U.S. 199, 201 (1916), the Court did not quote from *Perez* and seemed to review the merits of the claim: "Whether or not, under the circumstances, it was a necessary formality to dismiss the jury in order to enable the accused to be again arraigned and plead, the action taken was clearly within the bounds of sound judicial discretion."
174. Though the defendant lost in Wade v. Hunter, 336 U.S. 684 (1949), the Court contemplated that the right kind of manifest necessity mistrial claim would win. After discussing the facts for several pages, the Court wrote, "Measured by the *Perez* rule to which we adhere, petitioner's second court-martial trial was not the kind of double jeopardy within the intent of the Fifth Amendment." Id. at 690.
175. See Richardson, 159–68 (proposing use of Due Process Clause to replace double jeopardy as protection against harassing prosecutions). I agree with Richardson's general observation that due process is, after all, "*intended* to spawn vague standards" and the Double Jeopardy Clause is not. Id. at 167. It is thus better to locate necessarily vague protections (against retrials after mistrial, or against harassing prosecutions in general) in the Due Process Clause.
176. Although Justice O'Connor has used a balancing test in double jeopardy cases, she has never been joined by another Justice. See Garrett v. United States, 471 U.S. 773, 796 (1985) (O'Connor, J., concurring).
177. Shellenberger & Strazzella, 191.
178. Schulhofer, Jeopardy and Mistrials.
179. Id. at 516.

180. Id. at 517.
181. See my discussion earlier in this chapter.
182. Sigler, 223.

NOTES TO CHAPTER 9

1. 302 U.S. 319 (1937).
2. See State v. Lee, 30 A. 1110, 1113 (1894) (discussing Conn. Gen. Stat. §
1637 (1888)).
3. Sigler, 79 (listing Maryland, Massachusetts, North Carolina, and Vermont
as other states without a state constitutional double jeopardy provision).
4. See State v. Lee, 30 A. at 1112.
5. See, e.g., United States v. Martin Linen Supply Co., 430 U.S. 564 (1977).
6. See *Lee*, 30 A. at 1110–11.
7. State v. Palko, 186 A. 657, 660 (Conn. 1936).
8. Today, this would be recognized as an implicit acquittal of the more serious
offense, which the Court explicitly recognized twenty years later in Green v.
United States, 355 U.S. 184 (1957). Thus, today the issue would be whether Palko
could be retried for second-degree murder following a successful state appeal.
9. United States v. Wilson, 420 U.S. 332, 352 (1975) (rejecting unlimited governmental appeal).
10. Justice Butler dissented without opinion. 302 U.S. at 153.
11. Incorporation would come thirty-two years later in Benton v. Maryland,
395 U.S. 784 (1969), discussed in this chapter.
12. *Palko*, 302 U.S. at 328 (quoting Hebert v. Louisiana, 272 U.S. 312, 316
(1926)).
13. Id. (citation omitted).
14. Id.
15. See id. at 323.
16. Id. at 328.
17. Id. at 323.
18. For an earlier expression of the same theory, see Thomas, Elegant Theory.
19. Note, 43 Wash. & Lee L. Rev. 295.
20. The Court has stated that the Constitution does not require states to have
appellate systems, McKane v. Durston, 153 U.S. 684 (1894), and has clearly held
that the right to appointed counsel exists in only the first level of review, Ross v.
Moffitt, 417 U.S. 600 (1974).
21. See chapter 3.
22. Comley, 677. See also Note, 15 Ky. L.J. 46, 51–52 (noting existence of state
statute authorizing state appeals).
23. Of course, the defendant who pleads *autrefois acquit* has other potential
arguments—implied acquittal of higher degree and collateral estoppel. But on

the basic issue of the scope of protection arising from the plea of *autrefois acquit,* that defendant is in the same position as if pleading *autrefois convict.*

24. Exodus 18:18–22.
25. See Mendelsohn, citing Sifre II, section 144; Sanh. 32(a).
26. See Gemara, Sanhedrin, 33b.
27. S. Mendelsohn, 150–51 & n.358 (1968) (citing Sifre II, section 144; Sanh. 32(a)) (noting an exception for instigating idolatry). See also Goldin, 109 & 109–10 n.6 (1952) (citing and quoting Talmudic book of Sanhedrin) (noting no exceptions).
28. See Commentary to Model Penal Code § 1.09, 48. I thus take Sigler's recommendations in favor of state appeal to be limited to errors of law. Sigler, 115, 224. Indeed, he discusses the Model Penal Code Commentary suggesting that appeal in the absence of an error of law probably violates the federal Constitution. Sigler, 208.
29. This leaves unsettled whether the facts underlying an acquittal can be reviewed if the trial was to the judge. Westen and Drubel would be sympathetic to this distinction.
30. S. Mendelsohn, 150–51 & n.358 (1968) (citing Sifre II, section 144; Sanh. 32(a)) (noting an exception for instigating idolatry). See also H. Goldin, Hebrew Criminal Law and Procedure 109 & 109–10 n.6 (1952) (citing and quoting Talmudic book of Sanhedrin) (noting no exceptions).
31. Comley argues that American courts forbade appeals of acquittals because they erroneously assumed that this practice was embedded in the English common law. Comley, 678.
32. 2 Hale at 244–45.
33. Id. at 244.
34. 168 Eng. Rep. 455 (K.B. 1796). See chapter 3 for the discussion of whether *Blockburger* follows from *Vandercomb.*
35. 168 Eng. Rep. at 461.
36. 168 Eng. Rep. at 456–57.
37. Id. at 461. Friedland agrees that *Vandercomb* is a variance case. Friedland, 100. See also Carroway, 110; Comment, 75 Yale L.J. 262, 274.
38. United States v. Nickerson 58 U.S. (17 How.) 204 (1854).
39. Id. at 212.
40. A notable exception is Shellenberger & Strazzella, 165.
41. 131 U.S. 176, 187 (1889).
42. 195 U.S. 100, 134 (1904) (Holmes, J., dissenting).
43. 302 U.S. at 323.
44. 195 U.S. at 135 (Holmes, J., dissenting).
45. 144 U.S. 310, 318 (1892).
46. Id.
47. 302 U.S. at 328.

48. "The fundamental nature of the guarantee against double jeopardy can hardly be doubted. . . . This underlying notion has from the very beginning been part of our constitutional tradition. Like the right to trial by jury, it is clearly 'fundamental to the American scheme of justice.'" 395 U.S. 784, 795–96 (1969) (quoting Duncan v. Louisiana, 391 U.S. 145, 149 (1968).

49. Id. at 795.

50. Id. at 813 (Harlan, J., dissenting).

51. 163 U.S. 662 (1896). See chapter 8.

52. Maryland was another of the five states without a double jeopardy provision in its state constitution. Sigler, 79.

53. 395 U.S. at 813 (Harlan, J., dissenting).

54. See Conn. Gen. Stat. § 54-96 (West 1997). Among the few reported cases is State v. Avcollie, 384 A.2d 315 (Conn. 1977), where the issue arose when the trial court set aside a jury verdict of guilty and entered an acquittal. Because the Supreme Court has suggested that the Double Jeopardy Clause permits an appeal in that context (see chapter 8) the application of the state statute to overrule the acquittal would not likely cause a double jeopardy problem. The state court so held.

55. Sigler seems to agree, drawing the same distinction between *Palko* and Hoag v. New Jersey, 356 U.S. 464 (1958). Sigler, 54. *Benton* had not been decided when Sigler's book went to press.

56. Brock v. North Carolina, 344 U.S. 424, 438 (1953) (Vinson, C.J., dissenting), discussed in chapter 8.

57. Discussed in this chapter.

58. 199 U.S. 521 (1905).

59. See chapter 8.

60. 199 U.S. at 532 (N.Y. Const. art. 1, para. 6).

61. Id. at 531, quoting New York Code of Criminal Procedure 544.

62. 107 U.S. 221 (1883).

63. Id. at 225.

64. 438 U.S. 204 (1978).

65. See chapter 3.

66. 467 U.S. 493 (1984).

67. Id. at 500 ("Presumably the trial court, in the event of a guilty verdict on the more serious offenses, will have to confront the question of cumulative punishments as a matter of state law . . .").

68. Thomas, Elegant Theory, 870–71.

69. Foog Foo v. United States, 369 U.S. 141 (1962).

70. United States v. Martin Linen Supply Co., 430 U.S. 564 (1977). This case must be distinguished from United States v. Sanford, 429 U.S. 14 (1976), where the defendant lost on very similar facts because jeopardy had not attached. The only distinction is that in *Martin Linen*, but not in *Sanford*, the motion for ac-

quittal was within the time period permitted by Rule 29(c) of the Federal Rules of Procedure. In effect, the Court is saying that a post-trial motion for acquittal contemplated by the rules of procedure is still within the original jeopardy, a view that accords with a legislative-intent view of jeopardy.

71. This, of course, is Brown v. Ohio, 432 U.S. 161 (1977).

72. 467 U.S. at 501. See also Montana v. Hall, 481 U.S. 400, 403 n.1 (noting that an implied acquittal occurs only when the factfinder is presented with both charges and chooses to convict of only one).

73. See also United States v. Scott, 437 U.S. 82 (1978) (calling the outcome a "dismissal" does not create a jeopardy bar); Lee v. United States, 432 U.S. 23 (1977) (same).

74. Green v. United States, 365 U.S. 301 (1961). The defendant was convicted of three offenses in a single trial, later held to be the same offense. The issue in *Green* was whether the appellate court could choose which conviction to affirm. The defendant argued that double jeopardy barred affirming any conviction but the one on which the judge first pronounced sentence, on the theory that the judge's authority to sentence on the other convictions had been somehow exhausted by the sentence on the first conviction. The Court did not accept the argument. See also Holliday v. Johnston, 313 U.S. 342 (1941).

75. Pennsylvania v. Goldhammer, 474 U.S. 28 (1985) (per curiam) (resentencing was required because one count reversed on appeal as outside the statute of limitations).

76. See chapter 8.

77. Louisiana v. Resweber, 329 U.S. 459 (1947). Four Justices dissented, id. at 472, but on the ground that a second attempt violated the Eighth Amendment.

78. See chapter 8.

79. See Williams v. Oklahoma, 358 U.S. 576 (1959) (upholding use of prior murder conviction in sentencing for kidnaping).

80. 468 U.S. 447 (1984).

81. In *Spaziano*, the Court held that there was no Sixth Amendment right to a jury trial; otherwise, the Sixth Amendment would have prohibited the state from making the jury verdict advisory in nature.

82. 104 S.Ct. 1805 (1984).

83. *Burks* is discussed chapter 8.

84. 468 U.S. 317 (1984).

85. Ball v. United States, 105 S.Ct. 1858 (1985). For a detailed discussion of *Ball*'s sentencing implications, see Thomas, Sentencing Problems.

86. See Thomas, Sentencing Problems (arguing that to treat multiple convictions as a "package" is inconsistent with the clear, inflexible commands of the Double Jeopardy Clause).

87. In a factually odd case, Jones v. Thomas, 491 U.S. 376 (1989), the Supreme Court approved treating a sentencing pattern as a package. Thomas was con-

victed of felony murder and the underlying felony and sentenced to fifteen years for the felony and a consecutive life sentence for the murder. After the state courts ruled in other cases that the legislature did not intend to authorize convictions for felony murder and the underlying felony, the governor commuted Thomas's sentence for the felony, and the state courts vacated his felony conviction and credited the sentence he had served on that conviction to the felony-murder sentence. The Court held that Thomas was left in precisely the same position as if the trial judge had sentenced him correctly in the first place: with a single conviction and sentence for felony murder. I disagree, preferring Scalia's common-sense dissent. Id. at 389 (Scalia, J., dissenting) (joined by Brennan, Marshall, & Stevens, JJ.) (arguing that Thomas had fully served the sentence for the same offense as the greater and must, therefore, be released). For a defense of the outcome the Court reached (published before the Court decided *Jones*), see Flynn.

88. United States v. Sanges, 144 U.S. 310, 318 (1892).

89. 18 U.S.C. § 3731.

90. See Sanabria v. United States, 437 U.S. 54, 78 (1978) (holding that Court of Appeals "lacked jurisdiction of the Government's appeal)."

91. 144 U.S. at 323.

NOTES TO CHAPTER 10

1. In United States v. Sanford, 429 U.S. 14 (1976), the defendant made that showing, because of the judge's familiarity with the facts of the case, and there is no reason arbitrarily to deny him the acquittal equivalence he deserved. See chapter 8.

2. Moore, 353.

3. See chapter 2.

4. 432 U.S. 161 (1977), discussed in detail in chapter 2.

5. Missouri v. Hunter, 459 U.S. 359 (1983), discussed in chapter 3.

6. See chapter 3.

Bibliography

BOOKS AND ARTICLES

Amar, Akil Reed, Double Jeopardy Law Made Simple, 106 Yale L.J. 1807 (1997).
———, Forward: Some Sixth Amendment Principles, 84 Geo. L.J. 641 (1996).
———, Reconstructing Double Jeopardy: Some Thoughts on the Rodney King Case, 26 Cumb. L. Rev. 1 (1995).
Amar, Akhil Reed, and Jonathan L. Marcus, Double Jeopardy Law After Rodney King, 95 Colum. L. Rev. 1 (1995).
Anderson, Angela, Asset Forfeiture as Double Jeopardy, 32 Idaho L. Rev. 545 (1996).
1 Annals of Congress (1789).
Attenborough, F. L., ed. and trans., Laws of the Earliest English Kings (Cambridge University Press 1922).
The Babylonian Laws (Godfrey Rolls Driver and John C. Mills, eds. and trans., Clarendon Press 1955).
Batchelder, Charles E., Former Jeopardy, 17 Am. L. Rev. 735 (1883).
Bentham, Jeremy, Introduction to the Principles of Morals and Legislation (1789).
Bishop, Joel, Bishop on Criminal Law (9th ed., T. H. Flood 1923).
Blackstone, William, Commentaries on the Laws of England.
Bracton, Henrici, De Legibus et Consuetudinibus Angliae (George E. Woodbine, ed., Samuel E. Thorne, trans., with revisions and notes, Harvard University Press 1968).
Bradley, Craig, Racketeers, Congress, and the Courts: An Analysis of RICO, 65 Iowa L. Rev. 837 (1980).
Brickey, Kathleen F., The Jurisprudence of Larceny: An Historical Inquiry and Interest Analysis, 33 Vand. L. Rev. 1101 (1980).
Britton (Francis Morgan Nichols, trans., Clarendon Press 1983).
Carroway, William L., Pervasive Multiple Offense Problems—A Policy Analysis, 1971 Utah L. Rev. 105.
Cassell, Paul G., The Rodney King Trial and the Double Jeopardy Clause: Some Observations on Original Meaning and the ACLU's Schizophrenic Views of the Dual Sovereignty Doctrine, 41 UCLA L. Rev. 693 (1994).

Cassella, Stefan D., Status of Double Jeopardy and Forfeiture Law in the Sixth Circuit, 84 Ky. L.J. 553 (1995–96).

Cohen, Felix, Transcendental Nonsense and the Functional Approach, 35 Colum. L. Rev. 809 (1935).

Coke, Edward, The Third Part of the Institutes of the Laws of England (1669).

Colb, Sherry F., Freedom from Incarceration: Why Is This Right Different from All Other Rights?, 69 NYU L. Rev. 781 (1994).

Comley, William H., Former Jeopardy, 35 Yale L.J. 674 (1926).

Cox, Stanley E., *Halper's* Continuing Double Jeopardy Implications: A Thorn by Any Other Name Would Prick as Deep, 39 St.L. U.L. Rev. 1235 (1995).

Demosthenes (James Herbert Vince, trans., Harvard University Press 1954).

The Digest of Justinian (Theodor Mommsen, Paul Kreuger, Alan Watson, eds., University of Pennsylvania Press 1985).

Dworkin, Ronald, Law's Empire (Harvard University Press 1986).

Evans, Michael, and R. Ian Jack, eds., Sources of English Legal and Constitutional History (Butterworths 1984).

Feinberg, Joel, Harm to Self (Oxford University Press 1989).

———, Harmless Wrongdoing (Oxford University Press 1988).

———, Offenses to Others (Oxford University Press 1988).

———, Harm to Others (Oxford University Press 1987).

Findlater, Janet, Retrial After a Hung Jury: The Double Jeopardy Problem, 129 U. Pa. L. Rev. 701 (1981).

Finklestein, J. J., The Laws of Ur-Nammu, 22 J. Cuneiform Studies 66 (1969).

Fisher, Walter T., Double Jeopardy: Six Common Boners Summarized, 15 U.C.L.A. L. Rev. 81 (1967).

Fiss, Owen, Objectivity and Interpretation, 34 Stan. L. Rev. 739 (1982).

Fleta (H. G. Richardson and G. O. Sayles, eds. and trans., Bernard Quaritch 1955).

Flynn, Paul G., Judicial Sentencing Error: *Thomas v. Morris* and the Double Jeopardy Clause, 16 Pepperdine L. Rev. 613 (1989).

Friedland, Martin L., Double Jeopardy (Clarendon Press 1969).

Garcia-Rivera, Luis, Dodging Double Jeopardy: Combined Civil and Criminal Trials, 26 Stetson L. Rev. 373 (1996).

Goldin, Hyman Elias, Hebrew Criminal Law and Procedure (Twayne Publishers 1952).

Gooch, J. T., Is the Plea of Autrefois Acquit for Misdemeanors Justifiable in Kentucky?, 4 Ky. L.J. (March 1916) 20.

Guerra, Sandra, The Myth of Dual Sovereignty: Multijurisdictional Drug Law Enforcement and Double Jeopardy, 73 N.C. L. Rev. 1159 (1995).

Haddad, William A., and David G. Mullock, Double Jeopardy Problems in the Definition of Same Offense: State Discretion to Invoke the Criminal Process Twice, 22 U. Fla. L. Rev. 515 (1970).

Hale, Matthew, A History of the Pleas of the Crown (1847).

Hall, Gary H., The Effect of Double Jeopardy on Asset Forfeiture, 32 Idaho L. Rev. 527 (1996).

Hegland, Kenney, Goodbye to Deconstruction, 58 S. Cal. L. Rev. 1203 (1985).

Henning, Peter J., Precedents in a Vacuum: The Supreme Court Continues to Tinker with Double Jeopardy, 31 Am. Crim. L. Rev. 1 (1993).

Herman, Susan N., Reconstructing the Bill of Rights: A Reply to Amar and Marcus's Triple Play on Double Jeopardy, 95 Colum. L. Rev. 1090 (1995).

———, Double Jeopardy All Over Again: Dual Sovereignty, Rodney King, and the ACLU, 41 UCLA L. Rev. 609 (1994).

Hoffman, Paul, Double Jeopardy Wars: The Case for a Civil Rights "Exception," 41 UCLA L. Rev. 649 (1994).

Horack, Frank, The Multiple Consequences of a Single Criminal Act, 21 Minn. L. Rev. 805 (1937).

Hunter, Jill, The Development of the Rule Against Double Jeopardy, 5 Journal of Legal History 2 (1984).

Husak, Douglas N., The Philosophy of Criminal Law (Rowman and Littlefield 1987).

Johnson, Phillip, The Unnecessary Crime of Conspiracy, 61 Calif. L. Rev. 1137 (1973).

———, Multiple Punishment and Consecutive Sentences: Reflections on the *Neal* Doctrine, 58 Calif. L. Rev. 357 (1970).

Kafka, Franz, In the Penal Colony (Willa Muir and Edwin Muir, trans., Schocken 1961).

Kant, Immanuel, The Philosophy of Law (W. Hastie, trans., 1887).

Kelman, Mark, A Guide to Critical Legal Studies (Harvard University Press 1987)

Klein, Susan R., Civil In Rem Forfeiture and Double Jeopardy, 82 Iowa L. Rev. 183 (1996).

King, Nancy J., Portioning Punishment: Constitutional Limits on Successive and Excessive Penalties, 144 U. Pa. L. Rev. 101 (1995).

———, Professor Amar's Three-Dimensional View of Double Jeopardy: Adjusting the Focus, 26 Cumb. L. Rev. 18 (1995).

Kirchheimer, Otto, The Act, the Offense and Double Jeopardy, 58 Yale L.J. 513 (1949).

Kravitz, Max, Ohio's Administrative License Suspension: A Double Jeopardy and Due Process Analysis, 29 Akron L. Rev. 123 (1996).

LaFave, Wayne R., and Jerold H. Israel, Criminal Procedure (2d ed., West 1992) (hornbook edition).

LaFave, Wayne R., and Austin W. Scott, Criminal Law (2d ed., West 1986) (hornbook edition).

McElroy, Michael A., Double Jeopardy: The Ephemeral Guarantee, 5 Crim. L. Bull. 375 (1969).

McKay, Monroe G., Double Jeopardy: Are the Pieces the Puzzle?, 23 Washburn L.J. 1 (1983).

McKechnie, William Sharp, Magna Carta, A Commentary on the Great Charter of King John 359–367 (2d ed., Burt Franklin 1958).

McLaren, W. G., The Doctrine of Res Judicata as Applied to the Trial of Criminal Cases, 10 Wash. L. Rev. 198 (1935).

Mack, Barbara A., Double Jeopardy—Civil Forfeitures and Criminal Punishment: Who Determines What Punishments Fit the Crime, 19 Seattle U. L. Rev. 217 (1996).

Maitland, Frederic W., ed., 1 Select Pleas of the Crown, A.D. 1200–1225 (1888).

Mead, Susanah, M., Double Jeopardy Protection—Illusion or Reality?, 13 Ind. L. Rev. 863 (1980).

Mendelsohn, Samuel, The Criminal Jurisprudence of the Ancient Hebrews (Hermon Press 1968).

The Mirror Of Justices (William Joseph Whittaker, ed., 1895).

Model Penal Code (Proposed Official Draft 1962).

Moore, Michael S., Act and Crime (Oxford University Press 1993).

Mueller, Eric L., The Hobgoblin of Little Minds? Our Foolish Law of Inconsistent Verdicts, 111 Harv. L. Rev. 771 (1998).

Neafsey, Ed, and Edward R. Bonanno, Parallel Proceedings and the Fifth Amendment's Double Jeopardy Clause, 7 Fordham Envtl. L.J. 719 (1996).

Olson, Trisha, Comity, Justice, and Recognizing the Sameness of the Other: A Response to *Reconstructing Double Jeopardy*, 26 Cumb. L. Rev. 37 (1995).

The Opinions of Paulus, in The Civil Law, ed. and trans. S. P. Scott. 17 vols. Rpt. (AMS Press 1973).

Owens, Richard, Alabama's Minority Status: A Single Criminal Act Injuring Multiple Persons Constitutes Only a Single Offense, 16 Cumb. L. Rev. 85 (1985).

Pasley, Robert S., Double Jeopardy and Civil Money Penalties, 114 Banking L.J. 4 (1997).

Paulsen, Michael Stokes, Double Jeopardy Law After Akhil Amar: Some Civil Procedure Analogies and Inquiries, 26 Cumb. L. Rev. 23 (1995).

Peller, Gary, The Metaphysics of American Law, 73 Cal. L. Rev. 1151 (1985).

Perkins, Rollin M., and Ronald M. Boyce, Criminal Law (3d ed., Foundation Press 1982).

Pollock, Frederick, and Frederic William Maitland, The History of English Law Before the Time of Edward I (2d ed. 1899).

Ponsoldt, James F., When Guilt Should Be Irrelevant: Government Overreaching as a Bar to Reprosecution Under the Double Jeopardy Clause After *Oregon v. Kennedy*, 69 Cornell L. Rev. 76 (1983).

Posner, Richard, The Jurisprudence of Skepticism, 86 Mich. L. Rev. 827 (1988).

Poulin, Anne Bowen, Double Jeopardy and Judicial Accountability: When Is an Acquittal Not an Acquittal?, 27 Ariz. St. L.J. 953 (1995).

————, The Limits of Double Jeopardy: A Course into the Dark?, 39 Vill. L. Rev. 627 (1994).

————, Double Jeopardy Protection Against Successive Prosecutions in Complex Criminal Cases: A Model, 25 Conn. L. Rev. 95 (1992).

————, Grady and Dowling Stir the Muddy Waters, 43 Rutgers L. Rev. 889 (1991).

————, Collateral Estoppel in Criminal Cases: Reuse of Evidence after Acquittal, 58 U. Cin. L. Rev. 1 (1989).

Reiss, Steven A., Prosecutorial Intent in Constitutional Criminal Procedure, 135 U. Pa. L. Rev. 1365 (1987).

Remington, Frank J., and Allan J. Joseph, Charging, Convicting, and Sentencing the Multiple Criminal Offender, 1961 Wis. L. Rev. 528.

Richardson, Eli J., Eliminating Double Talk from the Law of Double Jeopardy, 22 Fla. St. U. L. Rev. 119 (1994).

Richman, Daniel C., Bargaining About Future Jeopardy, 49 Vand. L. Rev. 1181 (1996).

Robinson, Paul H., and Jane A. Grall, Element Analysis in Defining Criminal Liability: The Model Penal Code and Beyond, 35 Stan. L. Rev. 681 (1983).

Ronner, Amy D., Prometheus Unbound: Accepting a Mythless Concept of Civil In Rem Forfeiture with Double Jeopardy Protection, 44 Buff. L. Rev. 655 (1996).

Rudstein, David S., Double Jeopardy and the Fraudulently-Obtained Acquittal, 60 Mo. L. Rev. 607 (1995).

————, Civil Penalties and Multiple Punishment Under the Double Jeopardy Clause: Some Unanswered Questions, 46 Okla. L. Rev. 587 (1993).

————, Double Jeopardy and Summary Contempt Proceedings, 69 Notre Dame L. Rev. 691 (1993).

Russell, M. J., Trial by Battle and the Appeals of Felony, 1 Journal of Legal History 135 (1980).

Schwartz, Stephen Jay, Multiple Punishments for the "Same Offense": Michigan Grapples with the Definitional Problem, 25 Wayne L. Rev. 825 (1979).

Schulhofer, Stephen J., Jeopardy and Mistrials, 125 U. Pa. L. Rev. 449 (1977).

Schuman, David, Taking Law Seriously: Communitarian Search and Seizure, 27 Am. Crim. L. Rev. 583 (1990).

1 Senate Journal (1789).

Shellenberger, James A., and James A. Strazzella, The Lesser-Included Offense Doctrine and the Constitution: The Development of Due Process and Double Jeopardy Remedies, 79 Marq. L. Rev. 1 (1995).

Sigler, Jay. A., Double Jeopardy, The Development of a Legal and Social Policy (Cornell University Press 1969).

Solum, Lawrence, On the Indeterminacy Crisis: Critiquing Critical Dogma, 54 U. Chi. L. Rev. 462 (1987).

Story, Joseph, Commentaries on the Constitution (1833).

Strachan-Davidson, James Leigh, Problems of the Roman Criminal Law (Clarendon Press 1969).

Strazzella, James A., The Relationship of Double Jeopardy to Prosecution Appeals, 73 Notre Dame L. Rev. 1 (1997).

Talmadge, Philip A., Preface: Double Jeopardy in Washington and Beyond, 19 Seattle U. L. Rev. 209 (1996).

Theis, William H., The Double Jeopardy Defense and Multiple Prosecutions for Conspiracy, 49 SMU L. Rev. 269 (1996).

Thomas, George C., III, A Blameworthy Act Approach to the Double Jeopardy Same Offense Problem, 83 Calif. L. Rev. 1027 (1995).

————, Legal Skepticism and the Gravitational Effect of Law, 43 Rutgers L. Rev. 965 (1991).

————, A Modest Proposal to Save the Double Jeopardy Clause, 69 Wash. U.L.Q. 195 (1991).

————, An Elegant Theory of Double Jeopardy, 1988 U. Ill. L. Rev. 827.

————, Sentencing Problems Under the Multiple Punishment Doctrine, 31 Vill. L. Rev. 1351 (1986).

————, Successive Prosecutions for the Same Offense: In Search of a Definition, 71 Iowa L. Rev. 323 (1986).

————, A Unified Theory of Multiple Punishment, 47 U. Pitt. L. Rev. 1 (1985).

————, Multiple Punishments for the Same Offense: The Analysis After *Missouri v. Hunter*, 62 Wash. U.L.Q. 79 (1984).

————, RICO Prosecutions and the Double Jeopardy/Multiple Punishment Problem, 78 Nw. U.L. Rev. 1359 (1984).

Thomas, George C., III, and Barry S. Pollack, Rethinking Guilt, Juries, and Jeopardy, 91 Mich. L. Rev. 1 (1992).

The Treatise on the Laws and Customs of the Realm of England Commonly Called Glanvill (G. D. G. Hall, ed., Nelson 1965).

Venkatesh, Vendana, Taxation, Double Jeopardy, and the Excessive Fines Clause: *Department of Revenue of Montana v. Kurth Ranch*, 48 Tax Law. 911 (1995).

Vestal, Allen D., and John C. Coughenour, Preclusion/Res Judicata Variables: Criminal Prosecutions, 19 Vand. L. Rev. 683 (1966).

Vestal, Allan D., and Douglas J. Gilbert, Preclusion of Duplicative Prosecutions: A Developing Mosiac, 47 Mo. L. Rev. 1 (1982).

Westen, Peter, The Three Faces of Double Jeopardy: Reflections on Government Appeals of Criminal Sentences, 78 Mich. L. Rev. 1001 (1980).

Westen, Peter, and Richard Drubel, Toward a General Theory of Double Jeopardy, 1978 Sup. Ct. Rev. 81.

Williams, Joan, Critical Legal Studies: The Death of Transcendence and the Rise of the New Landells, 62 N.Y.U. L. Rev. 429 (1987).

LAW REVIEW STUDENT NOTES AND COMMENTS

Note and Comment, The Impact of Recent Double Jeopardy Decisions on Federal Agencies, 10 Admin. L.J. Am. U. 327 (1996).

Note, Two Views of *Austin v. United States*: Is a Civil Forfeiture Action to Collect "Proceeds" Pursuant to Title 21 U.S.C. § 881 (A)(6) Still Exempt From the Protections of the Double Jeopardy Clause?, 23 Am. J. Crim. L. 431 (1996).

Note, Truly Constitutional? The American Double Jeopardy Clause and Australian Analogues, 33 Am. Crim. L. Rev. 123 (1995).

Note, Mistrials and Double Jeopardy, 15 Am. Crim. L. Rev. 169 (1977).

Case Comment, Expanding Double Jeopardy: *Department of Revenue v. Kurth Ranch*, 75 B.U. L. Rev. 505 (1995).

Note, Double Jeopardy and the Concept of Identity of Offenses, 7 Brooklyn L. Rev. 79 (1937).

Note, Double Jeopardy: Prosecution for Underlying Felony Following Acquittal for Felony-Murder, 9 Buffalo L. Rev. 378 (1959).

Note, North Carolina and Pretrial Civil Revocation of an Impaired Driver's License and the Double Jeopardy Clause, 18 Campbell L. Rev. 391 (1996).

Note, To Punish or to Remedy—That Is the Constitutional Question: Double Jeopardy Confusion in *State v. Hansen*, 30 Creighton L. Rev. 235 (1996).

Casenote, The Tax Man Cometh, But Fear Not: The Double Jeopardy Clause Bars Criminal Taxation of Drugs Contingent on Criminal Conduct: *Department of Revenue of Montana v. Kurth Ranch*, 28 Creighton L. Rev. 475 (1995).

Comment, Wrongful Death and Double Jeopardy, 26 Cumb. L. Rev. 231 (1995–96).

Comment, Double Jeopardy and the Identity of Offenses, 2 De Paul L. Rev. 263, 266 (1953).

Comment, The Potential Double Jeopardy Implications of Administrative License Revocation, 46 Emory L.J. 329 (1997).

Note, Administrative License Suspensions, Criminal Prosecution and the Double Jeopardy Clause, 23 Fordham Urb. L.J. 923 (1996).

Casenote, Drunk Driving, Administrative License Suspension, and Double Jeopardy in Virginia: *Tench v. Commonwealth*, 4 Geo. Mason L. Rev. 521 (1996).

Summary, *Department of Revenue v. Kurth Ranch*: The Expansion of Double Jeopardy Jurisprudence into Civil Tax Proceedings, 25 Golden Gate U. L. Rev. 331 (1995).

The Supreme Court 1995 Term, Double Jeopardy Clause—In Rem Civil Forfeiture, 110 Harv. L. Rev. 206 (1996).

Note, The Identity of Offenses, 20 Harv. L. Rev. 642 (1907).

Note, The Supreme Court Assaults State Drug Taxes with a Double Jeopardy Dagger: Death Blow, Serious Injury, or Flesh Wound, 29 Ind. L. Rev. 695 (1996).

Note, Put Down That Drink!: The Double Jeopardy Drunk Driving Defense Is Not Going to Save You, 81 Iowa L. Rev. 775 (1996).

Supreme Court Review, *Witte v. United States*: Double Jeopardy and the United States Sentencing Guidelines, 86 J. Crim. L. and Criminology 1539 (1996).

Supreme Court Review, Fifth Amendment—Double Jeopardy and the Dangerous Drug Tax, 85 J. Crim. L. and Criminology 936 (1994).

New Decisions, Addition to Tax Not Double Jeopardy for Convicted Cocaine Dealer, 83 J. Tax'n 316 (1995).

Comment, Double Jeopardy: Vandercomb to Chicos—Two Centuries of Failure in Search of a Standard, 45 J. Urban L. 405 (1967).

Comment, Double Jeopardy and the Identity of Offenses, 21 La. L. Rev. 615 (1961).

Note, One Bite at the Apple: Reversals of Convictions Tainted by Prosecutorial Misconduct and the Ban of Double Jeopardy, 94 Mich. L. Rev. 1346 (1996).

Note and Comment, Is the DUI Double-Jeopardy Defense D.O.A.?, 29 Loy. L.A. L. Rev. 1273 (1996).

Note, Criminal Law and Procedure—Tests of "Same Offense," 32 Mich. L. Rev. 512 (1932).

Note, Multiple Prosecution and Punishment of Unitary Criminal Conduct—Minn. Stat. § 609.035, 56 Minn. L. Rev. 646 (1972).

Note, Criminal Law—Double Jeopardy, 24 Minn. L. Rev. 522 (1940).

Note, Double Jeopardy vs. DUI: Is a License Revocation for Driving Under the Influence Punishment or a Remedial Sanction?, 23 New Eng. J. on Crim. and Civ. Confinement 239 (1997).

Note, Two-Tiered Test for Double Jeopardy Analysis in New Mexico, 10 New Mexico L. Rev. 195 (1980).

Note, Mistrial and Double Jeopardy, 49 N.Y.U. L. Rev. 937 (1974).

Casenote, *Department of Revenue v. Kurth Ranch*: Double Jeopardy. A: Multiple Punishment Component. Q: What is Confusion? Continuing Where *Halper* and *Austin* Left Off, 15 N. Ill. U.L. Rev. 433 (1995).

Comment, An Analysis of Wharton's Rule: *Iannelli v. United States* and One Step Beyond, 71 Nw. U.L. Rev. 547 (1976).

Comment, Double Jeopardy and Reprosecution After Mistrial: Is the Manifest Necessity Test Manifestly Necessary, 69 Nw. U.L. Rev. 887 (1975).

Note, A Closer Look at the Supreme Court and the Double Jeopardy Clause, 49 Ohio St. L.J. 779 (1988).

New Jersey Developments, Primitive Justice: Private Prosecutions in Municipal Court Under New Jersey Rule 7:4–4(b), 44 Rutgers L. Rev. 205 (1991).

Comment, Multiple Punishment and the Double Jeopardy Clause: The *United Sates v. Ursery* Decision, 71 St. John's L. Rev. 153 (1997).

Casenote, Imposition of Montana Drug Penalty Tax Constitutes Double Jeopardy, 5 Seton Hall Const. L.J. 1231 (1995).

Survey of Recent Developments, Constitutional Law, Fifth Amendment and Eighth Amendment, Eviction of Tenant Convicted of Drug Offense, 27 Seton Hall L. Rev. 1161 (1997).

Comment, Applying Section 654 of the Penal Code, 32 S. Cal. L. Rev. 50 (1958).

Note, The New Al Capone Laws and the Double Jeopardy Implications of Taxing Illegal Drugs, 4 S. Cal. Interdisciplinary L.J. 323 (1995).

Comment, *McMullin*'s Double Jeopardy Protection May Be a Casualty of South Carolina's War on Drugs, 48 S. C. L. Rev. 405 (1997).

Comment, *Halper, Austin,* and *Kurth Ranch*: Can Illinois' Summary Suspension Statute Withstand the Double Jeopardy Clause Challenges in Light of the Recent Decisions of the United States Supreme Court, 21 S. Ill. U. L.J. 149 (1996).

Note, The Protection from Multiple Trials, 11 Stan. L. Rev. 735 (1959).

Note, Up in Smoke: The Texas Controlled Substances Act, 28 Tex. Tech L. Rev. 923 (1997).

Note, The Double Jeopardy Clause: Refining the Constitutional Proscription Against Successive Prosecutions, 19 UCLA L. Rev. 804 (1972).

Note, Multiple Prosecutions and Punishments Under RICO: A Chip Off the Old "Blockburger," 52 U. Cin. L. Rev. 467 (1983).

Comment, Single Sentence on Multiple-Count Indictment—Conspiracy and Double Jeopardy, 17 U. Cin. L. Rev. 79 (1948).

Case Note, *Department of Revenue v. Kurth Ranch*, 73 U. Det. Mercy L. Rev. 117 (1995).

Case Comment, Constitutional Law: Taxation of Contraband and Expansion of the Double Jeopardy Clause, *Department of Revenue of Montana v. Kurth Ranch*, 7 U. Fla. J.L and Pub. Pol'y 385 (1996).

Comment, The Decisive Blow to the Double Jeopardy Defenses in Kansas Drunk Driving Prosecutions: *State v. Mertz*, 44 U. Kan. L. Rev. 1009 (1996).

Comment, Scorched Earth: How the Expansion of Civil Forfeiture Has Laid Waste to Due Process, 45 U. Miami L. Rev. 911 (1991).

Comment, The Foreclosure of Double Jeopardy in Administrative License Suspensions and Civil Asset Forfeitures Following *United States v. Ursery*, 65 UMKC L. Rev. 104 (1996).

Note, Matching Tests for Double Jeopardy Violations with Constitutional Interests, 45 Vand. L. Rev. 273 (1991).

Note, Commonwealth Right of Appeal, 43 Wash. & Lee L. Rev. 295 (1986).

Note and Comment, Crime and Punishment and Punishment: Civil Forfeiture, Double Jeopardy and the War on Drugs, 71 Wash. L. Rev. 489 (1996).

Enlarging the Sargasso Sea of Double Jeopardy: *Department of Revenue v. Kurth Ranch*, 17 Whittier L. Rev. 477 (1996).

Annual Survey, Sweeney v. State Board of Funeral Directors: The Commonwealth Court Holds that Double Jeopardy Challenges to License Revocations by

Administrative Agencies Are Subject to *Halper* Analysis, 5 Widener J. Pub. L. 809 (1996).

Note, Popular Sovereignty, Double Jeopardy, and the Dual Sovereignty Doctrine, 102 Yale L.J. 281 (1992).

Note, The Double Jeopardy Clause as a Bar to Reintroducing Evidence, 89 Yale L.J. 962 (1980).

Comment, Twice in Jeopardy, 75 Yale L.J. 262 (1965).

Note, Consecutive Sentences in Single Prosecutions: Judicial Multiplication of Statutory Penalties, 67 Yale L.J. 916 (1958).

Note, Statutory Implementation of Double Jeopardy Clauses: New Life for a Moribund Constitutional Guarantee, 65 Yale L.J. 339 (1956).

Note, Double Jeopardy and the Multiple-Count Indictment, 57 Yale L.J. 132 (1947).

Index

260; *autrefois attaint,* 30–31, 72, 82–83, 224; *autrefois convict,* 29–30, 83–84, 260; benefit of clergy, 76, 81; former pardon, 31–32
Commonwealth v. Smith, 236–37
Compound-predicate offenses, 113, 178–83
Conduct divided into "units of prosecution," 49, 95–96, 152–55, 183–87; auto theft/joyriding, 65–66; difference between finding one violation and counting violations, 156–61; possession offenses, 187–88; using "single impulse" analysis, 159–60
Continuing criminal enterprise offense (CCE), 118; as exception to traditional "same-offense" analysis, 25–27, 182; uncovering evidence to rebut *Blockburger,* 195
Cox, Stanley, 123
Crime and tort: historical evolution, 119
Crist v. Bretz, 90, 251–52
Critical legal studies: the indeterminancy of law, 42–45

De Grey, William, 203
Department of Revenue of Montana v. Kurth Ranch, 123, 124, 130–31; Justice Scalia's dissent, 127
Diaz v. United States, 155
DiFrancesco, United States v. See United States v. DiFrancesco
Dixon, United States v. See United States v. Dixon
Double Jeopardy Clause: Blackstone as source of language, 7; compared to sentencing theory, 9–12; debate in First Congress, 5, 84–86, 120–22; legislative-prerogative understanding, 17–27; "life or limb" requirement, 119–33; as limitation only on prosecutors and judges, 14–27; Madison's proposed language, 84–85, 214; as mandatory joinder, 12–14; as substantive limitation on the legislature, 8–12
Double jeopardy paradigm case, 46–49
Double jeopardy policies: to guarantee singularity of blameworthiness, 134–36; to manifest legislative intent, 38–39; to prevent prosecutorial harassment, 37,

50–52; to protect against unauthorized judgments of criminal blameworthiness, 63–67
Douglas, William O., 244–45; in favor of "same transaction" test, 55
Downum v. United States, 68–69, 237, 239–40, 242, 244, 246
Drubel, Richard: and appeals, 217–18, 220–21, 223; and attachment of jeopardy, 252; criticism of *Brown v. Ohio,* 66; Double Jeopardy Clause conceptualized as hierarchy of values, 115–16; and jury nullification, 259; and mistrials, 239
Dual sovereignty doctrine, 40, 188–94; and collateral estoppel, 212; criticisms, 190; established by 1847, 189; federal-Indian prosecutions, 189, 191–92; limited by Department of Justice policy, 193; in municipal-state context, 189–91; state-state prosecutions, 189, 191; state statutes barring state trial after federal trial, 193
Duchess of Kingston, Rex v. See Rex v. Duchess of Kingston
Due Process Clause: as conceptual home for mistrial cases decided on basis of fairness, 254; as limit on legislative prerogative to create substantive criminal offenses, 21–23, 24; as limit on unauthorized convictions, 62, 109; and proportional sentencing, 232
Dworkin, Ronald, 44

Ebeling v. Morgan, 157–60, 199
Eighth Amendment: as just deserts, 18; as limitation on legislature, 21–23, 68, 232
Elizabeth I, 81
Ex parte Henry, 55–56
Ex parte Lange, 109-10, 111-112, 132

Feinberg, Joel, 135, 140, 151, 157, 209
Fiss, Owen, 43
Fleta, 95
Ford, Gerald, 9
Forman v. United States, 235
Friedland, Martin, 18; on collateral estoppel, 201, 211, 212; as comparative law study, 114; criticism of dual sovereignty, 190; noting English rule against splitting a case, 55; recommending

About the Author

George C. Thomas III has been writing about double jeopardy since 1984, publishing more than a dozen major articles on the subject in the law journals. He authored the report of the 1994 American Bar Association Committee on Double Jeopardy and is currently Distinguished Professor of Law at Rutgers University.